RAVEN'S CHILDREN

RAVEN'S CHILDREN

RICHARD ADAMS CAREY

A Richard Todd Book

HOUGHTON MIFFLIN COMPANY

Boston   New York   London

1992

Library of Congress Cataloging-in-Publication Data

Carey, Richard Adams.
Raven's children / Richard Adams Carey.
p.   cm.
"A Richard Todd book."
ISBN 0-395-48677-7
1. Yupik Eskimos — Social conditions.   2. Yupik Eskimos — Economic
conditions.   3. Social change.   4. Kongiganak (Alaska) — Social
conditions.   5. Kongiganak (Alaska) — Economic conditions.
I. Title.
E99.E7C2878   1992
306'.089971 — dc20   92-5858
CIP

Printed in the United States of America

HAD 10 9 8 7 6 5 4 3 2 1

For
John H. Carey, Jr.,
beloved father

ACKNOWLEDGMENTS

My considerable thanks are due to a number of people: to Gilbert Amik, who years ago introduced my wife and me to Bethel and its people by giving us a place to stay when we had nowhere else to go; to Sandy Elder, who tracked down that article I couldn't find; to Phyllis Morrow, who volunteered as much as she could know, and made some good recommendations; to Judith Kleinfeld, who also suggested some excellent sources; to Sue Hare, superintendent of the Lower Kuskokwim School District, who let me come back again; to Corky Carleton, who listened to early portions of my manuscript instead of to his radio; to Jeff Fair, who provided comradeship and cheerleading throughout, and who inspired me with his own writing; to Richard and Patty Taylor, Mike and Cathy Lucas, and Mike and Julie Blair, all of whom helped to house me in Bethel after I got tossed out of Elsie's; to David Black, for his readings, suggestions, and sports weeklies; to Paris Finley, whose written response to my initial draft provided a lift that saw me through all the subsequent drafts; to David Sleeper, who encouraged me first of all, and helped me to take the beginning steps; to Julia Hanna, who brought the various pieces of this enterprise together; to Liz Duvall, who brought my writing into focus and clarity, or at least got it closer to that; to my editor, Richard Todd, who in the gentlest fashion taught me to write a book; to my mother, Mary Jane Miner, who showed me what courage and grace are; to my wife, Lois, who provided me with more than the requisite amounts of patience, love, and encouragement, as well as her own insights; and finally, to the Real People themselves, who gave me their friendship wherever I went, and taught me even more than I guessed.

CONTENTS

PREFACE

"They might need somebody at a cannery out on Bristol Bay," the employment agent told me. He was a short, heavyset man in a rumpled gray suit. "They called here just a few minutes ago. The guy said a bunch of Eskimos he hired just walked off the job."

I stood in an office in the basement of an old building in Anchorage. I had come to Alaska in the summer of 1970 hoping to catch on with a crew fighting forest fires, but I ended up broke and out of work instead. I had never even heard of Bristol Bay before. The agent pointed to a map splayed across the wall behind his desk, indicating the great round incision the bay makes just above the long tusk of the Aleutians. I noticed also, for the first time, that the Alaska road system — the red tracings between places like Anchorage, Fairbanks, Tok, Juneau, and the little towns and villages of the Panhandle and the Kenai Peninsula — hardly marked out more than a twelfth of the state; that the west in particular, along the entire thousand-mile length of the Bering Sea coast, displayed only immense swaths of open and unmarked space, crossed at wide intervals by rivers such as the Noatak, the Kobuk, the Yukon, and the Kuskokwim, but nothing else; that here was a piece of America as big as Texas and yet as unapprehended, and as discrete from our history, as the moon. I think I almost trembled in my eagerness to get out there, to a place I saw as so new and rich in possibility, and the agent himself was moved by the stretch of it on the map, standing in his narrow office and marveling aloud, "Man, that's really out in the sticks."

He said that the cannery was supposed to call back later that day, and to check with him first thing the next morning. But the cannery never called back, and the next day the agent could only surmise that the Eskimos had decided to go back to work. I hitchhiked down the Kenai and finally found a job cutting fish at a cannery in Homer.

It took me seven more years to get out to the sticks. Then the state of Alaska hired me to teach high school English in Kongiganak (pronounced, roughly, "Kung-i'-gu-nuk"), a village near the mouth of the Kuskokwim River. A man named Oscar Active became a friend with whom I played basketball on weekends, and his wife, Margaret, was my secretary when I became the principal of that little school. I left Kongiganak in 1984 in order to work at other schools in the Lower Kuskokwim School District, but I still visited the village occasionally. In 1987 I began to act on the sense of possibility I'd felt so long before, conceiving a book that would represent a certain poignance I felt in the lives of not only the Actives but every family in the Kuskokwim region — a poignance enforced not merely by the routine perils that we all face, no matter who we are or where we live, but also by the broadly political and economic perils peculiar to the lives of Alaskan Natives at this point in time.

I thought of a narrative form as the best vehicle for this book for the same reason that every culture has chosen primarily narrative forms for the oral transmission of its folklore: no other form so successfully communicates the personal implications of a history, an issue, or a principle of living. And I thought of Oscar and Margaret as the best protagonists of this narrative for several reasons. They were friends of particularly long standing, and I knew them as individuals better than any other couple in the region. Oscar's family roots in the upriver town of Bethel brought them sometimes to that fascinating meeting place of Western and Eskimo cultures in southwestern Alaska. Finally, a number of the tensions that beset their family life exemplified those testing other families in Kongiganak and elsewhere.

I knew by then, also, that personal privacy is guarded at least as jealously among Eskimo families as among whites, and in fact in Yupik Eskimo folklore it was for failure to respect such privacy that dogs lost their power of speech. Nonetheless, I came to the reluctant conclusion that I needed real names and a verifiable train of events in order to capture the special character of that poignance. In other words, I needed a narrative that could not be accused of hyperbole, compression, dramatic artifice, or any elements of fantasy — a narrative, ultimately, that had everything to do with the lives of real people making their way in a real, if somewhat unfamiliar, world, and nothing to do with any elements that would make that relationship suspect.

So finally, with trepidation, I approached the Actives with this idea: that I live with them during the 1989 fishing season at Cape Avinof and along the Kuskokwim River and turn the material of whatever transpired into a narrative that conveyed through the windows of their lives and affairs something of those several perils and the human stature of what they threatened. Oscar and Margaret agreed to this, though I had no way of gauging at that time what their reservations might be, if any. I could not know whether they really thought the project's goals were worth the expense of their privacy, or whether they acted more out of respect for our years of working and playing together.

Eventually I found that the trepidation I felt in asking was matched by the discomfort I felt as we carried out the project together. I tried as best I could to stay in the background of the affairs I was describing, though inevitably, the mere fact of my presence and activity had some distorting effect. Also I found the nature of that activity and the new role I had assumed in these lives to be somewhat unsettling. During that summer, I used Oscar's telephone to call my own family in New Hampshire two or three times each week, usually trailing its long cord into an empty bedroom so I could have a little privacy. Then I hung up and returned to my observing and note-taking. In time the lyrics to an old Doors song began to run through my head — "I'm a spy in the house of love" — and behind the lyrics I heard Robbie Krieger's smirking, predatory guitar riffs. Ultimately I found the irony of that long telephone cord nearly intolerable.

But this was more than a personal matter; there were historical and racial dimensions to my discomfort as well. We were all friends, of course, and all of us Americans. But I was a child of the Western culture whose dealings with the Native Americans of the Lower 48 began with the "rule of discovery," a doctrine conveying not only title to the various lands of the New World but also dominion over any of those lands' original inhabitants to whatever European power "discovered" them. In the United States this sort of thinking reached a terrible conclusion at Wounded Knee in 1890. The bleak and uncompromising bitterness against whites that pervades so many continental Indian reservations does not exist yet in southwestern Alaska, but the people of the Kuskokwim know their American history, and under the gravitational stress of the increasing proximity of non-Native culture and population, and under increasing constraints on Yupik hunting and fishing, bitterness is starting to build. Elders speak nostalgically of the days when white men were newsworthy marvels, seen no more frequently than confused humpback whales or the errant polar bears that sometimes drifted south on broken pack ice. I witnessed one occasion in Bethel that summer when Oscar was chided just for keeping company with a white man, and I'm sure there were more.

Also, I knew that over the years the residents of villages such as Kongiganak have often found little to cheer about in their portrayals in print and on television. A good portion of these media representations, whether dealing with someone's personal affairs or not, has been informed more by stereotype than by experience, or has been shaped prejudicially by convictions hostile to Yupik values, or simply from pure ignorance has been inaccurate or incomplete. People have noticed that even accurate information about anything unsavory — the practice by some individuals, for example, of headhunting, or killing walrus solely for their tusks, which are then traded to black market ivory dealers for cash or drugs or alcohol — tends to lead to the incorporation of that practice into the Eskimo stereotype, so that the actions of an aberrant few are generalized to all, and the ability of Yupik villages to defend their lifestyles politically is thus eroded. Finally, the mere fact of such scrutiny reinforces the sudden and queasy sense of marginality — and implicit vulnerability — that has settled across the region in only the past few generations.

I thought back to that empty map I looked at in Anchorage in 1970, and I realized that mine was a peculiarly American sort of dilemma. Filled with the westering urge, I had contemplated from some distance removed open areas of virgin territory, quickened it with the creatures of my own ambitions, and was then nonplussed to find that territory already inhabited. Invading Europeans got around this dilemma by conceding a humanity only of the most qualified sort to the people whom they met on these shores — by denying, in effect, that these were really people. In my case, I hadn't gotten around it, only blundered up perplexedly against the daunting obviousness of it. I had finally begun to see the human costs and risks of bearing witness to intimacies, particularly when the protagonists are members of such a besieged minority.

I had also blundered against the terrible difficulty of perceiving and communicating all that the Actives had deemed worth their sacrifice. I considered the terms used in the political debates conducted in Alaska and Washington, D.C., and it occurred to me that catchphrases such as "Yupik values" and "traditional lifestyle" and "subsistence hunting and fishing" were euphemisms not merely for the familiar concept of cultural differences but for something well beyond that, something that finally constitutes, right here in America, an entirely separate mode of being: a character of mind and social interaction that Western culture has historically dismissed as naive, but whose ambitions

are simply distinct from the needs or desires that produced
Western economies and artifacts.

The essence of this mode to those who stand outside it is as
elusive as smoke, or it wouldn't be so casually discounted. The
images and sensations immediately available to its observers —
say, the scent of wind and grass and sky in the clothes that hang
in ranks across a wall; the comfortable movement of an old
man's eyes across the round sweep of these worldwide horizons;
the peculiar ecstasies of the blood that accompany both the
hoarfrost in October, when the ground is good again for traveling, and breakup in May, when the marshes are covered in
birds; the rich, fecal scent that issues from the open gut of a
fresh-killed seal, and the heft of its knotted organs, the pearly
mantle of its fat, the dark promise of its meat; the wonderful
banality of a woman or child carrying the best portions of that
meat to the houses of relatives and neighbors, and the neatly
unconscious manner in which that largesse is accepted; the
warm susurrus of the Yupik language, with its marvelous dis-
criminations of spatial and familial relationships, and its
rhythms like the rocking of a boat, or the beating of a heart —
these approach it in only a tentative and halting manner, coming
to a stop far short of its center. The stiff features of our convenient stereotype remain largely intact, draining both life and
expression not only from that mode of being but from being
itself, the love and fear and laughter and regret that denote the
common reality of all people, and that belie the callow distinctions we draw.

Even before the project began, in fact, I started to feel these
various sorts of unease, and to wonder if maybe this was a job
the Actives would prefer to walk away from, as those cannery
workers did in Bristol Bay. Of course, in Kongiganak the only
possible response to a friend's request is one of assent. But if in
reality that assent is impossible or undesirable, a refusal is po-
litely conveyed through subtle cues of gesture and intonation, as
part of a subtext to the vocal response. Those kinds of cues are
hard to convey over the telephone, or even in a letter. In January

1989, six months before the start of the fishing season, I went to Kongiganak to stay with Oscar and Margaret for a few days, partly to share the pleasures of Slaaviq, the Russian Orthodox celebration of Christmas, but mostly to give them an opportunity to convey these signals of refusal.

I wasn't sure, but it seemed to me that the signals were being sent. After Slaaviq I went home to the neighboring village of Chefornak, where I was working that year, and wrote a letter to the Actives suggesting that we break the project off. But Oscar called immediately to say that they wanted to go ahead. "I think there's lots of people got the same problems I'm fighting against," he noted, accurately enough, alluding directly to problems that transcend his ethnicity, belie our distinctions, and even address unresolved issues in my own life. "Maybe what happens to me, no matter how it turns out, will be able to help those other people somehow."

So it began, and so it was finished, despite all the hazards of privacy, race, politics, and my outsider's perspective. These pages don't reach the end of that story, or even the end of that summer in 1989, and the nature of my perspective dictates unavoidably that the story is more Oscar's than Margaret's. But actually it's as much the story of a place as it is of these brave and remarkable people — a place that I imagined once to be empty, but found to be comfortably furnished with dreams and ambitions that long antedated my own.

" 'Live,' Nietzsche says, 'as though the day were here.' It is not society that is to guide and save the creative hero, but precisely the reverse. And so every one of us shares the supreme ordeal — carries the cross of the redeemer — not in the bright moments of the tribe's great victories, but in the silences of his personal despair."

— Joseph Campbell,
The Hero with a Thousand Faces

RAVEN'S CHILDREN

I

GOING BLUE

1 ◎ THE VILLAGE RESOLVES *itself out of the tundra like a mirage: point by point, slowly achieving feature and coherence, building itself out of the mere fabric of space. This is how it still takes shape in my mind at night, how it's always taken shape as I've approached it in waking, whether by boat, snow machine, or small plane. Last night it was open boat, the image seen from some distance out to sea in Kuskokwim Bay: first the low, wet sweep of the empty coastline, hardly distinguishable in its color and contours from the bay itself; then, on a low bluff about three miles back from the shore, the yellow storage tank of Kongiganak's water treatment plant, like the bald bottom stage of a booster rocket; next the bulky, hangarlike block of the village's single school building and the chalk-white communications dish pointed mutely at the sky; finally the ramshackle houses, maybe forty of them, thrown like a pile of old boards and spare parts against the feet of these small monuments, along with their sea wrack of driftwood drying racks, looping utility lines, and upended fuel drums. The village seems inexplicable, and as tenuous as an outpost on Mars. I blink my eyes, and it's gone again.*

You can find it on the maps, or at least some of them, anyway; it's one of those tiny black dots that line the coast of western Alaska at impressively infrequent intervals. Sometimes it's there, and sometimes it's not. Neighboring communities such as Kipnuk, Kwigillingok, and Quinhagak are reliably included. I find the maps also inexplicable, since often they cite places like Kus-

kovak and Chalitmut, villages long since abandoned, their old-
fashioned sod houses now just hummocks in the ground, just
another variety of peat ridge or frost heave. But it was often like
that, at least until recently, the communities winking in and out
of existence like fireflies as the movements of game animals
changed, or a river channel silted in, or some families quarreled,
or an epidemic struck, or a war was fought with a group of more
distant villages.

A few miles to the southwest, spread directly along the shore
of the bay, lies an earlier incarnation of Kongiganak, a site abandoned at some point early in this century, when most of its residents moved westward to Kwigillingok. In fact, it has been only
a little more than two decades now since the village as it presently exists was reconstituted. Only the grass remains at the old
village, along with some old shell casings, some scraps of net
twine, a stove-in teakettle, the splintered trunk of a lost wooden
doll.

But even those are strange to me, and would be no less so here
in the modern village. Kongiganak is a Yupik place, which is to
say a community of Alaska's southern Eskimos, a people distinct in language, history, and even culture from the more familiar Inupiaq Eskimos, or Inuit, of northern Alaska, Canada, and
Greenland. I myself am an outsider. One hundred and sixty
years ago, the first Russian explorers and traders in this region
referred to themselves as Cossacks, and so to this day a person
such as myself is described in Yupik as a kass'aq (pronounced
"gus'-suk").

In Kongiganak the ordinary gestures of everyday life — at
least to me — are in equal parts familiar and strange, like sign-
posts in garbled spelling. They point in their enigmatic manner
to a past of such depth and scale, of such discourse between
forgotten generations, as scarcely to be imagined, yet one as im-
manent as yesterday's weather. I blink, and all the buildings just
that quickly revert to grass. In my mind's eye the old village and
the new begin to blur together, and I conceive of them as each
the complement and the destiny of the other. They blur even

into destinies such as my own, and in these knotted grasses, among these shifting sloughs, I don't think I know any longer exactly where the boundary exists.

Only yesterday Oscar Active laughed, his single front tooth like a sliver of quartz in his gum, when he told me that I'd been enrolled in his school of cussing for the summer. Now I get my first real lesson as we find that the tide is out in the Kongiganak River and that the *Crazy J*'s anchor rests beneath the keel of another wooden skiff. This other boat rests high and dry on exposed riverbed, and is too heavy to be lifted. So Oscar cusses at the top of his lungs, dispensing his expertise abroad, not only to me and his family but also to the half-dozen houses that line this portion of the riverbank, their windows thrown open to the weather today. Still cussing, he goes down into the mud to tunnel the anchor out, while his brother Charlie and I haul on its line. Elsie and Margaret and the four children and their cousin line the bank above us, staring silently down at the progress of this project, and the clouds above their heads are high and white and dreamy.

Today is the next to last day of May 1989. Breakup came a couple of weeks ago to this part of southwestern Alaska, but this is the first day that really feels like spring. Delayed by weeks of chilling rain and high winds off Kuskokwim Bay, the hordes of shorebirds and waterfowl that migrate each year to the Yukon-Kuskokwim Delta are finally nesting. Similarly, at Cape Avinof, forty miles west of here, shoals of persistent shelf ice have delayed the herring spawn, and so also the opening of the commercial herring fishery.

Oscar Active is a fisherman, and he knows that agents for the Alaska Department of Fish & Game are at this very moment performing their test fishings over at the cape. Today the winds have died, and a sky so vast that on many days it's honeycombed into several discrete weather systems is ruled all at once by a single blue and breathless clarity. Oscar raises his head, just as his mother and wife and all the children start down the riverbank, just as the anchor pops loose like a seed and Charlie nearly falls over backward. Oscar peers up at the sky first and then down the river, reminding himself, I'm sure, that the fishery could conceivably open at any moment now and that this would be a perfect day for him and Charlie and me to be traveling over to Cape Avinof in the *Crazy J*. He cusses again, under his breath this time, then glances up in his wife Margaret's direction.

The *Crazy J* is twenty-four feet long and broad-beamed, painted slate blue with a crisp black trim. It seems huge compared to the little aluminum skiff that Oscar and Charlie fished in last summer, and Oscar himself, as he stands at the steering console that he has bolted to the stern thwart, seems no less huge. Yesterday in Bethel, the big town seventy miles inland up the Kuskokwim River, a *kass'aq* running the cash register in a hamburger joint nodded familiarly to Oscar, and Oscar laughed, but with an embarrassed edge to it, as the clerk pointed to a group of strange teenagers playing an arcade game and said, "I'm telling all these white kids what it's gonna be like here this summer with all the crazy drunk Eskimos, and you're just what we need, Oscar — a big one. One look at you — I'll tell 'em what you're like — and they'll be buying tickets home faster than they can sell 'em."

Charlie is a big one too; indeed, all of the natural brothers in the Active family are big, astonishingly so for Eskimos. But Oscar is the biggest, the most physically imposing: something over six feet tall, something beyond 260 pounds, most of it square and thick, bone and hard muscle, though in recent years his belt buckle has been safely out of the weather. This morning, in a little house on the opposite side of the village, Oscar sat at his breakfast like a great bear come wandering inside and tamed. But his mother, Elsie, impressed by his fiery temperament and mane of wild black hair (already graying in streaks), prefers to call him Oscar the Lion. I heard her murmur that to herself a moment ago, conceding in frank admiration, while Oscar swore and dug at the anchor, "He's even louder than I am." Older fans of *Sesame Street,* when they're teasing him, call him Oscar the Grouch.

Now, grouchily, Oscar looks back over his shoulder at the eighty-horse outboard motor. His two little boys are the last to clamber into the boat; Margaret rinses their feet in the river before they set their rubber boots down on the clean floorboards. When Oscar kicks the Evinrude into life, the boat ponderously faces upstream, lifting toward its skeg. Oscar Junior and Clayton, aged four and three, settle themselves on the boat's middle thwart, on either side of their mother, and stare in wonder at the banks gathering speed, then blurring past. Up from the village the crests of the banks are lined by sedge meadows, and Junior stands to point at the dozens of ducks that flush from their midst as we flash by: northern pintail, mallard, American widgeon.

The Kongiganak's channel is a narrow and silty trough, coiled and accordioned and then pressed like a gutter into the level plain of the tundra, and today Elsie enjoys even the pull of these crazy veers and loops. The old woman squints like Popeye through her one good eye and laughs, making a swirling motion with her hands. Then she gestures forward to the dwindling image of the village, which by now has appeared at one time or another over all quarters of the boat — bow, stern, port, and starboard. She shouts above the roar of the motor, "This is a seal-intestine river! Shaped like seal intestines!" She laughs again, her mouth hollow and toothless, her short white hair trailing straight in the wind.

Oscar's mother still lives in Bethel, where Oscar grew up, where in fact she raised all of her six sons, and where Charlie has made his home once again since his divorce a few years ago from the Kongiganak girl he married. But the foraging is no longer so good in the vicinity of populous Bethel, which has grown to a town of four thousand, and a good portion of the old woman's food now, by necessity — and to her distaste — is the *kass'aq* food that she has to buy at the supermarkets. But down here on the coast the foraging is still very good, and in fact subsistence hunting and fishing remain the chief economic activity in villages such as Kongiganak, providing explanation enough for their existence and location, just as they did for all those centuries prior to the appearance of the Russians. Elsie is delighted to be headed upstream like this, to devote an entire day to searching out the eggs of the nesting wild birds, and it was precisely for this, and the promise of fresh spring food, that she came down from Bethel with Oscar and Charlie and me in this boat.

Margaret and all the children are delighted too: serious-minded Elizabeth, who is twelve years old and has her father's pouting lower lip; eight-year-old Janet, the exuberant one, whom Oscar named this boat after, and who answers as often to her nickname, Crazy; the two little brothers; and their ten-year-old cousin, Aaron Paul. This morning, after Oscar had unexpectedly agreed to the foray, Janet danced in sweet joy throughout the tiny house, her brown feet bare, one of them labeled FOOT with a felt-tip marker and the other labeled FEET.

But Margaret didn't say a word then, and she continues to be as silent as Elsie is effervescent. She sits with her back to Oscar, facing into the wind, and I watch as she lifts her face to the sky a moment and flares her nostrils, drinking in the brackish scent of the quickening marshes. Her cheeks are high and round, her brow smooth. Her shoulders hunch slightly in the chill. Behind her glasses her face is like water at the bottom of a well: clear, pure, betraying nothing.

Half an hour after leaving the village, we reach an area where the river twists past a covey of meltwater lakes. Oscar throws the Evinrude into neutral and then kills it, allowing the boat to skim into a portion of the bank where swaths of undercut sod have split and fallen into a sort of stairway up the incline to the surrounding tableland. Charlie pulls the hard-won anchor out of the bow and then climbs stiffly up the bank, digging its tines into the parched grass above us. The rest of us empty out of the boat, Elsie skipping nimbly as a goat up the steps of sod. Oscar and Margaret climb up separately, still without sharing a glance, and I doubt that they've so much as exchanged a word all day.

At the top of the bank we stand in a row and look out upon a huge, unportioned field of chalky greens and wintry yellows and browns, the lakes in the distance winking cobalt blue in the sunlight. Now that the big motor has stopped, the quiet is almost palpable. But slowly that ringing silence is overcome, and overwhelmed, by another sort of ringing, almost a roar, startling in its pervasiveness and the breadth of its register: a sourceless, throbbing cacophony of bird cries, a sound like the morning of the fifth day of creation.

Oscar grunts as he drives the sharp end of a broken oar into the grass at the top of the bank so that it stands upright like a fence post, marking the position of the boat. He stands there for a moment with his lips pressed together, hard and white, just as he did while he stood at his window earlier this morning, staring into the light glancing off the smooth surface of the bay.

Then, without a word or gesture to one another, we fan singly and in pairs out into the tundra.

2

I WATCH OSCAR move off upriver with Junior's hand in his, a bear, or maybe a lion, and his cub, while Charlie takes off alone in the opposite direction, a twelve-gauge shotgun cradled in his arms. Others depart at angles between these extremes: Margaret and Crazy toward an area of rolling frost heaves; Elizabeth, with Clayton on her shoulders, in the direction of some marshes covered over with horsetail; Elsie, by herself, toward one of the lakes. The nephew, Aaron, stays with me. Dressed in a brown leather flight jacket with Army Air Force arm patches, the boy is as lean as a willow switch, and his skin seems to have been brushed like varnish over the planes of his face.

We stand in the midst of a landscape more peculiar than mere tundra. About twenty miles east of here stretches the wide mouth of the Kuskokwim River. The Kuskokwim is the chief artery into the interior for this part of Alaska, twisting more than 700 miles from the foothills of the Alaska Range to this remote and soggy coast, draining (along with its tributaries) an area of more than 50,000 square miles. Far to the north, about 150 miles distant, lies the mouth of the Yukon, the Kuskokwim's more glamorous and storied sister. But in southwestern Alaska the rivers argue to be taken on equal terms. They approach within twenty-five miles of each other at Kalskag, a Kuskokwim village seventy-five miles above Bethel and once the site of an important portage between the two. There, though the Yukon then swings sharply north to empty into Norton Sound, the two rivers' flood plains begin to open out and blend together, finally combining into a single immense alluvial fan roughly the size of Wisconsin. The coastal fringe of the Yukon-Kuskokwim Delta runs 250 miles up the coast of Alaska, from Cape Newenham to Saint Michael, and the saturated tundra of this fringe and its interior, with its seal-intestine sloughs and meltwater lakes, provides summer breeding grounds for some 24 million migratory shorebirds and waterfowl.

In its own way, I suspect, the Yukon-Kuskokwim Delta is a natural wonder on the order of, say, the Grand Canyon or Yellowstone, though of an entirely inverted sort. Just as the Grand Canyon is a monument to the erosive power of running water unconfused by other natural processes, and Yellowstone to the might of Pleistocene ice in a similarly pure application, this hybrid planet of water and silt is a monument to the converse tendency of filling in and leveling off — a monument, over the millennia, to nothing but the long and single-minded exercise of sedimentation, its motions flash-frozen each fall, then sluggishly renewed in the spring over its underlying pan of permafrost.

Here this process is played out on what seems a universal scale, the flooding and silting simply swallowing up, like the sea, whatever topography lies beneath it, every hint of the kind of relief that so distinguishes those other monuments, or indeed is characteristic, on a lesser scale, of any other landscape.

The birds that so relish this wetland converge in seasonal streams from the Pacific, Asia, and all over the Americas — converge in a place so vast and uncut, however, as to absorb them even in all their millions, scattering their nests like motes of dust, providing flyways as widely spaced across this sky as the weather systems. I don't think much of my own chances of finding any eggs here, and in fact I've been foraging like this many times around Kongiganak in the spring — once before in this very area — and have never on any occasion found more than a few broken bits of shell, and never any eggs. So instead I go back to the boat to get my shotgun out of the bow, as Charlie did. Aaron looks pleased. He points straight ahead to the lakes maybe a mile distant, in a bearing only slightly off from Elsie's, and then dances ahead of me.

The river disappears as we move away from it. Underfoot the ground is spongy beneath its cover of reindeer moss, cassiope, Labrador tea, and crowberry; this will end with surprising crispness at the margins of the lakes and ponds, and from the air it looks as though the beds of the lakes have been stamped through the mat with cookie cutters. From any ground-level perspective, however, the breadth and uniformity of this cover swallow up all other features, so the river simply vanishes as we move a short distance away from it, the matching planes of its banks blending in sight, the landmark oar the only sign to indicate that a division exists. From this distance the lakes appear as little more than sequined blue threads teased through a carpet of burlap. Aaron, who prefers Yupik to English, though he speaks both languages, points ahead to a set of white pinpoints strung like rice along a portion of one such thread. "*Qugyuut — pissurlapuk!*" he says. "Swans — let's hunt them!"

These big, straight-necked tundra swans, also known as whistling swans, are the chief ingredient of a delicious soup prepared by Margaret's grandmother, though it has taken time for me to superimpose the image of game bird on my received *kass'aq* perceptions of swans. And to see them stirring in their bright, numberless flocks here among the barrens is in fact arresting in a way that surpasses the stirrings of any other bird. Once I went hunting in the fall near here with a man named Tommy Andrew as my partner. That time I just dropped the muzzle of my gun and let squadrons of the swans pass over my head unmolested, even as Tommy called them in my direction. He had placed himself on the other side of a lake from me, and in following his call the birds flew over his position as well. My partner fired away without compunction, and two of the swans fell heavily to the ground, dropping like bags of sand out of a theater's rafters. At the end of the day he was more glad of that meat than of any of the many ducks we'd taken.

But here the swans are alert and difficult to approach as they feed on the sago pondweed growing along the bottoms of the lakes. Aaron and I stalk them, alternately crouching and crawling, skirting the rims of intervening ponds. But the birds always sense us and rise from the water in whooping, spiraling clouds long before I've gotten my shotgun in range. Then they gather and circle off toward the ocean, sometimes swinging near enough for Aaron to exhort in Yupik, "They're close. Try and shoot!" I don't think so myself, but twice I try such mortar shots anyway — to no effect on the birds, which disappear to the south with powerful bell-beats of their wings.

A short while later Aaron takes an opposite path to mine around a lake, and when he joins me he proudly pulls from his pocket a seagull egg as big as his hand. "*Elpet pikan,* it's yours," he says, presenting it to me with a white smile creasing his face, his eyes just creases themselves. Then he points suddenly to a pair of pintails skimming rapidly toward us from the east, their wings weaving flashes of violet and bronze and green. I shoot between them and drop the female into the margin of the same pond that yielded the seagull egg. Heartbreakingly, the male veers back and lands beside his dying mate. Reluctantly I take him as well, watching down my barrel as he explodes from the midst of the pellets hailing about him, the slender plume of his long black tailfeathers trailing, and falls into the pond.

Later, when Aaron and I join the others for lunch back at the boat, Oscar the Grouch tells me that the swans were out of range and spares hardly a glance for the two ducks. "Don't shoot pintails now," he scolds. "They're too damn skinny."

Elsie pinches their breasts between her fingers and says, "They're good." She thrusts out her chin, as she does habitually when she contradicts Oscar, or anybody else, and her face, with one eye closed off, looks as nicked and creased as a prize-fighter's. She says she lost the eye years ago in an accident when she was taking care of her kids, and is reluctant otherwise to talk about it. I know the pintails will be eaten, skinny or not, for Margaret wouldn't discard wild meat, though Oscar might complain about having to eat meat so lean. After lunch, how-ever, I leave my twelve-gauge in the boat and concentrate fully on the gentler task of finding eggs.

But this is worse for me than stalking swans. Aaron goes off on his own into the lakes, and I begin an erratic drift across the wavelike peat ridges and around the borders of the ponds. Sometimes I'm tantalized by bits of broken shell, or occasional feathers, or an owl pellet, or the mere presence in my ears, like surf or the echo in a seashell, of all the thrumming bird cries. But the calls come distantly, from off toward the horizon, as though these lakes had entirely emptied, and my eyes tire quickly from the monotony of the groundcover, from the mem-ory of similar long afternoons.

This time, however, my circuits start to intersect with those of a more experienced egg-finder, and I learn from watching Margaret that it pays better to rely on the birds and their behav-ior than on the thin odds of coming across a nest by chance. When a black-bellied plover shows signs of distress, whistling plaintively and floating in its colors of charcoal and old leaves from frost heave to frost heave in a circle around me, I drop to my hands and knees and scour the immediate area for its nest. Margaret glances at the bird, approaches, and finds the nest in only a minute.

Later I notice a tiny western sandpiper trailing like Tom Thumb in the wake of my boots and cheeping frantically in agitation. When I turn, the bird hops away as though flightless, flitting as needed just beyond my reach. Again the nest eludes me, and when Margaret can't quickly find it either, she drives the bird away and sits on a driftwood stump some distance removed. Margaret grew up in the neighboring village of Kwigillingok, eleven miles to the west, and as a little girl she was badly mauled by a loose sled dog. In this bright sun the faint scar that she still bears on her cheek looks like the track of a bird. She turns in my direction, her eyes drawing slowly over the ridges, and the scar disappears.

"Where's that bird?" she wonders in English. "Did you see it come back?" Then a smile plays about her lips, betrays her thoughts. She thinks mischievously about Hannah, her grandparents' adopted teenage daughter, who has left her two-year-old with the old couple and gone off to Bethel. "It must be Hannah's grandmother, abandoning her children like that."

But then the sandpiper reappears, landing and settling into a patch of bog cranberry thirty or forty feet away. Margaret rises from her stump and goes directly to the spot. The little bird's four tiny eggs are maroon and slate gray, sharply pointed and full of promise. "We should take them all," Margaret says. "That way she'll be fooled into laying another clutch, if they're not too old. But she won't if there's even just one egg left."

Others find eggs as well. Oscar locates a yellowleg's nest when the long-beaked bird nearly scares the wits out of him by exploding like a ptarmigan from right under his feet, but then he calls Crazy over and lets her find the eggs. Elsie finds a dozen eggs of various sorts by foraging skillfully on her own among the lakes, but she falls on the tundra coming back to the boat, and four of them break. Elizabeth finds a lesser golden plover's nest, but Margaret has been watching, and she discourages the girl from taking the eggs. The plover was too aggressive in the way it pursued and harassed Elizabeth, Margaret says, and probably the eggs are too far along.

No one's eggs are welcomed more delightedly, however, than those that tiny Clayton finds. Elizabeth can hardly tell the story, she laughs so hard. "I was carrying him up on my shoulders, you know, and one of his boots fell off. And then just while I'm bending down to pick it up, right then, he points down into that grass and tells me, 'Look.' Gee, I couldn't believe it."

The semipalmated sandpiper eggs that result from this precocious foraging won't be eaten immediately, like the rest. Instead Margaret will boil them and keep them in the cool of the entryway at her house. Then, later this summer, she'll throw these eggs, along with candy and other foods, some household and toilet items, and a number of cut strips of cloth and yarn, to a shrieking and laughing assembly of women — the grandmothers and mothers of any girl in the village that Clayton might conceivably marry. This will be his *uqiquq*, his seal party, a centuries-old observance that marks a male's new status as a provider — an event happening singularly early in Clayton's case.

The Yupik term *uqiquq* relates to seal oil and refers to the taking of a bearded seal, an animal not only rich in that nutritious commodity but charged with a peculiar spiritual power in the ideology that still informs and supports this hunting economy. Once a boy or young man captures one of these great seals, the *uqiquq* that is given for him formally welcomes him to the village's pool of marriageable males. But an *uqiquq* may also be mounted to commemorate the first harvest of any wild food, including sandpiper eggs. In a number of the villages upriver on the Kuskokwim, and around Bethel, these seal parties are rarely or never celebrated anymore, though I remember that Elsie attended one near her home last week. In Kongiganak and other coastal communities, however, they are still performed, much as Susie Chanigkak, Margaret's grandmother, has always per-

formed them, and they are even enjoying something of a renais-
sance, with daughters now occasionally feted in the same manner.

Clayton sits in the boat and sips at a can of orange soda, heedless of his renown, the pop trickling down his chin. Elizabeth
places the eggs in a plastic bucket floored with moss and then
sets the bucket up on the boat's forward thwart. "Put that
bucket down, stupid!" Oscar booms. "Them eggs'll fall and
break. What you doing, putting it up so high?"

Elizabeth cringes as though struck, lifting the eggs down to
the floorboards. I prop my back against that same thwart and
start to nod off; I find that by now the thunder of Oscar's edgi-
ness, his suspicion that this egg-hunting may be a costly mistake,
registers hardly at all on a sensibility grown more diffuse than
in even a three-year-old like Clayton. I'm leg-sore from all my
walking, wind-burned, drowsy, and everything seems to come
at me at once in the avian frenzy of this world, almost as if in a
dream: the distant rattle of the sandhill cranes; the brief, busy
flights of the black-bibbed Lapland longspurs whisking from rise
to rise; the little dunlins rocking like hunchbacked sailors along
the shores of the lakes; the striking scarlet flush on the necks of
the breeding phalaropes; the strange, whiffling thrum of the common snipes as they lay their tailfeathers like sounding boards
against the air in courtship.

I absorb all this now as I have all day, and just as I always
have: with hardly a hint of a subsistence hunter's focal purpose,
a forager's attention to relevant minutiae, even when I try con-
sciously to assume that stance. Young Aaron sees the big flocks
of game birds approaching from the horizons long before I do.
Tiny Clayton almost falls on his face into a clutch of eggs, while
I need help to cash in on my own near misses. For brief periods,
maybe, I exist here almost as pointedly as Margaret does, or
Elsie, or Oscar when he's not thinking of everything he's already
sunk into this commercial fishing season and everything that's
already gone wrong, or promises to; but then I find myself distracted by something as extraneous as the sight of a stilt-legged

dowitcher prospecting through a bed of goose grass, and I'm lost to my own purposes here, like a child unable to concentrate long enough to learn simple addition. Instead I meander casually through a world that has become a pleasant art form, and I find the hunter's task of asserting any firm place for myself in its motions and flux as puzzling as Arabic. The effort to separate and anticipate its stirrings ends up tiring me, frustrating me, and I come back empty-handed, too proud to pretend that the seagull egg Aaron gave me was mine.

The stern of the *Crazy J* is heavy with water that leaked in through the bow while we were gone, and Oscar starts his little electric bilge pump by touching the bare end of a wire to a battery post. The water gurgles over the side as though through a faucet. I don't remember ever hearing Charlie fire his shotgun; I watch through half-open eyes as he returns with no game, stows the gun beneath the boat's small foredeck, and then stands at Oscar's side behind the stern thwart. Crazy fetches the bucket that contains Clayton's eggs and shows it to him. Charlie smiles as he looks into the bucket, his teeth splayed and chipped like broken crockery, his upper lip wisped by fine black hairs. His eyes are sleepy and vacant as he looks up again from the eggs, and his cheeks hang like curtains down the length of his face.

The other eggs as well are secured safely in the boat, and Oscar starts the motor. Before I dropped down the bank and into the boat twenty minutes ago, I turned and saw the women trailing reluctantly back, looking like a band of gypsies: Margaret advancing prettily across the peat ridges in her flowered cotton parka cover, her *qaspeq,* the two boys holding on to her hands, and Elsie some distance behind them in her green nylon jacket and bright bandanna, carrying her eight unbroken eggs in her pockets. The old woman's mouth was open in a laugh again, and her legs were so bowed that she rocked back and forth like a dunlin as she walked.

Elsie is still laughing, astonished at breaking those eggs, but the mask on Margaret's face is firmly in place once more. Margaret sits on the middle thwart as the boat swings downstream, her back to the bow this time, her eyes gazing emptily between the two brothers.

3 ⊙ OSCAR AND CHARLIE and I sit around the converted telephone cable spool that serves as the Actives' supper table, and Oscar laughs as he describes what it was like commercial fishing with Charlie a few summers ago at Quinhagak, a village on the southern side of Kuskokwim Bay. "That summer Charlie had pneumonia, but we went down from Bethel anyway," he says. "He steered the boat, and I hauled the nets and did all the work. But then I got a pinched nerve in my back, and I couldn't hardly move. But Charlie was feeling a little bit better by then, so I just started steering, and Charlie did all the work."

Charlie shakes his head and says, "It was stormy down there that year, man. One day we spent the whole time just surfing down those waves."

"Yep, they were as high as the roof on that *lagyaq* there," Oscar adds, pointing out the window to the little shed where Margaret and her grandmother cut and store their fresh meat.

Charlie looks at the *lagyaq* and still can't believe that he got talked into going out into weather like that. "Gambling with our lives," he says.

Oscar laughs again. "It's a good gamble when you survive."

Margaret clears our plates away, taking them to a sink where water is contained in a plastic basin and clean dishes and mugs are piled in perilous architecture in a drying rack on the counter, and I wonder what she thinks of Oscar's gambling this year. On our way up to the nesting grounds this morning, Junior pointed out to me various items of the boat's cargo — the Styrofoam grub box, the broken oar, the VHF radio, and the new marine battery and the propane camp stove, both of which Oscar had just bought in Bethel out of his and Margaret's income tax refund — and after each item set himself in front of me and said in his stentorian voice, "It's not yours!" Finally he took hold of the boat itself, latching onto the starboard gunwale with both tiny fists, reminding me that even the *Crazy J* itself wasn't mine.

Margaret knew that — knew that for better or for worse, the big wooden boat now belonged to her husband. Oscar had just bought it from Jerry Demientieff, an old school buddy of his, promising to pay Jerry $1000 for it at the end of the fishing season. Last night he told Margaret, "It'll pay for itself no sweat. It won't fill up with fish as fast as that little aluminum boat I been borrowing from Joe Brown, and I won't have to be running back and forth to the tenders all the time making deliveries. Instead I'll just keep my net in the water — save time, save gas — and get more fish, you know?"

Margaret nodded, though I doubt that Oscar's assurances quite quelled her concern. I'm sure it's already occurred to her, as it has to me, that maybe there is too much that belongs to Oscar this summer, that quite possibly he's put too much in the pot and is already overextended. Besides this new used boat, with its $1000 price tag, and besides the Skidoo Safari snow machine that he wants to buy from me in the fall, and besides the gear that he has already bought for this boat, there is the new thirty-horse Nissan outboard that he bought last month from Swanson's Marina in Bethel. Margaret had to arrange for a $1500 loan from the First National Bank in order to buy that motor, and they still have eleven more payments to make on the loan.

Of course, the herring are coming to Cape Avinof, if they're not there already, though they don't appear to have arrived just yet. Oscar's brother Buzzo now lives in Kipnuk, the village closest to Cape Avinof, and Buzzo called this morning to say that there was still too much ice off the cape and that Fish & Game wouldn't be opening the fishery immediately. On the strength of that, Oscar agreed to take the family egg-hunting, though no sooner had he done so than he began to get nervous, and to start thinking that maybe he should be traveling instead, especially with everything he's got riding on this season.

Though potentially lucrative, the herring season is a short one, and it's not until the various species of Pacific salmon start swimming in waves up the Kuskokwim River that the real money crop of southwestern Alaska finally arrives. The salmon will be there all summer long, available to fishermen three to four times each week in periods set aside exclusively for commercial — as opposed to subsistence — fishing. But given the commitments that Oscar presently supports, and given the sort of money that he could realistically hope to make this summer anyway, from both the Cape Avinof and the Kuskokwim fisheries, he can scarcely afford to have a single thing go wrong — and a couple of things already have.

Jerry Demientieff now lives in Kasigluk, a village about thirty miles northwest of Bethel, and last week Oscar and I went up there in the borrowed aluminum skiff — with the Nissan on its back — to pick up the wooden boat. We traveled on the Johnson River, a tributary to the Kuskokwim, and on the way back to Bethel, as I followed in the skiff behind the newly christened *Crazy J*, the Nissan just stopped dead in my hands. Oscar towed the skiff to Bethel and then left the motor at the marina, saying, "I don't know what's wrong with that thing, but I hope the warranty covers it. If it don't, I don't know what I'm gonna do."

Then Oscar discovered some cracked ribs in the bow of the *Crazy J*. Yesterday, in fact, he was afraid that the boat might break up beneath us in some heavy weather on the Kuskokwim, and the cussing that he then gave to Jerry, who had never said anything about those cracked ribs, was what later suggested to Oscar that he might legitimately teach the art to those less skilled. Now, if it's at all possible, he wants to be in Kipnuk at least a full day before the herring season opens, both for the margin of safety a day would provide and for the purpose of repairing his damaged boat. "The buyers don't want the herring anyway, just the roe," he told me. "And roe counts are gonna be real high when Fish & Game finally opens it up. So I want to get over to Kipnuk ahead of time, get Buzzo's help with fixing that damn leak, and be ready."

Finally, there is this other brother, Charlie, the youngest, Oscar's long-time fishing partner and also an alcoholic. Oscar himself has vowed that he's on the wagon now, that he isn't going to do any more drinking in Bethel, not this fishing season nor anytime after that. It seems also that he's been using my presence this summer to encourage a similar resolve in Charlie. Before we left for Kasigluk last week, Oscar and I rendezvoused in Bethel at the little efficiency his mother now rents. Charlie showed up drunk at Elsie's that afternoon, his slumberous eyes lit up, his arms and legs in spastic motion from the rocket fuel running through them. He said to me, "Oscar told me not to do any drinking this summer 'cause you were gonna be hanging around. But I'll tell you something, Rick, I don't stop drinking for nobody — not you, not the great Oscar Active, not George Bush, not the pope, not nobody. If anybody's gonna stop me from drinking, it's gotta be me, myself. That's the only way it's gonna start happening. You know what I'm saying?"

Then Charlie laughed and said, "Oscar, you remember that time Rick got drunk with all of us? That was after that basketball tournament in Napakiak. When was that? Maybe in seventy-nine?" He clapped his hands and slid down from his seat to the shag rug, down on all fours, his legs suddenly watery, a drunk imitating a drunk. "He couldn't even stand, man." He grinned up at Elsie, who just ignored him, and said, "Ma, you shoulda seen him. He was yellin' out, 'Help me up! Please somebody help me up!' "

Oscar wanted to get out on the water that day before the tide got too low on the Johnson, before we ran the risk of bending a propeller on the ice still frozen fast to the river bottom. He didn't like being delayed by Charlie, but even he had to smile as Charlie rolled about on the rug. "That was the year that benchwarmer hit that long shot at the end of the third overtime, or we woulda won that tournament," Oscar said. "Gee, I couldn't believe he made that shot."

"But we won a lot of other tournaments, Oscar," Charlie said. "We were the best, you know that? The Kongiganak Hunters, man — there wasn't nobody could beat us."

"Yep, then we got old," Oscar said.

The only vow that Charlie took that day was that he wasn't going to fish with Oscar at Cape Avinof, as he has in years past. "Them herring are too filthy, Oscar," he said. "I'm retired from herring fishing. You're gonna have to find someone else be your herring captain this year." Oscar didn't say a word, just set his lips and looked away, like he did this morning after he drove the oar into the bank of the river and prepared to set off with Junior.

But of course here Charlie is after all, maybe because he felt he actually owed Oscar the help, especially considering all his brother's bills, or because he was flat broke himself and needed the money, or because, with his bootleg vodka all drunk up, he was just too hung over to argue when Oscar went to his house to get him yesterday. At Cape Avinof, Oscar only needs skilled help, the sort that Charlie can provide. Later, on the Kuskokwim, he will also need the commercial salmon fishing permit that only Charlie possesses. Certainly that's part of what makes Oscar afraid now, contributing to that sense of gambling with his life again, though in a different way. I'm sure it makes him wonder sometimes how he got here from where he was, from the way things were in those days before he got old.

Now Oscar goes out to the front steps to smoke a cigarette while Margaret fetches bags of wet laundry from both of the little bedrooms. She places these first in a pile beside the mail-order shelves that hold the TV, the children's books, the family photo albums, and the various basketball trophies, and then starts carrying them one by one to the clotheslines outside. The sky above her is slowly filling with clouds like bolts of dirty linen, and the wind is blowing crisp and cold again off the bay.

4 I FIRST SAW Oscar Active in the fall of 1977, the year that I came as a first-year high school English teacher, fresh from Massachusetts, to the new school that the state had just built in Kongiganak. I remember Oscar was playing basketball on Kongiganak's outdoor wooden playdeck, where he rose shirtless and monumental from the midst of the other players. He was probably slimmer then, though by no means lean and hard like the rest, and with his round belly and narrow hips, his pants had trouble keeping a modest height in back.

He stood that day in the middle of an end-to-end pickup game, dribbling the ball casually twenty-five to thirty feet from the basket and well beyond the pale of the zone defense ranged against him. I remember thinking that this huge Eskimo probably hadn't played much ball and that must be why he was content so far from the basket, where his size was almost a liability against the quick little guards playing in front of him. Quite suddenly, however, the big man picked up his dribble and brought the ball over his head, rising at the same time so high and so effortlessly into the air that it seemed he'd been lifted by piano wire. Liquidly the wrist flicked forward, in a textbook jump shot, and the ball arced smoothly toward the basket. It sailed through the hoop, banged against the frayed chains that served as the net, dropped to the boards beneath, and bounced off into the mud around the playdeck. No one expressed any surprise or startled admiration. Not deigning to look back, Oscar loped easily to the other end of the court while someone on the opposite team tiptoed into the mud to retrieve the ball.

I didn't know it then, but Oscar was still a newcomer himself in Kongiganak that year, though his neighbors had known him for years as a famous athlete. His feats on that dilapidated playdeck, and later in the new school gym, were no different from those they had already heard about on the radio from Bethel in the early 1970s. People admire athletes here as much as any-

where else, and only two generations ago people gathered in
qasgiit, or kashims, large community buildings built into the
ground and roofed over with driftwood logs and banks of sod,
and engaged in such contests of endurance and agility as could
be contained in that space. But the kashims were also the ceremonial bastions of Yupik shamanism, and slowly these buildings were destroyed at the urging of Christian missionaries. In
at least some respects, the high school gyms that have been built
in many Kuskokwim villages during the past two decades function as the heirs to these kashims, and people in Bethel and all
its satellite communities have gone mad as Hoosiers over basketball. Similarly, the region's present city-league tournaments,
such as the tournament in the upriver village of Napakiak that
Charlie recalled with Oscar, have in part replaced the great winter festivals and intervillage gatherings celebrated in the region
before the coming of the missionaries.

Oscar actually spent the early years of his childhood in Kasigluk, where Jerry Demientieff lives now. A good many of his uncles and aunts and cousins live there as well, and Oscar's father,
James, has gone back there since his separation from Elsie some
fifteen years ago. But when Oscar was still in grade school and
James and Elsie were still together, the whole family moved to
Bethel, which even then was a predominantly English-speaking
community, even among its Eskimo majority. Since he has lived
in remote and traditional Kongiganak, Oscar has once again become fluent in Yupik, though he more often speaks in English.

During Oscar's teenage years in Bethel, the town's regional
high school was the only secondary school in the area. Those
youngsters from the outlying villages who wanted a high school
diploma but who didn't want to attend a federal boarding
school in the Lower 48 or elsewhere in Alaska came to Bethel to
stay in the school dormitory or live with relatives. So at that time
Bethel Regional's varsity basketball teams represented every little village up and down the Kuskokwim. Almost as though I
were there myself, I can see Oscar as an ambitious fifteen-year-

old, bucktoothed and gangly and shockingly thin, disdaining to learn those post-up moves underneath the basket recommended for tall men, instead standing at glamorously long distances in Bethel's cavernous gym and shooting prayer after prayer at the distant rim, until after a time a surprising portion of those prayers began to be answered.

I thought at first that Oscar's long-range shooting, in the days before the advent of the three-point shot in basketball, was just showboating. Now I wonder if acting contrary to his own gifts was just one way of taking revenge on himself, of punishing himself for his father's alcoholism. But certainly he also liked the attention that such shots commanded, and sometimes this made for trouble between Oscar and his coach, once Oscar had filled out and established himself on the varsity. One time at practice the coach got mad enough to throw a basketball at him for playing out of position, and in response Oscar announced he was quitting the team and left the gym. A number of other players followed suit, including the four other starters. The next day Oscar received both an apology and a formal request to return. Still angry, he shrugged his shoulders and said he'd think about it. Finally, thirty minutes into the next practice, the young prince in exile led his sympathizers back into the gym.

Later came Oscar's desperation half-court shot against the team's archrivals, Nome. The Moravian pastor in Bethel interrupted his evening service to report the final score, and listeners to the radio ran whooping into the streets of Bethel and the surrounding villages, firing their shotguns into the air. In 1974, Oscar's senior year, the Bethel Warriors were strong favorites to win a Class C championship, but their coach was home with a blood disorder on the night of their first-round game in the state tournament, and the confused and rudderless team went down to defeat and early elimination.

After moving to Kongiganak, Oscar recruited and organized and captained the Kongiganak Hunters, coaxing his teammates into buying expensive white uniforms, with red and blue trim, from a supplier in New York City. Charlie moved down from Bethel to be with Oscar and play on that team, and I played on it as well, traveling with them either by small plane or by snow machine to games and tournaments in the other villages. In the salad days of the Hunters, Oscar's chief concern as captain and strategist was often to curb his own and his teammates' scoring enough to avoid humiliating their opponents. Of course, in Kongiganak the audiences were smaller and less cosmopolitan than the audiences he'd played before in Bethel. The bleachers and piled gym mats in Kongiganak were lined in part with old men who remembered hunting by kayak in storm surges out on the bay, who had never gone to school or played basketball, who spoke not a word of English, and old women who had borne their babies on caribou skins on the floors of dark and seeping underground sod houses. But these as much as anyone else loved the speed and spectacle and bright patriotic color that Oscar's team provided.

It still rather surprises me, though, that Oscar finally came to live in Kongiganak, a place very different from Bethel, and far from both his own family roots and the scene of his schoolboy triumphs. But maybe it's no more unexpected than his courtship of Margaret Paul, who went to Bethel from Kongiganak in 1970 as a boarding student at the high school. Grave, quiet, studious, and shy — just as her grandmother, Susie Chanigkak, had raised her — Margaret was much more traditional in her demeanor than Yupik girls who had grown up in Bethel or in nearby villages: much more reserved, much more instinctively respectful of her teachers and elders, much less inclined to seek or solicit attention. I can only imagine how astonished she must have been when the one whom Charlie describes, then as now, as Oscar the Great began teasing her by stealing her pencils and breaking them. Margaret wouldn't say a word, would only rise quietly from her seat to get another. "The school district was rich in them days," Oscar told me. "They had lots of pencils."

Eventually Oscar himself was surprised — surprised by where

this teasing led him, surprised by how empty he felt when the girl with the broken pencils went home to Kongiganak that year for Christmas vacation. A lot of the other girls in school were also taken aback by the attentions Oscar the Great devoted to this unassuming girl from the coast, and eventually jealous enough to write unkind things on restroom walls. Maybe Margaret answered in part to a streak of shyness in Oscar, well concealed beneath his bluster and wildness. During a school dance in January, after the boarding students had come back from vacation, Oscar couldn't bring himself to risk asking her to dance. Instead he got his friend Ronnie Simon to ask her for him, and after she consented, and after they danced, he found — after a struggle — the courage to ask her to a movie at Swanson's Theater the next night. "I said I'd pay, but I didn't have no money. Tickets were fifty cents in them days, before that old movie house shut down. I went and I bummed a buck from my dad. He didn't mind."

Maybe James Active didn't mind, but George and Susie Chanigkak certainly did. I know George and Susie as Aataq and Aanaq, or Father and Mother, the terms of respect used for them by everybody in Margaret's family in Kongiganak. Aataq and Aanaq had taken a large share in raising Margaret since the death of their only daughter, Lilly, Margaret's mother, when Margaret was just a little girl. In keeping with Yupik custom, they'd arranged soon after Margaret's birth for her to marry Tommy Andrew, a boy from another Kongiganak family and later my partner when we hunted swans. Tommy was going to high school at a federal boarding school in Oklahoma and had been writing hopefully to Margaret. Oscar, in contrast, came not only from faraway Bethel but from a family of notorious drinkers, and Aataq and Aanaq wanted no part of him.

But Margaret found herself falling in love with Oscar, maybe precisely because of that shyness, that unexpected vulnerability. Or maybe, being from Bethel, Oscar represented to her the larger world beyond the village, a world whose mysteries and opportunities were already piquing her interest. In any event, this whole Western notion of falling in love was something of a puzzle to Aataq and Aanaq; traditional Yupik marriages were more pragmatic. Love might or might not follow afterward, as certainly it had in their case, but it wasn't considered a requirement for a successful union.

Whether she was in love with Oscar or not, however, and whether she was already pregnant or not, Margaret would never have married him without her grandparents' blessing, so firm was her loyalty. And they in turn would never have given that blessing without the intercession, at Elsie's urging, of a relative of the Yupik pastor of the Bethel Moravian church. Aataq and Aanaq finally pronounced this blessing a year after Oscar and Margaret's graduation from high school, on a day when Oscar was driving a cab in Bethel. "My mom was complaining," Oscar said. "She wanted me to make some money, or I woulda been home that day." He happened to go down First Avenue with one of his fares, and there he saw Margaret, just flown in from Kongiganak, with her bags on the steps of his house, the little one near the Kuskokwim that Charlie now occupies.

Oscar called his boss on his CB radio when he saw her and said he was going blue — taking his cab out of service for the day.

"Going blue? You can't do that," his boss said.

"Just watch me," replied Oscar.

Oscar views this as strong-mindedness: his willingness to go blue, his readiness to talk back to his boss or coach or anybody else, just like his mother, and then do what he thinks right. On the whole this kind of assertiveness had served him well in that increasingly *kass'aq* town upriver, whose population now is about half and half, Eskimo and white. But in conservative and entirely Yupik Kongiganak, after centuries of living in close quarters and having to get along and work together to accomplish their hunting and fishing, people define strong-mindedness in terms of very different qualities: they prefer self-control, compliance, and a willingness to merge seamlessly into the group;

they prefer the sort of restraint Margaret exhibited when Oscar stole her pencils and broke them. And nowhere were Oscar's deficiencies in these respects more apparent than at the Hunters' basketball games in Kongiganak, where he'd go into towering rages at some of the volunteer referees' more irregular calls.

At first, after Oscar and Margaret decided to move down from Bethel, the chief Hunter's new neighbors simply looked on aghast as this huge man bellowed into the faces of officials who sometimes came no higher than his uniform number, who might be John N. Andrew's oldest son or Kenneth David's well-liked brother. Margaret just looked away, shrinking into her seat in embarrassment. Then came whistles, jeers, hoots. Finally even the most rabid of the Hunters' supporters cheered as technical fouls were assessed against Oscar, and when in rare instances he was ejected. Someone native to Kongiganak wouldn't have openly disputed an official's call, and certainly wouldn't have displayed such rage unless ready to resort to actual assault. Oscar was nowhere near that point; he never laid hands on a referee, nor used his size aggressively against his opponents, no matter how angry he was with the course of a game, nor even hurt his opponents by accident, his body control was so perfect.

But appearances were otherwise, and someone native to Kongiganak would have been tamed immediately by public opinion, or at least by the supplications of his wife, never to protest again. But Oscar the Great went right on bellowing. Only the eventual decline of the Hunters, and a growing suspicion on Oscar's part that the games didn't really mean anything anyway, took some (but not all) of the fire out of his tantrums. He began devoting more of his energy to his subsistence hunting and fishing, which Oscar says is the reason that he wanted to move to Kongiganak in the first place, the coast being much richer in wildlife than the tired lands around Bethel. I suppose the name that he chose for his basketball team in 1977 is meaningful in that respect, suggesting the entirely Yupik way in which, at length, he hoped to define himself in Kongiganak.

No doubt the importance of his commercial fishing and the

money it brought in also increased in his mind as Elizabeth and the other children arrived, and as the expense of equipment and ammunition and fuel for his subsistence hunting and fishing grew from year to year. With his commercial fishing, in a certain sense at least, he had already gone blue, taking it upon himself in 1978, after an exceptionally poor season on the river, to sell his limited-entry Kuskokwim River commercial salmon permit to a buyer he remembers only as "some woman from Anchorage." This was against Margaret's advice, but even today Oscar refuses to second-guess himself on this, saying that he sold the permit at a good time and at a good price, getting $10,000 for it. That $10,000 paid a lot of bills for a lot of months, but it's gone now, and these days the sale of his salmon permit is one of the few subjects the voluble Oscar prefers not to talk about much.

Because Charlie still has *his* permit, however, Oscar can still make money on salmon, even if he hasn't made much recently. Officially Oscar is Charlie's helper, but since Oscar supplies the boat and most of the gear, the two brothers split fifty-fifty, as they did when they both had permits. But it's not quite the same as it used to be; now Oscar can fish only when Charlie is there in the boat with him, and when they go to a tender to sell their fish, now it's always Oscar the Great who waits in the boat and cleans out the scales and blood, while Charlie goes officiously to the tender's wheelhouse and collects their pay, later awarding Oscar his cut. In summers past, more and more often it seems, Charlie wasn't always sober enough to go out during the hours set aside for commercial fishing on the Kuskokwim; but then, neither was Oscar.

I think Oscar feels himself slipping ever more firmly into the same shirt of fire that his father has worn much of his life. When we were in Kasigluk last week, Oscar chose not to stay at his father's house but at Jerry Demientieff's. Jerry has a bulldog's squat muscularity, and prides himself on his frankness. He told Oscar that his dad wasn't doing so good, that the old man could hardly lift anything anymore, he was so stiff, and was having a tough time these days living by himself. Then he said, "I saw him yesterday, and he tells me he just got back from Anchorage, and I told him I knew that a long time ago. He says, 'How the hell you know that?' I says, 'Shit, you were so stinky drunk I could smell you.' "

James Active, Senior, is lonely now, and failing, but somehow he manages. Oscar and his brothers speak in a manner almost approaching reverence about all that James taught them about the river and the sea and the tundra, almost as though this were a bountiful kingdom bequeathed by the old man to his sons. I remember watching Oscar as we came up the Johnson River to Kasigluk, seeing him beam that jack-o'-lantern smile as he watched other fishermen dropping their *qaluit* — dip nets big enough to snag the front end of a Volkswagen — into the river's shimmering banks of smelt and other hunters waiting in their boats beneath the underbrush of the banks for the flocks of common scoters that fly down the rivers in spring.

But the kingdom isn't always that benign. Both Oscar and Jerry told me about James's National Guard training exercises in January 1961, when he and ten others went down in a helicopter near Napakiak during a ferocious winter storm. Nine were killed instantly, and James suffered a broken neck. Nonetheless he managed to drag the single other survivor away from the burning wreckage. Then only James's insistence that they drink each other's urine kept them from freezing to death during the night. "But seems like his real bad drinking started after that," Oscar said. "His neck hurt all the time, and he didn't want to take that medicine they gave him, so he just drank instead."

Jerry mentioned someone they both knew who had just been arrested in Bethel for some crime committed while he was drunk.

"Him?" Oscar said incredulously. "Ain't he a preacher?"

"Sure, but give him a bottle and he's just a worthless fart on earth," said Jerry.

"Yep, like any Eskimo." Oscar sighed. "I was doing really

good last summer, but then I just had that one little sip with Charlie, man, and *bam* — I was gone."

The next day Oscar went over to James's on the off chance that he might have a marine battery he could lend him for the big Evinrude Oscar had just installed on the *Crazy J,* just as James had once loaned a buck for Oscar to take his girl to the movies. The old man stood before an unmade bed in the middle of his one-room house, the contents of a vinyl suitcase half strewn across the floor. His face was white and long, his chin tapering to a point, his lower lip wet and pendulous. His eyes peered birdlike from what appeared to be mere scratches on his face, and his hair was a nearly invisible white stubble, like frost on a stone. He'd been rummaging through the suitcase on the floor, but suddenly he stopped and pulled his wallet out of his back jeans pocket. From the wallet he drew a blue-and-white airplane ticket. "Here it is. I got it," James said.

"That your ticket back from Anchorage?" Oscar asked.

James barked a short, chortling laugh. "I couldn't find that ticket in Anchorage, even I looked all over that hotel room there. So then I let Matthew buy me a new one, maybe two hundred bucks. Then I get home here and I find the other ticket right in my own wallet."

He dropped stiffly onto the bed, his eyes shining with merriment, while his son stood in the middle of the floor, shifting his weight from foot to foot. Oscar's brow was clouded over, as though he couldn't decide what face to wear. Elizabeth and Crazy had come to Kasigluk with us, and they huddled like mice against one wall, covering their mouths and whispering between themselves as they peeked furtively at a gallery of family snapshots tacked and taped to the wood. No, James didn't have a marine battery, but maybe Jerry did, and Oscar should ask him.

Of course Oscar had already asked Jerry. Oscar stared into corners, avoiding his father's look, but James wasn't looking at Oscar the Great anyway. He gazed as fondly at his useless Alaska Airlines ticket as at a lottery winner, and the trickster laughed again as he thought of his brother Matthew coughing up the money to buy him a new one.

5 TODAY IS AANAQ'S eightieth birthday; or at least June 1, 1909, is the date that everybody agrees on for her, since not even she knows exactly when she was born. Probably she's a little older than that. She places her birth somewhere between 1905 and 1910 in the now abandoned village of Orotok. She sits on her couch smiling, the intersecting lines of her face laid in the track of decades of such smiles. One of her eyes is blue with cataracts, like a cat's-eye marble, and she's wearing the butterfly-shaped barrette and the imitation diamond earrings she has received as gifts. Hanging from a hook above the oil stove in this neat house is a traditional *ipuun,* a large wooden ladle, which Aataq has just finished carving for her from a piece of dry spruce.

The radio on a shelf above the old woman is tuned to KYUK, the AM station in Bethel, and callers from there and from other villages here on the coast are phoning birthday greetings to be relayed over the air to Susie Chanigkak in Kongiganak. She smiles most brightly at the greeting from Harvey, her grandson, the second of Margaret's two brothers. Harvey works as an aircraft mechanic in Bethel and shares Charlie's house.

Charlie, who is sitting at Aanaq's table eating salmon soup, says to Oscar, "I hope Harvey's not drinking and tearing up my house." He likes to keep his house clean, and usually it's as neat and orderly as Aanaq's. I wonder if he's so fastidious that way because it's one element he can control — usually — in a life that otherwise has passed beyond that point. The house used to sit on the riverbank directly overlooking the Kuskokwim, though it was Elsie's house in those days, and still is Elsie's, really. It was at that house in 1979, just as Charlie remembered, that the Hunters gathered for a listless post-tournament party following their overtime defeat at the Napakiak Invitational Basketball Tournament. But the party livened up considerably with the purchase of some bootleg whiskey, and we wrought terrible destruction on Elsie's house. She was gone all that night. I met her for the first time the following morning, her single eye widening in astonishment as she pulled the bedclothes from my face and beheld my white man's features. Then she turned away, raging as she picked her way through the tumbled furniture and broken glass to rouse the other miscreants.

Today the house is in a little cul-de-sac near Watson's Corner, where the white satellite dish of Bethel CableVision looms over the traffic. A few years after that party, the riverbank began to disappear from under it, and the little building was moved three hundred yards back from the river to its present spot on Weber Circle. This area is now the geographic center of the town, which over the years has been retreating in fits from that crumbling bank. To the east of Watson's Corner are the big Alaska Commercial Company Store, called the AC; the Brass Buckle discotheque; the cemetery; the Bethel Native Corporation apartments, where Elsie lives; the Bethel Regional High School; and rows of low-income houses built in the 1960s by the Alaska State Housing Authority (ASHA). To the west lie the Moravian church in its grassy swale, Swanson's Marina, the Kuskokwim Inn, and the bridge over Brown's Slough, the little river that winds through the town and then empties into the Kuskokwim. That bridge then leads into the older, helter-skelter section of Bethel known since missionary days as Lousetown.

The town looks as though it were still on the move, as though everything were just in transit to a more permanent location. Its central arteries — the Chief Eddie Hoffman Highway, connecting the town and the airport; Ridgecrest Drive, running east out of Watson's Corner; Third Avenue, running west to Lousetown — are paved, but the rest of the roads are rutted dirt and gravel, looping like trails around small lakes and crisscrossing between the various houses: grand and sunny inventions of cedar and glass, or dark and rickety tarpaper shacks, or simply some compromise between these extremes, the grand and the squalid standing side by side. Similarly, the lots between the low-rise modular office buildings are dotted with rusting World War II Quonset huts, waist-high plywood steamhouses, mobile homes billowed over with mustard-yellow expandable foam, and sagging freezer vans that were once rented out as stopgap living quarters. Not a single home or business looks much like another, except in the development known simply as Housing, and all of the buildings seem to stand at odd angles, as though they had been jacked out of their foundations and were just waiting to be moved, well ahead of the next cave-in at the river. The roads reach out to the last of the houses at the town limits and then run decisively back. The tundra opens up beyond as abruptly as it does in Kongiganak, and on the maps even Bethel is just a black dot, albeit a little bit bigger, in a wide and unpeopled space: four hundred miles west of the state road system, accessible only by boat or plane, unconnected to anything else.

Oscar usually stays at Charlie's house whenever he visits Bethel without Margaret and the kids, but last week he and I slept at Elsie's apartment instead. We kept our gear at a fish camp belonging to Tony Watson, who, like Jerry Demientieff, is one of Oscar's old classmates. With his fair skin and thinning hair, good-natured Tony actually looks more *kass'aq* than Yupik. His fish camp is made up of a cleared patch of ground, a small cabin, and some drying racks, and in the summer he and his relatives cut and dry their winter supply of salmon there. Camps like these are strung up and down the Kuskokwim and off on its tributary sloughs; Tony's is on the aspen-choked riverbank directly opposite the town.

Last Friday, after Oscar and I got back from Kasigluk with the *Crazy J*, and after we'd left the broken Nissan down at Swanson's, we had some coffee in Tony's cabin. Oscar shook his head in disappointment, telling Tony that we weren't staying at Charlie's because Charlie was already drinking too much. "Gee, man, seems like he's really starting in early this summer," Oscar complained. When Tony asked Oscar when *he* was going to start in, Oscar said that he was on the wagon now, that he didn't do that shit anymore. At this Tony's eyebrows climbed up his forehead, as though he were talking to a child who had just seen Jesus.

In fact, it took only a few hours in town for Oscar to fall off the wagon, to do that shit some more. That day he needed to get identification, some guarantee for a fish buyer in Cape Avinof that he was in fact the man his commercial herring license said he was. Last summer Oscar had his driver's license suspended for twelve months for drunk driving, and then his wallet was stolen. Unable yet to replace his driver's license, he wanted to get himself a new Bethel Native Corporation shareholder's card; this would identify him as a part owner in one of the many regional and local Native corporations established by the Alaska Native Claims Settlement Act of 1971. But the only person at the BNC office authorized to issue such a card had taken the day off, Oscar discovered, and wouldn't be back to work until Tuesday because of the Memorial Day weekend.

Oscar was beside himself as he left the office. Already worried about Cape Avinof, he said at first that he was damned if he'd waste the whole weekend, and not have his gear ready, and probably miss that first opening, and that we'd just go home to Kongiganak anyway, though I don't know what he intended to do about his ID. We got our baggage out of Tony's cabin, and then we went back to town, where Oscar left me with the *Crazy J* near the mouth of Brown's Slough, at a break in the steel sea wall that runs the length of the Bethel waterfront. There a graveled ramp for launching boats climbs from the break and opens into a small patch of land in Lousetown owned by Elsie. Adolph and Maggie Lind, Oscar's grandparents on his mother's side, once lived in the house facing the road there, its walls patched out of sheets of corrugated metal. Now the house is occupied by

John, the oldest of the six brothers, who was adopted as a baby by James and Elsie. The old woman also has her own drying racks and smokehouse there.

"I got to let Charlie know what we're doing," Oscar said as he climbed into the battered Chevy pickup that he keeps in town. "I'll be right back."

I waited for more than an hour. When at last Oscar showed up again, Charlie was with him, and Charlie's camping gear was piled into the back of the pickup. Oscar said our plans had changed and we weren't going down to Kongiganak after all. "We're gonna go upriver and net some whitefish," Charlie told me, smiling his splay-toothed smile. "The first fresh fish of the year, man."

Charlie's intoxication was immediately apparent; Oscar's wasn't. The great Oscar Active handled the boat with his usual skill as we headed up the Kuskokwim and then turned into Steamboat Slough, a ribbon of deep water that provides a short cut upstream. The slough was the color of pewter beneath the low clouds, and a sprinkling rain had begun to fall, its rings on the pewter indistinguishable from the rise-rings of the feeding smelt. New-leafed quaking aspens and balsam poplars — known here as cottonwoods — crowded along its banks, and just before the slough rejoined the Kuskokwim, the blank face of a grounded ship appeared from behind their trunks. The bow of the steamboat faced squarely into the water, contemplating the current like a turtle that had dragged itself nearly to the edge of the slough and then expired.

Oscar told me it was the *Peggy Belle,* an old paddle-wheeler that his grandfather Adolph had once piloted up and down the Kuskokwim. I sat low on the floorboards, sensing at last, from the shape and tone of his words, that he'd been taking some nips with Charlie, just as he had at the start of last summer. I remembered his words to Jerry Demientieff: "One little sip with Charlie, man, and *bam* — I was gone." Behind us the *Peggy Belle* disappeared past a bend, its gutted, skull-like features in the midst of the trees looking weird and unsettling in the gloom.

But tonight Oscar feels good, and he's enjoying himself at this feast for Aanaq, who has accepted him entirely since the day she and her husband finally pronounced their blessing. Rather to his surprise, Oscar's luck still holds at Cape Avinof, along with the shelf ice, and the great shoals of herring still haven't appeared. Now Oscar has his net in good repair and the boat all loaded, and we're poised to leave for Kipnuk early tomorrow morning.

Charlie may consider that the wrong direction; he talks a lot about Bethel, and says he'd go home if he only had $40 for the plane fare and then $5 more to take a Kusko Cab from the airport to his house. But Oscar is glad he's here — not for anything to do with a license, since anyone who plunks down $50 can still get a herring permit, but partly because Charlie's experience and judgment will mean safer and more lucrative fishing and partly because he simply enjoys Charlie's company. Today Oscar finished patching his gill net, and then the two brothers built a makeshift shaker to nail to the port gunwale when they want to. This will support the net at shoulder level as they shake it clean of herring. I watched as they eyeballed the lines of the gunwale and thwarts and cut and shaped a pair of two-by-sixes to nail fast to them; then they both laughed uproariously when their first cuts proved nowhere near correct.

Oscar reaches for some Tabasco sauce to sprinkle into his soup. He says he's sure he can fix the leaks in the bow of the *Crazy J* with Buzzo's help, and then mentions again to Charlie that they should be able to do a lot better with the bigger boat. He turns to me and laughs, saying, "Yep, nineteen seventy-six was the best year I ever had commercial fishing. I made twenty thousand bucks that summer. I bought a new boat and a motor and a new snow machine. . . . I don't even remember what I did with the rest of the money."

I know that since then Oscar's paychecks have been small and

getting smaller, though to be fair, there have been factors in that
decline besides Oscar's lack of his own salmon permit and both
his and Charlie's drinking: lower fish prices, higher fuel and gear
prices, changing international currency rates, bad weather, increased interception by fishermen on the high seas and elsewhere, the timing and frequency of Fish & Game's commercial
periods on the river, and more. In recent years, in fact, Oscar's
commercial fishing has ended up being subsidized by the money
Margaret makes in her winter job as the secretary at the Kongiganak school. Margaret happens to do the bookkeeping for the
school's student activity account, and from that she has learned
how to keep track of her family's income and expenses in an
accountant's ledger. So she always knows more keenly than Oscar how thinly the family's cash resources are spread, how hard
it is to make ends meet.

I believe that money was at least half the reason why Oscar
and Margaret's reunion last Tuesday was so prickly. Oscar finally got his shareholder's card that morning, and we arrived in
Kongiganak ten hours after leaving Bethel, anchoring the boat
at low tide on the north side of the village. Then we met Margaret standing alone outside Aataq's house. She held Hannah's
two-year-old baby, Vivian, in her arms, and her eyes were bright
with anxiety. "I don't know where Junior and Clayton are.
They've been missing for half an hour," she told Oscar, and at
that he and the two girls raced off to look for them.

Ten minutes later Elizabeth found the boys at the east end of
the village, playing safely in the tall grass on the other side of
the runway where the small planes and Twin Otters land. But
all that evening husband and wife were separated by barbs of
mutual recrimination, Margaret no doubt disappointed to discover that a new marine battery, a new propane stove, and all
the routine expenses of Oscar's unexpectedly long stay in Bethel
had eaten so deeply into their tax refund, Oscar probably
ashamed about that, and angry in his suspicion that the care
Margaret had been obliged to provide for Vivian had made her

less vigilant with their own children. Ever since the sudden loss of their firstborn, Sammy, some fourteen years ago, both parents have been much impressed with the frailty of a child's life, the imminence of mischance.

But that little quarrel, patched up now, rode like a fleck of foam on darker currents of danger and distrust. Maybe the events of one terrible night last summer in Bethel had something to do with the various ways in which Oscar the Great in recent years has found himself to be diminished; maybe they had something to do with the stark arithmetic of a woman having a larger and more reliable cash income than this fisherman, and the degree to which that supplants a Yupik male's traditional provision of resources or his control over the disposition of cash; maybe they had something to do with another man, though Margaret hasn't shown herself inclined that way; maybe they had something to do with the phase of the moon, the direction of the wind, or just the way the booze went down that particular night.

Whatever provoked it, Oscar beat the hell out of Margaret. They were visiting at a friend's house in the ASHA housing section of Bethel. There Oscar, in a drunken rage, pummeled Margaret about the face and shoulders with his fists, even as she held the screaming Clayton in her arms, even as the other children screamed as well, wailing and cowering in terror.

When Oscar passed out afterward, Margaret, bruised and bleeding, gathered up the children and fled. She stayed at a women's shelter that night and flew back to Kongiganak the next day, but not before having Oscar arrested for assault and securing an injunction to keep him away from her and the kids. Then she went home to think — about sending Oscar to jail, and about divorcing her husband, and about what life would be like without this bear in her house, the man who first approached her by breaking her pencils.

Finally she decided against all that. She dropped the charges and allowed the injunction to expire, and in the fall Oscar came home again, though not without promises: a promise to Margaret to obtain counseling through Alcoholics Anonymous at the Phillips Alcoholism Treatment Center in Bethel, and a promise to the oldest, Elizabeth, who seemed to be the most scarred by what she'd witnessed, that he would never take a drink again so long as he lived.

Now, this summer more than any other before, Oscar needs to be out on the water, hauling in fish each and every period, getting rich and staying sober. I remember Jerry Demientieff listening to Oscar's plans for the wooden boat and then remarking that if you can't buy plumbing out here on the tundra, you can at least have the very best toilet paper. "So, you gonna be a rich fisherman, Ox?" He laughed. "You gonna be sitting in Kong on your honeybucket all winter and wiping your ass with hundred-dollar bills?" I wonder if investments like the boat, with its cracked ribs, and the thirty-horse Nissan, awaiting repairs, and even the snow machine he wants me to save for him are Oscar's way of keeping his mind on his fishing and on those hundred-dollar bills, and away from his memories, his doubts, his pride and shame and growing thirst. In their very raise-the-stakes recklessness, maybe they help him keep his mind away even from those vagrant thoughts of suicide that have dogged him since last summer like the rabid foxes that sometimes come wandering fiery-eyed out of the tundra and into Bethel or the villages. Those investments might also be a way of keeping Charlie's mind on his fishing, if only Charlie can see Oscar's desperation, the holes that he's in with both his business and his family, and can respond to that.

It's a good sign that Charlie is here now, but I know Oscar is afraid, especially if it turns out that he himself can't stay on the wagon. All that Friday night on the river Oscar and Charlie maintained a fiction in my presence that they were both stone sober. They argued at some length as to whether we should camp up the Gweek River, which joins the Kuskokwim about eight miles northwest of Bethel, or further upstream near a beaver lodge Charlie knew. Finally we turned up the Gweek, set a net for the night at an eddy in the current, and then pitched tent on the riverbank amid a stand of tamarack, black spruce, and paper birch. Charlie had brought their bottle, but they kept it hidden, taking it out for quick nips over the course of the evening whenever I went out of the tent. I found their hiding place later when Oscar wanted some target practice with Charlie's .222. Charlie got the rifle out of his vinyl gun case and I handed it out the tent flap to Oscar, glimpsing then a silvery bottle of Gilbey's vodka resting against the black foam of the case like a genie in a lamp.

The next morning Oscar woke up hung over, surprised to find the stern of the *Crazy J* partly filled with water and wincing when he looked up at the sky, saying, "Gee, I didn't think it rained that much last night." We picked eight fat humpback whitefish out of the net, each four to five pounds. Their scales were wide and edged in black, like the feathers of an emperor goose. We cooked two for breakfast and then went back to Bethel.

Later that afternoon Oscar dropped all pretense about the night before. Charlie was home sleeping. The pickup had been lurching and stalling in the middle of the road, and Oscar was poking around the engine, trying to find where the problem lay. Suddenly, without any provocation, he threw his wrench aside and straightened up so fast that he nearly banged his head on the hood. Then he cussed himself as hard as he could for giving in the night before, for breaking his promise to Elizabeth and starting in again with Charlie.

That night Charlie needed to replenish his supply. By referendum Bethel is a damp community, allowing the possession but not the sale of alcohol, and Oscar obligingly drove Charlie to a bootlegger's place in Housing to make a buy. Then he drove him back to Weber Circle. But then he dropped Charlie off and returned to Elsie's apartment, where he sat with his mother and the two girls and watched TV.

Oscar believes in signs, in portents, in an aura of meaning that attaches itself like a nimbus to all the actions of a person and foreshadows crucial aspects of that person's fate in its stirrings. Certain portents are obvious in their meaning; if you beat your wife all black and blue and bloody, this may be taken as a reliable sign that the very next morning the cops are going to prod you out of your stupor in the midst of dirt and stale puke and throw you in jail until your bail is posted, then threaten you with jail again if you dare to approach either your wife or your children. But the same weight of destiny is implicit as well in actions more trivial than that — a piece of good meat gone to waste, a failure to answer the door when someone who might be hungry is knocking, or even the mere approach of a forbidden or dangerous thought — and is finally expressed in eventualities that might seem cruelly out of scale to the import of that first misstep.

Besides the matter of the campsite, there was another disagreement Oscar and Charlie had on our way upriver that Friday night. Charlie needed poles for his big canvas tent, so we stopped near a grove of stunted cottonwoods, the trees all ten to fifteen feet tall, their shoots budded to the height of our hips by snowshoe hares. Oscar found two trees with the sort of forking crotch that he wanted — "There's one spreading its legs," he said — and trimmed them both down to tent-pole length with his chain saw. Then he dragged the poles behind him through the woods and down to the boat.

Meanwhile Charlie was admiring a ten-foot spruce log tied with a rope to the trunk of one of the cottonwoods near the riverbank. "Gimme that chain saw, Oscar," he said. "Remember it was raining a while ago? I guess we're gonna need dry firewood up there."

"No, don't take that," Oscar said. "You see that rope? That wood already belongs to somebody."

But Charlie already had the saw in his hands and was working at the log, taking a two-foot piece off one end. "I'm not gonna take the whole fucking thing — just a little bit. Shit, you want to freeze your ass up there? Cold up there, man."

Charlie threw the spruce stump into the boat, and Oscar just stared at it for a moment. One of the Kuskokwim's ravens, as big as a terrier and as black as crude oil, stared coolly at the three of us from the upper branches of one of the cottonwoods. Then Oscar spat, pulled his anchor out of the sand, and said to me, "I don't like that. We never did that before."

II
FIVE BUCKS

1 ◎ NOW THAT THE FLOORBOARDS have been pulled out of the *Crazy J*, the three brothers, Oscar, Charlie, and Buzzo, gather around the cracked ribs in the bow and confer among themselves like a team of surgeons. The boat lies on a shelf of river bottom just up the Kuguklik River from Kipnuk, at a spot where Buzzo knew it would rest dry and level and be easy to work on at low tide.

"Look at that," Oscar says to Buzzo. "See how black the wood is along that rib there? That's an old leak, man. That didn't happen just since I bought it. That leak's been there a long time. What the hell's Jerry doing to me?"

Buzzo grunts his agreement, adding, "Guess you gotta replace them ribs. Get new ones in there tight with some good epoxy, and that ought to fix it."

Buzzo's real name is James, Junior, and he's the eldest of James and Elsie's natural children, born in 1950, two years after they adopted John. "Buzzo" is a nickname retained from childhood, just as Henry Active, who lives up the Johnson River in the village of Atmautluak, is known as Hippa, and Fritz Active, who froze to death in Bethel in 1980, was known as Mamoo. Buzzo is slightly taller and somewhat leaner than any of his three surviving natural brothers, though Oscar is the only one of the big men carrying what might be described as excess weight. But while Oscar and Charlie and Hippa are bulky from neck to toe, husky in a distinctly Yupik fashion, Buzzo is just big-boned and rangy, his hips tapering in neat proportion from the width of his shoulders. In fact, with his thin nose and narrow face, sun-burned now to a coppery hue, he looks almost more Indian than Eskimo, though mostly he looks like an Active.

Buzzo has a long piece of two-by-six he scrounged off his porch, and Oscar measures two lengths of this to the dimensions of the boat's beam at the points where the cracked ribs lie. The rest of us pull the bolts connecting the ribs to adjacent undamaged trusses. Oscar's jaw is taut with anger as he lays the extracted ribs against the two-by-six and traces the correct angles for his end cuts; two or three times he cusses at Jerry again, and having warmed up with that, he moves on to cussing those issues of economics and religion that suddenly have threatened to make our travel over here a waste of time and gas.

Earlier today in Kongiganak he called Fish & Game again, to learn from their public information recording that the test fishing performed off the cape yesterday suggested that the herring were just about to spawn. Then a neighbor told Oscar that all the processing ships were standing offshore at Cape Avinof and not coming into the fishery, because of a disagreement about prices with the Kipnuk fishermen. Oscar shook his head at this, saying that with the ice lingering so late this year, the herring were likely to spawn all at once, and a season that was always short anyway — a week or so, at best — could be over this year in a single day, which could be missed if the weather was bad or if the buyers and fishermen were still wrangling.

After that, Oscar's hunting partner Joe Brown visited the house. It was Joe's aluminum skiff that Oscar borrowed last summer for his fishing, that we rode in to Kasigluk when we got the *Crazy J,* and that Oscar wants to use again this summer, with the more fuel-efficient Nissan, for his subsistence food-gathering. Joe needed help from Margaret on his income taxes, which were overdue, and while he was there he reminded Oscar of another thing to worry about when fishing at Kipnuk. There the Moravian church exerts a particularly strong influence on village affairs, and Sunday is customarily a day of worship and rest in Kipnuk, no matter what. If the herring happen to choose the Sabbath as the single day on which to spawn, the combined force of church mandate and public opinion could well keep enough fishermen off the water to cause all processors to haul anchor and sail away. "Shit, what religion are they over there, anyway?" Oscar cried. "Seventh-Day Adventists? Bahais?" Then he remembered the price disagreement and concluded, "They're Jews, is what they are."

After we loaded the boat, we traveled the fifty miles from Kongiganak to Kipnuk: forty miles west past Kwigillingok along the northern edge of Kuskokwim Bay, and then ten miles around the wet nub of the cape and up its other side to that five-mile-wide nick called Kinak Bay, which funnels finally into the Kuguklik. The sky was a vacant and wintry dome of gray, and the low, rolling waves outside the Kongiganak River were green and streaked with foam. Oscar hunched behind the steering console in the cold wind and drove the boat hard through the waves while Charlie sat on a net buoy and kicked at all the gear that slid backward under the thwarts and into his legs. Ours was the only boat in sight up and down the coast and out to sea.

The shore of Cape Avinof was so low and so round as to be indistinguishable from the straight shore of the bay. Similarly, last Tuesday, when we came down from Bethel, the mouth of the Kuskokwim seemed merely an extension of the shoreline, the river opening so wide and the shore lying so flat that the curve of the horizon shielded one bank from the other. Here around Kipnuk the land is laid in lines that are, if anything, even lower and more profoundly flat than those around Kongiganak.

With a population of four hundred, Kipnuk is twice as big as Kongiganak, and its houses and church and fuel tanks lined the horizon just half a mile to the south of us. Ten miles to the north were Tern Mountain and Cheeching, a matched pair of volcanoes, either dormant or extinct, both still streaked with snow, both just piles of broken black pumice a couple of hundred feet high — the only stone, in fact, to be found on the hundred-mile length of coast from the mouth of the Kuskokwim to Nelson Island.

The land here congeals thickly out of the bay and lies like a blank riparian pudding around these mounds. The French writer and adventurer Gontran de Poncins wrote in contemplating such tundra, "It induced a strange impression of lassitude, so that one was weary before one had begun to march." Partly that lassitude derives from the labor of moving across it, like walking on a trampoline without any return to it, and partly from the absence — at least from an outsider's perspective — of any sense of place, anything to distinguish one location from another, and so also any sense of progress, particularly on a flood plain like this. But in fact there are places at Cape Avinof, and elsewhere in the delta, their identities betrayed even in winter to men such as Oscar by cues and idiosyncrasies too trivial to be noticed anywhere else: the precise angle of a bend in a slough; a particular arrangement of vegetation on a bluff; the geometric pattern created by a set of adjacent ponds.

Indeed there are hundreds of these places, many with their own names and histories, and I know that some of these recall extraordinary events in the area around Kongiganak and Kwigillingok. *Arveq* means bowhead whale, which are never seen in the shallow waters of Kuskokwim Bay, but once hunters were amazed to find just such an animal beached in the small river that now bears this name. Aataq has described how plugs of wood were stuffed into the whale's blowhole in an unavailing effort to smother it. Finally one hunter began to cut down to the whale's spine; at this the beast lurched and broke its own backbone. The river called Anirnaq was the site of an ancient massacre, where a war party attacked a rival encampment and drowned all the captured children.

More often, however, these names commemorate the banal: Maklagtuli, place of bearded seal skins, where a drying skin was once blown free of its pegs and into the water; Tugertalek, place having an ice pick, a lake where a hunter from Kwigillingok once found an ice pick stuck into the grass. Occasionally the names mark the effects of human intervention, however modest, such as Kitngialleq, or kicking heel. Here Kenneth Igkurak of Kongiganak wished to connect a larger river to a smaller one, but lacked the tools to do the job, so he simply scraped a shallow ditch in the earth with his heel. Over the years the ditch filled and widened, to the point where now the patient elder can use his big dip net in the connecting slough.

These thick and granular Yupik names aren't so mellifluous as the Abenaki or Algonquian names that describe the hills and valleys and rivers of New England. They resist penetration by outsiders, just as the landscape they describe, at least from an aesthetic point of view, resists the affections of outsiders. In 1870 the American trader Bernhard Bendel found the lower reaches of the Kuskokwim "monstrous and dreary," but a Yupik hunter's whole being is so bound up in these spaces that he has difficulty distancing himself enough for evaluations such as this. *Yupik* translates literally as "real person," and only three generations ago it was believed that the entire earth looked like this — that the earth was made by Raven, whose wings created such turbulence in the primal darkness that a portion of it accreted into a solid mass. Then Raven with his talons — sort of like Kenneth Igkurak with his heel — scratched riverbeds on its surface, and also those mountains that run along the edge of the delta, whose peaks are visible to the south in this evening's clear air. Some stories tell that Raven then fashioned a man from the stone of these mountains, but that this product, predictably enough, sank into a bog; a second man, made from earth, survived and multiplied. Other stories say that man sprang full-grown and unanticipated from the pod of a beach pea plant that Raven had made.

Whatever the case, whether people were an end in themselves or simply some bastard offspring, Raven saw fit to provide for his progeny in a manner that was wonderfully rich and ample. Indeed, so far from being the sort of "sapless and skeletal place" that Poncins found in Canada's Pelly Bay, the Kuskokwim and this portion of the Bering Sea support moderate to huge numbers of salmon, tomcod, herring, Bering cisco, whitefish, lam-

prey, pike, blackfish, sculpin, smelt, sheefish, burbot, and needlefish; bearded seal, ringed seal, spotted seal, ribbon seal, sea
lion, walrus, and beluga whale; ptarmigan, mallard, American
widgeon, pintail, greater scaup, old squaw, common eider, king
eider, goldeneye, shoveler, green-winged teal, black scoter, Canada goose, cackling goose, white-fronted goose, emperor goose,
snow goose, brant, tundra swan, and sandhill crane; mink,
muskrat, beaver, otter, ermine, arctic hare, snowshoe hare, arctic fox, red fox, wolverine, black bear, brown bear, and moose;
a resurgent population of caribou; and a transplanted population of musk ox. Today the residents of the delta generally ad-
here to biblical accounts of creation — particularly in Kipnuk — and for some of these species, the limits of God's bounty
are suddenly and uncomfortably apparent; but over time the
singular breadth of this bounty has allowed Yupik people to
construct an Eskimo culture quite distinct from that of the more
hard-pressed Inuit of the high polar latitudes, a culture distinguished in part by larger and more stable settlement patterns
and a broader and much more elaborate ritual life.

Whether voiced in Christian terms or in echoes of the pre-
Christian spirituality that runs in vaults and catacombs and secret chambers beneath these hunters' orthodoxy, the immediate
presence of this good earth is so enormous and so pervasive in
the psyches of men such as Oscar Active as to provide not simply
a different point of view from that of the wage-earner but rather
an entirely separate mode of being. Oscar rarely suggests that
this land is pretty; it serves other purposes than that, and its
beauty trails in the wake of these. In 1985 the Alaska Native
Review Commission, an international body empowered by the
Inuit Circumpolar Conference to investigate the potentially
ruinous consequences of the Alaska Native Claims Settlement
Act, solicited testimony from villagers through the delta con-
cerning their perspective on the land. "God made us as well as
the land, and gave the land to us for our use," said John T.
Andrew of Togiak. "And the land that is given to us is our cloth-

ing and our food as well as our table." Given the scope of such religious and economic affinities, as well as others, the question of prettiness seems almost an impertinence. But as we traveled up the Johnson to Kasigluk in the days after breakup, and then down the Kuskokwim on the Tuesday after Memorial Day, I could see Oscar (his BNC shareholder's card in his pocket) rejoicing in the table setting itself: its openness and linear simplicity, its uninterrupted horizons and vast transparent skies, its freshening scents and softening textures.

Time collapses, accordions together, and then is stretched out again in what seems a different order. Now I watch as Oscar works, as he slowly abandons his anger and becomes absorbed in the technical challenge of fixing the leak and calmed by the company of his brothers. He chuckles to himself as he saws at the two-by-six, and then nods toward the tools and the work Buzzo and Charlie are doing, asking me, "Know where the Eskimo learned all this stuff?" He grunts as the ripsaw snags for an instant and then draws smoothly again. He says, "From the white man. The Eskimo didn't know jackshit until the white man came along."

I smile and shrug my shoulders. I know that Eskimo peoples have been ingenious enough substantially to extend the borders of the habitable world, at least as Europeans used to define it, and that the technology of their lifestyle has been of a democratic sort, shared equally among all its subscribers. Western technologies are less so, and in this respect I really don't know how Oscar regards white men like myself, whose skills are peculiar to some narrow and nontechnical vocation and who come to this region knowing less than jackshit — less than even the most callow Eskimo, it seems — about those Western machines and technologies that here are not just conveniences but are often entrusted with their users' lives. Once, while traveling with the Hunters to a tournament in another village, Oscar easily diagnosed the misbehavior of my snow machine as the result of a blown head gasket and was able to make a stopgap repair with a piece of aluminum foil. If I'd been traveling alone and if the weather had closed down on me, my perplexity might have been deadly.

But an Eskimo can't afford the mixture of savage awe and religious faith with which I regard a gasoline engine, or even a boat bottom, for that matter. A curious sort of irony has ensued since the days when traders and explorers such as Lieutenant Lavrentiy Alekseyevich Zagoskin, who traveled between the Yukon and the Kuskokwim for the Russian-American Company from 1842 to 1844, were among the first to demonstrate the products of Western science and industry in this region. In his journal, Zagoskin described setting off rockets and making camphor burn in snow by way of entertaining his hosts, and was prescient about Yupik people's ability to penetrate these and other entertainments themselves: "In showing them my watch, the compass needle, the force of gunpowder, etc., I tried as much as possible to acquaint the natives with the structure and use of these objects. I explained to them that this is all the result of the cleverness of man, and that they too, if they wished, could learn to do likewise." By now, of course, men such as Oscar, Buzzo, and Charlie have learned "the structure and use of these objects" with an aptitude that shames many of those whose culture produced them, and as such industrial artifacts have become increasingly complex and specialized, Westerners have more and more often surrendered to the difficulty of mastering anything more than which buttons to push, which switches to throw, which keys to turn. So here, beyond the pale of the service center or the boatyard, the circumstances that the Russian explorer met have recently become reversed.

Whistling to himself, as though he knows what I'm thinking, Oscar fetches from the cuddy beneath the foredeck the new propane stove that he bought in Bethel. While the rest of us scour silt and twigs from the bow in preparation for the insertion of the two new pieces, Oscar busies himself with assembling the stove, first sliding its parts out of the cardboard box and looking doubtfully at the long manual of printed instructions. He shows the manual to me and says, "These are *kass'aq* instructions." Then he ceremoniously lays it aside and starts fiddling instinctively with the stove's many components and fittings. Chuckling faintly, he says, "These are Eskimo instructions: 'This must go here. Oh, maybe this connects over here.' " He lifts his head and laughs, his brothers joining in. After the stove is assembled in Eskimo fashion, as Oscar attaches a tank of propane and prepares to strike a match, Buzzo and Charlie laugh even harder to see me move circumspectly out of the boat and up the embankment. But this is just theater on my part; I'm probably less surprised than any of them to see the stove light quickly and without mishap.

Finally both new ribs are set into position in the bow. The three big men stand in a row along the length of the pieces, pressing the wood with their combined weight against the bottom of the boat long enough for the epoxy to set. The clouds overhead have broken into concurrent shelves, streaked in mineral shades of blue and gray, and the shelves are crumbling into jagged pieces in the north, then drifting over the horizon.

In age, Oscar is in the middle of the five natural brothers, and now he stands happily and just so between Buzzo and Charlie, the oldest and the youngest, and laughs — laughs with a sort of lilt and sense of ease that I never seem to hear when he's among his other family in Kongiganak. It occurs to me that his father, James, has been more or less exiled from the lives of his wife and children, but not from those of his brothers; the vigilant Matthew still buys him a ticket home if he's drunk in Anchorage and can't find the one he already has. Now Oscar laughs again and says, "Three Actives ought to be heavy enough to set that rib."

Behind the three heavy Actives, one of the delta's long and spectacular sunsets is in progress. The clouds light up in tongues of fire as the sun grazes the water and rolls sideways, seeming to hit bottom at three fathoms. In fact outsiders aren't immune to the beauties of the Kuskokwim, though usually their sense of the land is not so holistic, more absorbed with its brilliant parts. We enjoy these volcanic sunsets or the sheer elemental violence of its storms, its great clouds of nesting shorebirds or its luxuriant beds of wild iris. Sometimes the scale and grandeur of such displays approach the inexpressible. The schoolteacher May Wynne Lamb confessed herself lost in wonder as she regarded the northern lights from the upriver village of Akiak in 1917. She wrote, "The awe-inspiring exhibitions of the Creator are beyond reproduction, for only God in his sanctuary can portray such an array of splendor."

2 ◎ JERRY DEMIENTIEFF has come down to Cape Avinof in his own new boat. The *Good Night Irene* is a factory-line Yukon-Kuskokwim Raider; big and square and broad-beamed and aluminum, it looks like a scaled-down World War II amphibious landing craft, as if it could be safely dropped without a parachute from the cargo bay of an airplane. Jerry wears silvered sunglasses and camouflage-pattern rain gear, and looks like a paratrooper as he stands on the swiveling pilot's seat so he can look into the hold of the *Crazy J*. He nearly falls off the seat as the aluminum boat rolls over a swell. Then he regains his balance, surveys the four or five hundred herring littering the floorboards of Oscar's boat, and says, "Shit, at least I got more than that."

The *Good Night Irene* and the *Crazy J* are tied together, rolling in sequence over the waves, the homemade shaker that Oscar and Charlie fashioned in Kongiganak now nailed to the port gunwale of Oscar's boat like a vestigial piece of rigging. The morning is raw and cold, and twenty-knot winds from the south are worrying Kinak Bay and surrounding waters into lurching slate-gray swells. Jerry and his brother Ricky are fishing only some two hundred yards offshore, and the floats of Jerry's net trail almost like stepping stones toward the land, veering gently to the north and finally pointing up the coast.

Oscar is no more impressed than Jerry by the number of fish he has gotten so far. Jerry's own fish bin is empty because he has just completed a delivery to one of the processors, but apparently it wasn't a very lucrative one. He says that very few of the fish he delivered were females ready to spawn. These are the only sort of herring the buyers are interested in, and what they pay is based on the volume of the females' valuable roe, figured on a percentage basis against the volume of fish in the delivery. Ten percent is usually considered the minimum that the buyers like to see. Jerry jumps down from the seat to more secure footing and says, "Percentages are low, Ox. Some people are only getting one or two percent. I got a little better than that, but not much."

Oscar whistles and Charlie concedes a dry, inward chuckle at this news. "Goddamn," says Oscar.

It looks as though the boats around us are already starting to thin out, though this may actually reflect more fishermen trying the spawning grounds farther down the coast. They're going despite reports on the VHF radio that the winds are exceptionally high behind the sandbars there. When we first stood at the mouth of the Kuguklik earlier this morning, the largely unprotected waters of the bay were peppered with a flotilla of forty to fifty small fishing boats, their numbers overflowing the bay, and behind some of the boats white floats trailed visibly like strings of dirty pearls. The ocean's horizon to the west had disappeared behind a thin and smoky fog, and hovering somewhere between that missing horizon and the welter of fishing skiffs, as brilliant as quasars at the edge of the universe, the big halogen lights of the three anchored processors shone spookily through the mist. Oscar looked at the assembled host and said, "Maybe I shoulda bought a permit this year for Elizabeth. They might be going limited-entry here pretty soon, and that would get her name on the record books, at least." Then he turned the boat south, into the swells, preparing to run along the southern line of the bay and then out to the cape, adding, "I'll give my own permit to Junior when he gets old enough."

Oscar wanted to go to those other spawning grounds himself, but he doesn't trust the *Crazy J* to hold together for travel that far in this hard weather. Friday night, after we replaced the cracked ribs, I slept in the only available bed at Buzzo's house; Buzzo's two older daughters were twined together like kittens in the bed opposite me, while the two younger children slept in the other bedroom with their parents. Charlie curled up on a couch, Oscar on a mattress on the floor. I slept late Saturday morning, and when I got down to the little slough off the Kuguklik where we'd finally anchored the *Crazy J,* I was surprised to find the boat hauled up on the grass and propped on its side with the oars. Oscar was running a propane torch along the boat's bottom while Buzzo and Charlie looked on.

"This ain't a boat, it's a submarine," Oscar said, spitting the words out like bad meat. He stepped back and pointed to an area on the starboard side of the bow, beneath the spot overlaid by the ribs we had replaced the previous night. There a jagged eighteen-inch gash ran along the outer layer of plywood. "We came down this morning at high tide, and the whole boat was half full of water. I never seen it so full." He pointed to some bolts driven through the bottom on either side of the gash: "This is where he tried to fix it before with some bolts, but not too well."

The little slough ran like a beltway around the northern edge of the village, and its banks were lined with dozens of other boats, most of them skiffs, some of them big gill-netters with enclosed cabins and hydraulic winches. When a gill-netter motored down the slough with the volume on its VHF turned up high, relaying an announcement from Fish & Game that the fishery would be open the next day, Sunday, from 10:00 A.M. to 6:00 P.M., Oscar said he was glad at least of that, glad he'd have time today to dry out the bottom and put a plywood patch on it. Then he cussed at Jerry some more.

"Is Jerry coming down for this?" Buzzo asked.

Oscar said, "He's supposed to. He better hope he don't see me."

I asked Buzzo if the opening meant that the processors and the Kipnuk fishermen had come to an agreement on prices, and Buzzo said, "I don't know. I don't give a shit. I just want to fish. I got too many bills to pay."

This morning, instead of running down the coast we kept to the beach, or at least to that variable line of points where the seawater exhausts its reach across the tidal flats. The flats themselves gave off a sterile salt scent and were bereft of vegetation; they would seem biologically dead if it weren't for the interest they rouse in waterfowl and shorebirds, who gather on them at low tide in densities of up to a quarter million per square mile in quest of the flats' hordes of invertebrates. Also there are the fat and robust clams I've seen raked from their depths by foragers or exposed in the belly of a walrus.

The tide was coming in then, and the flats were almost entirely submerged. On our port side the water slapped at the edges of the tundra's mat, not in waves but in disparate and contrary sloshings. A number of boats had anchored one end of their nets in close to these edges, and sat like Jerry only a short distance offshore, with their gear drawn at an angle across the tide's easterly flooding. But Oscar and Charlie saw little sign of fish in either the nets or the bins of these boats, and finally we swung out to sea, heading in the direction of the processors. There we set net in twelve feet of water and waited an hour to catch the few fish we have now.

Before shaking the net out, Charlie tried unsuccessfully to raise Buzzo on the VHF radio. It was then that a familiar voice interrupted his transmission, hailing the *Crazy J.* I watched Charlie break into an ironic smile, saying, "You know who that is, Oscar."

Oscar did. He grabbed the mike from Charlie and replied, "What the fuck do you want?"

"What the hell'd you do to your boat?" Jerry Demientieff asked.

"Me? What the hell did *you* do to it?"

"Nothing. I hear it's got a crack in it."

Oscar looked at Charlie, and then said, "Yeah, but it's an old crack. It's all black around the edges."

"Well, what do you want me to do, jump up and down for joy? Where is it?"

"Right out here in the fucking ocean. I gotta fish with it, whether it leaks or not."

"I mean the crack."

"Oh. Up in the bow. Near that first rib under them floorboards."

"Up in the bow? Shit, I didn't do nothing. That's Took's work."

"Took's? What you mean?"

Charlie leaned with one elbow on the starboard gunwale and listened as Jerry explained that Took Lareux, who built the boat and from whom Jerry had bought it, had run it with too big a motor; Jerry had seen him trying to fix it once with the bolts we saw yesterday, and had wondered what the hell he was doing. Then Charlie smiled again as Oscar was mollified, two weeks' hoarded anger draining away from his voice, and the discussion turned at last to the technical issue of fixing the leak, the practical issue of finding fish.

Of course it was unlikely that Jerry was trying to cheat anybody, since he had yet to collect even a penny for the *Crazy J*, though maybe he might at least have mentioned that leak in the bow. But it would have been a waste of time to try to tell Oscar that earlier; he needed a villain — or, more precisely, a traitor — on whom to vent his spleen, and I knew he would cherish his spleen like a spider its egg, deaf to any excuse, so long as it was only him and the boat and its fucking leak.

I think it's all a matter of faith with Oscar, and by now that's just the problem. I suspect that because he was betrayed again and again by James, who — like any alcoholic — always seemed to love his bottle more than he loved his sons, he sees himself as someone who will inevitably be betrayed by anybody on whom he has less claim than that — which is to say, anybody. But with his friends and his brothers, I notice (as Charlie does), he's as quick to forgive as he is to accuse, as if he knows that in these secondary relationships there is always enough space to allow one participant, or even both, to be a drunk, or one participant, or even both, to be a traitor; the relationship will still be viable, even if only on an intermittent or emergency basis. Oscar knows that such a bond can endure an occasional lapse of faith, and is anxious to have it out and then move on.

But fathers and sons are bound too tight, as are husbands and wives, and Oscar hardly seems to believe that having it out and moving on is even possible in these brittle relationships, once that primal faith has been broken. I remember him telling me last week, while we were heading up the Gweek, that he doesn't trust Margaret anymore. He has decided that she betrays him, though, not on the basis of any tangible evidence, or even gossip or hearsay, but simply because he can't imagine her otherwise at this point in their relationship, notwithstanding her decision to let him come back. Given that his own father so readily abandoned him for his binges, or maybe did worse — his own father, whom he never harmed as he has harmed Margaret — he can't imagine otherwise.

But once in a while the readiness to forgive, or take assurance, that sustains his other relationships breaks through even here, and the image of Margaret in Oscar's mind composes itself into something more like herself. Maybe it's a piece of that old strong-mindedness just standing up and dismissing some of the demons. On the Gweek, Oscar also told me that once last winter, while out on a walk with Margaret in Bethel, he put his arm around her shoulder and said he was glad she never fooled around on him. I suspect that he was feeling good about himself on that walk, proud that he had stayed sober all fall and winter, glad that the counseling at the treatment center seemed to be working, and just beginning to hatch his plans for the summer. I can only imagine Margaret's amazement at hearing Oscar for once discount the suspicions that — this past year in particular — have begun to lie like dragon's teeth in a ring around her, and sometimes make her afraid even to speak to houseguests such as Charlie and me.

Now Oscar pours from his Thermos steaming cups of black coffee for himself and Jerry and the rest of the two boats' occupants. Charlie takes a mug and slides down to a clean spot on the floorboards, out of the wind, observing, "No church bells this morning, Oscar."

"Yep, the herring are so late this year that even these Christians are scared of missing 'em," Oscar replies, grateful for the Moravian pastor's decision not to hold services today.

After emptying his two Thermoses with Jerry and his brother, Oscar heads down the shoreline a mile or two, staying near the beach this time. Charlie once again sets net, still a little farther out from shore than where Jerry is fishing. He grunts as he hefts and drops one of the two-bladed fifty-pound anchors over the starboard gunwale, then throws out one of the two red buoys painted with the *Crazy J*'s registration numbers. Both anchor and buoy are tied to one end of the nylon filament net.

Then Oscar shifts the Evinrude into a rumbling reverse, and Charlie straddles the net and feeds clumps of it into the water, careful to feed out the cork line and lead line in equal lengths and not to reverse them or tangle them with each other, furiously working the mesh free as it grabs at nail heads, splinters, and other irregularities in the boat's rail. The net is fifty fathoms long, the maximum allowed under state regulations. Just before it's entirely paid out, Charlie takes hold of its lines like a sailor with a mainsheet while Oscar guns the engine, stretching the net taut to its fullest length. Then Charlie drops the second anchor over the port side. The boat works gently in the opposite direction to confirm that the anchor has taken hold. Finally he tosses out the remaining buoy and sits heavily on the forward bench, sweating even in this thirty-degree cold, his jeans soaked with spray.

Oscar kills the engine, scolds Charlie for the second or third time for forgetting his rain pants in Bethel, and then contemplates with approval the symmetry of the floats. They trail out through the green water like the posts of a submerged picket fence, most of them held below the surface by the pull of the anchors, the depth of the water, and the emptiness of the net. "All them corks will come up to the top if the net fills," Oscar says. Now they surface in discrete sets as the moving swells scoop the water out from under them.

Oscar tells me that around here you can set net for herring just about anywhere there's water. "They'll even swim up into the rivers and lakes to spawn. Up around Nelson Island they got kelp growing on those rocks up there, and the herring like to lay their eggs in that kelp. So everybody'll set their nets right along the beach. But around here just about any place is as good as another." He blows into his hands to warm them, closes his green raincoat a snap higher at the neck, and then laughs harshly, adding, "Or as bad."

For the second time Oscar and Charlie wait in vain for the net to fill, for their floats to rise to the surface. After another hour they decide to pull up anyway. Charlie stretches himself out full length on the *Crazy J*'s short foredeck, lifts one end of the net, both cork line and lead line, clear of the water, and stretches both lines like a rubber band over the prow. Then he and I together wrestle the exposed portion of the net down along the gunwales the length of the boat and lift it onto the shaker, which is simply a rolling length of aluminum pipe threaded between two posts cut from the two-by-sixes. The bar of the shaker is at shoulder level, and the net goes over this like a belt over a wheel.

Even in calm weather the tension of a firmly set net is enough to make this difficult, and in this wind the net is as heavy and stiff as steel; raising it up to the shaker is like hanging cable over the stanchion of a swaying suspension bridge. Once the net's on the roller, however, Oscar and Charlie pull the lead line and the cork line to the pipe's opposite ends and then haul simultaneously on these lines toward the far buoy. At the same time they shake the captured herring to the floorboards out of an open middle seam in the net. In this way they move the boat slowly and arduously, lurching in the swells, under the full length of the still-anchored net.

But if the first few feet of the net are any indication, there are even fewer herring here than there were in the area of our first set. The little fish, most between six and nine inches, are scattered like bits of chaff throughout the mesh, and most are pitched with simply a flick of the wrist into that middle seam and then down into the area of the boat partitioned off as a fish bin by means of sheets of fiberboard nailed to the middle and stern thwarts. Some of the herring are more firmly lodged and have to be extricated by hand, and a very few others are so tangled up that their bodies have to be torn from their heads, with hardly more resistance than candy wrappers, as the bar of the shaker rolls closer and that section of the net slides over the bar and back into the sea.

Neither Oscar nor Charlie takes much pleasure in handling herring. The fish come out of the water coated in a thick film of mucous, and their sticky, transparent scales drop off at the touch — they are almost thrown off, it seems, in the way a porcupine appears to throw off its quills. Then they hold as fast as ticks to the surface of whatever drew them, where eventually they dry and start to stink. "Dirty, filthy fish," Oscar says with a grimace, even as he stands in front of the middle thwart and shakes the herring into his bin, the loose scales glistening like dimes on his rain gear and the surfaces of the boat.

The herring are better to look at than to handle. In fact the fish are pretty, and I'm surprised again, as I was at the end of our first set, by the summoning of such bits of light and color from the waters of this stygian sea. Most of the herring are long and narrow, as though they have been stretched appreciatively from either end, like dollar bills; and the notorious scales commencing behind the gills are joined in patterns as precise and symmetrical and lustrously metallic as chain mail. An indigo blue, almost a black, is splashed along the spines and dorsal fins, a silvery sort of white along the flanks and belly. These colors in turn are brushed with soft undershadings of violet, mauve, and magenta.

Maybe what surprises me most is simply to meet this subtle sort of glamour in such an ordinary and unheralded fish. Like baleen whales, herring feed largely on plankton, but they are preyed on by almost everything: waterfowl, sea lions, salmon, porpoises, sharks, tuna, mackerel, cod, striped bass, squid, fishermen who might otherwise be in church, and more. They swim sometimes in shoals huge enough to swallow whole pods of whales, numbering three billion individuals or more. The fish outlast their predators by no other virtue than the sheer volume of their numbers, achieving in that volume what a whale achieves in its size, even if that's not apparent from the slim yield of these two sets. It seems somehow extravagant that such gorgeous colors are spent on what amounts to the sea's common currency, as if that other world beneath our keel had really more to do with an artist's sensibilities than with the frank economies of survival, the tradeoffs that keep almost everything on this side of the water, at least in these regions, so muted and spare and nondescript.

Or maybe that glamour has to do simply with the lust that keeps such currencies common. Even the few herring diverted into Oscar's boat look to have suffered an unseemly interruption: clumps of thick white milt dribble down the fish and are smeared across the floorboards; beaded clusters of eggs the color and texture of marmalade erupt from the bellies of the females. Each cluster seems to promise by itself an entire shoal of herring. The baffled wrigglings and flappings of the fish seem to be as much a result of thwarted generative frenzy as of the drying and gasping of their gills.

When finally the *Crazy J* reaches the opposite end of the net, maybe an additional one or two hundred fish lie squirming in its bin. Oscar and Charlie wring water from their gloves and look at these with obvious disappointment. "We should go back out on the bay again," Charlie says. "At least we got a few more out there than we did here."

3 ☉ By NOW, in the afternoon of a day on which all the fishermen on the radio continue to report poor hauls, at least two thirds of the skiffs seen earlier have disappeared, leaving only a scattering of stubborn fishermen between the land and the processors. Oscar has just pounded through the waves out to the margins of the bay again, where Charlie has set the net. Both of them are stiff with wet and cold, and I can scarcely imagine Charlie's discomfort in his soaking jeans.

I exist like a seed inside a capsule composed of all the layers of my clothing: the doubled wool socks, the thermal underwear, the jeans and thick flannel shirt, the down vest, the expedition parka, the rag wool hat, the rubber boots, the rubber gloves with their surgeon's sleeves reaching around and above the elbow, the white rain gear sized extra large in order to accommodate everything else heaped over my medium-size frame. Just the same, my feet hang like wooden prostheses beneath my shins, and my hands respond so thickly to any attempt to move them that I scarcely recognize the result. My jeans are still unbuttoned from the last time I pissed over the transom. And I don't understand how all the water gets in, how it runs in glacial rills down my chest, collects in aquifers inside my boots, condenses in a rimy film beneath my gloves. I sit on the boat's middle thwart with the herring stiffening around my feet and my gear stippled with scales. I sit gathered in on myself, my back to the wind, too miserable and numb for any but the most necessary movements. Charlie's face is white as he goes to handle the net, and his dripping legs find the thwart almost insurmountable.

As the afternoon wears on, the wind finally dies and a viscous gray fog overtakes us, blotting out the land and any neighboring boats, leaving only the ghostly beacons of the processors showing in the west. Earlier Oscar had gaped in astonishment as a *kass'aq* agent for Fish & Game rode a tiny Zodiac out to our boat just to see how we were doing, and then disappeared in the direction of a neighboring skiff, dropping into the trough of a swell and then bobbing over its crest like a cork. At four-thirty a voice that sounds like it belongs to that same high roller announces over the VHF that today's fishing period, originally scheduled to close at six, will be extended indefinitely owing to the low volumes and percentages taken thus far. But at five, when another set of the net comes up virtually empty, Oscar decides to quit. "I burned ten gallons of gas today," he says. "We probably won't even get enough to pay that."

The nearest of the processors is the *Midas,* from Juneau. The sixty-foot ship rocks slowly in the waves somewhere between one and two miles out, a mountain of wet steel and coiled lines and loud machinery that seems too huge to be interested in our few buckets of fish. On this part of the coast, unfamiliar faces are rarely seen; the various *kass'aqs* that man the *Midas* look to me as world-weary, exotic, and vaguely sinister as the roustabouts who run the refreshment stands and carnival rides at small-town fairs in New England.

Oscar eases the *Crazy J* alongside, and a deckhand as big as he is, in a denim jacket and with herring scales that look like sequins running up the legs of his rain pants, stares blankly at us from the ship's stern, as though he can't imagine what we want. Then he throws a line to Charlie. As Oscar climbs stiffly aboard the tender, a teenager with pale freckles and huge red ears swings into our boat. The boy spares not a glance to Charlie and me but awaits the descent of an enormous black hose, the trunk of a house-sized elephant, which he takes in his hands and carries down to the floorboards. This is the ship's dry-suction pump, a gigantic vacuum cleaner for fish. Charlie and I sit together in the bow, our heads drawn turtlelike into our shoulders against the pump's rocket-engine roar, and watch as the small heaps of rigid herring disappear into its maw, so instantly that they seem to have been vaporized.

Actually, that's more or less what happens to the fish; as Charlie and I take up an old frying pan and an empty coffee can to splash down the interior of the boat, cleaning off at least some of the scales and blood, another hose on the *Midas* ejects the stripped and shredded bulk of our catch back into the sea like so much offal. All that's kept is the roe, a delicacy to Japanese and other Asian buyers, who make up the sole market for this commodity, and the roe is all that Oscar is paid for. "Twenty bucks," he says when he comes back, speaking evenly and without emotion: for 378 pounds of herring, at 5.6 percent roe; for six hours on Kinak Bay in hard weather; and for ten gallons of gas, this costing a little more than $2 per gallon.

"Where's the land?" Oscar wonders, turning in perplexity at the smooth banks of fog surrounding us. Finally he locates a compass in the padlocked plywood storage cabinet that he nailed to the stern thwart next to the steering console. He takes an easterly bearing and maintains that heading until a beach empty of any other boats appears.

Buzzo, who fished with one of his neighbors today, comes in half an hour later than we do, and his clothes join ours turned inside out and hung on lengths of clothesline screwed into the ceiling over his oil stove. A steamy scent of salt, sweat, and wet wool fills the small house. Buzzo says that his wife, Alice, is still out fishing with her brother, Moses Martin; earlier Oscar said that Alice didn't like to fish with Buzzo, and guessed it was because he yelled at her. He laughed, adding, "Margaret went out fishing with me once, but I bawled the shit out of her, and she don't want to no more."

Alice returns at midnight, her round, full cheeks burned raw by the wind and cold. Oscar passes her in the doorway on his way back down to the slough to check the *Crazy J*, and her numbed fingers have only just managed to unzip her parka by the time Oscar comes back on the run, yelling that the boat is swamped and about to go under.

Apparently the bow is still leaking, despite the plywood patch Oscar put on the bottom yesterday. After he anchored the *Crazy J* at low tide in the slough that snakes around the back of the village, the boat filled partly with water from the bow and then tipped enough so that an edge caught in the slough's steep bank, preventing it from being lifted by the tide. Now the boat is pitched sharply, half in and half out of the water, and the big Evinrude motor is nearly submerged.

Once we have lifted the stern high enough up on the bank to expose the engine, Charlie and I stand in the boat and bail as Oscar strips the engine down, draining and drying the carburetors and spark plugs, expressing doubt that the damned thing will ever start again. "If I can't fix this boat, I'm gonna give it back to Jerry," he says again in a murmuring and reflective manner, almost as though he were talking to himself. "Called Margaret after we got back. She didn't like it that we weren't still out fishing. Told her we wasn't even making gas money."

Charlie bails in alternating fits of passion and despair. When we anchored the boat earlier, his nearly dysfunctional legs had slipped from beneath him on the muddy slope of the bank, and he had fallen back sloppily against the boat. "Different village, same mud," he said simply. In accepting his 50 percent share of the take from Oscar, he said he was sorry that he didn't have enough money for airfare to Bethel, but he figured that after three more days like this he would — if he lived that long.

A minute ago he seemed likely to live. He was luxuriating in a warm house, in dry pants, in front of a TV, watching Buzzo's borrowed tape of *Good Morning, Vietnam*. Now he's out in the weather again, standing up to his thighs in freezing water. He says not a word, just windmills the water out of the boat in frenzied and furious bursts. Then he stands panting, measuring the boat's contents as though the water were simply an extension of the ocean, as though bailing it were as much use as bailing out the bay. Then he starts in again, grimly, the water arcing in foaming sheets far out into the flooding slough.

The calm that rolled in behind the fog still prevails, though the fog itself has cleared, and in this burnt-orange midnight twilight the air has taken on the stillness and color of amber. Above us a flock of black turnstones has settled onto the ocherous stretch of mud and sedge that intervenes between the slough and the houses. There aren't any stones to turn there, but all the same the little birds dip and probe tirelessly through heaps of broken net floats, old pop cans, scattered shards of Styrofoam. They take no heed of our fidgetings; instead their placid, guttural rattles seem the spoken expression of the evening calm. In those intervals in Charlie's bailing when I can hear them, they remind me of the spring peepers in New Hampshire, whose massed, rattling calls I followed with my son one night to a beaver pond, only to have the frogs fall into a throbbing silence at the first sound of our approach.

"What else can go wrong?" Oscar wonders, still as though he were thinking aloud. "Well, Toksook Bay was worse in 'eighty-seven, when we went up there. The weather was just as bad as this, and those guys up there from Nelson Island were getting jealous. They didn't want nobody from anywhere else on the coast fishing around there. Pissed me off."

The engine by now has been reassembled. Oscar checks the battery connections and then stands apprehensively at the steering console, gazing back over his shoulder at the Evinrude. The motor starts at the first turn of the key, and the turnstones rise in astonishment into the sky.

4 ◎ "PULL UP THAT NET. Let's move."

Charlie stares at Oscar from his seat on the foredeck. He wears a gray wool balaclava, and droplets of the misting rain have fastened to its fibers like dew. "Why move? There's fish here."

"Look at that *marayaq*," Oscar retorts, pointing at a sandbar lifting slowly out of the water like the back of a whale. "The tide's going out. We'll get stuck. So pull up the net."

Charlie remains motionless on the deck, staring at the onrush-

ing bulk of a wave as it hisses and sprays along the length of the
line tying the net to the boat. That wave rolls enormously under
the boat, and then another, and a third. Oscar stands wordlessly
at the steering wheel, a cigarette clamped between his lips. He
looks as though he might bite it in two. He glares at Charlie for
a minute and then turns away, his back to the sandbar, and
stares out at the rolling field of whitecaps, the smattering of
small boats pitching across their crests, the dim horizon. After
some moments' stalemate Charlie finally rises, and with infinite
slowness begins working the net's first anchor loose.

Later in the day the *Crazy J* and the *Good Night Irene* tie up
together again. Jerry says that the buyers and the fishermen have
worked out a deal where the processors would pay for herring
at the rate of $800 per metric ton for 10 percent minimum roe,
just like last year, but also an extra $100 per ton for every per-
centage point over ten. He says, "But nobody's even getting
close to ten around here. So I hear one of them processors is
picking up and going down to Kwigillingok today."

Zack Slim, one of Buzzo's neighbors in Kipnuk, joins the
group, tying his little skiff to the opposite side of the *Crazy J*,
which now rolls and bumps in the middle of the three boats.
Zack's teenage brother Cup'aq (pronounced "Joo'-buk") lies in
the bow of the skiff with his hands folded over his belly. "He's
getting seasick," Zack says, and the other men laugh sympathet-
ically.

"Gee, these fish are little this year," Oscar says. "I think
they're swimming right through my net."

"How big's your mesh?" Jerry asks.

"Two and seven eighths inches."

"Mine's littler than that — two and three quarter inches."

Oscar flashes Jerry a puppyish grin and says, "You should let
me use it."

"Sure," agrees Jerry. "For half your catch."

"That ain't much," Charlie says, and a ripple of rueful laughter ensues.

"Mine's two and three quarters. I got this one brand new

from Icicle," Zack Slim says, naming a seafood company that owns one of the processors.

Oscar looks into Zack's boat and admires the neat pile of bright green filament gathered under the sick teenager. "Brand new? How much?"

Zack laughs and says, "I don't know. Free."

"Free? Oh, you mean they're billing you at the end of the season." Oscar thinks about this, sitting on the boat's midthwart and kicking at the few herring scattered about his feet, skidding them toward the back of the bin. "Gee, I should get me one of them free nets and go over to Kwig. Those fish are always small over there, but at least it's closer to home." He takes off the Tibetan-style wool cap that lies on his great head like a napkin and runs his hands through his hair. "But as soon as I leave here, man, I know these waters are gonna boil with fish."

This morning Oscar helped me look around Buzzo's house for my last pair of dry socks. He wandered through Alice's kitchen and through the bedrooms and talked unhappily about all he has invested, in both fees and equipment, in this herring season. He stopped and stood distracted a moment, asked me to remind him to call the alcohol counselor he'd begun to see in Bethel, and then seemed to listen to the murmuring of the CB. A fourth processor, the *Captain Banjo*, had arrived in the night, and someone was trying to describe to the ship's pilot the location of a channel into the bay, assuring him that he'd have at least nine feet of water.

Finally Oscar said, "One time Charlie and me set net and those corks came up so fast, man, they almost flew out of the water. Then we pulled up, and every single square of the mesh had a fish in it, maybe fifteen percent roe. Gee, we made eighteen hundred bucks in just one day."

Later we waited half an hour with a number of other boats at the mouth of the river. The swells out on the bay were even higher and fiercer than yesterday's, but finally the wind abated slightly and the boats ventured out. Our first set yielded pre-

cisely four unfortunate herring, one of these a roe-bearing female, altogether maybe a pound of fish and a fraction of an
ounce of roe.

"So, Ox, we gonna be wiping our asses with hundred-dollar
bills?" Jerry wonders. He stands with his coat open and his
hands shoved into the bib of his rain pants. His laughter skirls
in sharp, mocking peals over the heads of his numbed companions. "Look at poor Charlie here — he tries to retire every
year."

Oscar sighs. "I should retire too. These herring are trying to
tell me something."

Zack Slim grins and nods in the direction of old Gregory Jack,
fishing a few hundred yards upwind of us. We stopped at
Gregory's boat prior to setting our own net here. Gregory is a
middle-aged man fishing alone, his smile gummy and self-
deprecating, his smooth jaw occasionally interrupted with long
gray whiskers. Zack notes that one of Gregory's anchors has
broken loose, and now his net is folding up under the force of
the wind and current. "He's just sitting there looking at it."
Zack laughs. "He don't care."

"Call him Mosquito," Oscar says, volunteering the older
man's nickname. "He'll answer."

Eventually the lone fisherman simply elects to pull in his
folded net, and we watch as he struggles with its weight and
tension, these probably even more pronounced than they were
yesterday. Even the distressed Cup'aq lifts his head in Gregory's
direction. Jerry spits tobacco juice over the side of his boat and
says, "It's hard out here without a helper."

But a strange sort of fortune seems to attend this Mosquito.
Visiting him earlier, we saw that one entire well between the
thwarts in his little skiff was filled with fish, four times as many
as we'd been able to find, and even from this folded net he's
obliged to stop time and again to shake herring into his boat.
When at last the net is entirely in, he starts his motor and heads
off toward one of the processors.

Once Jerry and Zack depart, Oscar and Charlie decide to pull up our own net. They do this with some anticipation, re-membering Gregory's catch, but the yield is only a few dozen fish. The fishery is still on the same indefinite opening under which it operated yesterday, and whether under force of Margaret's alleged chastisement or just a stubborn insistence on at least recovering his gas money, no matter how much gas it might take, Oscar is loath to quit. The morning wears into afternoon, the afternoon into another long gray evening that witnesses a calming of the wind and sea, and all the while Oscar and Charlie become more desperate in their tactics. When one anchor or the other insists on dragging, Charlie just pulls the loose anchor into the boat and Oscar uses the steady tug of the motor in low gear to keep the net from folding. When Charlie suggests that the fish might be swimming over the net, or even just bouncing off mesh pulled too taut by the current, they pull both anchors into the boat and leave the net to float on the surface like a drift net. The roe percentage of such few herring as we catch is improved by Charlie's throwing a number of males back overboard.

For whatever reason, traffic beneath the waves, if poorer in herring, is more cosmopolitan than yesterday. We catch half a dozen whitefish like the ones we brought back from the Gweek River — five to ten pounds each, big fish that look coarse and colorless next to the herring, but they're clean to handle and succulently fat; we save these to take back to Alice. The net brings up dozens of aptly named sand dabs — gritty, pancake-sized flounders — and also an occasional sculpin, known locally as devilfish. I prefer the local name; with its fins as wide and leathery as bats' wings, its gaping mouth, goggle eyes, and scale-less skin, the little fish in fact looks like something dredged up from hell. These and the sand dabs are all thrown back, but a suspicious little crab, half the size of my palm, is kept by Charlie as a pet in a plastic bucket. Later, however, the bucket is acci-dentally kicked over, and the crab scuttles into the boat's re-cesses.

Twilight gives way to darkness some two hours after midnight, and Oscar is finally forced to quit. By now the processors' lamps seem to be strung like Christmas lights against the black dusk in the west. Carrying a load of fish roughly equivalent to yesterday's haul, though gathered in almost three times the amount of time, Oscar motors first to the newly arrived *Captain Banjo,* whose home port is Seattle. The tide is ebbing again, and he is puzzled to find a dozen boats lined up ahead of him at the *Captain Banjo,* some to sell fish, some to buy the gas that the processor is selling for $3 a gallon, while another tender half a mile away seems to have no boats at all. "What's wrong with that one?" Oscar wonders, turning the boat in the direction of the second tender. But when we reach the *Roberta M,* a deckhand tells us that they're getting under way before the tide runs out and are done buying fish. Oscar has to return to the first ship and wait in line.

"Would you like us to go over to Kwig?" a hatchet-faced crewman on the *Captain Banjo* asks as he throws Oscar a line.

"Huh? Go to Kwig? I want to sell my fish."

"No, I mean tomorrow. Would you like us to set up over there near that village? We been asking all the fishermen. Would you go fish over there if we did?"

"Oh," Oscar says. "Sure. Go ahead."

On the way back to the village Oscar has trouble with the sandbars lifting out of the water. In the darkness they look just like land, and while Oscar skirts them, looking for channels around them, he has nothing to say about the proceeds of our fifteen hours' work. Charlie is in better shape than yesterday thanks to the rain pants he borrowed from Buzzo, who stayed home to watch his kids today, but his face is drawn with lines of exhaustion, and even Oscar — just about as hard to kill as James Senior, I suspect — looks as though he'd fall over if it weren't for the support of the steering wheel.

"The guy said we only had two hundred pounds," Oscar says finally. "But he didn't weigh it — he just looked at it. I guess he was in too much of a hurry."

"Two hundred pounds?" I protest. "But we had almost four

hundred pounds yesterday, and it didn't fill any more of the boat."

"How much?" Charlie asks.

"Three percent roe. He said he'd give me five bucks, take it or leave it."

"Five bucks?"

Charlie's incredulous words hang in the air as the Evinrude's prop hits a bar and digs up mud. Oscar swings the boat back toward the processors — the *Captain Banjo* has pulled anchor as well and is under way out to sea — and finally chooses simply to tail a Kipnuk boat through the bars and back to the river. The sky is still overcast, and no moon is visible, but even in this gloom a sourceless light seems to be playing over the water, catching the sharp ridges of the sloshing little waves in patterns of silver and black that suggest the trembling of trees, and the edge of sleep, against a failing night sky.

III
YOUR EVIL FATE

1 ⊙ "GOD'S LOVE IS INFINITE, and it's never consumed," Mary Azean says, preaching in Yupik during the Moravian church's Wednesday evening service. Jonah Anaver, Kongiganak's former pastor, has recently been transferred by church administrators to Kwigillingok; until another pastor is appointed, parishioners such as Mary will perform services and oversee church functions on a volunteer basis. Mary is small and stout, with a kindly aunt's mellisonant voice. The pastor's pulpit stands behind a simple altar inscribed "This Do In Remembrance of Me," but for her sermon Mary chooses to sit behind a podium set to one side of the altar and in front of the piano. She disappears entirely from view when she sits, and her voice comes, disembodied, from speakers hung in the corners of the ceiling, like communication direct from eternity: "On earth everything is consumed. Even a cup of water slowly disappears, evaporating into the air. Even the love we feel for each other is always changing, and sometimes it just goes. But God's love is always there, and is never consumed. God's love never changes."

Margaret and Janet sit side by side in one of the smooth oak pews. Aanaq and Aataq have been lifelong members of the Russian Orthodox church, and Margaret grew up attending services in Kwigillingok's Russian church, with its voluptuous gold and red furnishings, its luminous portraits of the Virgin and the saints, its flickering candles and rich scent of incense. By comparison this Moravian church is as bare and simple as the inside of a cupboard. But Oscar's family has always been Moravian, and Margaret is happy to attend services in either church, believing that one manner of approaching God is as direct as another and finding it pleasant that in Kongiganak the two churches stand literally side by side. She and Janet take out hymnals from the rack in front of them and stand with the rest of the congregation as Peter Daniel goes to the piano and plays an accompaniment to "Just As I Am." Outside, rain begins to fall from the sullen gray clouds that have prevailed through most of the day.

Margaret and Oscar were out all afternoon under those gray clouds, the two of them sifting through Oscar's king salmon net for tears in its mesh. They stood opposite each other in the low grass in front of their house and moved in tandem, like a couple dancing, to advance the net in equal lengths. Compared to the herring net, the five-and-seven-eighths-inch twine mesh of the king salmon net seems monstrous, and some of the monsters that thrashed about in it last summer tore big holes in it. Whenever Oscar saw a hole, he laid the net in the grass and had Margaret straddle the tear, holding the mesh apart with her boots. Then he kneeled at her feet, cut away the broken twine, and wove in and out of the neat opening with his *ilartuq,* a shuttle in the form of an elongated spool with horns on it. He used this to tie and knot new lengths of twine into a precise reconstruction of the mesh.

There must have been dozens of such tears in the three-hundred-foot length of the net. Margaret gazed across the breadth of that portion stretched across the ground, the grass pushing its blades through the mesh and causing the twine nearly to vanish, and asked, "How do you see those holes?"

"I got fisherman's eyes," Oscar said, still moving the *ilartuq* back and forth between her feet. Then he jammed the shuttle into his back pocket and took out his jackknife again, telling Margaret to move down to another spot on the net. He said, "I heard Fish & Game got a seventeen percent roe count on Saturday, the day before they opened it. But those guys over in

Kipnuk weren't ready. They got to have everything their own way. You know? They're gonna get that fishery closed down for good."

Oscar's is only one of many explanations for the failure of the Cape Avinof fishery this spring. After only a few hours' sleep at Buzzo's the night before last, we were awakened at 9:00 A.M. by an announcement from Fish & Game over the CB radio. The agent said that although all the processors were leaving Cape Avinof, the fishery itself would remain open on its present indefinite status. Then a Kipnuk fisherman's voice broke in, demanding, "How come those tenders are leaving like that?"

"Well, that's their own decision," the agent replied. "We don't have anything to do with that. I guess they're probably following orders from their owners."

"Then what's your sense in leaving the fishery open? Who we gonna sell to?"

"We're not saying that you ought to go fish. This just gives you an option in case one of the processors decides to come back."

"Those kind of ideas are how come we got problems like this in the first place," began the fisherman, who saw this as too much too late — he was mad about the money he'd lost, the money almost everybody had lost, and he took this opportunity to blame the debacle on Fish & Game for opening the fishery too late, after the shoals had already spawned under the cover of the cape's silty waters.

But others told me that Fish & Game had really opened it too early and the fish were still coming. Still others, like Oscar, blamed the Kipnuk fishermen for throwing a wrench into the whole process with their demands for higher prices. And some looked farther afield, blaming the Japanese, who in fact were the first to fish for herring commercially in these waters and whose big offshore trawlers, operating beyond the modern two-hundred-mile limit, scoop up and destroy whole shoals of roe-less herring, which are discarded as by-catch.

In any event, Oscar decided we'd better get home while we

still had enough gas to do so, though now he's having second thoughts. "Maybe I shoulda stayed one more night. I heard on the CB last night that a big empty tender was going back into Kipnuk 'cause they spotted a big school over there."

"You got any gas left?" Margaret asked.

"No, no gas anyhow. Just a little I got saved to get back to Bethel."

Everybody is short on gas this spring. The late thaw has required everyone to use snow machines for a much longer period than usual. By now the gas reserves of all of the Native village corporations are virtually exhausted, and they will stay that way until the summer supply barges start coming. The last source of supply, those processors who were selling gas at $3 a gallon, is now mostly gone as well.

Suddenly Oscar straightened and laughed, describing to Margaret the plight of the fishermen lined up a few boats behind us the night before last. "That *Captain Banjo* wanted to get out of there before the tide went out from under 'em, and gee, that *Banjo* crew wouldn't give those guys nothing. They wouldn't buy fish, they wouldn't sell 'em any gas. Some of those Kwig guys were desperate, man, and they wouldn't let go. Finally those guys on the tender just untied their lines and threw 'em in the water."

Elsie was already gone by the time we got back to Kongiganak last night. Margaret said she'd gotten homesick and got on a plane, taking Elizabeth up to Bethel with her for company. Margaret also said that Hannah had come home; Vivian's young mother had gone to Hawaii with a plane ticket she'd bought from a raffle winner in Bethel, and returned to Kongiganak just the day before. But she wasn't home for long, had already flown off again, though not without mishap.

Oscar bent down again at Margaret's feet and loosed a slow, delicious chuckle. "So Hannah forgot her Anchorage ticket?"

Margaret nodded. "She called from Bethel and said she forgot it. She wanted me to get it and put it on one of the Seagull Air planes coming down here."

This time Hannah was going to Seattle, and she was taking Vivian with her. I saw her yesterday at Aanaq's house, sitting at the supper table in tight Calvin Klein jeans and a white cotton pullover. With her suntan her skin was as smooth and brown as sandalwood. My breath caught for a moment to see her white smile, to see how much she still resembled the beautiful schoolgirl I'd known, even as she held Vivian on her lap and fed the child bits of dried seal that she'd chewed first herself. She looked like she was babysitting her infant sister.

In grade school Hannah had been a promising student and also a model of traditional Yupik decorum: silent, with her eyes downcast in the presence of men or older boys, entertaining only the most glancing and opaque interactions with the other sex. But even then Aanaq, struck by Hannah's beauty, expressed apprehensions about what might become of the girl as she grew older, and eventually Hannah seemed to become distracted by her own good looks — or maybe she used her beauty to express her independence of traditional roles and values. She fell off at school, struggled to earn her high school diploma, and then began to live sometimes in Bethel, sometimes in Kongiganak, never entirely at ease, it seemed, in either place. Most of her boyfriends in Bethel were *kass'aq,* and she showed little interest in the life that many of her classmates had already settled into and that Aanaq so plainly desired for her: marrying a boy from the village and raising a family here. Aataq and Aanaq had not been so bold, as they'd been with Margaret, as to choose a husband for Hannah themselves.

This trip to Washington was for the purpose of spending a few weeks with José, Vivian's father. José had come to Bethel two years ago to drive cabs for the summer. In the fall he had gone back to Seattle to go to school. He and Hannah had stayed in touch, though he'd sent hardly anything for the baby, and wasn't as sure of his paternity as Hannah was. Margaret didn't know whether José was paying for this latest adventure or Hannah had somehow scrounged the money for it, but she was at least satisfied that her grandparents weren't subsidizing the journey. This morning Hannah had prevailed upon Charlie to help carry her bags up to the runway for one of the early Seagull flights into the village and back to Bethel, but no sooner had she arrived in town than she phoned Margaret with the news that she had left her Bethel-to-Anchorage plane ticket at Aanaq's.

Oscar chuckled again to think of the peripatetic Hannah stranded at the very start of one of her junkets. He cut the two loose ends from a knot and asked, "So what did you tell her? Did you tell her you wouldn't bring it up?"

"No, I couldn't do that," Margaret said. "She's my sister. I brought it up to the plane."

Oscar grimaced. "A worthless sister. Somebody should give her a piece of their mind."

Margaret had come home to Aanaq from Bethel, with Oscar the Great in tow, but it remained to be seen if Hannah would. I've never seen either of Margaret's grandparents in Bethel, and so far as I know Aanaq only goes there when her heartbeat flutters, occasions when a plane comes immediately — weather permitting — to take her to the hospital. Then, if she isn't allowed to come home again very soon, Aataq goes up to be with her. I know Aataq also went up by sailboat once, maybe in the late 1930s, at the urging of a Russian Orthodox priest. That was to get a marriage license for himself and Susie, though they'd already been living together for years by then, just as their parents had arranged.

I think these two elders are grateful for their remoteness from Bethel, and have little use for the big town other than as a place at one time in which to sanctify a Christian marriage, and a place now, possibly, in which to die. Oscar's family, in contrast, has been wedded to Bethel, for better or for worse, almost since Bethel's inception a little more than a century ago — almost since the day in 1884 when two American missionaries from a Protestant evangelical church with roots in Bohemia decided that a spot near the Yupik village of Mamterillermiut would be the most propitious location for their mission on the Kusko-kwim.

According to Yupik legend, Mamterillermiut was where a young couple fleeing famine on the Yukon had found their fish traps full one morning. They decided to stay, and so began the Yupik occupation of the middle stretch of the Kuskokwim. The churchmen, J. A. H. Hartmann and William Henry Weinland, liked Mamterillermiut for several reasons: it was central to two other Yupik villages as well as an Alaska Commercial Company trading post; it was comfortably removed from stubborn Russian Orthodox strongholds down on Bristol Bay and 250 miles upriver on the Kuskokwim, at Fort Kolmakovsky, where the Russians had established a post at the edge of Athabascan Indian country; and it boasted the first tentative tree cover that had appeared to that point on the river. Probably most of all they were impressed by the Bible reading for the day they landed at the village: "And God said unto Jacob, Arise, go up to Bethel, and dwell there: and make there an altar unto God, that appeared unto thee when thou fleddest from the face of Esau thy brother."

One of the Moravians' companions on that journey was Edward Lind, known more familiarly in Bethel history as Trader Lind. At Mamterillermiut the four Yupik guides hired by the missionaries at the mouth of the Kuskokwim decided they had come far enough. They said it was late in the season and they were low on provisions, though more likely they were concerned about the sometimes hostile relations between coastal and upriver Yupik peoples. At that point Trader Lind intervened. He said that there would be no pay for any of the guides' work so far — at the rate of twenty-five cents a day — unless they went on to Fort Kolmakovsky, which at last they did. Lind was a Russian Finn who had come to the region just a few years before, and he managed the AC trading post at the old Russian fort. By then he already had six children by his Yupik wife, and he wanted the Moravians to build their mission at Kolmakovsky so his children could attend the mission school. No doubt he was disappointed in the missionaries' firm preference for Mamterillermiut, but no matter: the AC trader at that post died the next year, and Lind was transferred downriver to take his place. When William Weinland and four other missionaries returned to Mamterillermiut in 1885 in order to start building, Trader Lind — the father of Adolph Lind, Oscar's grandfather — was there to meet them.

Perhaps not wishing to tie the mission too strongly to a single village, the Moravians decided to build at a site on the Kuskokwim's western bank roughly opposite Mamterillermiut, and also somewhat removed from Lind's trading post. There they began to construct a small cabin and a church, and there also, allegedly, a Yupik shaman prophesied that the new mission would fall into the river. Possibly the Moravians interpreted this as a challenge hurled across the chasm separating their religion and that of the shamans, and perhaps it was, but it was also an accurate observation of the Kuskokwim's tendency at that particular bend. In time the original Moravian buildings indeed had to be hastily moved back from the river's brink, just as Elsie's house was years later. Today the long spit that once guarded the mouth of Brown's Slough, and that also held the town's first airstrip, has disappeared, as has every foot of the original waterfront. For many years junked cars and trucks were heaped along the riverbank in an effort to protect the town, and this made for a beachfront of sheet metal and rust that came to be known as the Bethel Riviera. While picturesque, it didn't entirely work. Bethel's new steel sea wall, completed just last year at a cost of $22 million, is only the latest attempt to thwart the shaman's prophecy.

The original cemetery established by the Moravians has had to be moved as well. Oscar told me last week that he and his brothers used to play at the foot of the riverbank beneath its site: "We'd find bones or skulls lying around, and we didn't think nothing about it. We'd just throw 'em away or play with 'em." Then Elsie added that when it was time to move the bones — sometime in the 1950s — her husband was one of the two men hired by the town to accomplish the job. Well, maybe they were hired; I know that during that time in Bethel, public drunks were arrested, dried out, and then assigned to what might be described quite literally as the graveyard shift. In whatever capacity, James exhumed the remains and then reburied them at the cemetery's present location above Dull Lake, in between the BNC apartments and the Brass Buckle discotheque. Elsie said it was grisly work: "There was lots. Sometimes he found three bodies, or even more, all piled on top of each other under the same ground. Sometimes they was in boxes, sometimes just falling apart. But him and Moses Buzz, they carried 'em all over."

On Memorial Day, I went with Oscar and Elsie and the two girls to that graveyard. After a weekend of nothing but rain and wind, during which Oscar had paced his mother's apartment like a caged cat, the air that Monday was clear and blue and still. The cemetery's wooden crosses were uniformly white, some of them pitched at odd angles, some of them bearing the transverse pedal of the Russian Orthodox faith. They looked like stakes anchoring the burial ground to earth, as though James had driven them in to make sure that this graveyard wouldn't float away, or its bones be tossed about by his kids. The Actives moved in a solemn, whispering group from grave to grave, while savannah sparrows flitted between the crosses and the grass and blossoms of yellow saxifrage and Alaska spring beauty nodded in the light air.

Elsie had come alone the day before to clean the plastic wreaths on Adolph and Maggie Lind's graves. That day they were as green and glossy as holly. Adolph Lind was actually only a stepfather to Elsie, but he was kind to her, and an affectionate grandfather to her boys. In addition to the crumbling *Peggy Belle,* he had piloted barges, scows, and other paddle-wheelers from the mouth of the Kuskokwim to far-flung mining camps high upstream in the Kilbuck and Kuskokwim mountain ranges. He was also among the first to bring Charlie Chaplin and other silent film stars to Bethel, in the days when Oscar wouldn't have had to bum a buck from his dad, when admission could be had for a bundle of rye grass or a piece of dried salmon. I remember a snapshot of Adolph and Maggie tacked to the wall of James's house in Kasigluk. The couple stood formally, both still young, Adolph in a woolen jacket and canvas pants. These and his wire-rimmed glasses made him look like a full-blooded *kass'aq* of bookish inclinations. His wife was dressed in an elaborate winter parka of ground squirrel and muskrat skins, and she beamed at his side, her oval face and button nose the same as Elsie's.

Maggie died in 1976, Adolph in 1981, and I never met either of them. But I remember Maggie's voice from a folklorist's recordings of traditional Yupik stories. Her speech was crisp and intimate, and she took a manifest pleasure in her tales of how the sandhill crane got his blue eyes, how the red fox became red, how two selfish and quarrelsome old women were frightened into sharing a tiny needlefish equally. She was known throughout southwestern Alaska as a font of Yupik folklore, though I don't know how she managed to become so learned; both her parents died in one of those withering epidemics that accompanied both the Russians and the Americans into this region, and she was raised by missionaries at the Moravian orphanage in Bethel. I remember reading in the *Tundra Drums,* the weekly Bethel newspaper, an interview that she gave shortly before her death. There she described her fond memories of the Moravian Children's Home, noting how she grew to love the church people who took care of her and the days devoted to baking bread and making jam from the wild tundra berries, and how she always kept in her mind phrases from a song she'd learned there: "Keep on the sunny side, always on the sunny side."

Succeeding generations, however, have found the sunny side less tenable. Jackie and Gregory, Adolph and Maggie's two natural children, both died as young men. "They had mental problems, both of 'em, all their lives," Oscar said. Gregory suffered a fatal seizure in a boat on the Kuskokwim, Oscar told me, and Jackie committed suicide. Their graves lay in another part of the cemetery from their parents', and Oscar moved swiftly past the crosses of these two unfortunate uncles.

Close to them lay Fritz, also known as Mamoo, the second youngest of Elsie's children. Fritz visited Kongiganak the year that the Hunters narrowly lost the Napakiak basketball tournament, and he traveled up to Napakiak with us by snow machine, riding with me and another player in the big plywood sled Oscar pulled behind his Polaris. At twenty to thirty miles per hour the sled soared like a glider over the tops of frost heaves and ice escarpments, and then came to earth with a bone-bruising crash. At some point beyond the halfway village of Tuntutuliak we began traveling on the Kuskokwim, and amid the heaved-up blocks of ice the sled turned over, spilling us sprawling and laughing onto the river.

Big, but not as athletic as Oscar or the rest of his brothers, good-natured Mamoo just watched the basketball games from the audience. On Friday night he spread his sleeping bag beside mine on a mat in the Napakiak gym and told me about going to Kicking Horse, Montana, to attend a cooks' vocational training program, and how impressed he was with the greenery and grandeur of the Rockies, and how he longed to go back there to visit sometime.

At the party the following night at Elsie's house, Mamoo was the first to buy a bottle of Johnny Walker from a visiting bootlegger, and — after the bottle had been passed from mouth to mouth around the team — the first to pass out from its effects. Early the next morning, long before daylight, he rose from his stupor and switched on an overhead light above my bed. Someone had broken a window, and I woke in twenty-below-zero cold to see Mamoo standing by the light switch, blinking and listing to starboard. "Oh, are you trying to sleep?" he asked in his usual manner. Then he straightened, belched, and concluded, "Well, fuck you." He staggered off into the other room, met Oscar similarly staggering in through the front door, and began with him a long and clamorous discussion of each other's character flaws. "Who the hell gives you the say-so to always be in charge?" Mamoo wanted to know. "Who elects you the god-damn boss o' the world?"

The next year Mamoo was found prostrate on the snow one morning in Bethel, a little too drunk and a little too cold. He lingered for a day, heartbroken at the prospect of having his hands and feet amputated, but he died instead. Elsie stood in silence a long time at that grave, the breeze ruffling her short hair, her lips drawn tight and her chin dropping slowly down to her breast.

Oscar also knows what a parent's peculiar grief is like. Sammy Active's grave is excruciatingly tiny. On our way up to the Gweek River on the preceding Friday Oscar had said that he needed to paint its cross again. Sammy's cross was small and straight, awaiting Oscar's promised new coat of white paint, but its present coat was not in any disrepair. Elizabeth and Janet stepped gingerly about the grave of this brother they never knew, whose loss still puzzles and stabs at their parents.

Margaret told me once how she took the eighteen-month-old baby to the Indian Health Service hospital, when they were still living in Bethel and were part of the big crowd — including Buzzo and Mamoo and Charlie — that shared Elsie's house with her. The boy had been crying all day and refused to stay on his back, turning over onto his stomach, seal-like, whenever Margaret laid him down. The doctor said he had some sort of stomach flu and sent them home. Sammy always slept in between his parents, and that night Margaret woke and was horrified to touch his leg and find it cold. Then Oscar woke up and roused the whole household, but it was too late.

The doctor who had examined the child earlier wanted to do an autopsy, but Oscar angrily refused permission. Margaret, after being led to believe that an autopsy was a requirement, signed the necessary forms when Oscar wasn't around. But she never received the results. Instead she had to ask the doctor about it much later, when she met him once at the hospital. She was told that Sammy had died of pneumonia. But years later, when another doctor consented to check Sammy's file for her,

Margaret was told that he had been a victim of sudden infant death syndrome. She still doesn't feel that she knows what really happened to her baby. "Maybe because I'm Native, they didn't feel like they had to be straightforward with me," she said. And she remains terribly afraid on any occasion that she has to take one of her children to the hospital, as though it were the hospital itself that killed Sammy, though really she believes otherwise.

For his part, Oscar wouldn't give Sammy up. Astonishingly enough, at least to me, he enrolled in the Moravian seminary in Bethel in order to train to be a lay pastor. But he completed only the first half of the two-year program. The next year, when Elizabeth was born, he was so keenly disappointed that the new baby was a girl and not another little Sammy that at first he refused to visit mother and child in the maternity ward. Margaret was deeply hurt at the time, but now she laughs about it, noting how fiercely Oscar has learned to love both Elizabeth and Crazy since then. That sort of fierceness, raised to a metaphysical plane, was what brought Oscar, at least for a time, into the church: "I think it was a way of trying to make himself certain that he and Sammy would be reunited again, and that he hadn't really lost him," Margaret said.

I see Oscar pausing quickly before the little plot of ground, standing there blinking self-consciously a moment before moving on; see James Active and Moses Buzz carrying all of Bethel's bones, all of the town's lost loved ones, away from the river in boxes that crumble at the touch; see these at the same time that the worshippers in Kongiganak conclude with one more hymn — "Lead Me, Savior" — and then trail home in small clumps through the rain.

2 ⊙ MADE OUT OF DRIFTWOOD poles nailed and
lashed together, and wearing pieces of old net
hung there to keep dogs at bay, Margaret's
drying rack looks like a rude sort of tent frame wrapped in a
negligee. A dozen very slender poles lie like roof beams across
the top of the rack, maybe eight feet off the ground, and these
were already about one third full last week with black and
knotty strips of seal meat drying since the beginning of May;
also the maroon slabs of some early king salmon caught by Margaret's brother Paul at the mouth of the Kuskokwim; and also
the darkening clusters of the female kings' eggs.

For the past half-hour Margaret has been climbing up and
down a stepladder set beneath the overhead poles, consolidating
all these foods at one end of the rack. Now she moves back and
forth between the nearby plywood cleaning table and the stepladder, a strip of corrugated cardboard folded like a waiter's
napkin over her arm and a half-dozen yarned-together pairs of
cleaned herring laid at a time over this cardboard. She expects
that the drying rack will be full to bursting by the time she finishes hanging these new fish, and she hums softly to herself as
she works, happy in the mild scent of the fresh herring, the prosperous image of the rack's neat and perfect rows.

The herring are too bony to be eaten fresh, however, and
Margaret needs something for tonight's supper. Last night we
ate the last of the king salmon that Oscar and Margaret received
from Paul and that they saved to be eaten fresh. Since Margaret
will be working at the school this afternoon, doing some of the
secretarial work that she promised to do this summer in the
principal's absence, and since Oscar and I will be down at the
river scraping herring scales out of the boat, she asks Oscar to
stop at the Kongiganak Trading Company store to buy some
ground beef on our way home tonight.

Oscar nods absently, then reaches up to touch one long clump
of salmon eggs. Once the color of cantaloupe, the eggs are now

darkening to a ferrous red and turning rubbery. He says, "You used to be able to sell these on the Kuskokwim. Any eggs that you got from subsistence fishing, you could take 'em and sell 'em for good prices, and some of these guys who didn't hardly ever go subsistence fishing, man, they were fighting to get out there. But then some *kass'aqs* started just going for the eggs and throwing away the fish, and now you can't do that no more."

"Not just *kass'aqs*," Margaret reminds him. "Also some Eskimos."

Her husband nods again, conceding the universality of greed, and then stands admiring the drying rack. Oscar is happy now too, having put Cape Avinof behind him and feeling suddenly optimistic about the salmon season on the Kuskokwim, where roe count won't be an issue and there are sure to be fish in the water. It's almost as if he views this disastrous spring at Kipnuk as a down payment for a good summer on the river.

But I know he's already disturbed again about Charlie, and about the paperwork that his brother will have to get done before that season opens, in ten days or so. Three nights ago Elsie telephoned from Bethel and told Charlie that a stipend for a day's jury duty last month had arrived in the mail for him. Combined with the $12.50 he made at Kipnuk, that gave him just enough money for plane fare home. He told Elsie to put the check on the first Seagull flight in the morning to Kongiganak, and then made reservations with Julia Phillip, the local Seagull agent, for the return leg of that flight. "It's an emergency," he explained, laughing, to Julia.

Charlie flew home Saturday morning, retired once more from herring fishing. Later that day Oscar took me as his partner over to Kwigillingok, where a processor was expected to anchor. We were using gas he siphoned from the tank of his snow machine, and the wind blew just as hard as it had off the cape, kicking up waves that ran like broken logs toward the village. Our anchors dragged all afternoon, and the wind kept pushing our bow into the net whenever we tried to shake it clean.

In the end it didn't matter. Oscar paused once in the midst of shaking, the lead line as hard as a banister in his hands and his face dripping with spray, and noticed that many of the boats farther out to sea were pulling in their nets and heading in to shore. One boat crossed our stern, and the man at the wheel made a cutting motion across his throat as he passed us. Oscar dropped his line, allowing the *Crazy J* to swing with the wind, and picked up the mike to the VHF. He learned that the expected processor, the *Casey L,* had just turned around and was heading back out to sea. "The tide's going out, and nobody's catching fish anyway," Oscar said. "So they changed their mind."

Desultorily we finished shaking and then pulled in the net, collecting all told maybe two hundred pounds of herring, along with a smattering of sand dabs and devilfish. Then Oscar headed toward Kwigillingok, where Margaret grew up and where her father, Mills Paul, still lives with his second wife and their children. Oscar wondered what Panta Paul, Margaret's half-brother, might be doing with whatever herring were in the net he had set inside the mouth of the Kwigillingok River. Since he didn't have anywhere to sell the fish anyway, Panta was happy simply to give us the approximately four hundred pounds that he'd harvested. After he and his brother Leo and I had moved the fish from the Pauls' boat into ours, Oscar surveyed the squirming heaps of silver, saying, "Margaret's been bugging me to get some herring for drying this summer. That ought to keep her busy for a while."

We ended up staying over there, sleeping at Mills's house. (Mills was out hunting beaver, and never came home that night.) Oscar wasn't worried about his boat anymore in those heavy seas; as a matter of fact, in Kongiganak he had come back laughing from the river Thursday morning, returning from his customary errand of pumping out the water that had leaked in overnight. He said that the drain plug at the bottom of the boat's transom had been pushed in backward and had probably been that way ever since he and Buzzo and Charlie had worked on the boat at Kipnuk. "I bet we fixed that leak over there after all," he said, and sure enough, Jerry's submarine has been dry inside every morning since.

But with the tide running out, the tidal flats outside the Kwig-illingok River had heaved up like continents, and Oscar didn't think he had enough gas to follow the channel way out into the bay and then pick up the Kongiganak's channel. At Mills's house he stretched out on the floor in front of the TV, grimacing when he heard that gas prices on the delta would probably rise by fourteen cents a gallon as a result of the massive *Exxon Valdez* oil spill in Prince William Sound in April.

When we got back to Kongiganak yesterday, the wind had died and the clouds were drawn in a thin, translucent lattice across the sky, their pattern reminding me of the leaning crosses in the graveyard at Bethel. Oscar talked and laughed without a care as we scooped the herring out of the *Crazy J* and into white five-gallon plastic buckets, hauled the buckets over the river-bottom mud and up the steep portion of the bank closest to his house, and trundled them in Aataq's old wheelbarrow over the boardwalks to the big plywood bin behind the house. Oscar emptied a bucket of herring into the bin and sang, "The dirtiest fish in America!" He laughed and said to me, "Did you see that animated film — what was it called — *An American Tail*? I like that song: 'No cats in America!'" He laughed again, throwing the empty buckets into the wheelbarrow and steering it back to the river, still singing, "The dirtiest fish in America!"

Oscar likes fishing for salmon too, and he's feeling confident now that he'll make money at that. But certainly part of his buoyancy these past two days has to do with the same satisfaction that Margaret takes in this heavily burdened drying rack, though maybe his is of an even more profound sort than hers. It concerns something more than the prospect of full supper plates this winter, and philosophically it relates to the import of the seals that Oscar hunted in open water this spring, among drifting ice, in Joe Brown's skiff, and which Margaret and Aanaq butchered together in the *lagyaq*, or the various ducks and geese, along with a few swans and sandhill cranes, that he brought home before the birds started nesting.

Having watched the stalking and killing for years, however, and participated in it myself, I still get a little uneasy sometimes with the élan, even the ferocity, with which hunters such as Oscar go about it. I remember that time years ago when I just dropped my gun and let squadrons of tundra swans pass overhead unharmed after the bewildered Tommy Andrew had called them in my direction. On seal hunts I've dutifully shot at and taken seals and then donated the meat to the owner of the boat, but not before being disturbed by the dead seals' puppyish features and the fins that are as delicately reticulated as an infant's hand. In Kongiganak the meat was cleaned and processed, as these herring are being cleaned now. I've taken pictures of the butcherings in the *lagyaq*, and of walrus being flayed and sectioned by men on the ice floes or on the riverbank. Many of my friends from Outside, and even elsewhere in Alaska, have found these pictures unsettling, as though they were pictures of battlefield atrocities.

I'm reminded in this of the young schoolteacher May Wynne Lamb, who so admired the aurora borealis in Akiak. In 1917, during a winter festival competition testing speed in butchering reindeer, she had to turn her face away when what she saw reminded her of a childhood visit to the Kansas stockyards. She wrote: "I didn't witness this gruesome performance. As a girl I had visited the stockyards as a part of my education — which part I really don't know — but the hogs were quickly ducked in cold water by one man; then another person slashed their throats; and still another man skinned them; and so on down the line until every part of the hog was dressed, and the waste turned into fertilizer. For days after this ghastly sight, fish was on my menu. Once in a lifetime is too often to attend an exhibition of that sort."

That was May Wynne Lamb's individual response — to give up meat for days and witness no further such spectacles. Simply stated, the problem that was revealed to her was the brutality that necessarily preceded her meals. The world of those stockyards has framed a number of broader cultural responses to that problem: to sequester its stockyards and slaughterhouses well out of sight, for example, and not usually to include visits to such places in its children's education; to employ only a very few people to accomplish the work and so keep others' hands free of blood; to package its processed and separated cuts of meat in Styrofoam and cellophane bundles so free of blood and hair, and sometimes bone, that they betray no trace of their animal origins; to conceive since biblical times of animals in general, and domesticated animals in particular, as subservient objects, property to be disposed of as people see fit; to adopt very recently — more or less concurrently with the shift of America's population from the countryside to the cities — a vigilant stance toward the welfare and safety of those undomesticated animals that no longer make up any portion of its own diet. Partly this vigilance has to do with the dwindling numbers of these animals as their habitats are destroyed or contaminated, but I wonder if it also helps compensate for the violence we visit upon our domesticated sources of meat.

Whatever the case, all this is essentially a cosmetic solution to the problem of murder. Traditionally, the world of the *lagyaq* has had no choice but to confront that problem more squarely, and in response it has devised an entirely spiritual kind of solution — a sort of Grand Unified Theory, as it were — that ties the central issues of religion, economics, and human social forms into a single ideology proper to the lives of both animals and men. It begins by conceiving of animals as not in any way subservient in the hierarchy of creation but in many ways more capable and potent than people. This is logical enough, given the great preponderance of occasions on which the prey animal easily escapes the hunter. Similarly, animals are conceived as possessing souls, just as people do, for which the body is only a temporary vessel. In Yupik the word for soul is *yua,* which translates literally into English as "its person." In stories the *yua* is described as a face of human features hidden beneath the mask of an animal's own face, and in shamans' masks it is depicted as a smaller and alternate set of features set at an angle in the midst of the primary features.

The early Christian missionaries taught that the soul was eternal, that death had no sting — except maybe for those left behind — and this was entirely consonant with Yupik belief. But Yupik people not only extended this potency to the animal realm but conceived of the soul's destiny in different terms. To the missionaries, death was a point of linear finality, followed by the soul's eternal sojourn in the other world; to the people, death was simply a temporary point of punctuation in the soul's endless cycling between this world and the next. To this day in Kongiganak and other villages, newborn children are given the Yupik names of recently deceased relatives or neighbors in the conviction that at least the soul of the deceased, and possibly certain aspects of the personality as well, are reincarnate in the child. Souls are pleasantly colorblind; old Willie Azean died in Kongiganak in 1981, and when my son, Ryan, was born a few months later, he was given the elder's Yupik name, Asian. Now, whenever Ryan visits Kongiganak, he enjoys certain privileges of kinship that are unavailable to me.

Similarly, the souls of animals cycle between the visible and invisible worlds. Given that an animal is swifter, more agile, and more sentient than a hunter, it follows logically that a hunter may succeed only at the consent of the prey animal; in other words, an animal actually allows itself to be killed and its soul released to the other world, as a matter of obligation to the hunter. This obligation was — and still is — cultivated by the observance of proscriptions and taboos by both the hunter and his wife, by the cleanliness of their weapons and tools, by the performance of certain propitiatory rites, and by the absence of waste in their use of the meat. Therefore Oscar stayed home all last spring, while other men went out on the bay, because of the taboo against a father's hunting seals during the year of a daughter's first menses. Therefore Aanaq is careful to put a drink of fresh water into the mouth of a bearded seal before cutting it up on the floor of the *lagyaq*. Therefore children and visiting *kass-'aqs* are admonished to clean every scrap of food from their bowls or plates at meals. Transgressions may bring bad luck to the individual hunter's family, or may prompt the sort of animal movements or weather patterns that cause hardship or misfortune for an entire region.

But the most important way in which this obligation is cultivated between the hunter and his prey is through the sharing of the animal's meat. The gift of wild meat to neighboring households creates an interlocking web of obligation among people that mirrors the ideal web of obligation between humans and animals in both this world and the next. Moreover, the routine back-and-forth movement of meat between households, and the airborne disbursement of gifts that will accompany Clayton's *uqiquq* later this summer, and the more formal distribution of food and candy and gifts that accompany Slaaviq, the celebration of the Russian Orthodox Christmas, are all reflected images of the cyclical motion of souls between the two worlds. Not only does the act of sharing reproduce that motion; it engenders it as well, and a seal or bird or walrus that allows itself to be taken once by a hunter can be expected to allow that again and again by that same hunter, as its *yua* is reconstituted, so long as its meat is properly shared and other observances are respected.

Christian spirituality has not so much displaced this concept as overlaid it. During the past century portions of its breadth have been pared away by Christianity's more linear way of thinking, by the influence of Western materialism and consumerism, by the cash economy, and by the degree to which the potency of animals has been seemingly diminished by the rifle, shotgun, and steel trap. The men and women of Aanaq's generation in particular are disturbed to see the daily gestures of respect and propitiation become thinner, less elaborate, and less frequently observed. At Cape Avinof, Oscar and Jerry talked about a group of young Kipnuk hunters who had gone head-hunting this spring, slaughtering a pod of eleven walruses and taking only the heads so they could sell the tusks to black market ivory dealers. Outraged, the elders of that village made the hunters recover and butcher the carcasses in at least partial recompense for their offense against the animals' souls. Christianity itself is often enlisted in behalf of this thinking. I remember Elsie's look of dismay as she watched news clips from Prince William Sound of shorebirds in their death throes, their feathers coated in oil. She shook her head, her jaw tightening, and said bleakly, "Maybe this is how God did open their eyes."

Wild animals have grown more or less extraneous to Western economic life, but not so here. There are too few jobs in the villages, too little money, and the food in the stores is too expensive to be anything more than a supplement, or an emergency ration, like the ground beef we're picking up tonight. Even if people could afford it, they wouldn't buy it regularly; they notice that it doesn't keep you as warm out on the tundra or the bay, that it doesn't keep you feeling so good. Besides, the food from the stores is spiritually sterile, has nothing to do with an animal's *yua,* and sharing it accomplishes little in abetting the life-sustaining cycling of souls.

But the wild animals of the delta are still wary and elusive, and even hunters armed with shotguns and rifles come home empty-handed very often, as Charlie did on the day we went egg-hunting. A successful capture remains a point of agreement between hunter and prey, a moral affirmation, just as sharing that meat remains a point of agreement and moral affirmation between the hunter's family and their relatives and neighbors. This is still the driving wheel of the Yupik subsistence economy, a logically coherent solution to the problem of murder that becomes much more than that as well — becomes, in fact, a universal key for integrating this world and the next, the human and animal kingdoms, the individual and society.

Curiously, this spirituality has always been relatively attenuated when it comes to fish. Of course fish in general, and salmon in particular, are far and away the most important food resource in the delta, and yet fish seem to exist only at the periphery of this spiritual interrelationship, this system of taboos and propitiations, whereas seals, by contrast, are at its very heart. But Eskimos around the world are distinctive for their marine mammal technologies, their exploitation primarily of seals, and only on the Yukon-Kuskokwim Delta and Bristol Bay — nowhere else in the world — have Eskimo peoples moved so far inland and developed such flourishing salmon-based economies. Ancestors of the Eskimos, who were seal hunters themselves, probably occupied the coastal regions of the delta some 2500 years ago. Around 2000 years ago, the development of fishing technologies based on nets made laboriously from rawhide, sinew, or willow bark allowed these people to exploit the delta's upriver environment, at roughly the same time that the distinctive characteristics of Eskimo culture as a whole were taking shape in the Bering Strait region. Some suggest that salmon and other fish were too recent and local an addition to the paleo-Eskimo and Eskimo economies to allow the development of a corresponding spiritual complex. Maybe the degree to which we recognize ourselves in a seal, or even a bird, has something to do with it as well. Or maybe the answer lies simply in the fact that the fish were always there, and in great numbers, no matter what. Be that as it may, the inclinations of fish seem to have been only loosely tied to the habits and behaviors of people.

But that relationship nonetheless exists, and these days, as the fish are seen suddenly as less reliable and less numerous, failures on the part of humans are viewed as affecting their movements and availability. Certainly Yupik elders must have been offended by the salmon roe stripping on the Kuskokwim that Oscar described, and must continue to be offended by the herring roe stripping by the commercial buyers. Also, the sharing of fish is nearly as potent as the sharing of seal in answering to the reciprocal relationships that tie one household to another. Margaret's herring, once they are dried and smoked, promise that soon she will again have quantities of wild food that she'll be able to share with other people, and that her household will reassert itself as one of those whose productivity helps to keep the whole system in motion. This has nothing to do with a commercial fisherman's paycheck; in fact, in certain ways selling fish for money is entirely antithetical to it, and I think sometimes that Margaret wonders if maybe that's part of Oscar's problem, one of the roots of his anxiety and anger.

In any event, the trip over to Kwigillingok was worth the gas. Oscar set out to go commercial fishing but instead came home with a load of fish for his family to eat and to share, and the fact that a portion of it was received from his brother-in-law renders it all the more charged with value in that other, decidedly noncommercial sense. The language itself suggests the crucial nature of this: the Yupik word for man, *angun,* is composed of word parts that combine literally in English as "a device that chases and catches food." Not just a household's economic productivity but the validity of a marriage and a person's credibility as an adult male continue to rest on the performance and the results of that chase. So Oscar has salvaged at least that much from this herring season.

Later, however, after cleaning the boat, he finds that he forgot to salvage dinner tonight. Both of us walked right past the store without remembering the ground beef, and now the store is closed. Chagrined, Oscar shuffles uneasily in front of Margaret, who is dismayed to find herself without a thing to serve. She pokes around the kitchen in perplexity, suggesting, "I know Aanaq's still got some salmon that Paul gave her, but it's frozen."

"How about defrost it in Paul's microwave?" Oscar says.

"Can't. It's one of those you-won-it-in-a-contest microwaves."

"Won what? Who won?"

"You know," explains Margaret. "The prize you win is you get to buy the microwave. It's just junk. It broke right away and they threw it out."

"Oh."

Margaret sighs and begins digging through the deepest recesses of the kitchen cabinets. Oscar, meanwhile, sits at the table and chews pensively at his lower lip. Suddenly he straightens, shouting, "There's dinner!" at the announcement over the CB radio of a child's birthday feast at Kenneth and Ruth Igkurak's house.

Margaret listens doubtfully to a repeat of the announcement and wonders, "Are we invited?"

"They put it over the CB, didn't they? Who you think's invited?"

"But what'll we bring for a present to dinner?"

In little more than a moment Clayton and Junior and Crazy are fetched from Aanaq's house, coats are thrown onto the two boys, and the family trails out their door and up the boardwalk to the Igkuraks' house at the western end of the village. Margaret carries an unopened box of Stove Top stuffing mix as her impromptu contribution to the feast, and no doubt it galls her to bring something store-bought like that, something as poor as that, and not strings of smoked herring, or at least some king salmon.

Oscar doesn't mind. He chuckles as he walks down the boardwalk hand in hand with Junior, the little boy striding almost comically with the same assertive, elbow-swinging gait as his father. "Sometimes you just gotta go foraging for your supper," Oscar says.

"*Takaryugpaa,* how embarrassing," replies Margaret.

Oscar misinterprets, thinking that she's talking about their presence at the feast rather than her gift. "Well, who you think's invited to this, anyhow?"

The box of stuffing mix falls to the boardwalk, but Crazy scoops it up. A shadow of a smile plays about Margaret's lips as she hoists Clayton into her arms and then skips to catch up to Oscar, saying, "Only the élite."

3 ⊙ IN 1878, seven years before the Moravian missionaries began building their church in Bethel, a twenty-three-year-old naturalist from Chicago visited Kongiganak. Edward W. Nelson was traveling by dog team from the big town of Saint Michael, which lies north of the Yukon River on Norton Sound, 250 miles away. Later Nelson would write that he was kindly received in his visits to the villages along the coast and up the Kuskokwim, even if that wasn't always the case: "In the large village of Kongigunugumut, near the mouth of the Kuskokwim, I was given a very surly reception, and it was almost necessary for me to use force before I could get anyone to guide me to the next village. On the contrary, at Askinuk and Kaialigamut, in the same district, the people ran out at our approach, unharnessed our dogs, put our sledges on the framework, and carried our bedding into the kashim with the greatest good will."

Kongiganak, or Kongigunugumut, as it was known in the 1870s, receives no other mention in Nelson's classic monograph, *The Eskimo About Bering Strait*. The other two villages no longer exist, and the Kongiganak Nelson visited would have been located at the community's former site along the bay. That site was abandoned some years after his visit, when many people moved to Kwigillingok. Kongiganak did not exist again as a community until the summer of 1967, when none other than George Chanigkak, Margaret's enterprising grandfather, tore his wooden house in Kwigillingok into sections and ferried them by boat over to this small knoll. During the next winter Kenneth Igkurak, who created the slough Kitngialleq with a scrape of his heel, followed suit, and so did a number of others. The migrants used logs as sled runners and hauled the houses behind snow machines, dog teams, and a Caterpillar tractor. Aataq says he came and others followed because they were tired of the spring flooding in low-lying Kwigillingok, though factors such as the availability of game and internecine political rivalries may have played a part as well.

I can only speculate as to why Nelson was greeted poorly at Kongiganak a century ago. Possibly he suffered the brunt of unperceived tensions between the villagers and the men who were guiding him at that point, or between Kongiganak and the next village he wanted to visit. But Nelson traveled throughout the Yukon-Kuskokwim Delta and along the shores of Norton Sound for three years, and then rode a revenue cutter for another year through the Bering Strait to Eskimo villages in Siberia and northern Alaska. On only one occasion did he feel that his life was threatened, and that was on King Island, in the Bering Strait. There the young scientist had an angry and public confrontation with a man he caught stealing from him. Later, as he settled down to sleep in the village's kashim, where the adult men lived communally, he was puzzled to see an individual he described as the village's headman settling himself into a seat near the kashim's chilly entranceway. Much later, in the middle of the night, Nelson heard someone else come creeping into the building. He looked up from his sleeping-bench to see the thief whom he had embarrassed earlier stealthily advancing through the entranceway. The headman, however — who didn't sleep that entire night — took the intruder by the shoulder and spoke sharply to him in an undertone. The thief drew back, and only then did Nelson realize the reason for the headman's vigilance.

Elsewhere, even in Kongigunugumut, the scientist stayed out of trouble, in part because of his characteristic good manners, in part because of the generous supply of trade goods he carried with him, and in part also, I believe, because of his precocious insight into the sophistication of Eskimo, and particularly Yupik, culture. But Nelson wasn't an ethnographer, and had no training in that field. His passion instead was birds, though his mission couldn't afford him the comfort of such specialization; rather, he was charged to find out and record everything he could about the general zoology, geography, and ethnology of this little-known region. It was not until almost a full century later that Nelson's primary interest actually entailed some double-edged consequences for the residents of Kongiganak, providing not only the first legislative challenge in southwestern Alaska to a prey animal's spiritual consent to be killed, but also demonstrating the extent to which events in this village had at last become tied — invisibly but intimately — to events and circumstances elsewhere in the world.

These consequences began with almost geologic slowness. In 1878 the United States had been the landlord of Alaska for a little more than two decades, having obtained the territory in the Treaty of Purchase with Russia, but it remained so far from the thoughts of most Americans that it had taken seventeen years for Congress to establish any civil government there. Spencer Fullerton Baird, collector and also the assistant secretary of the Smithsonian Institution, suspected that the new territory concealed significant clues about the relationships between New World and Old World faunas. Since the Smithsonian lacked the money to post scientists to Alaska, however, Baird managed to prevail upon government agencies to fill their Alaska stations with men of his own choosing and then allow them to conduct field work for the Smithsonian in their spare time.

Edward W. Nelson's interest in natural history, particularly ornithology, was probably kindled during his boyhood years in the Adirondack Mountains of New York. He was born in Amoskeag, New Hampshire, but when his father enlisted in the Union Army during the Civil War and his mother subsequently went to work as a nurse in a Baltimore hospital, Edward and his brother were sent to upstate New York to live with their grandparents. His father died in battle, and after the war the family moved to Chicago, where his mother began a dressmaking business and young Edward prowled the Lake Michigan shore. His high school principal introduced him to professional naturalists, from whom he learned collecting and mounting techniques. He taught school for a few years after his graduation, and then, realizing that there were few opportunities in Chicago for an ambitious ornithologist, he went to Washington, D.C. This was after he had heard from a friend that the Smithsonian was looking for scientists of the young and physically energetic sort.

So Baird arranged for Nelson to be hired as a weather observer at the U.S. Signal Service's station at Saint Michael, a fort and trading post established by the Russians four decades earlier on the very northern fringe of the delta. Coincidentally, Saint Michael had also been the headquarters of the Western Union Telegraph Expedition, which had tried unsuccessfully before the Civil War to establish a route for a trans-Siberian telegraph cable linking the United States and Europe. Baird had sponsored the scientific corps attached to that expedition and had personally transmitted their reports to Congress. Their early appraisals of the natural history and resources of Russian America not only piqued Baird's interest but were also influential in sealing the purchase of what Secretary of State William Seward foresaw as the cornerstone of America's eventual Pacific empire.

Nelson arrived in Saint Michael in 1877. For the next three years he cajoled friends into taking over his duties at the weather station for two or three months each winter, and then undertook grueling dog-sled journeys of a thousand miles or more up and down the coast and into the delta's unmapped interior. He was probably the first *kass'aq* to visit Kongiganak and a number of other Kuskokwim-area villages. Although the trade goods from Saint Michael that he carried were appreciated and desired, they were not entirely novel; Western industrial items had been circulating through the region along trade networks from Siberia and the Pacific Northwest for at least a century already. But Nelson's commercial interests were novel: not the furs, which had drawn the Russians and which were important also in trading with neighboring Inupiaq Eskimos, Athabascan Indians, and Siberian Yupiks and Chukchis, but rather the routine and trivial objects of everyday life. People were so astonished by Nelson's willingness to trade for these items that he became known throughout the region as *angun kiputetet caunrilngurnek,* "that man who buys good-for-nothing things."

To Nelson, however, each one of those good-for-nothing things was the key to a mystery, no less so than the observed habits of a bird. Each item that he bought was individually labeled and described with an ornithologist's zeal for fine detail: an ivory dart socket carved like the head of a wolf, for example, with the dart erupting from its jaws like a chameleon's tongue; or a wooden carving of a bulging lingcod, with a lid over the fish's stomach that opened to reveal a cavity for storing spear points; or tubes for inhaling snuff, made from the hollow wing bones of geese and incised with designs of a precise and abstract geometry; or an iron saw blade fastened into an ingenious wooden frame in imitation of a Russian bucksaw; or a tool bag sewn from the skins of four wolverine heads and supplied with a bottom of tanned sealskin; or wooden ladles etched with drawings of supernatural monsters, their bodies split down the middle and their organs visible, as though spread open for vivisection; or a bow hunter's wrist guard carved out of dusky fossil mammoth tusk; or an amulet in the shape of a creature with a froglike head and a swollen stomach, possibly a portrait of Aqsarpak, or Big Belly, a famous shaman; or an arrowshaft straightener carved in the shape of a fetal caribou, complete with umbilical attachment; or a marvelous dance mask with the head of a horned puffin protruding from its neck, a tiny walrus held in its jaws, the mask's grinning face surrounded by a halo of willow hoops and disembodied hands, flippers, and webbed feet; or hundreds upon hundreds of items more. Nelson's descriptions of the delta's flora and fauna were equally thorough; his reports on animals, for instance, covered all the variations of their physical appearance, a broad range of observed behaviors, the precise extent of their habitat, both their Latin and Yupik names, and the often multitudinous methods that his hosts used to pursue and make use of them.

The results, finally, of these long winter journeys, shorter summer excursions, and a one-year stint as an observer on the U.S. revenue cutter *Corwin* were a priceless ethnological collection of close to ten thousand specimens, the largest of its kind in the world; a report on the birds of the Yukon-Kuskokwim Delta that remains a classic in its field; and the encyclopedic monograph *The Eskimo About Bering Strait*. This large book is not only exhaustive but nearly unique; it stands alongside the journals of the Russian Lieutenant Zagoskin, who traveled the region thirty-five years earlier, as a perceptive and sympathetic rendition of an Eskimo world very different from, and much more populous than, that of the better-documented Inuit — a culture that has been described by the archaeologist Robert McGhee as being "probably as rich as any other in the nonagricultural and nonindustrial world."

Moreover, the two accounts describe a world that even then was fading away before its observers' eyes, and indeed the Russian and the American are in poignant agreement on the withering of all that they couldn't observe in that world, of all the unexamined mysteries of thought and desire that lay beneath its surface forms. Zagoskin wrote:

> If we wish to preserve the memory of their primitive life, it is well to hurry: with the spread of Christianity and the contact with our way of living the natives so quickly lose their native character that in a decade or so the old people will be ashamed to recount and will conceal their former customs, beliefs, and other habits, and their whole social life will change. We observed this at the present time among the newly baptized on the Kuskokwim.

Similarly Nelson, who was fascinated but bewildered by the mask festivals he witnessed in the kashims:

> Unfortunately, I failed to secure the data by which the entire significance of customs and beliefs connected with masks can be solved satisfactorily . . . ; the field is now open, but in a few years the customs of this people will be so modified that it will be difficult to obtain reliable data. When the Eskimo between the Yukon and Kuskokwim rivers become so sophisticated by contact with white men that mask festivals will fall into disuse, it will be but a short time until all the wealth of mythological fancy connected with them will become a sealed book.

No one else immediately came to penetrate that "mythological fancy," however, and in fact crucial aspects of the philosophy and practice of Yupik shamanism are now forever lost. In certain other regards, however, Nelson and Zagoskin were too pessimistic. They overestimated the prospective traffic of other white men in the region, and they underestimated the depth and tenacity of that spiritual life, which the shamans did not define, after all, but only tapped, and which has been able to reach some accommodation even with Christianity.

Paradoxically, the shape of the American's personality is less accessible to us now than that of the humane and sagacious Russian. There is only a single known photograph of Nelson in Alaska; moustached, he stands in a skin parka, mukluks, and snowshoes, a carbine cradled in his arms, his eyes gazing furtively to one side over the beak of his nose, the background behind him a white and luminous fog. The personal diary that he occasionally mentions in his monograph has been lost, and his own responses to all that he saw are veiled beneath the monograph's rigorous scientific objectivity. In his reports and letters, however, the young man's energy and animating passions are still on display, in particular his enchantment with birds. In a report to the Signal Service, for example, Nelson describes a trip he undertook in May 1879 to an island near the mouth of the Yukon. There he and a companion named Alexie awaited the arrival of the emperor geese, whose nesting behavior had never previously been observed.

> There followed about two weeks of the greatest misery it was my fortune to endure in the north. Day after day the wind blew a gale from the ice-covered sea, and was accompanied by alternate fog, sleet, and snow. Without fire, and with no shelter but a small light tent made of thin drilling and pitched on a bare marsh facing the sea, the Eskimo and myself crouched in our scanty supply of blankets, benumbed with cold, and unable to better our condition. Finally, the weather moderated, and the geese, ducks, and other water-fowl flocked to their breeding grounds.

The conclusion of this sortie was described in a letter to a friend at the Smithsonian. Neither Nelson nor Alexie was equipped with *imarnitet,* those seal-gut raincoats that fasten to a kayak's coaming and keep both the boat and its wearer dry. When they returned to Saint Michael with a third companion in a bidarka, a three-man kayak, heavy seas arose that nearly swamped the craft and finally forced the party to take shelter in the mouth of the Pikmiktalik River. Nelson's legs had become paralyzed by the cold water, just as Charlie's nearly were at Kipnuk, and the scientist's friends had to pull him bodily from the cockpit, strip off his clothes, and set him by the side of a roaring driftwood fire. While shivering before the flames, however, Nelson heard the call of a nesting sandpiper. No doubt to the amazement of his companions, he immediately forgot his extremity and set off naked across the tundra in pursuit.

But enthusiasms such as these took their toll, and Nelson was forced to leave Alaska in 1881 with his lungs under siege from tuberculosis. He removed to the American Southwest, where he worked fitfully on his monograph during a long convalescence. At the same time Spencer Fullerton Baird, under pressure from other museums, was forced to lend portions of the Nelson collection, and the collector was surprised — and embittered — to see other scholars publishing material on some items before he had an opportunity to do so himself. The appearance of the monograph was delayed not only by Nelson's poor health but by the Smithsonian's chronic lack of funds, and it wasn't until 1899 that the museum was finally able to publish *The Eskimo About Bering Strait.* This might even then have provided the foundation for an important career in the young science of ethnology, but by then Nelson's age, troubled lungs, and inclinations had taken him a different direction: a series of government wildlife posts in the Southwest, important natural history expeditions into Mexico, eleven years as chief of the Bureau of Biological Survey in Washington, D.C., only one more brief visit to Alaska, and a pioneering role in the nascent wildlife conservation movement.

Neither Oscar nor any other hunter in Kongiganak is doing any bird hunting right now. The birds are well along in their nesting, and they repay a hunter's time and gas only when they're flocking. At one time, however, when all the geese were molting in July, people in the delta would hang salmon nets on upright stakes in certain marshes, then fan out through the marshes and drive all of the flightless birds and their young into the nets, there to be slaughtered and piled into boats. I think it's safe to say that Edward W. Nelson found these goose drives painful to watch — at least as painful as May Wynne Lamb's glimpse of the reindeer butchering in Akiak. And though his evidence couldn't have been anything more than anecdotal, he wrote in his monograph that "these drives and the constant egg gathering that is practiced every spring are having their effect in rapidly diminishing the number of waterfowl in this district."

In 1918, when serving in Washington as chief of the Bureau of Biological Survey, Nelson became perhaps the key figure in the negotiation of the Migratory Bird Treaty Act, legislation that the United States cosigned with Canada (or, more precisely, Great Britain) and that stands today as an early landmark in the history of wildlife conservation. Central to this act was the provision that both countries would prohibit the hunting of ducks, geese, and other migratory waterfowl, and also the collection of their eggs, during the nesting season, which the act defined as extending from the beginning of March to the beginning of September each year.

Here in the delta the birds begin to flock to their staging grounds in August, and fall hunting has traditionally begun one or two weeks before September. But of greater import to Yupik families has been the treaty's wholesale ban on harvests in May, which in many years provide households with their first taste of fresh food since the previous September, and which in some years — after wet summers that spoil all the drying salmon, or stormy springs that thwart the seal and walrus hunts — provide the only means of averting hunger, or even famine.

In the well-provisioned delta, famines were rare but memorable, their horrors lingering across the generations. Some of the elders' stories hark all the way back to the spring of 1894, though there have been more recent hungers. That year, however, hunger prevailed throughout the entire region. The Moravian historian Anna Buxbaum Schwalbe describes the suffering in Bethel from the recollections of the missionaries John and Edith Kilbuck:

> The people suffered much. Some ptarmigan were snared, but not enough to satisfy hunger. With starvation prevailing, the people ate the dead dogs who had themselves starved to death. Little children chewed their boot soles trying to get a little sustenance. Discarded fish bones were re-boiled with certain grassy roots while the caches of field mice were robbed of the small bulbs known as mice nuts. It became necessary for the missionaries to issue a daily dole of food. Mrs. Kilbuck wrote, "I will share my own meals just so my own little ones, always, might have enough." Nearer and nearer death from starving came stalking through the village. And then on May 22nd the wild geese arrived!! A native woman came running to Mrs. Kilbuck, flinging up her arms and calling, "Now we will eat, now we will eat!!"

Of course Nelson didn't see any of these famines, and I don't know what role, if any, those things that he did see in the delta — the spring harvests, and the subsequent egg hunts, and then the goose drives — played in his determination to get the treaty signed. Support for the treaty in Congress owed a good deal to the spectacular decline of the trumpeter swan, which doesn't nest in tundra regions. This bird had been brought to the verge of extinction because of the general accessibility of its nests in the forests of Canada and the Lower 48; the market value of its plumage for making powder puffs, quill pens, and feather boas; the taste for its meat, enjoyed by farmers; and even from the enthusiasms of wealthy amateur oologists, or egg collectors. These oologists had begun a flourishing international trade in rare eggs, the ultimate prize being the egg of the California condor. This could fetch $2000 to $3000, and since a

trumpeter swan's egg was virtually indistinguishable from a condor's, these were sometimes unscrupulously sold for such huge
sums.

Certainly Nelson must have realized that the treaty would be
of little consequence in the delta, and that the goose drives
would go on, since in 1918 and for many years thereafter the
federal government lacked the wherewithal to mount even token
enforcement in remote areas of Alaska. If anything, in fact, the
treaty was wholly beneficial, not only to the trumpeter swan but
to the households of the delta. Slowly, populations of the trumpeter and other waterfowl recovered, and households in rural
Alaska had more birds available to them than they would have
had otherwise. But when Alaska became a state, in 1959, a number of Native hunters in various areas, engaged in the routine
and traditional business of feeding their families, were astonished to find themselves suddenly under arrest for violation of
the Migratory Bird Treaty Act. These arrests provoked such outrage among Alaskan Natives in general that in a few instances
the airplanes of state and federal agents flying over traditional
hunting grounds were fired on.

At least one Alaskan Native was politically more astute than
that. Barrow's John Nusinginya happened to be a representative
to the state legislature and also a student of the black civil rights
movement in the Lower 48. His arrest in 1960 for shooting a
duck out of season was the occasion of what became known as
the Barrow Duck-In, as 138 other men harvested ducks over the
next two days and duly presented themselves for arrest to federal game wardens. The wardens merely issued citations, however, and in the ensuing public outcry against the wildlife agencies, charges against all of the hunters were dropped. Other
enforcement efforts similarly met with little political support,
and in 1975 the U.S. Fish and Wildlife Service discreetly adopted
a policy discouraging its agents from enforcing waterfowl hunting regulations against the subsistence hunting of Alaskan Natives. At the same time, within the past three decades in the
delta, the summer goose drives have almost entirely disap-

peared, though the spring and fall harvests have continued.

But all is not well. Oscar says, anecdotally, that the numbers of geese that return to the delta have greatly declined since he was a boy, and that those numbers were nothing compared to what his father remembers. Wildlife biologists confirm that at least since 1965, when they began their record-keeping, the populations of four species of geese — Pacific black brant, white-fronted, cackling Canada, and emperor — have dropped to levels low enough to endanger their recovery. These biologists also estimate that roughly half of the world's population of black brant nests in the delta each year, while virtually the entire population of the latter three species do so.

Predictably, explanations for these declines are various. Sport hunters in Alaska and the Lower 48, and also some wildlife biologists, point accusingly to the spring harvests that Nelson named a century ago as the chief threat to goose numbers, only now the harvests are performed by an expanding and better-equipped Yupik population. For their part, Yupik hunters are suspicious of environmental degradation in the Lower 48, the continued depredations of sport hunters along the Pacific flyway, and above all the rapid loss of winter wetland habitat in Oregon and California. Some also suggest that the biologists' fieldwork is disrupting nesting behavior among the threatened species, or possibly establishing a trail of scent that leads foxes to the geese's nests. Certainly red and arctic fox are on the increase in the delta, maybe because of a decline in winter trapping subsequent to low fur prices and political pressure from animal rights groups, and their numbers may be high enough to affect a crippling predation with or without the biologists' help. "And look at all that goose down they use in sleeping bags and vests," Oscar said to me once. "Where does all that come from?" Like many other hunters, he remains dubious of assurances from non-Natives — whose probity he does not at all take for granted, and who are obviously not disinterested in the matter — that these come from domesticated geese.

Most biologists agree that their data aren't complete enough to identify any single factor positively as the crucial element in the geese's decline. Some suggest that nothing more remediable than the weather may be at fault, citing an unusual number of late springs and instances of coastal flooding in the past twenty years. This would particularly affect the stocky little brants, who prefer to nest in lower and wetter areas. Whatever the case, the response of a politically more circumspect Fish and Wildlife Service to this visible crisis was the Hooper Bay Agreement of 1984, which has since been modified into the Yukon-Kuskokwim Delta Goose Management Plan. This plan, negotiated jointly by state and federal wildlife agencies, the Association of Village Council Presidents (AVCP) — a Bethel-based Yupik political and social service organization — the National Audubon Society, and representatives from a number of villages on the delta, prohibits the gathering of any eggs of the four threatened species, any harvest at any time of cacklers, and only early spring or late fall harvest of brants, emperors, and white-fronts (in other words, at times when the birds are flocking, before and after nesting).

The plan also closed the fall sport hunting of cacklers in the Pacific flyway, reduced the sport take of emperors in Alaska to two per day, and called for efforts on the part of both sport and subsistence hunters voluntarily to reduce the take of brant and white-fronted geese. Finally, it designated governing bodies in the villages to police compliance on their lands without interference by the wildlife agencies, which renders the plan essentially voluntary. As of 1989, biologists in the delta reported that numbers of the imperiled geese had indeed climbed somewhat, though factors governing their numbers, and even certainty about the numbers themselves, are too murky to ascribe this modest recovery to the effects of the agreement reached at Hooper Bay. I myself have observed only scanty numbers of these geese coming into the villages in the spring; whether this suggests a conscious grass-roots deference to the management plan's precepts, despite the conflicting Yupik conviction that failing to take an animal that offers itself to a hunter is an act of disrespect, or simply the continued relative scarcity of these species, I can't say.

But certainly the Yukon-Kuskokwim Delta Goose Management Plan has been successful in renewing longstanding divisions in Alaska between sport hunters, subsistence hunters, and conservationists — divisions that also partake of those more primal rivalries between Natives and non-Natives, and even simply between rural and urban Alaskans. The goose plan was hardly out of the oven before suits were filed against it by sportsmen's groups such as the Alaska Fish and Wildlife Federation and the Outdoor Council, whose members viewed it as reckless, racially discriminatory, and — in the hard light of the Migratory Bird Treaty Act — patently illegal. The AVCP and the Alaska Federation of Natives entered the suits as interested intervenors, and in 1986 the U.S. District Court in Anchorage accepted the AVCP's contention that the Alaska Game Law of 1925 established a subsistence exemption to the migratory bird law. This was another conservation law, incidentally, in whose design and passage Edward W. Nelson played a part. The 1925 law establishes general hunting seasons in Alaska and states in part that "no such regulation . . . except as herein provided, shall prohibit any Indian or Eskimo, prospector, or traveler to take animals or birds during the closed season when he is in absolute need of food and other food is unavailable."

With that the spring harvest of waterfowl in the delta, at least as a function of absolute need, became legal by court ruling — but only for a year. The sportsmen's coalition immediately appealed the decision, and in 1987 the Ninth U.S. Circuit Court of Appeals in San Francisco reversed the earlier judgment, concluding that the Migratory Bird Treaty Act supersedes the Alaska Game Law and that therefore the harvest of any egg or waterfowl whatsoever, under whatever extremity, is indeed illegal on American soil between March and September. The court added, however, that whether U.S. Fish and Wildlife chooses to enforce the act is a prosecutorial decision immune to judicial review; in other words, the court can't make Fish and Wildlife enforce the law. For its part, the federal agency has gratefully seized on this opening and chosen thus far to abide by the spirit of the goose management plan, pleading accurately that the logistics of enforcement remain very difficult over the vast sweep of the delta and its policy therefore is only to investigate the most blatant violations of wildlife laws, such as hunting waterfowl from airplanes and any mass killings of members of the four jeopardized species.

But technically Oscar was a criminal in his bird hunts this spring, whether he was taking geese or ducks or tundra swans, and all of us were criminals in taking the duck eggs we found a week or so ago. The wildlife conservation laws that for decades have indirectly helped to shelter Kongiganak's subsistence economy have suddenly come home to its very doorstep and threaten to block up the entranceway. "Everything the white man shoots at becomes extinct," Oscar said to me yesterday, responding to an item on the TV about the fate of the passenger pigeon in the Lower 48. "And once they don't want to eat a certain bird or animal, they don't want nobody else eating it either. How come? Eskimos don't go around telling other people what they can eat and can't eat."

Of course the health of these goose populations is a matter of more intimate concern to a subsistence hunter such as Oscar than to a sport hunter somewhere in California; of course no one is more eager than Oscar, or more eager than any other Yupik hunter, to see these species recover their former numbers. But the regulatory mechanisms lying in wait to ensure that recovery are like a splinter in his heart. While closures in hunters' access to the geese may deprive a sport hunter of his recreation, they deprive Oscar of a certain facet not only of his livelihood but of his ability to define himself fully and completely as a man, at least in the Yupik sense of the word, and consequently also as a husband and a father.

As more and more non-Natives come into the state and demand access to Alaska's wildlife resources, as often now for subsistence purposes as for sport, and as more and more wildlife habitat is lost to agriculture and housing and industrial development all over the world, and as disasters such as the *Exxon Valdez* spill scour out entire biomes, Oscar realizes that the political climate, which presently affords him much the same access that his father has always had to birds, marine mammals, and fish, will almost inevitably change. He realizes, in other words, that he's vulnerable in his access to the *sine qua non* of Yupik Eskimo life — a life that may not be given up in part or on a piecemeal basis, a life whose economic and social and religious strands are wrapped so tightly together that it exists either as a single indivisible thread or not at all. He's afraid that whether he and his neighbors go on taking these geese or not — or, more precisely, whether geese go on offering themselves to Yupik hunters in the time-honored moral agreement — it won't make any difference in the long run: the fate of these geese is already out of their hands. And in that he realizes that he has somehow lost control over the exercise of his livelihood, to his grasp on the life he came to Kongiganak to live, though he's not sure exactly how that loss of control so suddenly came about.

When the geese are gone, or inaccessible, and the seals and salmon as well, that will leave only the money to live on, and food stamps — only the ground beef from the Kongiganak Trading Company store, and the boxes of Stove Top stuffing mix. Oscar doesn't even want to think about that, and would sooner pick up a gun than mutely submit to such an eventuality. Certainly the world has gotten too small now to simply take your house apart and move it somewhere else, as Aataq did just a few decades ago.

So Oscar mends his nets, scrapes the herring scales out of his boat, frets about Charlie, knowing that the vulnerability of his access to wildlife has recently added another imperative to the necessity of his making money on his fishing, at least in the long term. He does these things angrily, feeling that even the recognition of that imperative is, in a subtle fashion, a diminution, a submission, an abrogation of sovereignty, a surrender of his birthright. He does them knowing that even to succeed in his fishing, to come home with a roll of hundred-dollar bills, is conceivably just a more roundabout route to hell.

4 ⊙ A SNIPE HANGS SUSPENDED in the blue sky above the bow of the *Crazy J,* its long wings treading the air, as stationary in space as a spider on a thread. Yesterday, while I foraged alone through the grasses here along the Ishkowik River for eggs, a long-tailed jaeger flew up behind me and startled me with its nasal honk. If the jaeger plays the kazoo in the delta's avian ensemble, then the snipe plays the ocarina; the fluttering of its tailfeathers during the long climbs and erratic swoops of its courtship flight produces a sound like two notes on an ocarina alternating rapidly back and forth, and there's no more certain accompaniment than this along the Kuskokwim to the presence of fair and sunny weather.

I watch from the stern as Oscar pokes his head sleepily out of the makeshift tent we built on the boat yesterday and rises stiffly to his knees from the floorboards, where the seven of us slept in a row across the beam of the boat. He glances at the snipe just as the bird drops in a thrumming, spiraling veer toward the river, and then approvingly surveys the white banks of cumulus clouds fringing the northwestern horizon: "North wind? That's good, that's a good wind, man. Really good weather. Let's go to Bethel."

That was the idea yesterday, after we loaded the boat and telephoned Elsie, warning her to expect us that evening, four days in advance of the scheduled start of the king salmon season. But then a fog as thick as milt wrapped itself about the *Crazy J* as we went out the Kongiganak River and turned down the coast. Oscar lost his bearings, and soon a sandbar loomed in front of us. Running the length of this, Oscar found that the bar was actually the eastern bank of the channel leading into the Ishkowik, the main artery of an important hunting ground between Kongiganak and the mouth of the Kuskokwim. He decided not to fight it; he took the boat about a mile up the river, and then he and Margaret and the four kids and I passed the afternoon egg-hunting while waiting for the fog to lift. I hunted alone, returning at last with three little dunlin eggs, still warm as biscuits to the touch. Margaret had nearly a dozen mallard eggs taken from two nests she'd found.

When the fog lifted we returned to the bay, only to be driven back by waves running in angry columns from the south. Oscar chewed his lip, surprised by the south wind and those building waves, and took shelter in the Ishkowik again. He steered the boat farther inland this time, bearing up the west fork of the river to a point where the school building in Kongiganak was almost visible across the scant four miles of tundra that separate that fork from the village. There we made this tent on the boat, lashing a waterproof tarpaulin to the gunwales and supporting its ends with the two oars crossed at the bow end and Oscar's shotgun propped up on the aft thwart. Then Oscar tried to call over to Kongiganak on the VHF, intending to ask someone to contact Elsie so she wouldn't call out search parties when we didn't arrive.

But no one answered. "Something wrong with this thing?" Oscar wondered, fiddling with the radio's dials. He repeated, "Kongiganak, this is *Crazy J*. Kongiganak, *Crazy J*. Kongiganak, you hear me?" He pushed at the wire connections between the microphone and the radio, muttering, "If I say, 'Go to hell, Kongiganak,' then they'll hear me."

"What's wrong with the radio?" Margaret asked.

"Either they can't hear me or they don't like me," Oscar said.

He connected the VHF to a smaller emergency antenna and attached that with duct tape to the top of the big antenna, but still no one answered. By then the wind was advancing up even this deep trough of the river, riffling portions of its surface in hard, stabbing thrusts. "I don't think we're going up the Kusko-kwim today," Oscar said finally. "Them waves are gonna be really bad at the mouth of the river. And I can't get hold of Mom from here. We might as well just go back to Kong."

But it was too late for that. The waves out on the bay had swollen into boxcar-size breakers, as bad as what Oscar feared at the mouth of the Kuskokwim, and he stood only a few min-utes of their pounding before turning back to the Ishkowik again. He looked up the coast in the direction of Kongiganak and said, "I'd try it if it weren't Margaret and the kids, but I don't want to get into trouble out here with them." Then he lifted the flap on the tent and shouted to Margaret, "Next time you and the kids are going up by plane. I don't care how good the weather looks."

Margaret nodded, holding Junior, who by then was scared and crying, saying that that was okay with her. "But that's more expensive," she added.

I know Margaret would have preferred to go up to Bethel a few days later, or even not at all, if that were possible. I won-dered what portions of memory and dread were concealed in the slope of her shoulders, in the wrap of her arms around Junior. But Oscar said he wanted to hang a new float line and lead line on his king net, and probably he wanted to make good and sure that Charlie's paperwork was squared away, that Charlie him-self was squared away.

I understand better now that there were a whole host of rea-sons why Charlie was so eager to retire from herring fishing and get back to town: not only the grueling nature of the fishing, his thirst and boredom, his anxiety about his house and what Harvey might be doing to it, but also the pain of once in a while running into Marianne, his former wife, in Kongiganak. Mar-ianne had been only fifteen when they got married, and Charlie just three years older. Marianne's parents never reconciled themselves to Charlie, and she and Charlie never had children; Charlie's son, Curtis, is the child of a woman Charlie lived with for a time following his divorce eight years ago, and custody rights belong completely to his mother.

Charlie took the failure of his marriage very hard, and I wouldn't be surprised if he still loves Marianne. But sometimes now Margaret can get him to laugh about it. A week ago he wanted to watch a Rambo movie that was being shown on one of the cable TV channels that Oscar can't afford, and Margaret suggested teasingly that he go down to Moses Strauss's house to watch it. Moses is the entrepreneur who brought cable TV to Kongiganak last year, and he is also Charlie's former father-in-law. "They have all the channels down there," she said.

Charlie smiled at Margaret's proposal, and his eyes half closed as he imagined himself walking down to the Strausses' house and settling into a chair opposite their big TV as if he owned the place. "What, you finally back from the store? After eight years?" he said, imitating Marianne's mother. Then Oscar and Margaret laughed as he answered in his own voice, "Well, they had a long line."

But this week of Charlie's being on his own in Bethel has been hard on Oscar. Charlie's phone has been disconnected since last month, and Oscar has had to wait on his brother's pleasure for any information. The commercial fishing district outside Quinhagak, a village on the opposite side of Kuskokwim Bay, opened for king salmon yesterday, Thursday, and Oscar would have liked to have gone over there and fished. But he never even got ready for that, because he was uncertain as to whether Charlie had gotten around to mailing his renewal for his commercial salmon permit to the Limited Entry Commission offices in Juneau. "If we go up to Bethel to get him and he still don't have his permit, then we're really up shit creek," he told me last Sunday. "I'd like to go over to Quinhagak, but I don't want to gamble on Charlie, you know? I'm too much in the hole already."

The next day Oscar telephoned Elsie and was told that Charlie in fact hadn't sent his renewal off, was having trouble coming up with the $25 renewal fee. "She said he didn't get his dividend check yet from Kemp-Paulucci," Oscar reported, naming the seafood company to which he and Charlie sold their fish last summer, which routinely pays a dividend based on the season's receipts to all the boat captains — which is to say permit holders — who sell to it. "Those boat captains are supposed to get their checks before May. He thought he'd have it by now." Then he added that Charlie had vowed to Elsie that he was going to sell to Whitney Seafoods this year instead, and Oscar was pleased at least by that indication of good faith and firm intention.

But by Wednesday evening, with still no news from Charlie, Oscar was physically unable to contain his anxiety. He sat on his couch, trying to watch TV but all the time stealing glances out his south window at the clear blue sky above the *lagyaq*. Then he'd shift and twitch explosively in his seat, muttering again and again, "Doggone that Charlie." Finally he said that tonight would be a perfect night for traveling to Bethel, and he jumped up and called Buzzo in Kipnuk, only to find that Buzzo entirely agreed with him and had already left for Bethel.

For the past few seasons Buzzo has used his own Kuskokwim permit to fish with Hippa, who keeps a fish camp on a slough just a mile or two downriver from Bethel. Oscar had talked to Buzzo just the night before, suggesting that they travel together up to town, and I wondered then if Oscar had hopes of laying claim to at least a share of that partnership in the event that Charlie didn't get his permit renewed. But if so, Buzzo wasn't playing along. Oscar put the phone down with a dark frown on his face. "You better start packing up," he told Margaret. "We better get out o' here first thing in the morning."

But Thursday morning Charlie called from Elsie's to say he had gotten his dividend check in the mail and would be mailing his renewal that day. Oscar breathed a huge sigh of relief and called off his emergency departure for Bethel. "Don't get lost on the way to the post office," he warned Charlie.

Instead Oscar spent that morning picking up what the melting snow had laid bare around his house and reminiscing about previous salmon seasons. He asked me if I remembered Charlie and him describing their fishing in Quinhagak a few summers ago, when Charlie had pneumonia, Oscar had a pinched nerve, and the waves were as high as the roof of the *lagyaq*. Then he kicked at an old boot still frozen to the ground and elaborated on that tale.

"That same year we also had a strike, a fishermen's strike," he said. "I think Kemp-Paulucci was paying sixty cents a pound for kings that year, and we all wanted a dollar. The fishermen's union, you know, had a meeting about those prices, and some guys from Kemp were there, and I had a lot to say at that meeting. They were talking about striking, and I said, 'What you're doing with this strike is good, but you're fighting a big company. If you just strike here, that's just a blow to the gut, 'cause the Kuskokwim's just a little district, and so's Quinhagak. But if you strike in other places too, that's a blow to the whole body. You should be calling Togiak, Bristol Bay, the Yukon, Unalakleet, and gettin' them other districts to strike too.' When I said that, I could see those guys from Kemp getting scared, man. There was a guy there from Napakiak wearing a Kemp-Paulucci hat, and he was trying to help Kemp at that meeting, but I called him a *kass'aq*, and Charlie told me the next day he had the word Kemp on his hat blacked out. Those Kemp guys threatened to pull their processors out, and we said, 'Go ahead — we ain't fishin' anyway.' We called those other districts, like I said, and then just before those processors were due to pull out, Kemp said okay, and we got a dollar per pound for the kings."

Oscar tied up a full bag of trash and laughed as he slung it on the boardwalk in front of Crazy. "The strike lasted five days, and that was just long enough for my back to get better."

Meanwhile, up in Bethel, Charlie was still trying to get to the post office. He called that same afternoon, telling Oscar that the deadline for getting his renewal to Juneau was the very next day, June 15, and he'd have to send it by Express Mail. His dividend check had been so slim, however, that he didn't have the money for both the renewal and the postage. Oscar thought for a minute, and then he remembered that he and Margaret had just gotten a refund check on some prepaid groceries that Margaret had ordered from a bulk shipper in Anchorage. "I'll send that check up to you on the next Seagull flight," he said. "Go pick it up at the airport."

Margaret had just come in from the *lagyaq*, where she'd changed the water on some herring eggs that she was soaking. She started to take off her coat, but Junior interrupted her, tugging at the coat and effectively preventing her from removing it. Then Clayton took hold and tugged in the opposite direction, and directly the boys were squalling and fighting. She fled them for a moment, found the refund check in the bedroom, and handed it over to Oscar with her face as vacant as the sky. Then, with her coat still on, she swept both boys into bed, first reading a Dr. Suess book aloud and at last murmuring softly to them in Yupik.

That was the last Oscar heard about the permit renewal, and now he can only hope that in fact Charlie has mailed it. This morning as we motor from the Ishkowik out into the bay — for the third time — the red-billed arctic terns that huddled together in the grass at the mouth of the river in yesterday's high winds are still gathered there, but today they are preening their feathers and basking in the sun, waiting serenely for the tide to ebb and uncover the sandbars. Oscar has decided to leave the tent up on the boat, partly because he's in a hurry and partly because Junior likes the shelter. Its sides snap like luffing sails as Oscar advances the throttle and the boat climbs up on its skeg.

Oscar is still puzzled by yesterday's weather, and suspicious as well. He stands at the wheel and says, "That was crazy weather, man. I wonder if one of those little girls caused it, those ones having their periods, maybe doing something they wasn't supposed to. Or maybe just the wrong person being out here on the water. Usually those fogs just burn off. You don't see that kind of wind after 'em."

The high tide allows us to run along the beach, staying within a few hundred yards of low grassy bluffs littered with driftwood.

When we came down from Bethel last month, the bay was so calm that the boat seemed simply to float over the water's motionless surface. The clouds in the southwest were blue and white and billowy; in the declining sun their reflection on the water was so perfect that the horizon ahead of us disappeared entirely, ocean and sky blending seamlessly into a single heavenly panorama. I remember Elsie clutching at her elbows with the sheer pleasure of that progress, saying, "Gee, looks just like we're flying."

Today we're not flying, but at last we're moving. The bay rocks just slightly beneath us, its surface scalloped with a light north wind, the water blue and winking in the sun.

After half an hour we enter the Kuskokwim almost without seeming to, its mouth is so wide and baylike. But even as broad as this opening is, and even at high tide, the ease with which Oscar brings us into the river is deceptive. Over the years the mouth of the Kuskokwim has been as much a barrier to the interior as a means of admission, and it remains so yet. Its waters, seven hundred miles from their source in the Alaska Range, lose what little momentum they ever had at the margin of the bay, dropping the bulk of their remaining silt into long, braided reefs of sandbars and mud islands. These in turn are crosshatched by hundreds of underwater sloughs and lakes, an invisible topography laid only inches from our keel, all of it plastic and mutable from year to year, even day to day, as the river contests with tides that are themselves opaque with grit.

Oscar has been traveling in and out of the Kuskokwim between Bethel and Kongiganak for almost sixteen years now, but still he sometimes runs aground and can't find his way free, has to wait for either a high tide to lift him over or a low tide to show him a channel. Depth sounders of the sort built into the small electronic fish-finders that some Kuskokwim fishermen now use, and which Oscar would love to have, are of little use in navigating here, as there generally isn't enough water for a sounder to provide accurate readings. Instead Oscar relies on an oar with a broken handle, which he calls his "Eskimo depth sounder." He keeps it close by, poling it over the side with one hand while he steers with the other. Nonetheless, he finds himself thwarted in every direction from time to time.

In good weather this just means more time and more gas for Oscar, but for larger craft it can mean worse than that. A twelve-foot range of tides sweeps back and forth across these reefs, and through the sloughs these provide currents strong enough and unpredictable enough to turn three-hundred-ton pilot boats sideways. The Russians preferred to stay out of the Kuskokwim's mouth entirely, choosing to supply their traders at Fort Kolmakovsky with six to eleven tons of merchandise each year ferried by *umiat*, large Yupik skin boats, from Saint Michael. These would travel up the more accessible Yukon, and then their cargoes would be hauled twenty-five miles overland to the Kuskokwim village of Kalskag. After the Treaty of Purchase in 1867, American traders and missionaries hired Yupik guides to get them and their supplies into the river, and in time the newcomers developed their own pilots, though not without incident. In 1899 the inexperienced pilot of the annual supply boat for the Bethel Moravian mission never found his way inside, and the following winter the missionaries Joseph Weinlick and Dr. Joseph Romig were obliged to undertake a thousand-mile dog-sled trip to Saint Michael and back to obtain food and avert starvation at the mission.

These days it seems almost surreal to see deep-draft ocean vessels and hulking four-hundred-foot barges enter the Kuskokwim and negotiate all the bars and islands that line the riverbed. We run past one such barge only a few miles above the mouth; stacked with containers, it lies at rest behind a motionless tug, looking like a skyscraper turned over on its side and cast adrift. There is in fact a natural deep-water solution to the Kuskokwim's maze, though the existence of this entry and channel up the river was not discovered until 1910, by the Army Corps of Engineers. Their interest was prompted by turn-of-the-century gold stampedes on the Yukon and in Nome. Back in the 1830s, a Russian trader, Simon Lukin, discovered gold along an upriver tributary to the Kuskokwim that he called the Yellow River, but this mysterious branch has since eluded certain identification. Later the reflected glory of the Klondike brought for the first time more than a smattering of outsiders up the Kuskokwim, their passage after 1910 courtesy of the army engineers, but the prospectors' efforts were rewarded with only minor strikes remote from Yupik villages and much closer to the river's headwaters than the region Lukin had explored.

Today barges laden with all the goods that gold can buy find their way unfailingly into the Kuskokwim with loran. Once inside, they follow the turns of a deep-draft channel that ranges in depth from a squeaky 15 feet at high tide to a scarcely credible 120 feet. The channel ends only a short distance above Bethel, almost exactly where — whether through coincidence or divine providence — the Moravians established their headquarters in 1884. With the discovery of the channel, the quiet mission and trading post inevitably became the commercial and transportation hub of the entire delta. But the channel shifts and changes every year, as Adolph Lind knew full well, and pilot boats take as long as ten hours to feel their way cautiously up and down its length.

Now we're running up the western bank of the river, looking across at Eek Island on the other side and meeting occasional skiffs — mostly from Kwigillingok, some from Tuntutuliak — with king nets in the water. These boats are tapping for subsistence purposes the first of the salmon advancing up the river. "Hey, strikers!" Oscar exults as he sees spray from two big fish hitting the mesh simultaneously in one of these skiffs' nets. We stop and tie up at most of the skiffs, since Oscar used a lot of gas yesterday running in and out of the Ishkowik, and he's afraid that we'll go dry before we reach Bethel. "Maybe somebody'll have a little gas they can sell," he says hopefully, but no one does.

One skiff we stop at is half full of red salmon, whose firm, delicate meat commands the best price per pound from the processors and which run simultaneously with the kings. Two huge king salmon lie on top of the reds, both of these as big and sleek and metallic as torpedos. Eventually we meet Moses Martin, Buzzo's brother-in-law, here all the way from Kipnuk for the salmon and now on his way home. He sells six gallons of gas to Oscar for $12, and also agrees to tell Alice to call Elsie in Bethel. Oscar says, "Tell her we'll be up there around eleven."

Above the river the early morning's pale fringe of cumulus has expanded into a crisp white wedge across the northwest quarter of the sky, but the rest of the dome remains a blue void. Oscar cuts over to the opposite bank as we speed past Helmick Point, diagonally across from Tuntutuliak, and there two big processors overtake us, both of them hurrying to Bethel for the Monday commercial opening. When the first alders and willows begin to show above Tuntutuliak, I see that the banks have grown almost lush since May. The rippling tent gives the boat a covered-wagon aspect, its passengers something of a dispossessed and desperate air, as though we were arriving at last in green California. Above Napakiak the yellow trunks of the cottonwoods grow together as thick as matchsticks, and some of these — where the river has chewed the ground from beneath them — already lie prone in the water, their new leaves trailing in the current like flags folded and cast down.

Not far from Graveyard Point, maybe five miles from Bethel, Oscar slows the boat and points to a bird with a wingspan about as long as Janet is tall, its color and precise shape hidden in the sun's glare. The bird glides with its wings outspread into a tall stand of shoreline cottonwoods. "What's that? A hawk?"

I suggest, "Maybe a rough-legged hawk, or an osprey."

Oscar gazes after the bird curiously and turns the boat into a slim, stagnant slough that winds through the midst of the trees. Almost immediately the slough opens up and takes on light, curving back into the main channel. The slow bend provides refuge for both clouds of mosquitoes and the bird, now perched in the crown of one of these cottonwoods: neither a hawk nor an osprey but an ordinary raven, its head cocked and its eyes, as narrow and suspicious as a moneylender's, fixed hard on us.

But Oscar is staring straight ahead and up as he cuts the motor. The boat drifts in sudden silence into the foot of another poplar, its roots and base flooded by the river, its dead trunk and jagged branches as bare as the spine and ribs of a whale. Some twenty feet up in this tree rests an assembly of sticks about the size of a truck tire, and from this parapet the bare and ghastly heads of four nestlings protrude, all of them nearly as big as their parent. The nestlings regard us with a scientific impassivity, brushing and jostling against one another to get a better view of our proceedings.

Oscar leaves the wheel and advances up to the bow, where he stands on the foredeck and gazes directly up at the nest. "You see them?" he says. "They make good pets."

"What do you mean?" asks Margaret.

"I had one once when I was a kid. They're good for cleaning up scraps. But how'm I gonna get one?"

The first adult raven is joined now by the other parent, which flaps into a tree behind us on the little island defined by the slough. Both ravens begin to fly from tree to tree, cawing and croaking in alarm.

"Leave them alone," Margaret says.

Oscar puts a hand on the cottonwood's trunk, finds the roots still solid, and gives the tree a shake anyway. The distress of the adults rises to a higher pitch. The birds seem almost big enough and angry enough to carry off one of Oscar's offspring for a pet. The nestlings aren't worried; with a scratching like the skittering of roaches, they crowd to one side of their swaying nest and gaze down at Oscar with a sense of unassailable remoteness.

For some reason I remember a story narrated in a dance that Lieutenant Zagoskin once observed in a kashim. A hungry shaman notices that whenever he goes out to hunt, a certain raven follows him and interferes. If he stalks a deer, the raven's cawing startles the deer before the hunter can get a shot. If he sets a snare, the raven tangles the snare or simply steals it. If he sets a fish trap, the raven finds a way to do harm even to that. Finally the shaman cries out, "Who are you?" But the raven's *yua* simply smiles and answers, "Your evil fate."

"Leave them alone," Margaret repeats.

Oscar lets go of the trunk and stands beneath the dead branches. He slaps absently at the mosquitoes and stares up at the nest, a bleak sort of longing written strangely across his face.

IV

THE SUPERIOR COMMUNITY OF FAITH

1 ☸ OSCAR COMES OUT of the tiny house where he and Margaret are visiting, where a group of people are playing Nintendo, and sits beside me on the low aluminum rail dividing the riverbank from this severed end of First Avenue. The other riverfront houses at this end of the old road are similarly close, dark, and dusty. Charlie's house, back in the days when it was more purely Elsie's house, used to occupy a point in space only a few dozen yards from here, before the river took its long bite out of First Avenue. Now the riverbank drops in a cliff to the new sea wall, a hundred feet below us.

The sea wall is red and crisp and neat, backed by a row of orange thermal siphons, as tall and spiny as saguaro cactuses. These siphons are said to dissipate heat from the underlying permafrost and so prevent thawing and shifting. But the sea wall is having trouble all the same. Down past Schwalbe Street and Weber Circle, where Charlie's house was moved to, the unprotected banks below the wall have crumbled, and, having flanked the steel, the river is now eating behind it. Oscar points upstream to sinkholes opening behind the sea wall in front of First National Bank and Swanson's Marina — holes that threaten the remaining end of First Avenue and the heart of the Bethel waterfront. He says, "See? You can't fuck with Mother Nature."

But salmon prices are something else again. Oscar has known for as long as he's been a commercial fisherman that you can fuck with those, and he was reminded again yesterday before we even got off the river on our way up from Kongiganak. Prices were all that was on his mind as he jabbed his anchor into the gravel at the top of the boat launch near Elsie's smokehouse, deaf to his mother's angry scoldings, and prices were all that he talked about during dinner at her apartment. Elsie's little efficiency was as neat as the Shinto gardens in the Japanese prints on her walls, but the new tenants soon remedied that. We stowed a portion of our gear in a waist-high pile in the tiny hallway closet and the rest in a spreading heap in a corner of the living room. The kids ran in shifts in and out of the bathroom, the two boys leaving crisscrossing trails of crumbled tortilla chips on the vacuumed carpet. The old woman found little consolation in the game we brought, discovering that the three dunlin eggs I gave her were too far along and that five of the duck eggs that Margaret had found had gotten broken during the boat ride. We also had a Canada goose; Oscar saw it swimming helplessly in the Ishkowik with a broken wing, and I shot it. But Elsie said it was too skinny and vowed grumpily just to throw it into the trash.

Mostly Elsie was mad about the four hours she and Elizabeth spent yesterday waiting down at the smokehouse for our arrival. She got the message from Kipnuk that we would arrive today at eleven, and they went down at that time to meet us, but actually we didn't make it in until the middle of the afternoon. Gregarious as always, and eager to see how the kings were running, Oscar had stopped at every skiff along the way, even after we got gas from Moses. Then we stopped somewhere near Napaskiak to take down the tent on the boat, and then we stopped at Hippa's fish camp, which consists of a tiny cabin set on a high grassy bank up from the mouth of a slough just below Bethel. A homemade backboard and a rusty hoop stood bolted to the top of a pole in front of the cabin, and thick beds of wild iris and languid lady, the hanging blossoms of the latter spattered like blue milk paint among the greens, ran along the bank toward the camp's bare drying racks.

The camp was empty. The cabin was steamhouse hot, and a loose swath of screening hung over the doorway to keep the swarms of mosquitoes outside the cabin from mixing too casually with the swarms inside. The cabin contained two cots, a little table, a camp stove, a battery-powered TV, some dry fish, and a few store-bought provisions. While Janet and the boys took care of some pieces of Bit O' Honey left lying on the table, the adults, basking in the heat, made tea and sampled a few pieces of the dry fish, put up by Hippa's wife, Emma, last season. The fish had grown moldy in the warmth, but we could just wipe away the mold's blue fibers.

We ran into Hippa after we left the camp, meeting him and Emma and their three kids and Buzzo out on the Kuskokwim. All six of them were jammed into Hippa's sixteen-foot skiff and on their way to below Napakiak for subsistence fishing. Hippa's family had just come into town from Atmautluak, and Buzzo would be staying with them at their camp this summer. Buzzo's wife, Alice, meanwhile, would leave their kids with her parents in Kipnuk and go to work at a cannery in Togiak, a village down the coast toward Bristol Bay.

Oscar looked at the crowded boat and said, "You got no room for fish."

Hippa, smooth-faced and boyish-looking, his teeth white and handsome, said that he didn't think he'd need any room, at least when it came time to fish commercially on Monday. He sat by his motor and said, "Prices are low, Oscar. Or at least the prices the processors are announcing now are low — lots lower than last summer. Some guys are already talking about going on strike."

Oscar's face fell visibly at this news. "There's gonna be a co-op meeting tomorrow at Napakiak," Buzzo added, referring to the Kuskokwim Fishermen's Cooperative, the union that annually negotiates a contract with Kemp-Paulucci, still the most important buyer on the river. Buzzo said the co-op would be deciding at that meeting what their response to the low salmon prices would be.

Then we stopped at Tony Watson's fish camp, across the river from Elsie's smokehouse. Tony was hung over and crawled wincing out of his sleeping bag, his mild, tolerant eyes giving him the look of a dissolute priest. After he put some coffee on his stove, he sat at his table with us and confirmed what Hippa had said. "Kemp-Paulucci's offering just sixty cents a pound for kings and twenty cents for chum salmon. Or that's what I heard. Somebody said that's two bucks less per pound than they're paying on the Yukon for kings."

Yukon salmon are too oily for Oscar's palate, but they're considered to be of better quality and customarily command somewhat higher prices from the buyers. But even the rumor of a disparity that great makes Kuskokwim fishermen such as Oscar and Tony angry.

Oscar was angry enough hardly to notice Elsie's fuming as she prepared dinner for us: hot dogs and white rice and a gelatinous beet-colored dish made of wild cranberries and pike eggs mixed together. He responded with only a word or two to her questions about what took us so long. At the table he predicted gloomily that the co-op would probably vote to strike. "But I want to go to that meeting," he said. "I was telling Joe Brown last year, it was a mistake when the co-op voted to stay with Kemp."

I asked what was involved in the co-op's contract with Kemp, and Oscar said, "They agree to a certain dividend rate, you know, and then they encourage their members to sell their fish just to Kemp. But I was telling Joe Brown how Kemp's prices have only come up since that other buyer, Whitney Seafoods, came in. Two years ago, when Whitney pulled out before the silver salmon season, Kemp's price dropped down to fifteen cents a pound for silvers. Now Whitney's got a new guy in charge and they offer good prices, but the co-op don't sell to 'em."

Oscar was in no mood for a strike, no matter what the prices. Just as he said in Kongiganak, he was in too deep, and I surmised that he wanted to go to the Napakiak meeting in order to suggest anything short of a strike. Maybe that was too much of a public turnabout, however, for the onetime firebrand of Quinhagak; whether intentionally or not, he never made it to the coop meeting.

Instead the day got frittered away by the various errands that accrue to a man who owns a functioning, if erratic, pickup truck in Bethel. In the morning Margaret quietly suggested that they go buy some groceries for Elsie. Then we moved five washloads of laundry to the laundromat across the street. Then we drove Margaret's brother Harvey to the airport, where he works at a bush flight service, so he could pick up an overdue paycheck from his boss.

The weather was sunny and mild, almost as nice as Memorial Day, and we were hailed on the way to and from these destinations by groups of friends and relatives on both the Active and the Paul sides of the family, many of whom climbed gratefully into the bed of the pickup with their own destinations: the hospital, Swanson's, the AC store, the post office, the small-boat harbor beyond the upstream end of the sea wall, a friend's house for lunch. Some seemed to have no destination in mind whatsoever but rode in the sunshine all day just for the pleasure of the unassisted motion.

After dropping a passenger off at Swanson's, down near First Avenue and the waterfront, Oscar was hailed by Sam Beaver, an old friend who works as a salesman in the little office from which the store sells its lumber. "What you got going tonight?" Sam asked.

"Nothing."

"Nothing?"

"I'm on the wagon."

Sam grinned and nodded, just like Tony had last month, and then mentioned someone else he knew who's on the wagon, who hadn't had a drink in almost two months now. "I'm on the wagon too," he teased. "I haven't had one since last night. Your wife up with you?"

"Yep."

"Oh, that's why. You know, my wife actually gave me a bottle last night. It was one she hid. She didn't want me going out and buying one."

Charlie had a bottle going last night, and has one going tonight as well. Last night Oscar went out to buy some PIK, a mosquito repellent that burns like incense, and put one smoking green coil directly under the chair in which he sat to drink his coffee — "Where it'll do the most good," said Oscar, who always seems to attract more than his share of mosquitoes. Later, when Charlie showed up drunk at Elsie's door, he stood in the entryway shouting, "I suppose this smell of PIK means that the great Oscar Active has arrived?" He came in sweaty and dusty, his button-down shirt open halfway down his chest. "I know that smell every summer. Every summer you know when the great Oscar Active is around."

The adults just ignored him, even when he swept Clayton into his arms and amazed the child by pulling the nipple of his baby bottle out of his mouth and inserting it into his own. He sat down next to me on Elsie's loveseat and said, "My permit renewal still ain't come from Juneau, Oscar. I don't know if it's gonna be here on Monday."

Oscar made no reply, just looked at the TV, and then Charlie turned to me and said sadly, "I wasn't gonna be drunk. I didn't want to be. But then I heard from somewhere that you guys had turned around and gone back to Kong. So I just started again."

Margaret sat on the couch opposite us, absorbed in a paperback novel, while the wisps of thin gray smoke that wreathed about Oscar made it look as though his seat were on fire.

2 ◎ HISTORY REPEATS ITSELF. Last month Oscar and I had tried to give Elsie a ride to the Moravian church on Sunday morning, saving her the mile-and-a-half walk past the AC store and the Brass Buckle and then down Third Avenue. But the old truck had bucked and lurched and stalled so much that an exasperated Elsie had finally abandoned it and walked to church. This Sunday again we offer her a ride, and again the old woman ends up walking and muttering under her breath. Oscar takes a chance with the cops and relieves me at the wheel, and Elizabeth and Crazy are delighted to feel the truck pull into the road smoothly with their daddy's practiced foot on the clutch, and take equal delight in teasing me. But after a hundred yards of carefree progress, history repeats itself. Eventually we coax the truck into the church's dirt parking lot, fifteen minutes after Elsie got there, thirty minutes after the morning service began.

In Genesis, Bethel is the place where Jacob has his vision of a ladder joining heaven and earth. "How dreadful is this place!" Jacob decides. "This is none other but the house of God, and this is the gate of heaven." Later the prophet Isaiah exhorts the people to "prepare ye the way of the Lord, make straight in the desert a highway for our God," in preparation for that time when "every valley shall be exalted, and every mountain and hill made low." With its valleys already exalted, its mountains and hills laid low, the delta much resembles just such a highway, and at times is strange and dreadful enough to suggest a gateway to heaven. I don't think it's merely a matter of landscape, or even the town's origins as a mission site, but whatever the reason, there is a number and diversity of churches here in Bethel that must exceed that of any community of comparable size anywhere in America: Moravian, Russian Orthodox, Roman Catholic, Seventh-Day Adventist, Church of Jesus Christ of Latter-Day Saints, Truth Missionary Baptists, Assembly of God, Apostolic Mission, Trinity Life, Covenant Evangelical, First

United Pentecostal, Holiness Pentecostal, Church of God of Prophecy, Bahai, and probably a few others as well.

The Moravian church is the most conspicuous, standing against the sky in the midst of a wide and grassy meadow on the south side of Third Avenue, the main street in Bethel, and right at the geographical heart of the town. The building is somewhat gray and weathered, its tin roof splashed with rust, and is actually the third such building to serve the town. This church was dedicated in 1958, and looks like one of those Lutheran chapels raised by pioneers on the Nebraska prairie a century ago, now somewhat down-at-the-heel. By virtue of both its location and its stately isolation, however, the church still proclaims itself as Bethel's preeminent place of worship, even as more and more *kass'aq* newcomers move into the town and the community splinters into an ever wider variety of small denominations.

This church is maybe half again as large as Kongiganak's, and about a hundred people have come for service today, with roughly equal numbers of Yupik and *kass'aq*. Many of the *kass'aqs* seem to be members of the town's longstanding families, those who have been here for two, three, or four generations. The pastor isn't one of these; he's young and blond, a relative newcomer. He preaches the necessity of sacrifice in order to live in Christ, and describes Jacob's reunion with Esau, recounting how Jacob progressively made presents of all his great wealth — his goats, rams, camels, kine, bulls, asses, and foals — as he went to be reconciled to his brother, as God required, until finally he stood before Esau bereft of everything, and the wronged Esau ran weeping to meet and embrace him. When the pastor finishes, the pretty wife of the Yupik lay pastor, who will later conduct an evening service in Yupik, stands at a podium near a wall hanging depicting Eskimo fishermen pulling nets into their skiffs. She sings in a clear, piping voice, "Take Up My Cross, the Savior Said." The congregation sits in rapt silence.

All this, down to the well-thumbed Bible that Elsie keeps on her supper table and reads from every morning, is the fruit of that original seed, the five missionaries who came just a century ago. More than the Russian Orthodox priests who preceded them and the Roman Catholics who missioned the Yukon and Nelson Island, these Moravians — John Kilbuck above all — were bold in their attack on the Yupik shamans, and the memory of that contest on the Kuskokwim is still warm enough and recent enough to cause discomfort. There are people still living in the villages who were at one time practicing shamans, and I know one in Kongiganak. But currently that old man is as devout as Elsie, and I wouldn't presume to question him about his former life. I've seen his sons nearly come to blows with anyone who mentions aloud that their father at one time was a shaman, that he's the same man who people said knew how to fly.

Now Oscar stands next to Margaret in one of the church's back pews, his chin down and his eyes shut, and I know as though I could read his mind that he's thinking not of the necessity of sacrifice and the surrender of wealth but of what he'll do tomorrow if the co-op votes to strike — whether he'll honor the strike, as he did at Quinhagak, with his bad back, or go out and fish. I suppose that questions of sacrifice and wealth aren't irrelevant to these considerations, but I doubt that the former seminary student is even listening much to the pastor. Oscar is too busy trying to save himself in this world to prepare his way to the next.

His dilemma in respect to this possible strike is a peculiarly modern one, and it was the Moravians, after all, in their struggle with the shamans, who brought the Kuskokwim into the modern world. Oscar endures the sort of loneliness that I've known all my life, in countless thousands of decisions, great and small, and that even the biblical Jacob, himself a modern individual, knew after first cheating and then fleeing from Esau. I couldn't explain that loneliness, if Oscar were to ask me — as well ask a fish to explain about water. And yet this church is the place where a dialogue — or a ladder, as it were — between the modern and the premodern is still joined. I think I can say without irony that Elsie comes here to feel the marrow in her bones, the salt in her blood, all that unites her to her mother, Maggie, who was raised by Moravians and was yet a medium to that earlier and entirely Yupik world. It may be all mixed up and garbled here, yet this is where all the voices are heard, Maggie Lind's as well as John Kilbuck's.

Margaret lays a hand on Clayton's head and stands on tiptoe in order to see Martha Larson, the singer. Oscar blinks, shuffles, and sighs, lost to his own purposes. His story begins where this other story ends . . .

3 ⊙ FERDINAND DREBERT, who came as a young missionary to Kwigillingok in 1912, wrote in his memoirs, "It was not long before I came into conflict with the powers of darkness. There were three shamans, or witch doctors, in the village, who kept the people in a state of fear. They did not oppose me to my face and even pretended they wanted to become Christians. But behind my back they opposed the Gospel. They were afraid to lose their influence over the people. Yes, the devil always fights back when his kingdom is invaded." The Roman Catholic missionary Bellarmine LaFortune had nothing but scorn for the shamans he met to the north, along Norton Sound and the Seward Peninsula, yet made a distinction between those who were true minions of Satan and those who were mere fakes: "They were imps, most of the time cripples, deformed individuals who had intercourse with his satanic majesty, or unscrupulous charlatans who resorted to fraud and black magic to dupe and cheat their victims." Even in 1912, Drebert found the three shamans in Kwigillingok to be formidable opponents. A generation earlier, the shamans who opposed John Kilbuck had no need of the sort of hypocrisy described by Drebert, and the kind of intercourse suggested by the

Catholic is in its own way a recognition of the strength possessed by these imps and cripples.

It is not entirely inaccurate but certainly too simple to say that the Yupik shamans kept their communities in a state of fear. Dread might be a better word for it. But just as Edward W. Nelson guessed that there was more than mere spectacle to the mask festivals he witnessed, so was there generally more than mere dread within the relationship of an individual shaman to his (or her) community at large. The complexity of that relationship was spun from the various facets of a shaman's role, from the multiple tasks an *angalkuk* answered to: not merely those of priest and magician, but also healer, seer, counselor, teacher, historian, poet, entertainer, weather forecaster, and even game manager. In the person of a shaman, all of these functions were collapsed into a single jurisdiction that mirrored the extent to which each facet of the Yupik universe, spiritual and corporeal, informed every other. Dread was contained within the shaman's ability to reign credibly over that jurisdiction, and the relationship spread beyond that to the degree that a village as a whole required and benefited from the shaman's command of it.

If a shaman demonstrated, for example, the gift of healing, as many of them did, then probably the quality of the dread became more reverent and humane. But certainly dread, and the ability to arouse it, were indispensable to a shaman's success; it was the same sort of dread, I imagine, as that felt by Jason at the site of the biblical Bethel. And surely nothing was more important to the establishment of that dread than a shaman's ability to work miracles. Any number of the men and women of Elsie's generation soberly attest to the shamans' powers of flight, and some have told me that they witnessed such flights themselves. One or two have said that they saw a shaman literally soar into the sky during the course of a séance, while others have described feats of levitation that would carry a shaman from one end of a kashim to the other or cause him to float and fall in spurts across the ground outside, like a ptarmigan in flight. Elders have described to me other feats as well — sitting unharmed in a pot of boiling water, for example, or shitting icicles, or causing walrus tusks to soften into a malleable sort of plastic, or causing boulders too heavy to be moved by ordinary men to come crashing through the skylight of a kashim.

Very few outsiders ever had the opportunity to witness a Yupik séance. Those few who did — many of them missionaries, such as LaFortune — explained what they saw as the result either of the intercession of Satan or of outright fraud. If fraud, the problem became how to explain its success, especially when the use of props or concealed seconds was easily apparent to the outsider. Many have simply dismissed the shaman's audience as credulous and childlike. Others have suggested that maybe the rhythmic chanting, the pounding drums, the thick smoke, and the macabre nature of the shaman's performance sometimes combined to induce a sort of mass hypnosis. Mrs. Schwalbe, the Moravian historian, recounted that such séances so transformed their witnesses and carried them out of their ordinary selves that they seemed to be strangers to the Moravians. Interestingly enough, Libby Beaman, the wife of a government agent posted to the Pribilof Islands to supervise the islands' commercial fur seal harvest, described meeting men wandering about at night in a trancelike state — a state that had nothing to do with the home brew already popular among the islanders.

> It is a bit disconcerting to run into one and have him look right through you without acknowledging a greeting. . . . Usually the next day, the man will recount ghostly encounters he has had or visions of almost mythological beasts. I've heard them pad past our windows on occasion and wondered what they could be up to. Sometimes they are actually clairvoyant when they are traipsing about in a dense fog and suddenly scream out, "Ship's light! Ship's light!" which they cannot possibly see with their physical eyes. And always, sure enough, when the fog lifts, a ship is lying offshore!

Still others suggest that a shaman's performance simply involved a conscious manipulation of symbols in an agreed-on field of meaning, similar to a Catholic priest's ritual translation of wine into blood, bread into flesh.

Few observers dispute, however, the unsettling nature of the shaman's physical ordeal during a séance and the genuineness of his ecstasy. Even these could occasion scorn: just as LaFortune found the shamans to be imps and cripples, others have suggested that they drew their membership from the ranks of the epileptic and schizophrenic — in other words, from those who endured forms of altered consciousness whether they wanted to or not.

But the historian of religions Mircea Eliade, surveying accounts of the practice of shamanism in Asia and the Americas, disagrees. Eliade observes that both Inupiaq and Yupik shamans were heirs to a religious and magical tradition whose roots trail 20,000 to 30,000 years back to central Asia. While the psychic processes underlying a shaman's ecstasy may in fact have something in common with those underlying epilepsy and mental illness, he says, an important distinction has to be made in regard to who is the master, the shaman or the illness.

> It is not to the fact that he is subject to epileptic attacks that the Eskimo or Indonesian shaman, for example, owes his power and prestige; it is to the fact that he can control his epilepsy. Externally it is very easy to note numerous resemblances between the phenomenology of "meryak" or "menerik" [Arctic hysteria] and the Siberian shaman's trance, but the essential fact remains the latter's ability to bring on his epileptoid trance at will. Still more significantly, the shamans, for all their apparent likeness to epileptics and hysterics, show proof of a more than normal nervous constitution; they achieve a degree of concentration beyond the capacity of the profane; they sustain exhausting efforts; they control their ecstatic movements, and so on.

Eliade goes on to say that in effect, a shaman was a sick man who had been cured, a man, or sometimes a woman, who — whether through accident or illness or internal psychic processes — had been plunged into an abyss of nothingness, into a lonely and chilling examination of what the historian terms "the fundamental data of human existence"; a man who then, through the mastery of certain esoteric techniques and disciplines, achieved not only a return from that abyss but the ability thereafter to enter and return from it at will. These techniques and disciplines are themselves a method of healing, Eliade suggests, and he describes a famous Siberian shaman who needed to practice his craft precisely in order to keep his original mental illness at bay.

Along the Kuskokwim some of the functions of shamanism were shared by those who were not shamans. It wasn't considered necessarily beyond the ken of ordinary individuals to influence the behavior of animals, the weather, or the health or fortunes of a neighbor through magical means. Nor were manifestations of catatonia, hysteria, or trance considered in and of themselves singular or potent. Similarly, Libby Beaman observed men who were not shamans experiencing instances of clairvoyance. In an otherwise classless society, however, skilled shamans were conceded to be an entirely distinct and powerful set of individuals, and they were easy enough to recognize; says Eliade, "He alone is a shaman who, through mystical vocation or voluntary quest, submits himself to the teaching of a master, successfully passes through the initiatory ordeals, and becomes capable of ecstatic experiences that are inaccessible to the rest of mankind."

In regard to those miraculous physical feats, in particular to such feats as flight, Eliade observes that the levitation or flight of saints is richly documented in both Christian and Islamic traditions. But he finds the metaphor of flight more compelling than questions of literal truth, suggesting that a shaman's ascent from earth, whether in the flesh, in the spirit, in the form of a bird, or as simply a metaphor, affirms that person's transcendence of the human condition and his reclamation of a primordial human state. Along the Kuskokwim that state was linked to the time immediately following Raven's creation, a time when men and animals, flesh and spirit, were all easily conversant with one another, a time that anteceded the chill of nothingness and the dark spaces that intervene now between those realms and between the whole scope of a person's wishes and their fulfillment. Above all, such flight proclaims the autonomy and immortality of the soul, the existence of unapprehended dimensions to this world that nonetheless may be communicated and managed — after a fashion.

Because of the rigors and dangers of shamanism, however, and also because of the ambivalent nature of the dread that prevailed between these adventurers and their communities, this was a vocation — for all its power — that was not precisely besieged with applicants. Sometimes entry into it was not at all a matter of ambition or choice. Those who rose from killing illness or accident with a shaman's ministrations, for example, especially if young, were likely to find themselves subsequently apprenticed to that shaman; also those who suffered from seizures or hysteria or were prone to spiritual dreams or waking visions; or those who successfully predicted minor events in the village; or those who were descended from a powerful shaman and perhaps had inherited their forebear's command of various tutelary spirits; or those who were physically unable to hunt and fish; or those who were simply chosen as apprentices for reasons apparent only to the shaman.

The anthropologist Robert F. Spencer tells the story of a young man from the Inupiaq village of Wainwright who was told by a shaman in that community, "I am going to take your life and give you the life of the *angatquq* [shaman]." The young man had no desire for such a life and attempted to resist, but found himself helplessly succumbing to the other man's power. This apprenticeship was cut short, however, by the shaman's death of natural causes. Spencer also describes a Barter Island shaman who settled on the person of a visiting white man as his successor. The white man obligingly went out into the tundra with the shaman, but returned badly shaken and went no further with his training. Spencer reports that the man thereafter was subject to involuntary periods of trance and ecstasy, and that his informants told him that the visitor could well have become a shaman if he had wanted to.

Once a man or woman became recognized as a shaman, that person assumed an exaggerated degree of individual responsibility for a host of community needs. Yet in spite of that, the shaman endured an uneasy relationship to the community as a whole, and certainly this unease was exploited by the Christian missionaries in their later contests with the shamans. Some part of the difficulty may have lain in the solitary nature of the shaman's practice, which isolated him from the hunting partnerships and the food exchanges that routinely tied together individuals and households and networks of families in the ordinary operations of food-gathering. Usually shamans were hunters and fishermen themselves, but as a class they were less skilled in these pursuits than those who did them exclusively and to a great extent relied instead on the food and gifts that their ministrations brought in. For example, Zagoskin describes a method of trapping otters that was scorned by the most capable hunters as being simply too easy and was therefore considered appropriate only for old men and shamans.

Another portion of the unease may have resided in the economic character of a shaman's practice. A shaman would not necessarily expect any reward for the performance of a public function such as the annual Bladder Feast, when the *yuat* of slain seals were ritually returned to the sea. But he would often be rewarded handsomely for such private services as, say, curing an illness. Even if the cure failed, it was considered polite to provide a reward, though a polite shaman would in turn refuse it. In material terms, a consistently successful shaman could become very wealthy in comparison to his neighbors, sometimes so wealthy as to be able to support two or more wives.

But since the acquisition of this wealth didn't involve a mutual exchange of food or animal goods, neither did it incur any of the mutual obligation that accompanies those exchanges. Instead it simply involved a one-way payment for a service rendered, much like a transaction in the cash economy, and resulted in what therefore amounted to a mutual cancellation of obligation. This wasn't a gift of what an animal itself had given freely but rather an uncomfortable sort of stoppage, or turbulence, in the cycling of *yuat* between households and between worlds. So it was an exquisite sort of irony that in the end, those individuals who assumed the greatest responsibility for maintaining such a cycle should also be compelled to disrupt that cycle in order to eat, and that some became wealthy in precisely this manner. The wealth was, however, more impressive to an outsider than it would be to a Yupik observer. To the latter, a wealthy man would be he who had given away great quantities of food and goods and who therefore had earned a fund of grateful deference and obligation from his neighbors. In this respect a shaman might well be comfortable but impoverished.

Finally, what isolated a shaman more than anything else within the fabric of his community was simply the daunting breadth of his power. Sometimes shamans themselves were the victims of an imperfect command of such power. Folklore recounts many instances of shamans failing to survive ordeals structured into their séances, or of one shaman engaging a rival in a contest of spiritual power and the vanquished shaman dying of illness soon after his defeat, or else being killed. Nelson tells of coming upon a peculiar teepee-like structure of standing driftwood logs along the shore of Norton Sound; inside this was a wooden box suspended by cords halfway between the ground and the top of the structure. Nelson was told that the box contained the remains of a shaman who had allowed himself to be burned alive in the expectation of being reborn at an appointed time with greater powers. But when the appointed time passed without the shaman's resurrection, the remains were entombed in that unusual manner.

In general, however, a shaman had most to fear from his neighbors, and they from him. Since he lived mostly outside the networks of kinship and obligation that tied individuals together and also protected each from the other, villagers rarely knew for certain whether he was using his power only for disinterested purposes. Although any individual could conceivably enlist a helping spirit to bring about sickness or bad luck in another, shamans naturally were particularly skilled — and particularly suspect — in this regard. The acknowledged threat of this kind of witchcraft sometimes blurred the line between payment and extortion for a shaman's services. It was also understood that a shaman might be hired by a third party for such purposes, and likewise that he could use his power to discover who else in the community was guilty of witchcraft in another's misfortunes.

In this way a shaman lived as a sort of lightning rod for a community's internecine hostilities and resentments, to a certain degree drawing them to his own person and to a certain degree redirecting them to either recognized malefactors or convenient scapegoats. Spencer, in fact, claims that the vocation drew not only the visionary but steadfast personalities described by Eliade but also those most likely to confirm a missionary's inklings of satanic intercourse, that is to say, those who were inordinately aggressive, misanthropic, or temperamentally unsuited for customary pursuits.

A shaman could well endure community hostilities so long as his power commanded sufficient admiration and so long as suspicion of any malice was less than universal. But one who failed too often to affect a cure or provide good counsel, for example, or whose actions alienated an entire community, could find himself in a dangerous position. Nelson heard of many instances of shamans being murdered by common consent of their neighbors. Similarly, Mrs. Schwalbe recounts missionary reports of a female shaman believed to be responsible for the deaths of several children, who was first clubbed to death and then had her joints severed and her body burned in oil. (The latter actions were probably taken to protect the village against the potent malice of the shaman's *yua*.)

Even this murder is eloquent with the awe with which a shaman was generally regarded and the authority that these remarkable individuals were conceded. In 1885 the first Moravian missionaries flew perilously into the teeth of that authority.

Their names were John and Edith Kilbuck, William and Caroline Weinland, and Hans Torgersen. William Weinland had been up the Kuskokwim the year before with Trader Lind and, together with Henry Hartmann, who never returned to the region, had helped to select the site of the mission. Unlike Hartmann, both Weinland and John Kilbuck were young and untried men fresh out of the Moravian College and Theological Seminary in Bethlehem, Pennsylvania. Hans Torgersen was a veteran lay pastor from Canada and spiritual leader of the group. Within only a few weeks of their arrival, however, Torgersen fell off a boat and drowned in the Kuskokwim. He had also been a carpenter, and it was he who was to have supervised the construction of the little cabin that would be their only shelter that winter. Neither Kilbuck nor Weinland knew much about carpentry. In a letter Edith Kilbuck described a picnic she shared with Caroline Weinland that first wet, raw autumn: a tarpaulin spread on the tundra and an umbrella raised against the rain, the air foggy with mosquitoes, the two men laboring clumsily at their rickety cabin, all of them still grieving for Torgersen, all of them homesick and afraid. The two women attempted to comfort each other with favorite passages from Scripture, but finally, Mrs. Kilbuck admitted, both of them broke down into tears, which mingled with the rain.

Probably such scenes had many precedents in the history of the Unitas Fratrum, or the Unity of the Brethren, as the church is formally known. The Moravian church was born with the death of the reformer Jan Hus of Prague, who in 1415 was burned at the stake by Roman Catholic church authorities for his presumed heresy. Hus's supporters then organized themselves into an underground evangelical sect in the kingdoms of Moravia and Bohemia, or present-day Czechoslovakia. A full century in advance of Martin Luther's Protestant Reformation, the sect emphasized the importance of good works and a godly life, and objected both to the Catholic church's absorption with ritual and to its extensive involvement in political and secular affairs. At the time the Moravians were also radical in their conviction that Scripture and sermon should be communicated not in Latin but in the congregation's own language, and they were the first, in 1501, to publish a vernacular hymnal.

The Moravians were subject to harsh persecution during the centuries of the Counter-Reformation and were unsuccessful in attracting enough members to establish themselves as a major Protestant denomination. Instead, in the eighteenth century they moved the seat of their church to Germany and chose to focus their resources on bringing Christian teachings to the heathen, thus inaugurating the modern Protestant missionary movement. Over the next two centuries members of the church were dispatched to the West Indies, Greenland, Lapland, Surinam, South Africa, Siberia, Ceylon, Algiers, Labrador, Persia, Jamaica, and many other countries.

In the United States, numbers of Moravian immigrants gathered into communities in North Carolina and Pennsylvania, and eventually administrative centers for an American branch of the church took shape in Winston-Salem and Bethlehem. In 1883, Sheldon Jackson, a Presbyterian minister and a renowned Alaskan missionary, appeared before Bethlehem's Society for Propagating the Gospel to say that he had approached other churches about mission work along the little-known Kuskokwim but had been refused. "At last I come to the Moravians with the same request," Jackson said. "For more than one hundred years you have cared for those to whom no one could resolve to go. If you refuse, these heathen must go down to ruin in the dark."

So the Moravians went where no one else could resolve to go. Along with those reasons I've already stated for the choice of Mamterillermiut as the site of the mission, Hartmann and Weinland were much impressed by the character and success of Nicolai Komolkoshen, the part Russian, part Yupik manager of the AC trading post at that village. But the replacement of Trader Nicolai with Trader Lind following the former's death was no great setback for the mission; Lind was to prove a valuable ally over the years, and his bilingual wife was an important resource in the missionaries' determination to learn Yupik. Sometimes that alliance was a prickly one, however, as the missionaries became traders themselves, at least to a limited degree, and as Mrs. Lind demonstrated her attachment to much of what the Moravians condemned in Yupik life.

Besides Fort Kolmakovsky, Hartmann and Weinland had considered the village of Nushagak, on Bristol Bay, as a possible mission site. But as at Fort Kolmakovsky, the Moravians were reminded that Sheldon Jackson had overstated the case in saying that no one else could resolve to go there. The priests of the Russian Orthodox church had arrived fifty years earlier, and by no means had they ceased their activity with the Treaty of Purchase. Instead, a missionary society in Russia continued to support church schools and orphanages in America, and the American branch of the church, whose properties were exempt from transfer in the treaty, continued to receive a stipend from the Russian government. At Nushagak a Russian priest named Vasilii Shishkin remained in permanent residence. A man of mixed blood like Trader Nicolai, Shishkin welcomed Weinland and Hartmann when they landed there in 1884, but all came to the conclusion that the Moravians would do well to locate their mission somewhere else. Here and elsewhere, the Orthodox church had taken an approach over the years that stressed accommodation to Yupik belief systems rather than challenge and direct confrontation. The Moravians were to find themselves surprised, whenever they met it, by the tenacity of the Russian brand of Christianity in Yupik communities.

Certainly there was room for accommodation. Such Christian concepts as the creation, the fall, the eternal soul, the afterlife, resurrection, sin, sacrifice, the virtue of charity, and others found a rough correspondence, if not a precise equivalency, in traditional Yupik thought. Specific Orthodox concepts such as the imminence of the dead — that is, the belief that the dead are always present among the living — were particularly resonant.

No doubt Yupik villagers were also impressed by the sumptuous regalia, the sinuous chants, and the air of mystery attendant upon the Russian services, elements that were cultivated in shamanistic séances too. Edward Nelson heard in Yupik descriptions of Orthodox services an appreciation of these similarities: "Curiously enough, the great mask festival of the Eskimo south of the Yukon mouth has supplied terms by which the natives speak of the Greek [i.e., Russian Orthodox] church and its services among themselves. When they saw the Russian priests in embroidered robes performing the complicated offices of the church it was believed that they were witnessing the white man's method of celebrating a mask festival similar to their own."

For the most part, moreover, the Russian priests mounted no direct attack on the authority or integrity of the shamans. Since their numbers were so few and their visits to most Yupik communities so infrequent, they probably would have sacrificed their constituency if they had attempted to do so. Instead they instructed curious villagers in the broad precepts of Christian morality and in the litany, ceremony, and calendar of the church. They also instructed chosen laypersons in the performance of baptisms, burials, and prayer services. All those who were willing were readily baptized as Christians, and Lieutenant Zagoskin reported that the documents that attested to these baptisms were much prized, even if their contents were inscrutable: "The inscribed paper icons which are given to the newly baptized are hung in the winter houses and the kazhims; the certificates of baptism are carefully preserved in specially constructed wooden boxes. Yet many of these Christians cannot remember their own names and approach every Russian to ask about it."

The Moravians, however — the Kilbucks, the Weinlands, and their successors — were unimpressed by this approach. To their way of thinking, the Orthodox priests had baptized a good many "tea Christians," who saw in either a priest or a pastor another useful source of Western goods. These were Christians of the sort who would one day approach Ferdinand Drebert in

Kwigillingok and say, "I have been praying for tea all winter. So far my prayer has not been answered. You must now make my prayer come true." Weinland and Hartmann attended services at the Orthodox church in Nushagak in 1884, and Weinland reported, "There was no preaching, but chanting and reading of the Scriptures." The young missionary was of the opinion that "the religion taught by this Church consists entirely in forms and ceremonies, not manifesting any of the fruits of true Christianity in the lives of the natives."

By the same token, Yupik villagers, at least initially, were unimpressed with the Moravians. Accustomed to the pomp and splendor of the Orthodox services, one Yupik delegation to the Moravians is said to have finally remarked, in rough English, "No cross, no nothing. Nothing! All same dog." But with the remarkable John Kilbuck, who was particularly firm in this regard, the Moravians stayed a course that focused instruction not on the ceremonial forms of Christianity — a distrust of which was ingrained anyway in the original seed of the church — but on uncompromising Protestant habits of Christian thought and living.

This emphasis might have turned out badly for the missionaries if they hadn't also been so fiercely committed to learning Yupik and preaching in that language as soon as humanly possible. Among the Orthodox priests, Father Iakov Netsvetov, another mixed-blood Alaskan, had learned Yupik and devised an alphabet for it during his years at Russian Mission on the Yukon, but none of his work was published during his lifetime. With very few exceptions, other Orthodox priests were content to teach and read through interpreters. At the very first Moravian service conducted on the Kuskokwim, however, at Warehouse Creek at the river's mouth in 1884, William Weinland read from a New Testament translated by the church into Labrador's Inuit Eskimo dialect. This would have been somewhat intelligible to an Inupiaq audience, but it was not at all intelligible to this first Yupik gathering.

Undiscouraged, the Kilbucks and Weinlands sought instruction from Mrs. Lind and other bilingual neighbors, and at the same time administered a probing sort of apprenticeship to those few who responded immediately to their teachings. In fact, it was not until 1888, three years after the establishment of the mission at Bethel, that John Kilbuck was willing to admit eight such converts into full membership in the church. These had applied earlier, but Kilbuck held them at bay for a year, testing their consciences and broadening their instruction. The converts were finally admitted without baptism, however, since an Orthodox priest had previously taken care of that.

The Moravians rather expected the Orthodox faith more or less to wither away along the Kuskokwim, but Orthodox priests remained at Nushagak and on the Yukon and still occasionally visited the villages on the Kuskokwim. Certainly the newcomers underestimated the degree to which Orthodox tenets and practices found reinforcement in the traditional belief system, and the degree to which the priests' less confrontational methods appealed to Yupik values and temperaments.

In 1887 the ambitious Moravians tried to establish not a mission per se but an industrial school at Nushagak. By then a number of canneries were in operation there, and Nushagak and other villages were suffering already from the liquor dispensed by the canneries' Chinese and *kass'aq* workmen. Also, a U.S. revenue cutter had had to intervene to keep the canneries' salmon traps from entirely closing off the mouths of spawning rivers. Vasilii Shishkin found the Moravian staff at this new school fanatical and boastful, and charged them with stealing children by force from their families. The Moravians in turn accused the priest of forbidding parents to send their children to the school. Whatever the case, the Moravians roundly lost the battle of the Christian faiths, as they subsequently did in certain Kuskokwim villages, despite their commitment to the vernacular, and they finally closed their Nushagak school in 1906.

To the Kilbucks and the Weinlands, of more immediate concern than their Christian rivals were the still-entrenched shamans. These quickly recognized that the Protestant missionaries sought not just a religious transformation but a social and economic one as well — transformations that would admit no accommodations with the shamans' authority. In his journals John Kilbuck describes one old shaman warning against the Moravians in particular, and against *kass'aq* ways in general, in a manner that seems quite prescient, now that all the villages down the Kuskokwim are filled with the rumble of the 150-kilowatt diesel generators and all the other sorts of motors: "He strongly preached against adopting the white man's teachings. His strong point was that white people were the children of thunder. Therefore, we're not really human. He said 'everything they do and everything they have is accompanied by noise.' "

In challenging the shamans along such a broad front, the young missionaries reflected not only a Protestant scriptural attitude but a general Western ideology, which even yet dismisses nonindustrial — and above all nonagricultural — modes of living as inherently squalid and primitive. Even Zagoskin, who so admired Yupik ingenuity and artistry and who understood that the Kuskokwim people were just as skilled at making the Russian traders dependent on their goods as the Russians were at making Yupik people dependent on theirs, couldn't help but fundamentally patronize his hosts, concluding that Yupik people lived in a state of ignorance and want that only wholesale social change and a white man's education could remedy. After describing a group of hunters trading hundreds of beaver pelts at a Russian post for a little tobacco, some beads and flint, some cloth, and a few quilted shirts, he wrote:

> We must remember that ten years ago we found this native with a stone ax, bone needles, in a cold beaver-skin parka, starting a fire by rubbing together two wooden sticks, and without any practical domestic utensils. We must not judge too harshly the fact that he sometimes exchanges what is of no use to himself for something which has little value in our eyes. The northern native needs education as does a child; his education depends on us. At the present time his prosperity on earth de-

pends on the possession of a gun and ten rows of potatoes. This could be achieved with comparative ease.

Actually, as Zagoskin knew, beaver skins made such poor parkas that they were as trivial to "this native" as beads were to the Russians. Actually, this native started fires with a bow drill and not with wooden sticks, but to Western observers these fine points did not diminish the Yupik people's plain, aching need for education, a proper religion, and some potatoes.

Sheldon Jackson had described the Kuskokwim in terms of darkness and ruin, and the Kilbucks and Weinlands saw nothing to convince them otherwise. In their visits to Yupik villages, the missionaries saw only what Jackson promised, along with generous dollops of filth, misery, and depravity. Weinland was appalled when he first entered a *nepiaq,* a traditional family dwelling hollowed into the ground and roofed over with sod banked on a driftwood frame. This sort of house was entered through an underground passage designed to thwart the escape of heat. Weinland wrote in a report to church authorities:

> Emerging from the tunnel, through which you have squeezed past several dogs, groped in the darkness, and raised a curtain of dirty matting, you find yourself in the barabarrah, or house proper. It is about twelve feet square, with matting lying on the ground around the four sides. When I entered this evening, it was dark, and calling for lights, a sight was disclosed, which, alas, is but too common. In this small space, dirty, filthy, and filled with an indescribable stench, were *fifteen* persons, men, women, and children, besides several dogs.

John Kilbuck was similarly impressed.

> To the missionary party the natives in these villages were a source of wonder and pity. Wonder that human beings could exist with such filth upon them, and around them. The cattle and swine at home, had luxurious quarters compared to the homes of the Eskimo as we saw them at first. The women's faces were actually encrusted with dirt, oil, and soot. The maidens with their rosy cheeks were the only bright spots in

the ranks of the spectators — which surrounded the white ladies at every village.

Many of the families the Moravians visited in these houses had, in fact, precise and exacting ideas about personal and household hygiene, but these were different from Western ideas and reflected circumstances that included a relative absence of virulent germs, the difficulty of obtaining water through eight months of freeze-up, and the thrifty use of urine not only as a grease-cutter and cleanser but as a curative agent for animal hides. Nor would these families have found any significant discomfort in the crowding that Weinland lamented.

In truth, the missionaries saw a benighted image of themselves in the inhabitants of these houses, and were as disgusted by the villagers' moral squalor as by their physical squalor. Mrs. Schwalbe wrote that the churchmen found the villages rife with instances of cohabitation, adultery, polygamy, spouse exchange, and infanticide — activities that were usually regulated and that answered to a particular morality and cultural logic, but not to any morality or logic that the missionaries could entertain. Mrs. Schwalbe says, "The people seemed to fail to see the enormity of it all, saying that such were their customs and that it had never marred their happiness."

This unmarred happiness was precisely the problem, and very puzzling, given the apparent extremities that these people were subject to, from both the environment and their own customs. Weinland wondered if they might be happy, or at least content, only because they were ignorant. But then he remembered that they had been exposed to Western ways and values for some time now, and still they persisted in their darkness and ruin, immune to despair and any notion of suicide.

Taken as a class, the Yuutes are decidedly phlegmatic in temperament. They are content to take things as they come, be it threatened starvation or overabundance, be it intense cold or drenching rain, all seem to be regarded as so many phases of life which must necessarily be experienced, & to try to alleviate which they hardly dream. Life is to them one prolonged series

of sufferings; such as few could endure, & yet suicide is un-
heard of among them. They are deeply rooted in their habits
& manner of living, & it is a difficult matter to get them to
adopt even the most striking & most evidently necessary
changes. White men have been living in their midst for half a
century, and yet today their mode of living is rude, uncivilized,
filthy.

In part the Yupiks' lifestyle had remained so "rude" because
its practitioners found it, according to their own terms, physically practical and emotionally rewarding. More significantly,
this mode of living was suffused from top to bottom with hidden
ideological — which is to say religious — dimensions, which
were not at all apparent to casual observers, and which inevitably escaped William Weinland, who stayed at the mission he
founded for only two years. The enormity of it all, however,
didn't escape John Kilbuck.

John Henry Kilbuck had a considerable advantage over his
friend and classmate William Weinland, and indeed over every
other Moravian missionary who came to serve on the Kuskokwim: he was not himself a white man but a Native American.
In an 1885 photograph of the five missionaries taken prior to
their departure from San Francisco, his dark, aquiline features
and penetrating eyes seem to leap out from the pale and static
disposition of the group. His mother was a Mohican and his
father a descendant of the Delaware chief Gelelemend, whose
life was saved during the French and Indian War by Major William Henry. Gelelemend was subsequently baptized by his res-
cuer; the chief also decreed that all his descendants should have
Henry as their middle name, and eventually he joined the Moravian church. His two sons led the Christian Delawares to the
Kansas Chippewa reservation where they founded a Moravian
mission, and where John Henry Kilbuck was born in 1861.
    Young John stood in succession for the Delaware chieftaincy,
and an aunt, Rachel Henry Kilbuck, sought to prepare him for
that by instructing him in the Delaware medicine men's knowl-

edge of plants and herbs. But when Kilbuck was twelve, the Reverend Joseph Romig, the white man then in charge of the reservation mission, arranged for the promising boy to attend Nazareth Hall, a Moravian preparatory school in Pennsylvania. From there he went straight into the Moravian College and Theological Seminary, where his standing as the school's only Indian conferred a special status on him and where he excelled as an athlete and a linguist. On his graduation Kilbuck was ordained a deacon, and he served a year at a mission in Canada while Weinland participated in the reconnaissance of the Kuskokwim. Before leaving for Alaska in 1885, Kilbuck returned to the Kansas mission, where he swiftly courted and married Edith Romig, the tall and capable daughter of his sponsor at school.

Both William and Caroline Weinland were plagued by ill health during their short tenure in Alaska, and in 1887 they left to assume a parish in Iowa. But the Kilbucks remained for fifteen years, and John eventually attained near mythic status in the villages up and down the river. In time the young missionary displayed an extraordinary array of talents, among them mastery of a subtle and intricate language that very few outsiders ever learned to speak; skills in sled handling, boat handling, and overland travel that surpassed those of many Yupik hunters; and an unusual and palpable empathy for the people he moved among. To Kilbuck, this empathy was a matter of blood. Once, at a winter social gathering of villages, he observed a group of young men describing their hunting exploits to one another, and he wrote in a journal entry to Edith, "Somewhere in me, there must be some of the old Injun left, for I was strongly stirred, and I could not help but think of my forefathers, who not so many generations back, were such proud boasters. I think it is on this account that I feel so drawn to these people, and helps me to enter into their feelings." To the villagers as well, not only his empathy but his feats of travel and survival were a matter of blood, and Kilbuck was probably both pleased and amused to find how this was explained. He wrote to Edith, "I now have learned why the natives believe that I belong to their country.

Their supposition is that some one of their number was carried off on the ice, as it frequently happens, and that this man was rescued or landed among white people and that I am his offspring."

John Kilbuck's ideas about the scope of social change required on the Kuskokwim were a little more complex than Zagoskin's or Weinland's. He sought not a wholesale replacement of Yupik customs and habits with Western ones, but rather a Christian life that married Yupik virtues such as creativity and resilience to the Western virtues of discipline, thrift, and economic diversity. As Kilbuck became more and more fluent in the language, however, he also became more discerning, coming slowly to appreciate the extent to which Yupik spiritual thought — and therefore also elements of shamanism — underscored nearly every custom and habit, nearly every gesture of everyday life.

These all seemed to come to a point in the winter mask festivals, dances, and gift exchanges, all of which were distinct from the shamans' séances and often bore no evidence of the shamans' ceremonial participation. On that account the Roman Catholic missionaries on the Yukon and Nelson Island, for example, were generally tolerant of such events, as was John Kilbuck at first, viewing them as innocent secular entertainments. But in Yupik thought there is no crisp distinction between the sacred and the secular, and within five years the missionary began to appreciate this. "Even as he gained a deeper knowledge of the language," intones Mrs. Schwalbe, "there came with it a fuller revelation of the powers of darkness and the superstition which held the people in its grip." In 1890 Kilbuck wrote in a letter to William Weinland, "You remember the 'masquerades.' At the time we could not condemn them because we were unacquainted with their nature. Now, however, that we know that they are no more than heathen rites, the one grand religious ceremony of the year, we have condemned them, and seek to suppress them."

The shock of this condemnation from a man of Kilbuck's stature, and Kilbuck's insistence that people make a firm choice between their traditional practices and the Moravians' "New Way," probably ran in cold waves through the villages up and down the river. Not only did this violate the Yupik virtue of noninterference in the affairs of others, but it disabused people of any lingering ethnocentrism in this matter — ethnocentrism that prompted them to view Christianity as a variation of their own ceremonialism, just as their grandfathers had acceded to Zagoskin's companions the status of shamans when they were teasingly told by the Russians that watches and other implements were inhabited by spirits.

And with this the contest between the Moravians and the shamans came out into the open. It was a conflict in which Yupik adherents of the Russian Orthodox church often found themselves in sympathy with the shamans. In his own history of the mission, Kilbuck wrote:

> When the missionary was able to speak somewhat intelligibly in the native language — he began to travel from village to village. . . . At first — he was respectfully listened to — but as the opposition from the shamans and Greek Catholics [i.e., Russian Orthodox] increased — many ways were resorted to in order to baffle the preacher. — Some one would find something to chop — others would lie down on the shelves [of the kashim], and pretend to talk or sing in their sleep — or some one would interrupt the speaker with irrelevant questions. But there were a few interested listeners from the first — and these were a great source of encouragement to the missionary.

Of more import to those who couldn't decide whether they were interested or not, however, was the course of the struggle on the strictly spiritual plane, upon which the shamans customarily conducted their battles. In the fall of 1888, Kilbuck undertook a long overland expedition to Nushagak, through the mountains now known as the Kilbuck Mountains, for the two purposes of making a late mail delivery to a ship bound for the States and providing encouragement to the troubled mission school there. His travel was impeded so much by storms and extreme cold that Edith Kilbuck and her companions in Bethel

grievingly gave him up for dead. A particularly antagonistic shaman announced himself as the vanquisher of the missionary, but
when Kilbuck miraculously returned to Bethel in February, only
half dead, that shaman's power was broken in the eyes of his
neighbors, and Kilbuck's own prestige was enhanced enormously. Similarly, in the fall of 1894 Kilbuck seemed to lie on
his deathbed from the effects of pleurisy and then pneumonia;
his recovery from these illnesses was perceived as a miracle, and
as a moral defeat for those shamans who spoke against him and
who had cut pieces from his clothing to practice witchcraft
against him.

Something of a medicine man himself, Kilbuck recognized the
significance of this plane of conflict, and on at least one occasion
was not averse to the same sort of theater for which his enemies
were noted. In 1896, Dr. John Romig, Edith Kilbuck's brother,
and Romig's wife, Ella, a trained nurse, joined the mission staff
at Bethel. Western medicines and the presence of a doctor at the
mission were to prove crucial to the Moravians' efforts, but in
this instance they were also crucial both to Kilbuck's survival
and to his reputation. In 1899, at the very close of his ministry
in Bethel, the missionary caught a fishhook in his right hand
while ice fishing and subsequently developed blood poisoning.
Again, this illness was ascribed to a shaman's magic. Romig determined that an amputation would be required, and a certain
number of Yupik villagers were allowed to watch this operation.

Mrs. Schwalbe records that Ella Romig administered an an-
aesthetic to Kilbuck, and then the audience gasped — no doubt
as much at Kilbuck's uncanny forbearance as at the giddy mechanics of the process — as first the flesh was laid open, then the
blood vessels sutured, then the bone sawed through. Romig had
assistants carry quarts and quarts of water dyed with disinfec-
tant out of the operating room and dump them on the snow,
until the entire area surrounding the doctor's clinic was red with
what appeared to be Kilbuck's blood. Maybe Kilbuck and
Romig had no other thought than that of mounting an arresting
spectacle before people undecided in their convictions. Then

again, maybe they knew — whether from Kilbuck's youth or from what he had learned of the traditional religion — how literally and graphically this operation paralleled certain common narrative elements in a shaman's initiation or acquisition of new power: the extraction of the soul, the contemplation of the skeleton, the agony of dismemberment and resurrection. The shaman whom Nelson had found entombed in midair had attempted to sear the flesh off his skeleton and rise again, but he had failed. Once more, however, Kilbuck didn't fail; to the amazement of all who heard the story, he rose again. He might no less impressively have levitated.

In all probability John Kilbuck's operation was a central moment in the history of the Kuskokwim. People today who know little else about Kilbuck and what he accomplished here at least know the story of how he lost his arm. As the story was repeated up and down the river, Dr. Romig tended to disappear, and the legend grew that the missionary himself had sawed the arm off unassisted, as a shaman would; also, that Kilbuck had been attacked by a shaman who had beaten his own wife and who had been beaten in turn by Kilbuck for that crime. Thus, at his moment of greatest peril, the missionary's spiritual power again had triumphed. The Moravians ascribed this power only to Christ, with the promise that anybody, not merely a trained élite, could have it.

In time the missionary learned how to write, type, chop wood, handle a dog team, and even hunt geese using only his left hand, but that would be done elsewhere. His wife, Edith, was almost as admired as he was, and by the time the couple left the Kuskokwim in 1900, those few converts admitted so scrupulously into the church in 1888 had grown to more than a thousand and the previous authority of the shamans had for all practical purposes been shattered.

In fact John Kilbuck's greatest peril lay within his own soul and in the church itself — in his own fallibility and the internecine politics that followed in its wake. Like the Weinlands, Edith Kilbuck was troubled by ill health, and during the winter of

1891–92 she fell so sick that it was decided that she and John and their four children would return to the States for a year's furlough the following spring. They journeyed together to the mouth of the Kuskokwim and were ready to sail when they found that illness had prevented the man chosen as John's replacement at the mission from coming up from the States. Eventually Edith sailed away with three of their children, and John returned with their son Joe to Bethel.

Ann Fienup-Riordan, Kilbuck's biographer, writes that during that year's separation, "John found himself adrift in ways that, for all his travelling, he had not experienced since his arrival in Alaska." Despite the couple's time apart during John's proselytizing among the villages, theirs was an exceptionally intimate marriage, sustained in part by the journals they kept for each other during their separations. These often were more love letters than narratives. Edith, who managed the Bethel mission during her husband's many absences, was loving, affectionate, and fiercely devoted to John; at the same time she was highstrung, outspoken, uncompromising in her spiritual principles, and inevitably jealous of the degree to which she was obliged to give her husband up to others. John was sensitive to this, and distressed by seeing so little of his children. Nonetheless, he was confident of the power of their relationship, and their family, to endure these separations. While on a journey in 1890 to gather statistics for the federal census, he wrote:

> What a blessing a wife is to a man, when the two are all in the world to each other. No wonder that God said that the two are one, and that each will leave their own parents for the other. That there are trials peculiar to the pair, but where there is true union of sentiment and temperament, their joy and peace far out weighs every other care. Such has been my experience; Certain it is that you are the one meant for me, and I for you. . . . And those blessed children. How I would like to hear Kate rattling away with her tongue, and to see Harry's tho'tful eyes dance with some mischief he has tho't out. And

little Joe, I guess he will be afraid of me again. Thank God for my family, for the joy that my dear ones give.

With the passage of two more winters, however, the "trials peculiar to the pair" had become more pronounced, and their decision to take a furlough in 1892 was probably made as much to renew their marriage as to improve Edith's health. Whatever the case, their plans were thrown into disarray by the illness of John's replacement. It would appear that John, who probably thought himself much used to being on his own, was surprised by the different quality of their separation now that they were four thousand miles apart. Also he was surprised by its peculiar nature, now that it was he who was alone at the mission waiting for his spouse's return. He wrote to Edith that people "lamented because you were not here with me. The women feel that you are to them, what I am to the men." Lamenting himself, and adrift, Kilbuck eventually broke faith and took solace — on an undetermined number of occasions — in the arms of those "maidens with their rosy cheeks" whom he had always so frankly admired.

But this breach of trust with Edith and betrayal of his own Christian principles and preachings weighed heavily on the missionary. The following year, when Edith returned to Bethel with their daughter Ruth, leaving Harry and Katie in foster homes so that they could receive formal schooling, Kilbuck saw fit to confess his adultery. In an 1893 journal entry to his wife, he referred to this confession and its occasion: "After my prayers I went to bed, thinking of you and praying for you. — Darling, I feel so mean and base, and I hardly dare permit myself to express any affection. Would to God, I could wipe out such a black spot in my life. I can't work it off. — God must have mercy on me, and purify me with the blood of Jesus Christ. I am praying for a renewed heart." A few weeks later, on New Year's Day, 1894, Kilbuck returned to his transgressions for a second and final time: "Last year, after you left me, for months I hardly smiled, because I felt as one bereaved by death. This did not go away.

As some men take to drink to drown the one thing that weighs upon them, I erred."

The marriage endured, and in time Edith's anguish and anger was replaced by compassion for her husband. But the church was less forgiving. Kilbuck eventually confessed not only to Edith but to the missionaries who served alongside them in Bethel, and to the Yupik lay pastors he had trained, and, by letter, to the Moravian church's governing board in Bethlehem. While this was going on, Edith wrote to her father, who had first recognized Kilbuck's promise: "How I pity him, for he has lived a worthy life, save this fall, and now all his faithful work seems to be covered by one sin."

At first all these parties pardoned him, but it was decided that he could no longer serve as superintendent of the Alaska mission, and in 1896 he was succeeded in that position by Dr. Romig. In 1897, however, the board reassessed its position, following a visit to Bethlehem by Ernest and Carrie Weber, former colleagues of the Kilbucks in Bethel. Ernest Weber told the board that John Kilbuck's adulterous misconduct had been more extensive than his confession indicated. Possibly this was true, and possibly not; Weber may have been acting through jealousy of Kilbuck's success. The board, for its part, may have seized this opportunity to act on long-standing philosophical differences with Kilbuck, which persisted even after he was removed from the superintendency. Kilbuck had begun a sawmill operation in Bethel and was eager to involve the mission in such enterprises as fish packing, reindeer herding, and coal mining; these would be a way not only of paying the mission's bills, he believed, but of seeding local industries. These in turn would affect the economic transformation that he understood would have to be concomitant with any religious transformation. The church, however, was very uneasy about such involvement in secular affairs, and was also unwilling to yield such broad authority.

Whatever the precise explanation, in 1897 John Kilbuck was summarily dismissed from mission service, expelled from church membership, and ordered to leave the Bethel mission. When the unfortunate Webers, during their return to the Kuskokwim, were shipwrecked and drowned in a storm on Goodnews Bay, however, this expulsion was temporarily rescinded, and the Kilbucks were instead posted in disgrace to Quinhagak for a year, and then back to Bethel, where Kilbuck caught a fishhook in his hand and made his final gesture of defiance against the shamans. Then, in 1900, the famed missionary and his wife took their final leave of Bethel. The church and their own colleagues, acting on Kilbuck's admitted indiscretions, had at last accomplished what all the shamans' magic had failed to do.

The career of John Kilbuck should not be taken to simplify a long and ponderous struggle that still isn't quite over. There were other warriors besides Kilbuck, including the many missionaries who served with the Kilbucks in Bethel, those who succeeded them, and those such as Ferdinand Drebert who served at the permanent missions eventually established in Kwigillingok and Quinhagak.

But not even Kilbuck was content to rely on his own and other outsiders' devices. More than the Roman Catholics or the Orthodox priests, the Moravians from the very beginning relied on the help of knowledgable and committed believers within the communities they approached, not merely as interpreters, as the other churches did, but very quickly as fellow evangelists, who enjoyed nearly as much autonomy and authority as their *kass'aq* colleagues. In 1889 three of the eight converts first admitted into church membership were appointed by Kilbuck as lay pastors (at that time they were called helpers), and over the years this investment of authority in the villagers themselves, this creation of what Ann Fienup-Riordan has described as an alternative focus for power, was at least as crucial as Kilbuck's own energy and courage to the ultimate success of the Moravian effort. But like the shamans, these early helpers endured a charged and ambivalent relationship with the communities they served. The life of a remarkable man called Helper Neck is suggestive in this regard, and depicts how narrowly the lines were drawn between the antagonists in this contest.

Sometimes the lay pastors who joined the Moravians were young men who had grown up in the mission's orphanage, or at least had graduated from its school; in other instances they were simply men who assumed the life of a Christian as others did that of a shaman; and in some instances they were former shamans. This last was the case with Uyaquq, which translates into English as "neck," and who therefore became known to the Moravians as Helper Neck. Neck had been a practicing shaman in the upriver village of Akiachak and was probably somewhere in his mid-thirties when, in 1895, he forsook his usual spring hunting to come to Bethel for instruction from the Moravians.

Neck told the missionaries that his father had been a shaman also but had been converted to Christianity and baptized by an Orthodox priest. It had always been the father's wish that his son also become a Christian. Instead Neck had adhered to the traditional ways and completed an apprenticeship with another shaman. But he was turned to the Moravians' New Way, he said, by the words of the missionaries, by the urgings of his father and another relative who had forsaken shamanism, and by the serene manner in which his father met his death. It was after burying his father that Neck appeared in Bethel, where he began writing down lessons, parables, incidents in the life of Christ, and finally the entirety of the church's *Passion Week Manual* in what the puzzled John Kilbuck described as "some kind of self-invented hieroglyphics."

Neck couldn't read or write English or any other language; nor did he ever learn to speak English. He said that it was impossible for him to learn English because in order to do so he would have to think like a white man. The missionaries attributed his belief that he couldn't learn English to his tendency to disparage his own intelligence, though it may just as well have been a conscious choice. Helper Neck in fact was extraordinarily intelligent, and something of a linguistic genius. In all likelihood the "hieroglyphics" that he used to record the Moravians' teachings owed something to such precursors of literacy as already existed in the villages: the conventional symbols used with *yaarrutet*, or story-knives, to scratch out narratives in the dirt, as Yupik children sometimes still do today, though the practice is disappearing; or the marks inscribed with berry juice on birch bark before certain feasts to remind the hosts what gifts the invited guests desired. These were just crude pictographs, but both the public nature of Yupik life — with the crowded kashims, where the men and older boys stayed together, and the many-peopled houses — and the relatively stable nature of Yupik values and history provided for traditions that were well served by oral transmission.

At first Neck probably made his marks just as aids for recalling this strange new material, but he was also much impressed by the manner in which the missionaries recounted their stories with word-for-word precision each time they read. Eventually he grew dissatisfied with the inability of his personal pictographs to reproduce this precision, and over the space of his lifetime he continually revised and refined his method, developing the pictographs finally into a writing system that he taught to other helpers. At one point in this development the system underwent a revolution, when Neck suddenly realized the relatively limited number of phonemes that make up Yupik (or any other language). He also realized that these phonemes could be represented by discrete symbols — that is to say, the letters of an alphabet. To look at samples of the various stages of Neck's system is to recapitulate thousands of years of slow evolution in Western writing systems, and yet this method was accomplished in a single lifetime by an unlettered man who knew that writing was possible but nothing of how to go about it.

Today linguists regard Neck's notebooks and the various stages of his script as providing the only complete, step-by-step record in existence of the development, literally from scratch, of a sophisticated orthography. But Neck himself dismissed this achievement. "Because I was so stupid, God gave it to me," he said of the final form of his system. He also said that the crucial insight into phonemes occurred (as it would to a shaman) during a dream he had while seriously ill, and that when he woke from his dream he was able to write his symbols.

Sadly, it was not feasible for the church to use Neck's orthography, with its symbols that seem partly to suggest the English alphabet and partly the Arabic one. Instead, for the Moravians' Yupik translations of Scripture, they adapted the English alphabet into a rough sort of Yupik system that was not as accurate as Neck's but that came more easily to English-speaking pastors and typesetters. The church then began to instruct its Yupik students and lay pastors in this orthography. A number of the lay pastors eventually blossomed into ordained ministers; Neck's son, Lloyd Neck, became the church's first Yupik pastor, in 1946. The church's Yupik-language instruction bore other important fruit as well: it helped to sustain and legitimize the Yupik language in the face of educational policies by both the Bureau of Education and the Bureau of Indian Affairs that sought just the opposite — the eradication of Alaskan Native languages.

Many elders' most vivid memories of their public schooling center on the scoldings, beatings, or whippings they suffered for speaking Yupik in class. This policy prevailed as recently as Margaret's grade-school years at a federal boarding school in Wrangell, a town in southeastern Alaska. But since the 1920s students at the Moravian seminary have learned Yupik literacy in their classes and have been distributing Bibles and hymnals printed in Yupik. In the 1970s linguists and Native Yupik speakers at the University of Alaska developed an English-alphabet orthography for Yupik that is both simpler and more accurate than the original Moravian; this system is taught today in the schools along the Kuskokwim, though even it is probably less fundamentally precise than Neck's. Certain Yupik pastors and elders still use Neck's system in their own writing, however, partly for practical or aesthetic reasons but mostly in the firm conviction of Helper Neck's divine inspiration.

Apart from his wonderful notebooks, however, Neck's life

seems to have been a difficult one. I know his figure only from a 1903 photograph of him standing in a row with three of the church's other early helpers: a slight and round-shouldered little man in a button-down denim jacket and sealskin boots, his hands thrust diffidently into his pockets, his face tanned to an outdoorsman's burnish, his eyes glum and scholarly, like those of a professor denied tenure. He had been small and sickly as a child, and as a helper he was bedridden for months at a time at his various stations — Napaskiak, Tuluksak, Bethel, Quinhagak, and others. He also endured withering losses in his family: his first wife drowned, a son died of unreported causes at age eighteen, and a second son and a daughter died from tuberculosis. Probably he took these to heart, as he had his father's death.

The missionaries described him as a powerful speaker, with a patient and indirect approach in his dealings with the people of the villages he served in. He was successful enough in these to be eulogized by the Moravians at his death in 1924 as their "Apostle to the Eskimos." But this was at some personal cost, if the memoir Neck composed three years before his death is any evidence. In that he describes the poverty, hardship, and difficulty involved in overcoming the shamans — John Kilbuck notwithstanding — and in communicating the Word to people who merely ridiculed his efforts and who believed he was preaching only for the small salary he was paid by the church. Even those who accepted the Word, said Neck, "are often like deer corralled, but ever looking for an exit." He described with obvious dismay being lectured by a shaman who presumed that he was ignorant of Yupik customs and values, as some helpers who grew up in the orphanage probably were. People who knew better were no kinder, as John Kilbuck recorded: *"Shinplaster said to Neck:* — To think I see a shaman that refuses to shaman. Come, the weather is so stormy, make the weather better."

Though Neck claimed that he always simply discounted ridicule and disappointment, it is hard to ignore the sense of abiding sadness in his life. He would not or could not think like a white man; nonetheless, he passionately accepted the white man's Word and found a way to express it in an unprecedented and uniquely Yupik fashion. For those very reasons, however, Neck's own word no longer has any practical application. As he wrote, "I have done my work looking to the example of Jesus who counted as nothing his having come down to live with the lowest of human beings because he would that they might have life eternal. Therefore I have worked at different places, even though I was despised for it and I will also regard as nothing my having been despised and my work having been disparaged."

There was something else as well in the demise of shamanism and the ascendancy of modernism. It chased the Weinlands away, kept Edith Kilbuck and Helper Neck frequently bedridden, harrowed Neck's family, and has been, throughout centuries of encounter between Old World and New World, the most virulent weapon of the former versus the latter: epidemic infectious disease.

It is hard to gauge the incidence of disease in the delta prior to Western contact, but the evidence of both folklore and physical anthropology suggests that this was a rigorous place to begin with. Infectious disease was present — pneumonia, pleurisy, various skin and eye infections, and enough acute diarrhea to incur a high infant mortality rate. Nevertheless, the leading causes of death among adults appear to have been accident and exposure. Like any other Native American population, however, Yupik people were helpless before the ferocious city-bred pathogens that accompanied the Russians and other outsiders into the region. As early as 1842, Zagoskin noted the widespread occurrence of tuberculosis and syphilis, and described as well the horrifying ravages of smallpox in the villages he visited.

The healing skills of the shamans were not inconsequential. They exploited the quickening influence of the mind on the immune system far in advance of Western science, practiced a form of acupuncture still used effectively in the villages today, had recourse to various medicinal plant and animal substances, and were not bereft of surgical remedies. Many shamans could successfully amputate frostbitten or infected fingers and toes, and occasionally even limbs. Zagoskin reports an incident that occurred during Ivan F. Vasilev's initial reconnoitering of the Kuskokwim between 1828 and 1830: one of Vasilev's paddlers suffered from testicles swollen so much that the expedition leader feared for his life, but for three leaves of tobacco a shaman lanced the swelling, drained it, and so cured the man.

But people fell like blighted grass to smallpox, and the shamans were powerless to prevent it, though they tried. The old healers were prescient enough, or maybe cunning enough, to suggest that the coincident arrivals of the disease and the *kass'aqs* had something to do with each other. In Athabascan villages Zagoskin's party was greeted with dances whose purpose was to protect the communities from the death carried by the Russians, and on the Yukon a shaman persuaded villagers to set fire to trails on which the Russians had walked. On at least one occasion the response was deadlier than that. During the particularly virulent epidemic of 1838–39, Russian traders at the Yukon post of Ikogmiut (present-day Russian Mission) attempted to vaccinate as many people as possible. But since the epidemic set in just as the vaccinations began, the shamans blamed the vaccinations, and the post was attacked, its employees slaughtered.

In general, however, vaccination programs mounted by the Russians helped to curb smallpox in Alaska, and the success of these, coupled with the shamans' helplessness and attrition, opened the first important crack in the shamans' authority. Of course, for thousands of people the vaccinations came too late. Russian traders estimated that by June 1839, 60 percent of the people who had been living along the Kuskokwim were dead. Corpses piled up in the kashims and the sod houses, and in the spring starving dogs ate the bodies of their masters. In relating the devastation of certain villages along Norton Sound, Zagoskin found some comfort in the religious persuasion of those few who survived: "The infliction sent them by Providence was great, but the blessing that resulted was likewise great, as all those who are left are Christian."

Today the depth and scope of this cataclysm in plain human terms is almost impossible to grasp. How much does this exceed the Passover plague inflicted on Egypt, in which a child from each household was taken? How much does it exceed the horror of Hiroshima, where two in five died in the fireball of the atomic bomb? And it wasn't even close to being over. As successive waves of outsiders came into western Alaska with the gold strikes in the late 1800s and early 1900s, with them came successive waves of other murderous epidemics — measles, diphtheria, whooping cough, influenza, and more.

After the Moravians built their mission in Bethel, families came from villages as distant as the Yukon to obtain such homeopathic medicines as Weinland and Kilbuck could administer, though faith in Providence was often the best the missionaries had to offer. Later, when Dr. Romig joined the mission staff, desperate people sometimes journeyed five hundred miles to see the famous doctor, though too frequently with no better results. Mrs. Schwalbe describes a group of Athabascan Indians who came that distance with moose hides and sinew threads to offer in payment for a cure of the tuberculosis that was slowly killing them: "It was pathetic in the extreme because they had come a great distance through rain and storm only to learn through the cumbersome translation of English to Eskimo, through Eskimo to the Kaltchan language, that by care and food alone they might expect to prolong their lives for a season. As they prepared, disheartened, to return, the physician prayed with them and tried to point them to the great Healer. Believing in Him, he told them, they could return with hope in their hearts."

Nineteen hundred, the year of the Kilbucks' departure, is remembered on the Kuskokwim simply as the year of the Great Sickness, when a plague of measles ran through the villages concurrently with an influenza epidemic that spread down from the gold-rush beaches at Nome. Generally *kass'aqs* were only mildly troubled by these afflictions, but entire Yupik villages disappeared almost at once during a spring in which a cold and misty rain fell incessantly. In Tuluksak, Dr. Romig found sixteen bodies piled outside the kashim, as no one remained strong enough to bury them, and in other villages wood was being pulled from kashim walls to provide boards for coffins. In the mission's annual report, Romig said that in every village down to the coast children were starving, and that frequently the only cover provided to the remains of their parents were the tents that finally crumbled about them.

Edith Kilbuck took her leave of Bethel some months ahead of John, and John's letters to her are filled with almost nothing but the deaths of their friends in all the villages on the river and coast: long lists of names, including Trader Lind's wife, Elsie's grandmother. In September he wrote, "This summer there were 57 deaths in Bethel alone. I believe the deaths from here up, will soon number 250! Nearly all our loved ones are gone, Sumpka and wife, Ivan and wife and Willie, Stephen, Mrs. Lomuck, Big David and wife of Akiagamiut, Mrs. Lind, etc. When Sumpka and Anna died, every body tho't of Joe, and felt sorry for him. Poor Lind! he is having a hard time of it, with his children. He left just a few days ago, and he is still some where between here and Kmexmiut." It was eventually estimated that half of the adults and virtually all of the babies along the Kuskokwim — whose name is sometimes inaccurately translated from the Yupik as "the cough river" — died that year.

Amid this darkness and ruin the battle was joined more desperately between the old healers and the new. The shamans located the germs of these diseases not only in the *kass'aqs* themselves but in their religion, and Mrs. Schwalbe admits that even into the 1940s epidemics were followed by revivals of shamanism in villages such as Kwigillingok. Mingled with this etiology was a generally hidden but very real and durable resentment engendered by the advent of the *kass'aqs* in the first place; they were held responsible not only for the unnumbered deaths that accompanied their arrival, but for all the forms of uncertainty and disarray, for all the marring of the people's happiness, that followed those deaths and persisted in their presence.

Certainly the shamans played as well on confusions surrounding the motives of the Moravian missionaries. Since the shamans didn't feel compelled to go abroad and proselytize, it was hard to imagine just what the missionaries wanted. Weinland told how the mission site was besieged in its first year by visitors, many of them believing that the churchmen were traders willing to pay a better price for fur than Trader Lind did. Weinland tried to explain through interpreters that they were here for the people's own benefit: "We have endeavored to show the people that we take a deep interest in their welfare, by relieving their wants, and attending to their sick and suffering; in short, to do everything in our power to win their hearts and confidence." But this wasn't entirely convincing, and the confusion persisted. In time the Moravians, at Kilbuck's behest, did in fact go into the fur business, and also erected a sawmill, in order to trade with the villagers for salmon and firewood, for sealskin for their boots and soles, and also for labor around the mission. Later Ferdinand Drebert found himself obliged to combat rumors in Kwigillingok that he was getting rich from being paid a dollar by the church for each baptism that he performed, just as Helper Neck was accused of preaching for money, and I'd be surprised if the same self-aggrandizing motives weren't sometimes ascribed to Kilbuck and the other Bethel missionaries.

Western concepts of thrift, frugality, and private property also provided an avenue of attack for the shamans, particularly in times of shortage. Here again Ferdinand Drebert — who actually enjoyed a successful ministry in Kwigillingok, although beset with difficulty — found himself in an uncomfortable situation. During the winter of 1917–18 the people of Kwigillingok invited two neighboring communities to a three-day feast, after which a snowstorm stranded the two hundred guests and five hundred additional dogs in the village for an extra three days. Provisions were almost entirely depleted in feeding the guests.

Then the spring seal harvest was poor, and Drebert and his wife watched in horror as famine began to set in.

The mission itself had a good store of food, but not nearly enough for the entire village. A Yupik household, at least ideally, would have laid aside questions of general sufficiency and of the household members' personal needs and emptied their larder immediately into the hands of their neighbors, giving freely of what was received freely. In contrast, the Dreberts doled out as much as they felt they could spare, bit by bit, in soup cooked from small portions of flour and dried fish and salted salmon, and reserved as much food for their dogs as they would need for an emergency trip for help. Soon people were reduced to eating mice, dead dogs, and fishskin boots, and began to look menacingly at the mission storeroom.

At last Drebert decided he had to go for help, though it meant leaving his wife alone at the mission. But at the last minute he was stayed by the arrival of a man with two dog teams carrying quantities of reindeer meat, flour, and beans — a man who had been sent by none other than John Kilbuck. By then the Kilbucks had returned to the Kuskokwim, and John was working as a teacher for the Bureau of Education at the upriver village of Akiak. This food helped considerably, and the crisis passed entirely with the arrival of the geese, though some people gorged themselves to death then. In the end twenty-two people died, and all but two of the village dogs. In the village a bitterness prevailed against the mission, and it took some time for Drebert's good will, skill in Yupik, and strong condemnation of the winter feasts to dispel it.

By virtue of his permanent position at Kwigillingok, which began in 1915, Drebert occupied what might be described as a front-line position. Up until that time Bethel missionaries such as Kilbuck, Weinland, Joseph Weinlick, John Hinz, Ernest Weber, Adolph Stecker, and John Schoechert made only periodic, if frequent, visits to the villages, and those who confronted the shamans on a day-to-day basis were men such as Helper Neck. The helpers were provided with the same basic medicines as the missionaries, and were trained in their use. At a church conference in Bethel in 1895, one of them spoke on the importance of this:

> When these first teachers first came, they did not command our attention by what they preached, but when they gave us medicine, and said this and that ailment would be cured, we looked on to see if what they said was true. And because their medicines proved to be just what they said they were, we learned to believe what they preached was equally true. We learn now that the Saviour Jesus, when on earth, not only preached, but He also healed. So I give my counsel that whenever missionaries set out to work among the heathen, that they take the Word of God in one hand and medicine in the other.

Medicines were crucial because it was most often at the side of a sickbed or deathbed that shamans and helpers squared off face to face. In Kwigillingok in 1924 the helper Ivan Petluska gleefully described applying a mustard plaster to the stomach of a shaman who boasted that his flesh was "case-hardened" beyond ordinary mortal constraints. The shaman was unwilling to assay his own medicine on the helper for fear of hurting him beyond recovery, but he maintained that no white man's medicine could possibly have any effect on him. Within an hour, said the helper, the shaman was obliged to yank the hot plaster off and conceal the blister; subsequently he became one of the community's faithful churchgoers.

But in general the shamans weren't so easily put to flight. They became students of the church's scheduling of services and meetings, and would begin séances or other religious activities in the kashim precisely at the hour that the helpers sought to begin their own activities. Helper Neck would often discover to his chagrin that a shaman had conducted a séance to drive away the spirits of dead relatives during Neck's absence from his village. On other occasions he would find himself reduced to despairing silence against charges that a number of deaths in Bethel had to do with the disregard of traditional taboos. Some villages literally split into two, with those attending to the New

Way — or preferring the Orthodox way — simply packing up their households and moving to a different site.

Once during John Kilbuck's ministry in Bethel, in the winter of 1890, the missionary was called to the village of Kwethluk to minister to one of the three original helpers he had appointed. Brother Hooker had enjoyed unusual success at Kwethluk, and earlier in the year had actually persuaded the people to burn their traditional dance masks. But recently his son had died, and just prior to that event Kilbuck heard that the man had been seized with "something like vertigo" while out trapping. Now, according to what Kilbuck heard, Hooker had gone insane.

Kilbuck hurried to Kwethluk and went immediately to Brother Hooker's sod house. He wrote in his report, "God spare me any more such sights. Bro. Hooker was now quiet, but there was a wild frightened look upon his face. There were a few people present, but they were like so many statues." The missionary administered an opiate to Hooker and stayed with him until midnight. At that point a shaman known to the Moravians simply as the Mountain Boy, who was judged by Kilbuck to be at least partly insane himself, ordered Kilbuck to leave the village, but not before the missionary had performed some ritual actions meant to drive away malignant spirits.

Of course Kilbuck refused to execute this "senseless performance." Just then a man named Sam, a friend from the village of Napaskiak who feared for Kilbuck's safety, arrived to conduct him away. Kilbuck reported that after they had gone only a short distance, the entire village set out after them with a yell, the Mountain Boy leading. Sam took to his heels, but Kilbuck turned to face his pursuers, who drew to a surprised halt. The Mountain Boy berated and insulted him, accusing him of causing Hooker's illness, and then attempted to lay hold of the missionary's sled. A stern word from Kilbuck — who had loosened the crossbar of the sled in case he needed it as a club — dissuaded the shaman, who then continued his harangue. In his history Kilbuck wrote, "Among the epithets that the missionary remembers — was only this one — 'You are a crow' [i.e., a liar, a trickster]. — Suddenly the Mountain Boy — struck up a Russian Easter chant — and all his followers joined him — bowing and crossing themselves, they finished the chant. — Then they started for the village on a run."

In the following week Kilbuck was called away to other villages, and he learned afterward that Brother Hooker at least partly recovered his reason, appearing lucid at times. Nonetheless, on the Saturday before Easter the Mountain Boy and another man, followed by the rest of the village, took Hooker naked from a steambath, the Mountain Boy saying that he was now a saved man and would go to heaven. They led him some distance from the village, murdered him with spears, and then set dogs on his body. Kilbuck reported that one of Hooker's brothers "was so paralyzed with horror, that he stood rooted to the spot, unable to move or yell. In agony he closed his eyes and stopped his ears, but to this day he could see that horrible sight and hear his brother's shrieks, and the growls of the dogs. Such was the sad end of Bro. Hooker. God alone can fathom the grief that we have experienced and endured."

In fact Hooker's martyrdom was a grievous, if temporary, reversal for the Moravians. Shortly afterward Kilbuck's friend Sam took sick, and when this seemed to develop into a possession inflicted by a shaman, which was followed by Sam's death, a number of people who previously had stood with the Moravians began to shun the mission. Sometime after the murder, however, some emissaries from Kwethluk arrived at the mission in Bethel wishing to repair relations, though the Mountain Boy remained, said Kilbuck, "quite wild." Eventually even this figure became tractable, however, first entertaining exaggerated fears of vengeance from Kilbuck and then apologizing to the missionary and showing every sign of reason and composure. One Sunday the following winter, in fact, the notorious Mountain Boy made a public profession of faith and at last became a lay helper himself, though he never enjoyed the degree of trust extended by the Moravians to their other helpers.

Kilbuck finally diagnosed the Mountain Boy's apparent insanity as the result of "repressed cutaneous eruptions," noting that "now that he is better, small pimply eruptions cover his body." Whatever the cause of these eruptions, the affair between the Mountain Boy and Brother Hooker is suggestive of contests between individual shamans as described in folklore, and on certain occasions these also ended in such literal acts of violence. Also the rivalry between Moravianism and Orthodoxy played a provocative role here, with Kilbuck citing "a little old woman, a fanatic Greek" as an instigator in the trouble. To this day Kwethluk remains chiefly Russian Orthodox.

But in the end, the impression takes hold that this war between Christian and "heathen" was fought most vehemently between those out on the frontiers of both belief systems, men who often had much in common and who, whether through training, temperament, or experience, knew something of that cold sense of the divine experienced by Jacob where a ladder from heaven reached down to earth. The shamans knew the way to a place like that, had maybe been swept there involuntarily during their apprenticeships, but had learned to control their comings and goings, had learned to wrestle like Jacob with angels, or maybe demons, and had returned from those contests with a power, and a touch of arrogance perhaps, that made them dreadful to their uninitiated neighbors.

Ranged against them now were men like Helper Neck, who had traveled to that place himself, or spiritually minded others who at least knew of that place but who, like Neck, forbore to go there, abetting the Moravians in their taming of the dreadfulness of the sacred. Brother Hooker may simply have gone mad before being murdered, as Kilbuck heard and judged, or, more precisely, he may have involuntarily fallen deep into that awful place from which we derive our sense of deity, where Eliade locates those "fundamental data of human existence."

Thanks to Dr. Romig's curative powers, his stature nearly rivaled John Kilbuck's by the time the Kilbucks left in 1900. But even Romig lost considerable prestige in his inability to stay the devastation of the Great Sickness. But no matter: most of the shamans, particularly the most elderly and authoritative, died in the Great Sickness, and also in the killing diphtheria epidemic of 1906. Since there were not enough healthy adults to gather food, seasons of hunger came on the heels of the epidemics. The former dialogue between the generations in the kashims and the sod houses and during the shamanistic ceremonies — a dialogue crucial to the orderly transmission of Yupik culture — was interrupted, and more and more orphans, and also the children of single parents, ended up in the Moravian Children's Home. Among these was an orphan named Maggie, whose mother had died during the Great Sickness and who eventually would marry Trader Lind's son Adolph, but not until she had grown up in the Children's Home and learned to look on the sunny side.

And so it happened: with the death and discrediting of many of the shamans and the disability of the surviving adults, the traditional dances began to give way. Apart from their religious significance, such dances in their comic forms were sometimes unseemly to Moravian sensibilities, and in any event they made children too sleepy for school the following day. The missionaries noted also that the winter festivals were an excellent occasion for the spread of disease, as was the men's habit of congregating together in the kashim, and that even the sod houses, with their resident crowds of aunts and cousins and grandmothers, were too wet and dangerous. They encouraged the destruction of the kashims and the building of frame houses, each to be inhabited by a single nuclear family. In time the landscape of the villages began to be dominated by these drier, more spacious, more Christian, and much more energy-intensive mission-style dwellings. Slowly the rhythms of village life began to beat to the round of precisely scheduled church activities — the services, the prayer meetings, the catechism classes, the young people's meetings, the ladies' sewing circle, the choir rehearsals, and so on — and slowly the churches, which replaced the kashims, began to fill during services. So did the collection plates, after a fashion, brimming with a thin semblance of the goods once given away at such former orgies of charity as the Messenger Feast: calico, boot soles, handkerchiefs, socks, fur, candles, mattress ticking, dried fish, soap, bread, grass hats, dishpans, and a small leavening of cash. And so the villages themselves began to fill, becoming larger and more permanent as first the churches and then the schools went up, as people moved in from the smaller communities to be near these structures, and as many families abandoned their seasonal sojourns in spring or fall camps.

Some of the surviving shamans had their own theories about what was happening. The anthropologist Richard K. Nelson describes an Athabascan shaman who related the sudden demise of his own and others' power to their spiritual efforts during World War I, saying that in trying to help the American troops in Europe they shifted the source of their power from the earth beneath their feet to those faraway battlefields. Then they lacked the strength to bring anything more than a diffuse and attenuated form of that power back, and as a result their power waned. Similarly, Nelson reports that the behavior of ravens has been seen to have altered since the shamans' demise; the fact that the birds are now most commonly seen in the towns and villages, fearless and unkempt and scavenging through garbage, rather than foraging out on the tundra as they did formerly, when they only approached houses as dangerous tutelary spirits and at a shaman's behest, signifies that the birds' *yuat* are adrift and that the natural balance of the world is subtly askew without the shamans' intercession.

May Wynne Lamb, the Akiak schoolteacher, provides a few arresting glimpses of the famous John Kilbuck in his last years. After leaving the Kuskokwim, the Kilbucks returned to the Chippewa reservation in Kansas, where they purchased and worked a small farm. At the same time they preached without compensation in the old Moravian chapel, which the church had abandoned because of diminished numbers in its congregation and which the Kilbucks renovated themselves. Then they came back to Alaska in 1904 as teachers for the federal Bureau of Education. The bureau posted them first to its northernmost school, at Point Barrow, then to the Inupiaq village of Wainwright, in northwestern Alaska, and then to the Tlingit Indian village of Douglas, in the southeast. Finally, in 1911, the couple returned to the Kuskokwim to oversee the construction of the bureau's new federal school in Akiak.

John and Edith Kilbuck had lost none of their volcanic energy in the intervening years. With astonishing speed the little village thirty-five miles upstream from Bethel was literally transformed by the new teachers. Proper houses were the first order of business, as Edith wrote to her friend Caroline Weinland.

> From our first arrival in July we have talked "build houses" and now eight new houses grace the village. O, so much better than the old underground huts. A few houses had already been built. By another year there will be no one living in the huts, but *all* will have houses. Some already have paper on their walls, *all* have coal oil lamps — and good stoves. The people are no longer what they were *years* ago when you and me first landed. . . . The people of the village are *all* Christians. — and only two families are Greek Catholics. The rest are Moravians.

Soon there were twenty-four log cabins gracing the village, all of them painted rose with a paint Edith made from coal oil, floor oil, varnish, and cherry stain, and fifteen of them with private toilet areas. The Kilbucks also encouraged gardening. Here finally were the ten rows of potatoes that Zagoskin had proposed, which, along with turnips and cabbages and beets, were sold to miners, traders, and other *kass'aqs* — though soil for spring planting had to be stored in root cellars through the winter and then thawed indoors. John saw to the construction of a sawmill like the one the church still ran in Bethel, then arranged for the opening of a post office in the village, and finally convinced the Alaska Native Service to build its Kuskokwim hospital there in 1918.

By 1919 Kilbuck had become the superintendent of western

Alaska for the Bureau of Education, an office that also entailed management of the bureau's herds of reindeer. These were a project promoted by Sheldon Jackson and bought into by the federal government as a means of providing both a cash industry and a reliable food supply to the villagers. To spark interest in the new industry, Kilbuck organized the annual winter reindeer fairs at Akiak, and it was the butchering contest at one of these that so strongly recommended a diet of fish to May Wynne Lamb. The schoolteacher, who was merely May Wynne at the time, describes Kilbuck's return from one of his journeys down to the coast in a sled drawn by one of these reindeer, climbing out of the sled in his furs and icy beard like Santa Claus; "however, he lacked the little round belly, for he was straight of stature and tall." He did bear an unexpected gift, though — an orphan girl found in a village near Goodnews Bay who appeared to have been sat on top of a stove by a cruel aunt, and who was duly given over to the surprised young woman's care.

Since 1910 deep-draft vessels had been unloading their cargoes at Bethel, but much of that freight simply continued in smaller boats up to Akiak, as under the sheer force of John Kilbuck's personality, the little village eclipsed Bethel as the river's chief center of trade, transportation, education, health care, and federal services. I see him in a photograph of that time standing outside a window of the Akiak school on a clear winter day, the window apparently hung with some sort of fur for a curtain. Two dozen or so children of all ages, in muskrat parkas and sealskin boots, bright bandannas and plaid dresses, are ranged in front of him, along with an Eskimo adult. Kilbuck towers above them all, his face as dark and wind-beaten as those of any of his students, but his aquiline nose and bristling gray moustache sharply distinctive. His eyes, through wire-rimmed glasses now, are no less dark and penetrating than those that stared into the camera in San Francisco thirty years before. In the cold he wears only what looks to be a businessman's gray flannel jacket, the right sleeve of which is empty.

May Wynne valued the approval of those far-seeing eyes. In

her journal she described the variety of preparations and the considerable labor involved in her own spring plantings, and her pleasure at Kilbuck's arrival to survey her work: "When the superintendent, Mr. Kilbuck, arrived, my spading was completed, and I expected that some praise would be forthcoming for manual labor accomplished with so much sweat, muscle, and happiness, but it wasn't. Instead, he said in his quiet and reserved manner, 'It looks well tilled on the top, but the ground underneath hasn't been spaded very deeply.' " Much disappointed, she found herself simply not strong enough to spade the frozen ground underneath, and finally she hired a deaf-mute who had come down to Akiak for the summer from upriver in hopes of finding odd jobs. She describes this man as cheerful and very religious; he lived by the river in a canvas tent with JESUS handwritten in framed capital letters across its top. He was also an excellent spader, the schoolteacher found, but an inexperienced gardener, and hard to communicate with. Finally she was "annoyed to the point of tears" to find him digging up her potatoes and leaving the weeds in neatly tended rows.

May Wynne left Akiak in the wake of a tragedy brought on by epidemic. In the summer of 1917, Dr. Frank Lamb came from Michigan to take charge of the new Alaska Native Service hospital. The schoolteacher and the young doctor fell in love and were married that October, John Kilbuck presiding. A year later Dr. Lamb departed for Ruby, a village far up the Yukon, intending to answer a call into the military draft. But when the war suddenly ended, and the draft with it, the territorial governor instructed him to head for Nome, where the worldwide influenza epidemic of 1918 was killing both Eskimos and whites. Lamb journeyed slowly down the Yukon, ministering to the sick and burying the dead in villages along the way. When he reached Saint Michael, he and the doctor in charge there decided it would be best if he didn't go on to Nome after all but remained to help along the Yukon. He turned back upriver, but then fell sick and died himself, of either influenza or pneumonia.

Grieving, the young widow left Akiak the following spring

with her infant son. She left Lilly, the orphan from Goodnews, with the Kilbucks, and returned to her family in Kansas. But within a year she was back in Alaska, teaching at Bethel and a variety of other communities in the territory for ten more years. Then she moved to Seattle, where she ran a successful construction business. She never married again, and died in California in 1973.

John Kilbuck, meanwhile, at last effected a reconciliation with the Moravian church. In 1920 he wrote to the Provincial Elders' Conference, requesting to be allowed to return to mission service. This was granted, and the next year he resigned his superintendency with the Bureau of Education to take charge of the Moravians' new Akiak district and to establish a Native helpers' school there. But Kilbuck was allowed no more than to set this in motion. Returning from a week of prayer in Akiachak in January 1922, he fell ill with typhoid and pneumonia. Soon he was delirious, speaking almost entirely in Yupik. Edith Kilbuck recorded his last words: "Now that I have come to the end, it is not as hard as I expected it to be." He died on the morning of February 2, at the age of sixty.

The body was taken down the river by sled to Bethel. As it passed Akiachak, the driver was compelled to swing in close to the village, where the assembled community sang hymns as the sled passed. Hundreds came from up and down the river for the funeral, including a number of Russian Orthodox believers from Kwethluk, who brought a large wooden cross carved in the Protestant style. He was buried next to Hans Torgersen, the two of them, said Mrs. Schwalbe, "cut off, so it seemed, before their work was done." I found the grave when I visited the cemetery with Oscar on Memorial Day: a simple stone slab with name, dates, and biblical citation (Revelation 2:10), nearly hidden by tendrils of yarrow, cranberry, and bog rosemary.

Edith Kilbuck left Akiak that summer, traveling "down States" with the adopted Lilly and with Ferdinand Drebert and his family, who were on a year's leave of absence. There she rejoined her two surviving children — Harry and Katie had died in childhood — and lived her last years in Winston-Salem. The tide of business and services that had been drawn to the Akiak by Kilbuck flowed inexorably back to Bethel, and it was there that the Alaska Native Service opened its new hospital to replace the deteriorating and isolated Akiak facility in 1940. By then the little village was as unfrequented by outsiders as it was when the Kilbucks first came to it, though the distinctive little red log cabins remained.

By seeing so deeply into the layers of Yupik religious life, John Kilbuck and the Moravians finally won a victory over shamanism more thorough and more decisive than that attempted by other Christian denominations. Truly a social revolution had been eased into place. During Kilbuck's visit to Akiak in the winter of 1892–93, in his first ministry, someone suggested that the villagers form a church congregation there at once, but the missionary characteristically insisted that such a resolve be tested first by measures such as ratifying marriages according to God's ordinance, instituting evening prayers as at Bethel, and observing Sundays as holy days on which neither work nor any sort of hunting or fishing was performed.

As the strength and numbers of the shamans waned, congregations eventually took shape under these measures, in Akiak and elsewhere. Sunday indeed became a day on which foodgathering and other economic activities, and also public recreation, were (and still are) inappropriate, though extraordinary circumstances sometimes provided exceptions, as occurred during the herring season in Kipnuk. Marriages had no formal ceremonial observance in Yupik tradition, and there was no formal proscription against a wife — or husband — leaving an unsatisfactory or abusive spouse; marriages now became duly ratified. So, in 1939, after he had already been living with Susie for many years, George Chanigkak traveled by boat to Bethel in order to buy a marriage license, and at last was married in the Christian manner to Aanaq in Kwigillingok.

Pastors and priests, in fact, sometimes took the place of parents and grandparents who had died in the epidemics in arranging marriages. Since ceremonial obligations were not to be taken lightly under either religious tradition, this made for more stable and permanent marital relationships, as the missionaries desired, and effectively removed from married couples the option of simple separation and remarriage. Moreover, in the biblical concept of a wife's obedience and subservience to her husband and in the counseling provided by pastors and priests, Christian marriage grafted a hierarchical power relationship onto a union that was previously distinguished by a fixed and inflexible division of labor and more or less separate living arrangements but not by any idea of one partner ruling over the other. Now Margaret remains a necessary complement to Oscar as a hunter, since it's she who processes and prepares his meat, while Oscar is extraneous to Margaret's work as a secretary. In his own dependence and Margaret's potential independence, Oscar sees the authority that he should enjoy as a Christian husband, breadwinner, and lord of the house undercut. Margaret, for her part, must have considered Kongiganak's reigning proscription of divorce or separation as she stayed alone at her house last summer after the beating and weighed her future.

Finally, a new sort of interpersonal ethics was introduced in the idea of sin as an affront to God. This was a wider moral umbrella, which protected orphans no less than brothers, and enlarged on those considerations of kinship and exchange that traditionally governed relations between people — enlarged on them until these new ethics, combined with the nuclear Christian households, began at least to adumbrate the shattering of extended kinship bonds, which the sociologist Max Weber considered to be in Western history "the greatest achievement of the ethical religions, above all the ethical and asceticist sects of Protestantism." Weber continued, "These religions established the superior community of faith and a common ethical way of life in opposition to the community of blood, even to a large extent in opposition to the family."

Strange, but true; as Kilbuck himself wrote, both spouses will leave their own parents for each other. As husbands and wives became more established in their new hierarchical relationship, the bonds that traditionally tied that couple and those two individuals to the rest of their family, to the community at large, and even to the earth with its animating spirits were in certain ways loosened and frayed — in certain ways depersonalized — in the "superior community of faith." Traditionally, a person's relatives, with their willingness to take vengeance, had been the sole and ultimate guarantee of that person's safety. Therefore Nelson, a stranger, had been vulnerable to that thief's mischief on King Island. Now, with the creation of an alternate focus of moral authority, it became possible for an individual in these communities simply to forswear those bonds. This sort of autonomy is defined by another sociologist, Peter Berger, as an essential feature of modernity, and it blew like a rending wind through the Kuskokwim villages as the shamans fell away, and as the bold helpers allied themselves with the missionaries and their medicines.

> Biblical religion polarized God and man. One of the essential experiences of ancient Israel was that God is distinct from the rhythms of nature, the rhythms of the world. . . . Ancient Israel thus effected two separations . . . of God from man . . . and of man from the world. . . . The idea of the autonomous individual, who can step outside of his community, and even turn against it, is an essential feature of modernity. An autonomous nature, not subject to the gods and their intervention, is a presupposition of modern science and . . . of modern technology.

Naturally the kashims couldn't exist in a universe where God and man, and God and nature, were polarized into separate spheres. Instead they represented a time and a place where those spheres were indivisible — a place such as the biblical Bethel, of course, where they were joined for only an instant in a dream — and where that unity could be recovered and demonstrated at a shaman's behest. So one by one they were emptied and burned, but with a profound reluctance. Even in Akiak during the Kilbuck years the village's kashim still stood, remaining a place where men could mend their traps and gear together, a place where visitors from other villages could be lodged, and a place where some of the old ceremonial gift exchanges still took place. It was not until 1950 that the last of the kashims on the Kuskokwim was destroyed. This was in Napaskiak, a village where visiting Orthodox priests had preached without embarrassment in the kashim, and which remains today, like Kwethluk, a stronghold of Russian Orthodoxy.

Probably the best indicators now of the Moravians' success are the speed with which they made themselves extraneous and the degree to which John Kilbuck's church has become an energetically indigenous church. In 1946 the helpers Lloyd Neck and James Kinegak were ordained as pastors, becoming the first Yupik churchmen to be so elevated, and in 1950 James Kinegak stepped into the post Ferdinand Drebert once occupied, making Kwigillingok and neighboring villages the first church district placed under the ministry of a Yupik pastor. In 1978 the governing board of the Moravian church in Alaska, all of whose members by then were Yupik, voted to make their province autonomous and self-dependent, and in 1983 the Reverend Jacob Nelson of Bethel — whose relative reconciled Aanaq and Aataq to Margaret's marrying Oscar — was consecrated a bishop. Today the Moravian church justifiably points to its congregations on the Kuskokwim, and also in Bristol Bay and Togiak, as showcases of the missionary's art. Contemporary church historian Kurt H. Vitt surveys these gatherings and concludes:

> During the one hundred years, the seed sown by the missionaries has multiplied thousandfold. The ministry of the missionaries has ended and Native pastors, laypastors and lay people have taken their place. Native administrators are responsible for the executive decisions they make on behalf of the twenty-two congregations and fellowships in Alaska. These congregations are spread over an area larger than Pennsylvania.

There are only three "Kassaqs," "Outsiders," that serve today in the ranks of the Alaska Moravian Church as ministers. All of them are involved by the express invitation of the Native leadership.

Well might Edith Kilbuck have applauded all that had transpired in Akiak by the time she and her husband arrived there, and all of the church's accomplishments still to come. But it is also important to note that the Moravians' victory was not so complete as Mrs. Kilbuck believed, nor is it even now. Because the land generally couldn't be farmed or developed or made to yield potatoes, because Sheldon Jackson's reindeer experiment never worked out, because there just wasn't any alternative, and because nobody even wanted an alternative, the subsistence economy survived the collapse of shamanism. With it the spiritual bedrock of the Yupik religion has survived as well, even if shorn of its public ceremonial aspect. John Kilbuck saw well enough and far enough to spade down to that bedrock in preparing this ground for Christianity, but not even he could spade more deeply than that.

And in their choice to make Yupik the language of this church, and in their choice to devise an orthography for it, the Moravians preserved the spoken medium of Native religious thought to a degree unexcelled elsewhere. While such bonding as exists between that bedrock and its Christian topsoil is of a loose and sometimes mutually corrosive sort, it nonetheless exists, because of those complementary concepts that the Orthodox priests first discovered, because of such similar histories as the biblical and folkloric flood narratives, whether historic or mythic, and because of such comfortable activities as the church's winter songfests and Bible conferences, with their hundreds of visitors from neighboring villages and their concomitant feasting, though no formal gift exchange. The shamans stand in back of all this like uninvited guests who won't go away. Sometimes rumors circulate in one village or another that a shaman has begun practicing again, though they are more likely to be heard in the Catholic villages in and around Nelson

Island than in the Moravian ones. Still, the rumors are there, even in the Moravian villages.

Maybe in such times as these, when even the ravens are confused and at odds with themselves, a shaman's ability to recapture the time when men and the *yuat* of animals conversed freely with each other is profoundly attractive. And modernity hasn't necessarily outdistanced these adventurers, at least insofar as Berger defines modernity. They were, after all, the Kuskokwim's first autonomous individuals, who could — and did — step outside their communities and were always capable of treacherously turning against them. The shamans assumed those dangers so that others wouldn't have to, and the shock of modernity along the river lies in the fact that now, suddenly, everybody is nearly as autonomous as the shamans were, but without recourse to the ancient ecstatic techniques and the extraordinary psychic resources that allowed the shamans to overcome the polarizations, and the loneliness and alienating chill, inherent in such autonomy.

Maybe one sort of ecstasy comes in those 750 milliliter bottles from Anchorage, and it comes, like Jesus, to whoever seeks it out, free of any initiatory ordeal or apprenticeship; but everything looks just as screwed up the next day. At present, only the people's pastors and lay pastors hold any authorized and enduring solution to the rending oppositions, to the distances that now separate the sacred and the secular, human and animal, the people themselves. But in keeping with Western materialism, that solution is finally a matter of faith, and deliverance in the life to come. There is nothing on earth that will bring Sammy back. There is nothing before Oscar to provide him with a clear indication of his destiny, as either a hunter or a fisherman, a husband or a father.

4 ⊙

AFTER THE SERVICE Walter Larson, who has relatives in Kongiganak, meets me at the door of the church and invites me to his house for some smoked salmon and coffee. Walter will preach this evening in his role as the lay pastor for the church. He is also a fisherman, and he has a twenty-eight-foot boat hauled out of the water for repairs on the other side of Brown's Slough. He uses this both as a fishing boat for himself and as a tender for Kemp-Paulucci, taking deliveries from other fishermen. After we eat, he drives me across the bridge so he can show it to me.

In its blocks the boat seems at once ponderous and vulnerable, like a horse lifted off its feet in a belly harness, and with its elevated pilothouse and ample hold it seems almost as tall as it is long. A welder, a *kass'aq* with a road-map face and milky eyes, stands outside it sipping coffee. He asks Walter if the fishermen voted to strike yesterday at Napakiak, and Walter replies that a strike was okayed by the membership but there would be notice on Monday as to whether the co-op's management actually wanted to go through with it.

"The fish ain't gonna wait," the welder says. "They'll be gone by the time you all get this hashed out. Strikes are good for the next guy, but they screw the hell out of the guys doing the striking."

The pastor looks at his boat from bow to stern and nods his head sadly. "Yep, I'd like to take this boat out tomorrow, but I might get a bullet in it."

Elsie's smokehouse is just a few minutes' walk down the road from Walter's boat. A tiny yellow terrier of some sort is tied to the doorstep of Oscar's brother John's house, and it yips and yips like a stuck record. Oscar's troublesome truck is parked next to the empty fish racks, its front end jacked off the ground and set on stumps, and Harvey is stretched out on the dirt beneath it, badly hung over but harried all the same by Oscar into straightening the front wheel alignment. Charlie lies as if asleep on the bottom of an overturned dinghy. The rear gate of the truck is set flat, and a few cans of Diet Pepsi and empty candy wrappers are spread across it, Junior and Clayton nosing through them like hungry puppies. Elsie stands down at the sea wall with Margaret and Oscar, scolding Junior over her shoulder: "Don't you drink my Diet Pepsi! I need it so I don't get fat!"

Margaret and Oscar and the two sisters have joined a small group of teenage girls and an old woman in a rose *qaspeq*, sitting on the ledge of the wall and fishing by rod and reel for whitefish. One of the girls lifts a wriggling fish from the river twelve feet below them and a companion slips a net under it; then the girl clubs the fish daintily with a thick stick. Oscar has a cheap plastic rod and reel he bought at Swanson's and is showing Margaret how to cast with it. He mutters, "Last time I tried to do this, she threw the whole thing in the water."

"Are you going on strike tomorrow?" I ask him.

Oscar, in a manner of speaking, is polarized. He fidgets with the fishing rod and makes as though he didn't hear. The old woman in the *qaspeq* sits placidly at his side with her legs splayed out and her feet hanging over the water. She's fishing with just a hand line, and as she finishes rebaiting her hook and throws it out into the river, a *kass'aq* at the helm of a skiff racing by lifts his right hand and waves at her in response. Elsie taps the woman's shoulder and laughs uproariously at the boatman's mistake. She speaks rapidly in the language that Helper Neck was so jealous of, advising the old woman that the next time she should go "like this," and she puts her hands to her mouth and blows a kiss out over the water.

V

WHICH SIDE
ARE YOU ON?

1 THE KUSKOKWIM opens today. A six-hour commercial salmon period will begin at one o'clock this afternoon, but there hasn't been any word on KYUK radio as to whether the co-op leadership has actually ordered a strike. Finally Oscar picks up Elsie's telephone and calls his friend Sam Beaver. "You hear if they're striking today? They are? Goddamn. . . . What about you? You fishing anyway? Yep, me too. My Nissan's down in the shop at Swanson's — the mechanic says maybe I burst the seals on that — and I got a bunch of other bills I got to pay." Then he laughs and says, "Maybe I'll run over your new net."

So at least there'll be one other boat out there with us today. But if anybody here is as wary of danger as Walter Larson was yesterday, they don't show it. Elsie sits quietly at the supper table and reads, as she routinely does, from the Book of Psalms. Oscar and Margaret talk and laugh together as the big man pulls on his rubber boots. He suggests that Margaret kick him in the ass for good luck today, just as Elsie used to do for James. But Margaret just laughs, low and soft, telling him to go and make money.

Out on the Kuskokwim the sun chips shards of light off the water's crests, and the tide is so high that it floods the roots of the trees and brush fronting the river's edge across from town. There are plenty of other boats on the river besides the *Crazy J* and, presumably, Sam Beaver's. Tenders similar to Walter Larson's, along with a number of skiffs, run in crisscrossing pat-

terns in the river outside Brown's Slough and along the length
of the town waterfront, where three or four processing ships
belonging to Kemp-Paulucci and other major buyers rest at anchor. Oscar heads the *Crazy J* across the wakes of the tenders
and skiffs and around the ends of the two big nautilus-shaped
islands that sit squarely in the channel opposite Bethel, just
south of Tony's fish camp.

Once around the islands, he is able to head the boat straight
downstream through a smaller channel defined by these and
then a third midstream island, whose southern tip dwindles into
the river a mile or so above Napakiak, itself nearly opposite the
slough that leads to Hippa's fish camp. Somewhere between a
dozen and two dozen skiffs are working either this channel or
the one on the other side of the islands, though Oscar says this
isn't as many as usual. These and the boats motoring back and
forth along the sides of the big processors, their crews holding
up handwritten placards we couldn't read as we headed toward
this channel, are the only evidence — at the moment — that the
co-op has ordered a strike.

This channel leading down to Hippa's camp is Oscar's favorite fishing spot on the river, and while the tide is still flooding in,
he and Charlie decide to set net at the lower part of the channel
and let it carry us slowly up the length of the islands. Charlie
has sobered up for today's fishing, but his eyes are sunken and
he hardly ever speaks.

Oscar wanted to be out here at one o'clock sharp, but we're
about half an hour late owing to the tortoiselike quality of Charlie's movements. While we waited for him to get dressed and
gather his gear this morning, I looked around at his walls and
shelves: Hunter basketball trophies, Bruce Springsteen album in-
sert photos, Budweiser beer ads, a series of black-and-white portraits of Yupik elders taken from a calendar, and, above all, Curtis. The other displays, in fact, occupy only the odd corners and
irregular spaces not papered over with Charlie's son. A series of
framed snapshots flanks and crowds the basketball trophies. An
immense and grainy blowup of Charlie dandling the diapered

child on his lap dominates the wall opposite the plywood partition blocking off the kitchen area. A column of felt-tip markings and dates running up this partition records Curtis's growth. Slogans lettered onto adhesive strips — "Curtis, I love you, Dad," or "Curtis, my only son, nothing's gonna stop us now" — are taped to the windows and ceiling. The little house, carefully swept and vacuumed, has taken on the appearance of a shrine. I noticed that even Charlie's wristwatch has a tiny cutout of Curtis's face inserted beneath the minute and hour hands.

Last month Charlie, drunk, described to me how the boy's mother had gotten a court injunction against his approaching either herself or Curtis. "So I wrote the Department of Family and Youth Services, and I wrote the governor, and then I got a lawyer, and then finally I could see him on Saturdays. I went through shit, man, but I'm glad I did." Then he described the gifts that he got his son, the things they did together on those Saturdays, the savings bonds that he said he bought him for each and every birthday. "He don't want to go back to his mom's when it's time, and he's crying all the time. I tell him, 'I'm sorry, son, it's the law. You gotta go.' And then I just watch him — watch while he keeps on crying there in his mom's arms." His eyes lost their milky fondness, becoming dim and perplexed. "She has no love in her brain," he said, and then smiled and corrected himself. "I mean, her heart — she has no love in her heart. Well, I mean, her brain or her heart, there's no love in 'em both."

I saw that the marks on the plywood partition ended with Curtis's growth through May 1988. What about since then? "Yeah, I haven't seen him for a year now." Charlie paused, chewing his lip like Oscar for a minute, and I didn't know whether that was to cover something he didn't want to talk about or simply to wonder how that had happened. "I been letting it slide, I guess."

Now Charlie sits in the bow and slowly ties the two red buoys onto the ends of the green salmon net. The *Crazy J* turns just as slowly in the channel, and the breeze blows a sweet scent of cottonwood and lupine from the island.

Oscar feels safety in the number of boats out on the river today. He's concerned only with his gear as Charlie drops one buoy into the water and then slowly feeds the heaped net into the river. At the same time Oscar runs the Evinrude in reverse, backing the boat away from the island and into the middle of the channel. When he reaches the end of the net, Charlie wedges the second buoy behind the forward thwart, and then Oscar revs the motor, drawing the net straight and taut across the current. Then he drops the Evinrude to a speed just above idle, and the boat slowly draws the net in a shuttling motion across the breadth of the channel at the same time that the tide pushes it up the length. The net will complete three or four shuttles across before it drifts the two miles up to the northern end of the islands. The floats bob on top of the water like soda biscuits, and Oscar cries aloud in excitement — "Ii-i!" — as some of them tremble and dip with the force of the first strikers hitting the net.

Oscar's VHF radio still isn't working right; the unit can receive but can't broadcast. Just the same, Oscar runs it to get news of what's happening elsewhere on the river. We overhear two *kass'aq* fish buyers, maybe working for Kemp or maybe for someone else, trading information. There are a lot of fishermen on the river, and neither tenders nor skiffs are being seriously bothered by co-op members on strike. "Well, if they start hassling any of those guys fishing down there, you let us know, all right?" one voice growls. Then Oscar throws his head back in laughter when an old Eskimo fisherman reports in Yupik that he pulled a rusty forty-horse motor off the bottom with his first drift and he hopes to get an airplane with his next one.

As the boat approaches the riverbank, where the stumps and branches of submerged trees and brush project menacingly above the surface, just waiting to snag a net, Charlie rises at a word from Oscar and throws the second buoy into the water. Then Oscar shifts the motor into forward and races to the opposite end of the net, where Charlie drops a lasso over the first buoy and ties the end of that line to the boat. Oscar shifts into reverse and the net begins to move across the channel back toward the island. As the floats once again fall into line, extending straight out from the bow, Oscar laughs once more, remembering his written driver's test this morning, which he had to take for the reinstatement of his license and which Margaret, who doesn't drive, took just for the hell of it.

Oscar flunked the test by a single point. "Well, at least I got two more chances," he says. "And I don't feel too bad. Margaret flunked it by four points, and she's smarter than me." Charlie wordlessly gestures toward a long set of floats dipping beneath the surface in the midsection of the net, and Oscar crosses his arms in a manner that suggests he's restraining his own giddiness: "I feel my wallet getting fatter."

When the *Crazy J* reaches the top of the channel and the two brothers haul in, there is nothing here of the physical strain and the assembly-line urgency that attends shaking a herring net. While it's important to get the net clean and back into the water without wasting any time, each individual salmon merits attention, even the chums, or dog salmon, and even at this year's prices. Oscar and Charlie stand in the bow on opposite sides of the net in the mild sunshine, carefully maneuvering the fish free of the mesh, working gravely and silently, sliding each salmon like a silver ingot into that section of the boat set up as a fish bin and piling the cleaned portion of the net in a heap at their feet.

Most of the salmon are chums, running five to ten pounds each. At one time these were the staple of the Kuskokwim's dog teams. Compared to herring, their scales are much finer and more firmly attached, while their colors are subtler, a watercolor aquamarine and viridian. The skin is more metallic, looking like synthetic sheathing wrapped over test-tube muscle tissue. These chums are short and stocky, though the single red, or sockeye, salmon harvested in this drift is distinguished from the chums only by Oscar's practiced eye; he points to the red's slightly thinner build and the narrow neck on its tail. Much less numerous than the chums and kings, the reds are moist and firm, commanding six to ten times the price of a chum from a buyer.

About every third fish in this drift is a king, or chinook, salmon, and these have dark flecks like peppercorns spattered across their spines, and faces the hue and texture of old nickel. They're also more various in size, most of them weighing only ten to fifteen pounds, though the net also yields three or four warhorses weighing thirty to forty. These come from the water like outboard motors dredged up from the bottom, and Oscar has to lean over the side and gaff them — in the face, preferably near the gills, so as not to damage the meat — just to haul them into the boat. In their thrashings they nearly knock the sluggish Charlie off his feet, and sometimes they tear the net before they're knocked over the head with the butt end of the Eskimo depth sounder. Even these are small compared to some kings. Oscar remembers a hundred-pounder he caught one year at Quinhagak when kings were priced at $1 per pound: "Yep, that was a hundred-dollar fish, that one."

A few of the kings show the first signs of the hooked and toothy lower jaw that sets in as the fish ripen to spawning, speeding upriver in the macabre race between lust and their own decay, though most show no signs of that phase yet. But in every case the salmons' faces, with their fixed expressions and their staring eyes, like buttons painted black and laminated with plastic, seem already composed for death, and mortality settles into them imperceptibly as they lie in a stunned and silvery heap in the bottom of the boat, some of them streaked with blood from their own gills or from the gaffed faces of the kings. They lie in plated features, in perfect silence, though sometimes an eerie and unexpected sigh, unnervingly human, escapes from somewhere in that heap. They lie dumb with the strange clairvoyance that brings them back across so many miles and so many years to their original spawning grounds, even if some take wrong turns and turn up on occasion in the chocolatey waters of the Kongiganak.

By the time the net is clean, about a hundred fish lie in the bin. But Oscar's face is full of disappointment as he squeezes his gloves out over the side and then straightens. He turns toward the stern and squints up into the sky, saying, "This is lazy man's fishing. The sun's too hot and the tide's too high, and the fish are swimming low and deep."

The *Crazy J* speeds down to the bottom of the channel again and resumes its shuttling progress back up. Our second drift produces about forty more fish, including three reds. Charlie nearly loses one of the kings overboard as he takes it from the net, and Oscar, who no longer feels his wallet growing fatter, growls, "What's the matter with you? You're not poor enough?"

By now the tide has turned and the river is running out to sea again. This time, on our third drift, the boat shuttles down the channel, but the floats lie limply on the water's surface, and then the net folds up, the opposite buoy swinging in toward the bow of the boat, as the lead line catches a snag on the bottom. Charlie takes hold of the net and Oscar works the boat gently back and forth, and at last the net breaks free without tearing. Charlie hauls it in quickly, finding it virtually empty of fish and pulling a black and branching tree limb from its midsection. Oscar checks his watch and finds that an hour still remains in the period. "You want to try Jo Jo's Hole?" he asks, referring to a spot farther downstream known for lots of fish but also plenty of snags on the bottom.

On the way we meet Hippa and Buzzo, who have just sold a load of fish to a small Whitney Seafoods tender. Oscar asks, "What's the prices?"

Buzzo pulls his receipt from his wallet and reads, "Twenty cents for chums, seventy for kings, and a buck seventy for reds."

"Shit," Oscar says, drawing the word out to two syllables and shaking his head as though he hadn't believed that the buyers were really serious about those prices.

"But they gave me a retro."

"What's that?"

"They say if the prices go up later, they'll make up the difference to me." Unimpressed, Oscar shoves his hands into the bib of his rain pants, and Charlie looks at him with a broken smile. "But just sell your fish to Whitney," Buzzo adds. "Then if Kemp finally raises their prices, Whitney and them others will too."

The net comes up empty at Jo Jo's Hole as well, and at seven o'clock Oscar turns upriver to find the tender that Buzzo sold to. Charlie splashes water across the fish while Oscar says, "Last year we got forty cents for chums and a buck thirty-five for kings. This world's always talking about inflation. How come for the fisherman it's deflation?" He looks down at the water beading and dripping off the fish. "Four drifts and they just barely cover the floor. First time I ever unloaded just once on an opening day like this."

Oscar and I rinse the fish bin clean while Charlie presents his permit and identification and collects his pay, a little more than $600 for the brothers' ninety-four chums, forty-one kings, and four reds. Oscar recalls that they made $1500 on the first day of last year's season, and that was with a lot more boats on the river. But finally he decides, "Well, that's not so bad for coming out late."

The river is quiet in the sunlit evening, like a wide and empty highway. In Bethel a few leftover skiffs are tied to the sterns of the processors, waiting unmolested to sell their catch. Oscar steers past them, past Brown's Slough and Elsie's smokehouse, and finally into the enclosed small-boat harbor beyond the upriver end of the sea wall. The roughly triangular harbor is ringed with skiffs scuffed up onto its shores or anchored a short distance off, and Oscar has taken to keeping the *Crazy J* here so as not to be bothered with the tide running out from beneath it on the ramp at the smokehouse. This morning I parked the pickup in the lot abutting the harbor, and as we coast into shore near the Chevy, Oscar points to another pickup pulling up in front of a boat that has just landed. "As soon as the fishermen come in, the bootleggers come out. See that one?"

Kriska Evans isn't a bootlegger, but he's parked next to our pickup almost as if he were waiting for us. Fair-haired, though

Yupik, with a broad, crooked smile, he lived for a time in Kon-giganak some years ago, and I know him now as one of the chief proponents and organizers of the strike. He stands in his open car door, talking with a friend. He nods a smiling hello to Oscar as the Actives carry the gas tanks up to the pickup, and then says to his companion that about 60 percent of the town's fleet stayed off the river today. Unloading their gear, Oscar and Charlie move back and forth between boat and pickup as if Kriska were invisible.

2 ◎ MARGARET STANDS BENEATH a low roof at a table tacked together from odd boards and nailed against the side of the smokehouse. With her black hair gathered up into a knit cap, she wears a navy blue sweatshirt against the mosquitoes and a green rubber apron against the fish. Oscar crouches at her side, hefting a big king salmon out of a metal tub and onto the surface of the table, which has been spread with burlap, and Margaret swiftly heads and guts the fish with her *uluaq,* a half-moon–shaped carving knife. She slides it over to me for rinsing and then begins cutting the fish for drying.

With kings, this involves slicing the spine and ribs and also a sizable fillet of meat away from both flanks of the fish while working inside the organ cavity. This produces a thick slab of meat that still has a tail and dorsal fin, looking something like a chum salmon that has been skinned. Then the spinal section is crosshatched on both sides with double rows of shallow cuts from the *uluaq,* so that sections of the pink meat droop and protrude like a child's pouting lip. Next the skin, which still has a good deal of boneless meat on it, is spread flat on the burlap in a sort of butterfly shape, where its meat is also crosshatched with the *uluaq*. Margaret inserts short willow stakes sharpened at both ends into the skin to hold it flat, and then she ties skins together and spines together in pairs with yarn, like to like. Finally Oscar and I go up and down a stepladder to hang the cut fish on the beams of Elsie's drying rack.

Margaret works carefully, hardly feeling the mosquitoes, making cuts of almost surgical precision and regularity. This morning even Elsie, who lately hasn't had much good to say about anybody, marveled aloud at Margaret's cutting, saying that her daughter-in-law's fish looked better than the ones she'd cut herself. This isn't just a matter of aesthetics; the women cut salmon according to a method refined through the centuries, requiring cuts of an exact position and depth, and too loose an application of the method results in the salmon not drying properly or else becoming infested with worms. In Bethel and the tundra villages surrounding it, coastal women such as Margaret are admired for their skill with seals but often disparaged for their fish cutting. Margaret is an exception, and Elsie, justifiably, credits herself as Margaret's model.

At the moment Elsie is at her apartment with the kids, but John Active, the adopted brother, who is also skilled at cutting fish, stands at the table next to Margaret with his sleeves rolled up and his shirt out of his jeans, his face pale and thoughtful behind his horn-rimmed glasses. John isn't a fisherman like his brothers; he was once a reporter, anchorman, and producer for KYUK radio and TV, overseeing their various Yupik-language productions. He is also the author of a graceful essay on the Yupik people included in *Alaska's Native People,* a publication of the Alaska Geographic Society, and he had intended to expand that into a book. But somehow he lost the job at KYUK and the essay never got expanded, and now he works unhappily as a clerk at Swanson's. Next to Oscar he seems slight, almost skeletal, though his hands are strong. When he speaks, whether in English or Yupik, his words are as soft and crisp as the cuts he makes in his fish.

Margaret and John are working tonight on the kings Oscar

and I caught yesterday when we went subsistence fishing. Oscar originally wanted to go with Charlie, and Charlie was willing enough. Yesterday morning Oscar was sitting at Elsie's table, studying his driver's handbook for a second try at the license exam — "Everywhere you go, licenses. Pretty soon you're gonna need a pedestrian's license just to walk around. Cross only at crosswalks. Walk with a limp here." — when Charlie burst boozily through the door. "Well, I got my light and phone bill paid," he proclaimed. "Harvey was supposed to help me with that, but he already spent all his paycheck, and I paid for half of that new net I got on credit from Kemp. Let's go fishing, Oscar!"

Oscar just pursed his lips in disgust and decided to stall. He studied his handbook for another thirty minutes. Then we piled into the pickup, and (after the pickup stalled as well) I dropped Oscar and Margaret off at the Department of Motor Vehicles for Oscar's test. Next I drove Charlie to the River Pawn Shop, near the bridge across Brown's Slough, where he redeemed an expensive pair of binoculars. Dust hung over the roads like smog, and Charlie rolled up his window against the grit as he took the binoculars out of their case and ran his long, tapering fingers along their scopes in an almost reverent manner.

Then we went back to Motor Vehicles, where Oscar was beside himself; he'd flunked again by one point, missing on an item that he originally marked correctly but changed. At the apartment he grabbed the driver's handbook, went into Elsie's bedroom, and shut the door.

"How come he locks himself in there like that?" Charlie wondered. "What is he, embarrassed about me?"

"He's studying for his test," Margaret said. "He's only got one more chance."

Charlie stayed for lunch, waited some more for Oscar, and finally decided to go home, shouting through the bedroom door for Oscar to pick him up when he was ready to fish. When Oscar came out of the bedroom, he was shaking his head, saying, "Every day drunk."

Margaret would have preferred for Oscar to fish with Buzzo, and he might have been able to do that if he had only been willing to abandon his partnership with Charlie earlier. She said, "It's what you wanted. You wanted to fish with him."

So Oscar and I went out alone, first to the island across from Brown's Slough to cut some cottonwood to burn in smoking the fish, then to Tony Watson's fish camp to borrow a net with an eight-and-three-quarter-inch mesh, good for kings but wide enough to let the chums go through. Then we went downriver to an area across from the Bethel airport, where the huge radar towers of the air force's abandoned White Alice communications site climb into the sky like drive-in movie screens. A brisk wind blowing up the river cut the water into hard-edged ridges and troughs, and in that cooler weather the salmon swam closer to the surface than they had on Monday. We pulled in about twenty big kings and maybe half a dozen huge chums, king-size chums, so big that Oscar whistled in amazement as he cleaned them from the net. The backs of the kings were a pretty pea green peppered with black, and the fronds of their flaring gills were as red as tulips. Oscar ran his fingers along the smooth, dappled flank of one king, murmuring to himself, "Beautiful fish."

Elsie and Margaret began working on the fish last night, and in the course of that Elsie had a run-in with Charlie. The old woman was cutting the skins and gills off the heads of the kings and saving the heads' casings, which are white and fatty and cartilaginous and can be boiled and eaten. She saved the skins of the heads as well, spreading them flat, cutting enough around the eyes to allow the eyes to bulge out, and hanging them in strings from the end of the drying racks' beams. There they dangled in the wind like fantastic, frog-eyed earrings.

But working with the fish had soaked her shoes, and she also needed a bucket for the head casings. Since both her rubbers and her extra buckets were on Charlie's porch, she and Oscar and I drove over to the house on Weber Circle, where Elsie found the porch door locked tight. She pounded and shouted, shouted and pounded, but it was some time before Charlie — still drunk, and angry himself by then — was persuaded to open up. He and his mother carried on their shouting match as she got her supplies, and she was still shouting as we rode back to the smokehouse. "I want to move back into my own house! I'd like to just throw him out! I don't care what happens to him no more!"

Oscar said, "He should transfer his permit to me before something does happen to him."

Today Oscar and Charlie have switched their roles; Oscar wants Charlie to go fishing for more kings, though not with him, and Charlie isn't much in the mood anymore. The door to his house was open this morning, and we found him asleep in bed. Oscar gave the bed a shaking and told him, "I got to work on my truck today. It hardly runs no more, it stalls so much. I need you and Harvey to take the boat out and go subsistence fishing."

Charlie rolled over with glacial slowness and stared up at us through bloodshot, flickering eyes. "Hello, Rick," he said. "You still hanging around?"

"Hurry up," Oscar said.

Charlie sighed and rubbed his face with both hands. "When you gonna hang that new net I bought?"

"I'll hang it today. We got commercial fishing again Friday — that's tomorrow — so you better sober up."

"I gotta sober up. There's only one bottle left in that whole case of twelve." Charlie laughed harshly and then let his feet fall to the floor. He sat up as though he were climbing out of the grave, and in the light through the window his skin looked gray.

"You can go borrow some king gear from Tony. Hurry up. I want to get going."

Oscar charged into the front room to rout Harvey from the couch. Then we went out to wait in the truck. Charlie and Harvey came out in ten minutes, stiff, blinking in the sunlight, carrying their last bottle of whiskey and two cans of Budweiser. Harvey's cheeks were covered with whiskers, and his face already wore its characteristic grave and furrowed aspect, as though he'd just found something wrong he wasn't sure he could do anything about.

Margaret's brother climbed immediately into the bed of the pickup, but Charlie went over to the shaded side of the house, where a pair of savannah sparrows had built a nest in the upper branches of a willow bush. Oscar's kids, and Charlie as well, had been paying daily visits to this nest, and throughout the spring the mother had stared fearlessly back at the observers and refused to leave it. But this morning she was gone, and four pink and naked heads, no bigger than marbles, the lids of their blue eyes pressed shut, lined the edge of the nest. Charlie smiled at this first glimpse of the nestlings, standing enchanted at the bush until Oscar's hand on the truck horn prompted him into the pickup.

Clouds the color of dirty sheets had covered the sun and most of the sky by the time Charlie and Harvey were outfitted in the *Crazy J* and pushed off toward Tony's. But they came back forty-five minutes later without any fish and without Tony's net. "Tony won't give me that king gear," Charlie said. "He says you gotta come ask for it. He don't trust me. Wanted to fight me about it."

"He drinking?"

"Yep." Charlie smirked. "He gave us some of that."

"I ain't going over there. He'll want me to drink. Just use that six-inch net up by the drying rack."

"I ain't using that net. I'll catch too many chums, Oscar."

Charlie was adamant that he wouldn't fish with chum gear, and Oscar was adamant that he wouldn't go over to Tony's. Finally Oscar just said he'd go over to Tony's later and then pick Charlie up after dinner, though I know he's intending to go to an Alcoholics Anonymous meeting tonight. Charlie went home by cab and Harvey stayed to help work on the pickup. Oscar sighed and then spat into the dust, saying he wouldn't have half of these problems if he just had his own fish camp, where he could stay clear of town. "Tony knows about a good spot downriver. It's pretty far from Bethel —"

"That's good," interjected Margaret as she worked on her fish.

"— but it's got good water at low tide. Or maybe I should just build at that camp where all those Kongiganak guys are. But I don't know if they'd accept me. I could ask some of those old guys, I guess."

A warm, spattering rain starts to fall as Oscar leans over the pickup's engine compartment. It beats a staccato rhythm on the tarpaulins that he strung over the drying rack yesterday, and Margaret and John stand in the shelter of these as the pink cuts of meat tremble like pennants in the breeze and as Elsie's necklaces of heads lift like kites. Harvey ignores the rain, pointing to an inconspicuous filter at the base of the carburetor. Once he has removed the filter, he hands it to Oscar, who's delighted to find it clogged with a sticky brown sludge. "There's your problem," Harvey says.

Margaret calls Oscar's attention to his radio–cassette player on the seat of the pickup. KYUK is interviewing some officers of KUFMA, the Kuskokwim United Fishermen's Marketing Association, an organization that has joined the co-op this week in promoting the strike. The officers express bitterness against those fishermen who defied the strike on Monday, and vow that tomorrow they'll be closing the river down entirely.

Oscar stiffens and swears under his breath, saying, "They better not. I'll start cleaning my guns."

3 ⊛ BRUCE SPRINGSTEEN is playing on the stereo — "I was born in the U.S.A." — and Charlie says he feels like a tractor ran over his head. He goes to the stove and glances without appetite into a pot of reindeer stew that he made yesterday and forgot about. Oscar stands by the window and stares outside as though the house were besieged. "I hope we can get our boat," he says. "Maybe them strikers have that boat harbor blocked off. Maybe it's gonna be a war today."

Charlie sighs. "I don't feel like fighting a war, Oscar."

The town is decked in ribbons of orange, fluttering lengths of rubbery surveyor's tape tied to arms, sleeves, thighs, hats, antennas, bumpers, fenders, flagpoles, windows, rails, and eaves. The pickup swings quickly around corners manned by strikers and strike sympathizers passing out pieces of tape, and when I stop at the post office to pick up Elsie's mail, a middle-aged Yupik fisherman hands a length of it to me. In the parking lot a young *kass'aq* woman with blond ringlets attempts to give some to Oscar, but Oscar just laughs nervously, noncommittally, unwilling either to say no or to accept any tape.

Last night, while Oscar was at his AA meeting, I went to the KUFMA membership meeting held in a dilapidated social services building near the waterfront. Close to a hundred people eventually crowded into the meeting hall, their numbers divided equally between the races, with a smattering of *kass'aq* women. The members were dressed variously in old jeans or baggy sweatpants, denim jackets or dusty flannel shirts, rubber boots or scuffed-up tennis shoes; they sat in folding chairs or stood in back or sat cross-legged on the bare floor; and all of them were angry. An older Yupik fisherman, a precise and even-voiced man, as articulate in English as John Active, chaired the meeting.

Walter Larson waved to me and gave me a chair to one side of the chairman's table, just in front of the spot where a television crew from KYUK was setting up its camera. Though Walter was a buyer for Kemp, he had come around to supporting the strike, saying that over the years the co-op's management had simply gotten too cozy with Kemp and maybe that had something to do with this summer's low prices.

Those present voted almost unanimously to strike until fishermen were paid at least $.40 per pound for chums, $1.10 for kings, and $1.65 for reds. "If one processor meets those prices, then we'll fish, whether that's Kemp, Whitney, or Inlet Salmon," the chairman advised. "According to Kemp's contract with the co-op, they're required to match the prices of any legitimate local competitor. If Whitney raises their prices, Kemp will follow."

The fishermen's anger had more than just the processors as its object. The *Shinmei Maru*, a big white-and-turquoise freighter flying both Japanese and American flags, lay at anchor along the sea wall just on the other side of Brown's Slough from Elsie's smokehouse. At the meeting a *kass'aq* fisherman with a trim red beard stood to say, "No matter who we sell it to, most of our catch winds up on that Jap freighter, right? Well, I read that in Tokyo just one thin slice of Yukon-Kuskokwim salmon sells for six dollars and ninety cents. Why the hell don't we see any of that money here?"

Nor had they forgotten those fishermen who defied the strike on Monday, though none of these were mentioned by name. The chairman said, "We're going to need one hundred percent of the boats off the river tomorrow, and we're going to have to work hard to get it." He concluded by adding that he and other representatives would be meeting with the processors after this meeting, and that the membership should stand by tomorrow morning for news of any break in the impasse.

All these orange ribbons, brilliant against the nickel-colored clouds, indicate that no such break occurred last night. Oscar doesn't like the way things are going, including the time we're making in getting down to the harbor. We stop to fill the gas tanks at a pump on the harborside bank of Brown's Slough — "Two sixty-nine per gallon: Hazelwood prices," Oscar says, naming the captain of the *Exxon Valdez* — and he glances unhappily at his watch. "Even if we get out, we're gonna be late again. Gee, they used to start these commercial periods at seven A.M. How did we ever get to those? We were always late, and then they moved 'em back to nine, and we were still late, and now they start at twelve or one, and we're *still* late. It's crazy."

The small-boat harbor isn't closed off after all, but Kriska

Evans and a group of picketers and a KYUK television crew all line the embankment close to where the *Crazy J* is anchored. The TV camera rolls as Oscar hauls the boat in to shore, as Charlie and I move the gas cans and other gear out of the truck, as Kriska grins cordially at Oscar and invites him to join the picketers. Oscar just shakes his head and replies, "I can't tell my creditors I'm on strike. I got to pay for this boat, I got to get my motor out of the shop, I got to take care of my light bill —"

"You'll get your money back when the strike is over," Kriska says.

"No, I won't."

Finally Kriska grins again, waving to us as we pull up anchor and turn out of the harbor, and shouts, "Good luck!" Oscar and Charlie exchange glances and laugh uneasily.

Oscar's brother John doesn't like the way things are going either. When we pull into the ramp to pick up Oscar's net, he walks down from his house and says, "You gonna go risk your lives? See you on the evening news."

If the river was relatively quiet on Monday, it's absolutely dead today. The Kuskokwim could hardly have been quieter when Trader Lind sailed into Mamterillermiut a century ago with his missionaries in tow. There aren't even any boats around the processing ships, which rock placidly at anchor, with no one in sight on deck. The only skiff in their vicinity is speeding purposefully downriver with orange ribbons flying from its antenna mast. Charlie sits with his head down in the fish bin. Oscar looks downriver, then upriver, and confesses frankly, "I'm scared."

When I produce from my pocket the tape I was given at the post office this morning, Oscar decides to go undercover and ties it to his antenna mast. As we round the islands and point into the channel leading down to Hippa's camp, we discover that the river isn't entirely deserted; three or four other boats are in the channel, but none of them have their gear in the water. Instead they float almost invisibly, like lurking crabs, beneath the cover of the brush along the banks. Oscar runs the *Crazy J* all the way down the channel and turns into the slough to Hippa's camp.

"What are you gonna do?" asks Charlie.

"Sit and cry," says Oscar. "I'm on strike."

4 ◉ SOME ANONYMOUS ARTIST has composed a song about the Bethel strike, and some of its lyrics are appearing now on sheets of copier paper taped to telephone poles and bulletin boards and cash registers around town.

> They say that on the Kuskokwim
> There are no neutral men
> Either you're a union man
> Or you're a scab for Louie Kemp
> Which side are you on?
> Which side are you on?

But Oscar never pretended to be a neutral man. Along with many others, he thought that the *Exxon Valdez* disaster and the shutdown of the Prince William Sound salmon fishery this summer might have a silver lining for Kuskokwim fishermen: lower stocks available to wholesale buyers — which is to say the Japanese, who buy 95 percent of Alaska's exported seafood — and therefore higher prices. KYUK and the *Tundra Drums* have offered a couple of explanations so far as to why prices have instead plummeted since last summer: an infusion of farmed salmon from Norway, Chile, and Canada into international markets, and also a strengthening dollar against the yen. But Oscar, again along with many others, can't help suspecting that Kemp-Paulucci is bruiting these about as an excuse to put the screws to the co-op, and that the other buyers are going along for the ride — especially when rumors circulate about much higher prices at other fisheries.

Still, Oscar is fishing anyway, or would like to — if not for
Kemp, then for other buyers, who have broken his heart just as
much as Kemp has with their prices. He's got his bills to pay.
Kriska Evans counters that so does every other hardscrabble
fisherman on the river. But the firebrand of Quinhagak, the same
man who (at least by Oscar's account) made the big buyers
squirm in their seats a few years ago with his suggestion that the
fishermen run their picket lines all up and down the western
coast, goes out on the river just the same.

This question of whose side you are on never used to be this
hard. At one time, in those former communities of blood, everything was all woven together into a single durable, if inflexible,
strand; a man's loyalty to his family was reinforced by every
other imperative that governed his life. A single gift of seal meat
to another family in the village would simultaneously have followed the tug of all those braided interests. But now that original harness has been teased and separated out into a number of
discrete traces, matters of politics, religion, nation, race, town,
job, colleagues, friends, family, and self. Now those separate
traces routinely run at cross-purposes, knotting and tangling.
The exercise of this modern kind of autonomy becomes a personal and solitary algebra, like the inner operations of comput-
ers, so that one is involved in gauging the gravity of these various imperatives, unknotting the lines, and deciding on the one
arcing course — if any choice is possible — between those possibilities that finally brings about the best compromise, the nearest thing to a full solution.

Oscar tells anyone who's willing to listen about his creditors,
though there's more to the algebra than that. Of course he numbers Margaret among his creditors. To their mutual unease, they
both know that there's hardly any chance of his ever thinking
otherwise. And what would he do if he weren't thinking about
that anyway, and chipping away at his bills? I'm surprised that
he's lasted this long, that he hasn't joined Charlie yet for another
one of those little sips. Oscar told me the other day that he likes
seeing the drunks staggering down the Bethel roads and congre-

gating like zombies in the entries to Swanson's and AC and the Kusko Inn, because it reminds him of what a fool he used to be. But the mockery remains in Tony's and everybody else's eyes when he tells them that he's on the wagon. There also remains that stonelike composite of memory and dread in Margaret's heart, which contains in it the possibility that Oscar's children could become as remote to him as Curtis is to Charlie. And what else would Charlie be doing, for that matter, if the great Oscar Active wasn't hauling him out of bed? Only convincing himself with all the more certainty that it was time to cash in his permit, while it was still worth anything at all and while he was still alive to spend his money. Oscar doesn't even want to think about that.

It's a way of paying attention, just as Margaret didn't even feel the mosquitoes when she was attentively cutting kings down at the smokehouse. That night someone stopped to look at Oscar's fish and chat with him, and the visitor ended up asking him about how he had managed to become so fluent in Yupik, unlike many Eskimos raised in Bethel. "I did it the hard way," Oscar said. "I married a woman from the coast and then I moved down there with her."

Margaret overheard, and she only gave that liquid laugh of hers, telling the visitor, "That's the *easy* way."

Another old story came to mind. This tells that Raven once flew into the mouth of a whale. In the whale's belly, Raven was met by a beautiful young woman, the whale's *yua*, who was pleased to appear at regular intervals to feed Raven as a guest. The whale's interior was lit by a lamp that was fed oil from a tube running the length of the whale's spine. The woman warned Raven never to tamper with this tube, but Raven tasted the oil and found it deliciously sweet. Desperate for this oil and impatient with its slow drip, Raven ripped the tube away from the spine, rupturing one of the whale's heart vessels. The belly flooded with oil, and Raven was tossed and bruised for four days before the creature finally washed up dead on a beach, its lovely *yua* gone.

5 ⊚ THE RAIN IS running in thin ribbons off the hood of Charlie's raincoat. He sits on top of the foredeck and just smiles, staring upriver, as Oscar says, "Hurry up."

Charlie doesn't move. The smile seems painted on his face.

Oscar says, "You wanted to come out and now you don't want to set net? You scared?"

He can't get any response out of Charlie, and when he sees a boat approaching from the top of the channel, he cusses and kicks the *Crazy J* into forward, skimming it into the brush at the channel's bank. But the other boat is Tony Watson's, and he steers his big aluminum Raider into the bank next to us, where Oscar and Charlie regard the large load of kings in his bin admiringly.

"You been listening to your VHF?" Oscar says.

Raised in Bethel himself, Tony shakes his head and smiles. "Nope. I can't understand it anyway. How about them strikers coming down through here? Any of them looking at you bum?"

In fact, just a few moments ago a striking fisherman from Kongiganak caught us out in the channel and fixed Oscar with a poisonous stare as he went past, but Oscar also shakes his head and smiles. "Nope. We just don't look at 'em."

Tony casts off and heads on down the channel, and a few minutes later Chris Jacobs, another one of Oscar's old classmates and current fishing buddies, pulls alongside. Oscar sees that Chris also has a good load of fish, and as Chris approaches he calls out, "Here's the Active tender. You can just unload your fish right here."

Chris has a soft chin and full lips and wears tight bell-bottom jeans. He says that he was fishing first down at Jo Jo's Hole, but all he caught there was six fish and a snag on the bottom. Oscar has an explanation: "There ain't no fish down there anymore, since Jo Jo sold his permit."

"Then I went out into that other channel," Chris continues,

"and there's a lot of fish out there, man, a lot of reds. And now there's lots of boats out too, especially down around the Johnson River."

After Chris goes, Oscar suggests to Charlie that we at least set net and see how we do. "Then if we don't want to sell any fish, we can just use 'em for subsistence."

Charlie still sits in the bow, wrapped in his enigmatic silence, but this time, when Oscar positions the boat near the bank at the top of the channel, he finally bends down and begins to feed the net over the side.

The tide is at its lowest ebb, just about to turn, and the boat floats lazily down the long and empty channel, past a fish camp with a fire smoldering in its smokehouse and slabs of fish like pennants on its drying rack, past an abandoned camp with a leaning cabin and an overturned, rotted-out skiff, past dripping groves of alder with green ranks of horsetail growing thickly on their floors. Not so much a breeze but simply a movement of moist air carries the whiff of cottonwood smoke and cut salmon the length of the channel after us. The floats on Oscar's net tremble and dip, and long dorsal fins and thrashing tails claw at the surface along the line of the floats, but the brothers say nothing. Overhead a blue Cessna with big pontoons flies down the river, carrying observers for Alaska Fish & Game.

When Oscar steered into Hippa's fish camp, the tide was emptying out of the slough, and the water still left in the creekbed was as brown and thin as instant cocoa. But in the grasses around the cabin and basketball hoop, small dewdrops of alp lily and yellow-eyed Jacob's ladder flickered brightly in the rain. Hippa and Buzzo were leery of being out on the river, too, and Buzzo was in the cabin drinking coffee with his brother while Hippa's kids, heedless of the rain, played around the basketball hoop. Hippa sat next to Emma on one of the beds and said that he'd heard that chums were selling for fifty-five cents per pound down at False Pass in the Aleutians. "And they're the same fish as our fish. Shit, they *are* our fish."

Biologists have determined through tagging that many of the

chum salmon destined for the Kuskokwim migrate in early and mid-June through the blade-thin slice of sea between Unimak Island and the long tusk of the Alaska Peninsula. Recently False Pass and delta fishermen have waged legal and political battles over access to these fish, the delta fishermen arguing that the bigger False Pass boats working in such confined waters have the potential to destroy the riverine fisheries entirely, the False Pass fishermen objecting that severe limits imposed on their chum catch arbitrarily restrict their take of the valuable reds, which run at the same time. Nonetheless, since 1986 the state Board of Fisheries has maintained a variable cap on the False Pass chum harvest, which so far has resisted legal challenge.

Buzzo's small eyes blinked as he held his coffee mug to his lips and observed, "They still got a cap on those chums down there. There ought to be more fish here now. I wonder where the hell they are."

Oscar noted that the strikers were getting serious and that the guys out on the river were getting cussed out pretty badly on the VHF. "They were pretty serious in Quinhagak too, man," he remembered. "One time I saw a guy hold a pistol to the head of another guy who was threatening his son with a gun. I thought for a minute he was gonna shoot." But strikes got more serious than that down in Bristol Bay, the brothers agreed. They said one year a man was killed and a lot of boats were shot up.

Hippa was running a CB radio off a battery, and by two o'clock someone announced that one of the buyers had raised the price for chums by a nickel, up to twenty-five cents per pound. Oscar just grimaced disdainfully and said, "Too cheap."

What was of more import to the brothers was the increasing number of voices on the CB from fishermen out working the river, and eventually Buzzo was impressed enough to say, "Well, they ain't gonna pay me for sitting on my ass." He and Hippa went out to load their boat, and by two-thirty we were back on the river ourselves.

The drifts go quickly with the net filling so rapidly, and soon the bin is awash in squirming fish gasping in the rain, their bellies rouged, their eyes shadowed with a crescent of tincture of gold. A good percentage of them are kings and reds. No strikers come down the channel, and at the end of the period the *Crazy J,* sluggish with its cargo, finds a dilapidated Inlet Salmon tender anchored in a secluded cove a short distance downstream. There we unload nearly a ton of salmon, at the promised twenty-five cents per pound for our nearly two hundred chums, and Charlie comes out of the tender's cabin with a little over $1000 in hand. "We shoulda started on time. We woulda made two grand," Oscar says. "I got to hang that five-and-a-half-inch mesh gear that Charlie got. And we'll use that instead of this six-inch net. A lot of those little chums are going right through this."

At the Bethel waterfront the strike is much in evidence, as about a dozen skiffs displaying orange streamers and hand-lettered placards buzz in angry circles around the Kemp processing ship. They are also harassing the boats of those fishermen who have come to sell directly to the processor in exchange for slightly higher prices; they cut sharply across their bows, or throw heavy wakes athwart them. A police boat floating at the stern of the processor keeps a watchful eye on these proceedings, and at one point sets off in pursuit of one of the strike boats, its siren wailing. But the striker is better equipped than his pursuer; he carries a lower jet unit on his motor, which allows him to skim through shallow waters, and with this he veers into a silted channel running between the midstream islands opposite the waterfront. The police boat is unable to follow. Meanwhile Charlie has an ear to the VHF, and he reports that a crowd has gathered on the dock next to the *Shinmei Maru* and is shouting, "Japs go home!"

There are no picketers in evidence at the small-boat harbor, as there were this morning, but we discover that someone has cleaned out the back of Oscar's truck, taking some tools and gloves and other small items. This happens routinely in Bethel, and the theft may be unrelated to Oscar's fishing today, but all the same he says that he's going to have to start watching his boat a lot more closely. Charlie agrees, adding, "I'm gonna lock my door tonight."

Charlie is good and dry by now, and Oscar likes being with him when he's like that. On the way home he decides to rent a movie for us all to watch together on Charlie's VCR. He stops the truck at Village Video, where Charlie picks out a Cheech and Chong movie, but when we get to Charlie's house we find that Harvey is drunk. Not even Charlie feels like hanging around there; instead he just changes his clothes and leaves with us, asking to be dropped off at the Brass Buckle.

"Where you gonna sleep tonight?" Oscar asks him.

"At the disco," Charlie says, tucking his shirt into his jeans and zipping his glossy black leather jacket as he waits in the graying light to cross the road.

When we get home, Elsie is standing in the kitchen, heating a late supper for Oscar and me. She says, "I was really scared for you guys early today, but then I heard on the news there was two hundred boats out there, so I wasn't so scared. If there's lots of fish now, you should go subsistence fishing tomorrow, and maybe Sunday too. I don't like fishing on Sunday so much, but we got to have fish."

A settling tiredness is written into the lines of Oscar's face as he takes Clayton into his arms and stretches out on the rug in front of *The Beast with Ten Thousand Eyes* on the local TV channel, making do with that instead of Cheech and Chong. Margaret lies down beside him, flipping through the pages of the *Tundra Drums,* and points out an ad in the classifieds. "Here's an ad you should run: 'Experienced fisherman with boat and complete gear wants a partner with a fishing permit.'"

Oscar nods and shuts his eyes.

6 ◎ "MAYBE SO THEY won't get hassled," Oscar proposes as we watch the *Shinmei Maru* detach itself from the dock like a piece of the town cut loose by the river. We stand on the sea wall in front of the smokehouse, where Oscar has just tied the *Crazy J,* and gaze downriver past the *Captain Adkins* and the other docked processing ships while T-shirted sailors on the freighter's deck pull in hawsers, haul up the huge anchor, and drop a line down to a tug nestled against the port side. With few salmon loaded on it yet, the ship still sits high in the water, and the dark maroon of the hull's bottom portion — a maroon the color of dried salmon — is visible above the river's lapping waters. Slowly the freighter is drawn by the tug toward a point in the channel above the midstream islands, where it will anchor for the night.

A skiff with three drunks in it weaves erratically past the ship and then slows along the sea wall opposite where we stand. The man at the wheel shouts to Oscar, "What the hell are those Chinks doing here?"

Oscar replies, "Living off you. They're your cousins."

"Shit, they ain't my cousins," the boatman growls. "This ain't their land."

Oscar waves them away and shoves his hands in his pockets, knowing that no one on the freighter is going to be living off what he did today. But the weekend was nice; he felt rich with $500 in his pocket from Friday, and even more so after visiting Swanson's Marina on Saturday morning. The mechanic there told Oscar that the Nissan had probably been overrevved when he was carrying the Evinrude, a drum of gas, and the two girls up from Kongiganak, but that the company was good about its warranties and there was a good chance the warranty would cover the expensive repairs. Out in the marina parking lot, Oscar ran his hands longingly along the gunwales of a Kofler aluminum boat with high thirty-six-inch sides and more cargo capacity than even the big Raiders that Jerry Demientieff and Tony

Watson use. "Start saving your money now," Margaret recommended.

But then he went into the nearby Bethel Power Products store and his thoughts began to run to more accessible items. He said he needed to replace his VHF antenna, and also could really use the sort of electronic fish-finder and depth sounder that Tony Watson has on his boat. Margaret said, "Go ahead, but you'll never buy that boat."

At last he didn't buy anything, only a few tickets for a Fourth of July raffle drawing for a new four-wheel-drive Isuzu pickup. "That's my truck," Oscar said, suspecting that he might be on a roll.

And that's about when things started getting screwed up again. He stopped at Charlie's, as Elsie wanted, to pick up two geese from the freezer in the porch for dinner that night. But there was only one goose left, a white-fronted goose with a salmon pink bill, so he brought a duck back with it.

"You should've brought more ducks back if there's no more geese," Elsie said curtly.

"Well, they're drinking down there," said Oscar. "I ain't going down there again."

This provoked an angry exchange that ended with Elsie saying she'd go down there herself later, when maybe they wouldn't be drinking. Both Oscar and I knew that she would be waiting quite a while for that. Not only were Charlie and Harvey hard at work on a new case of booze, we'd discovered, but they'd been joined by Buzzo and a visitor from Kwigillingok. Buzzo had laughed at Oscar when he came through the door, laughed at the transparent distaste on Oscar's face, crying, "I'm on strike! I was supposed to go down to Kipnuk yesterday, but I decided I was on strike instead."

From the bedroom Charlie's voice came ringing out: "Hey, Oscar, you better hang that fucking net!"

"I got to go subsistence fishing today! I can't do everything myself!"

"Well, you better hang that net. When's fishing again?"

"Monday. Day after tomorrow."

"You hang that net, and I'll take Harvey with me Monday. We'll use two boats, two nets, make twice as much, you know?"

"Not if you don't sober up, damn you!"

Oscar turned and stormed out, and he was hopping mad by the time we got into the truck. "Goddamn motherfucker — wants me to fish with him and then never does nothing but drink. I don't even like to be in there no more. I can't stand that smell."

At least Tony had sobered up, and he was happy to lend us his king gear when Oscar and I went subsistence fishing in the afternoon. Oscar told Tony that he might try to sober Charlie up by bringing him and all their gear over to Tony's cabin on Sunday, in order to stay the night there. Then he sighed, remembering all the orange tape that was flying around Bethel, more of it now than ever, and said, "Or maybe we'll just strike Monday. I don't know. It's getting too deadly."

We set net in the channel at the round tip of the island right opposite Tony's camp, where a strong current bellied the gear out like wind filling a sail. Overhead, the clouds were breaking up into ribbons and skeins and tattered scraps. In two drifts we caught about ninety fish, most of them chums, along with one Dolly Varden (which Oscar preferred to call a Dolly Parton), resplendent in fine scales, pearly belly, and peppermint pink flecks. He threw all the smaller chums back into the river, talking to them as though they were children while he eased them out of the mesh: "Easy, easy there — I'm not gonna hurt you." He dropped them over the side into the water, where some wriggled immediately down into the depths and some waited a moment in confusion before flicking their tails and disappearing.

Oscar still had that money in his pocket, including the money he counted on saving now with the Nissan repair, and that seemed to necessitate going right back into debt. On Monday morning we took Elsie and Margaret and the kids over to the smokehouse to do some more fish cutting, but on the way we stopped at the First National Bank for Margaret to pick up a credit application. After talking it over with his wife, Oscar had decided to sell the old Chevy pickup, which left most of its passengers exposed to the weather and most of its cargo exposed to theft, and which was rusting underneath and couldn't last much longer anyway, and buy a used Plymouth Duster that was for sale at Kuskokwim Janitorial Services for $3500. This could be managed, Margaret conceded, if they paid off what they owed on the Nissan and then took out a loan for most of the price of the Duster.

Then it was back to Charlie's for the hard part: getting the permit holder out on the water for today's commercial period and making some more money. Oscar hadn't been able to get Charlie over to Tony's yesterday, and he, Buzzo, Harvey, and the visitor were still going hard.

In the house Buzzo laughed and pointed at Charlie, saying, "We're both on strike!" He sat barefoot on the couch wearing a baseball cap with BEER HUNTER written on its crown and a frothing mug in the crosshairs of a rifle scope pictured beneath that. "All we're doing is helping those *kass'aqs* rip us off, Oscar," he went on. "A little bit of salmon in some of them restaurants, man, costs twenty bucks. Rick here told me he can't even afford to eat fish down States. They're just ripping you off, Oscar." Then he leaned back on the couch, spreading his arms out wide and laughing again. "Of course, I'd probably want to go fishing myself if I hadn't already made eighteen hundred bucks."

But Oscar wasn't to be denied, especially with that Duster in mind, and after a lot of effort he finally shoehorned Charlie — with Buzzo trailing after him — out of the house and into the truck. No sooner had we arrived at the smokehouse, however, than Charlie discovered that he'd forgotten his raincoat. I drove him back to the house, with Buzzo trailing along again. We stopped at the post office on the way for Charlie to pick up some enlargements of photographs that Harvey had taken of Curtis the year before. Then Charlie and Buzzo fetched from the house Charlie's raincoat, a flask of R&R, and a bottle of Gatorade.

By then the commercial period had already begun out on the

river, and on the truck's radio KYUK reported that the Kuskokwim was unusually quiet, with only some sixty boats in evidence from the air, and that Louie Kemp himself would be flying
into Bethel from Minnesota tonight to meet with the fishermen's
organizations. The announcer also said that Kemp-Paulucci had
offered to pay, on a retroactive basis, average Bristol Bay prices
at the end of the season for all the fish they bought, but spokes-
men for KUFMA were suspicious of getting cheated in this arrangement and noted that Bristol Bay prices already were dropping.

Charlie listened to this, nipped at the whiskey, and said, "I
don't want to go fishing today. I already gave Oscar a lot of
money. He should be satisfied."

In the end Oscar had no choice but to be satisfied. At the
smokehouse he told Charlie to start loading the boat, but instead Charlie and Buzzo went up the road to get some coffee at
a snack bar and never came back. When Oscar finally gave up
on Charlie, he looked to Chris Jacobs as his last hope. Chris has
a Kuskokwim permit of his own, and he stood near his boat at
the top of the ramp, looking out at the empty stretches of the
river but making no movement toward going out. Oscar told
him that his permit-holding brothers were on strike — "alcohol
strike" — and suggested that they go out together in the *Crazy
J.* But Chris wasn't in the mood to risk it.

As a last resort Oscar tried to sell him his pickup. "You
wanna buy that? Eight hundred bucks — or make an offer."

Somehow Elizabeth and Crazy had come into a huge supply
of the strikers' orange tape, and they were busily applying it in
strips and ribbons to the pickup's every protuberance. By now
it had begun to look something like a Chinese kite. Chris looked
at the Chevy and pursed his lips. "Well, I must have a dollar
somewhere. But that'd be tops."

An hour later an older fisherman beached his skiff in the ramp
and reported that there were a lot of fish out there and that he'd
done pretty well, selling to Kemp. He swiftly unloaded his gear
and disappeared. Whether by coincidence or not, this fisher-

man's arrival was followed shortly by that of a burly striker, a widebody almost as big as Oscar, who came walking in baggy chinos down to the smokehouse from the road. He glanced with approval at Oscar's extravagantly orange truck, but then stared hard at the skiffs lining the ramp: Oscar's, Chris Jacobs's, the old fisherman's, and one or two others.

"Some of these boats here should have holes punched in 'em, you know that?" he said.

Oscar scratched his jaw and said that that sort of thing was harassment.

"So? Nobody knows who did it. They'll learn."

At dinnertime the family loaded into the orange dragon and stopped at the sea wall in front of Swanson's on the way home. There crowds of picketers and onlookers circled Kemp's dock-side warehouse and watched from the wall as orange-streamered skiffs ran in circles around a processing ship whose bridge and decks were entirely empty. The period was coming to a close, but no boats whatsoever were approaching the processor to sell fish. When one skiff finally did appear, its pilot steering boldly through the bow waves of the strike boats, the lines along the sea wall erupted into a furious outpouring of abuse and invective. This was cut short, however, by a roar from the street in front of the warehouse, with cries to the effect that Louie Kemp was here. The picketers abandoned the sea wall and swept like a wave into the street, catching only a glimpse of a lean, bearded man ducking like a hounded celebrity into the door of the warehouse.

Now we're cleaning up to go home again, having returned after dinner for more cutting and hanging of the fish that Oscar and I caught Saturday. The *Shinmei Maru* is presently another island in the river, its decks as empty as those of Kemp's processor. The sky above the ship is rose-colored, deepening in the north into vermilion, and a punky, acrid smell hangs faintly in the air. Oscar says that a tundra fire is probably burning somewhere up toward the Yukon — one of those smoky, erratic grass fires, lit by lightning, that settles momentously into the tundra and then spreads and burns slowly, like tobacco, sometimes seeming to burn itself out, only to start again days later, in a sort of directionless and smoldering parody of the way the sloughs move through this landscape, or even the way feelings and appetites seem to erupt from nowhere sometimes.

At Elsie's apartment Oscar can't get all the money that he lost today off his mind. He calls Sam Beaver and discovers that sure, Sam went fishing today, and he made over $1000 in just two drifts of his net.

On the floor Crazy has a deck of cards spread out in a game of solitaire. Junior has decided that he wants those cards, and he whines and fusses for them, refusing to be distracted or quieted. Suddenly Oscar erupts from his seat at the table, shouting, "Shut up! Shut up! Here — give him the fucking cards!" He scoops the cards off the carpet and thrusts them savagely into Junior's hands. Then he picks up his driver's handbook and disappears into Elsie's bedroom, as Junior's whines build like a fire alarm into a thin, stabbing wail.

VI
THERE ARE NO POOR
AMONG THEM

1 ◎ IN OUR MIND'S EYE Alaska glitters with wealth. We look upon it as unpopulated, undeveloped, as at least a reasonable facsimile of the frontier that throughout American history has been the most capacious and accommodating receptacle for our dreams. Therefore we invest it with an economic potential as yet undimmed by finitude or qualification. We remember that in his time Secretary of State William Seward suffered substantial criticism for persuading Congress to spend more than $7 million for a chunk of territory christened variously in the newspapers as "Seward's Folly," "Seward's Iceberg," and "Walrussia." But today we enjoy the irony of such derision, and calculate with self-congratulation that this rich land was spirited away from Czar Alexander II for about two cents per acre.

And of course it is rich. In the 1800s and early 1900s, we had the impressive spectacles of the gold strikes on the Klondike and in Nome. More recently we had the Prudhoe Bay oil strike and, in the wake of that bonanza, the continuing novelty of a state that not only requires no income taxes from its citizens but in effect pays them for simply living there — now pays them somewhere between $800 and $1000 per capita each year as a dividend from the state's investment of its oil revenues. In the long run, baubles such as gold and oil may be only the precursors to less glamorous but even more extensive and remunerative resources. Frontiers are supposed to be rich and promising, and in this Alaska obliges us. With its romantic history and persistent remoteness, it gleams at the edge of our setting like an oyster saved as a surpassing delicacy after the rest of the entrée has been disposed of.

For better or for worse, the oyster may in fact yield such pearls someday. At least for the present, however, this gemstone image of the land ignores all that has allowed the state thus far to resist the tides of population and development and to retain, at least from a mainstream perspective, a frontier status. It ignores the fact that the high costs of production and transportation dictate that only resources of bonanza stature are developed at all, and that even with oil, a sexy commodity, recoverable reserves in excess of 500 million barrels are required to make a particular field worth drilling. As the Prudhoe field approaches its extinction — already — and as oil prices worldwide remain relatively low, many of the large and spacious houses built around Anchorage during the boom times of the late seventies and early eighties stand empty and unsold. Some have even been bought by the state at giveaway prices and shipped by barge to provide low-income housing in the Aleutians, where their plumbing will be just as ornamental as the faucet and spigots on Margaret's sink, and where their roominess will make them expensive to heat. But it may be worth something just to see them there. At least for the moment, the oil bonanza has washed out, leaving behind little more than the gold did in the way of sustained economic enterprise. Alaska has resisted another industrial assault, and another ghost town memorializes the armies that briefly waged that assault — except this time it's a ghost suburb, some of it torn loose from its city and blown all the way out to the Aleutians.

The oil bonanza was not without consequence, however, in Yupik villages such as Kongiganak. For one thing, the oil at Prudhoe Bay fueled the passage of the Alaska Native Claims Settlement Act. Congress had been promising since 1874 to deal with the land claims of Alaskan Natives, but it wasn't until the oil industry needed unclouded title to a transportation corridor through the state that the legislature finally got around to it.

With the passage of ANCSA in 1971, Alaskan Natives were conceded title in fee simple to 44 million acres, or about 11 percent
of the state, and were paid $962.5 million in compensation for
the rest. That works out to about $3 an acre, which represents
at least a healthy appreciation on what Alexander II got for the
land, even if some Alaskan Natives question the czar's role in
this in the first place. But because of the radical structure of this
settlement — all assets are assigned to the approximately two
hundred village and thirteen regional Native corporations established by ANCSA, and most of these corporations have been
beset by difficulties (only some of their own devising) during
their first two decades of operation — it has been of little or no
direct economic benefit to individual shareholders such as Oscar
and Margaret. In the early seventies, ANCSA was hailed as a
shining Native victory in Kongiganak and elsewhere; now
ANCSA seems to promise at best maintenance of the economic
status quo in rural Alaska, and at worst the utter loss of tribal
lands through corporate debt or failure.

There was more. Using the revenues generated through its lucrative lease sales and taxes on the oil companies, the state
funded such rural capital projects as the Kongiganak school,
with its comprehensive K-12 educational program; this put an
end to youngsters having to go to a boarding school in Bethel or
elsewhere in the state, or even to the Lower 48, for a high school
diploma. The state also built Safewater, a big water treatment
facility that purifies the brackish water pumped in from a nearby
lake. This provides drinking water to whoever will fetch it,
which indeed is an important resource in those times of the year
when it's too cold to collect rainwater but not cold enough to
chop clean ice from the lakes; Safewater also provides community laundry and shower facilities. The state, however, is already
finding these buildings uncomfortably expensive to maintain
and operate, and certainly there is no tax base to sustain them
in Kongiganak, where unemployment, at least in terms of the
cash economy, runs in the neighborhood of 80 percent.

The oil boom also brought the annual Alaska Permanent

Fund Dividend checks, which are certainly a wonderful windfall for the cash-poor families of the bush, helping with everything from heating oil to Christmas presents. But in terms of the way life is lived now in Kongiganak, and of the money required to support that life, and aside from its legislative consequences with ANCSA, the boom has had no revolutionary impact. There was little money in the village before the Prudhoe Bay strike and there is relatively little money in the village in its aftermath. Like the gold rushes, it was primarily a *kass'aq* phenomenon. The image of Alaska as a land of wealth continues to conceal deep shadows of poverty, at least as that term is defined in Western economic practice.

But at least southwestern Alaska has a bonanza resource of its own, rich enough in value and quantity generally to repay its production and transportation costs, providing a large portion of such cash as does circulate in the villages, and the commercial exploitation of which is at least technically consonant with Yupik economic pursuits: Pacific salmon. The abundance and reliability of this resource through the twenty centuries or so that Yupik peoples have been fishing here have provided levels of stability and comfort that might be envied by the neighboring Inuit. Edward W. Nelson observed that in the lower Yukon the salmon ran so thick that cylindrical wicker fish traps, sometimes as large as five feet in diameter and usually some ten feet long, had to be emptied by their owners several times a day in order to prevent them from literally exploding with fish. Aataq, Margaret's grandfather, says that today's salmon runs on the Kuskokwim are modest compared to the runs he witnessed in his youth, before there was any significant commercial harvest of the salmon, and if so, the volume of those runs must have challenged the imagination.

Salmon populations typically fluctuate according to a regular cycle, and some years are better than others, but at least over the past two decades salmon populations here have not demonstrably suffered from the commercial and environmental pressures brought to bear against them. The Kuskokwim is very much the poor sister of southwestern Alaska's three major salmon fisheries; both Yukon and Bristol Bay fish are oilier and considered to be of better quality, while the volume of fish harvested in Bristol Bay exceeds that of either riverine fishery by a factor of twenty to thirty. Nonetheless, the annual value of the Kuskokwim commercial harvest has climbed exponentially from $92,000 in 1961, to slightly over $1 million in 1976, to $4.2 million in 1984, and to a record $12 million in 1988.

Here the hordes advance under the cover of silt, and you never see the fish unless they're netted or hooked. But once, in a clear-running tributary to the Susitna River in central Alaska (actually no more than a creek), I saw a salmon run that was much more modest but no less impressive. Nudging and jostling against the slim span of the creek and also against one another, the fish ran as thick as corpuscles through an artery. In the water their backs looked green, and they worked tirelessly against the backward cut of the current, slowly defeating it, oblivious to all but the mortal scent of their own nativity, lust, and death, as unanimous and unswervable as fate. Maybe it was simply the irresistible nature of that movement, when and where it could be seen, that declared to the Yupik mind that the *yuat* of salmon needed little in the way of ritual assistance or appeasement in making their runs up the rivers.

But it's been only within the past two decades that dollars and salmon have really had much to do with each other in the delta. The southwest's first salmon cannery was built by the Arctic Fishing Company at Nushagak in 1884, the same year that Hartmann and Weinland visited there, and some commercial fishing was done on the Kuskokwim as early as 1913. But these were hardly an indication of what was to come in the 1960s, when, in the decade following statehood, the confluence of an increasing international demand for salmon, a growing Yupik reliance on industrial items not easily secured through barter but available only for cash, and the state's own interest in developing and managing the industry brought about investment, expansion, and then, almost overnight, the appearance of a major cash enterprise in the delta.

The nascent commercial fishing industry, however, wasn't greeted with universal enthusiasm on the Kuskokwim. Some feared — and still fear — that commercial demand and the enticements of profit might destroy even such enormous stocks of salmon as these, just as New England and Canadian fishermen were witnessing the decline and collapse of the legendary Georges Bank's huge stocks of haddock and cod, and just as government revenue cutters had been required to keep the canneries at Nushagak from using set nets to close off the mouths of spawning streams entirely. Here, since salmon were still the linchpin of the delta's ancient subsistence economy, the consequences of such a loss would be more than mere economic displacement; it would bring an abrupt cultural disintegration and a sort of poverty that answered to either definition of the term, Western or Yupik.

But for a couple of reasons commercial fishing has not yet posed any threat to the subsistence variety. First, though there are now more Yupik people living along the Kuskokwim than in the sixties, the subsistence demand for salmon is not as high as it used to be. Partly this represents some dietary incursion by Western foods, but more significant is the abandonment of dog teams. The cash that came in with the fishing industry allowed people to buy snow machines, and they found that in the long run it was both cheaper and easier to come up with enough gas to fuel a snow machine through the winter than with enough salmon to fuel a dog team. In fact, the bulk of a family's annual salmon harvest traditionally went to its dog team. Now, usually, only those families with the interest, leisure, and money necessary for competitive racing — which is to say, very few Alaskan Native families — keep dog teams, and the annual subsistence salmon needs of an ordinary family can often be met by two or three weeks' fishing outside the designated commercial periods.

Second, the state took an early interest in the sustained viability of all of its commercial fisheries, and in its management of the southwestern fisheries has so far provided for enough fish to escape annually to maintain a stable resource base. The way in which it has accomplished this, however, has been of enormous, and possibly tragic, import to Alaskan Native fishermen. At first it limited only the efficiency of the individual commercial fisherman, by placing restrictions on such things as the kind of gear he might use, the size of his boat, and the time that he's allowed to have his gear in the water. But following an early scare (several years of such poor salmon returns in Bristol Bay and other fisheries that they constituted an economic crisis), the state decided in 1972 to limit the number of fishermen, instituting in all its salmon fisheries a system of limited entry, so that selling salmon for commercial profit is a privilege allowed only to those holding current state permits. Although the Alaska constitution specifically states that fish and wildlife are common property of all citizens — a concept very dissonant, incidentally, with Yupik attitudes, which wouldn't presume to view wild animals as property, and a concept that also lies at the crux of the state's discomfiture in providing any special protection to Native economies — it was amended that year to allow limited entry in the commercial salmon fisheries.

By 1974 the state had completed issuing permits and the system was largely in place, though not without controversy. And controversy still lingers. Limited entry has thus far survived about two hundred suits filed against it in state and federal courts, and also a 1976 state referendum. But from the state's point of view it has been eminently successful: it enjoys general political support throughout the state as a whole; its implementation has been accompanied by a dramatic recovery of salmon stocks since the early seventies — the number of fish annually harvested in Bristol Bay, for example, climbed from 8 million in 1976 to 28 million in 1980; and at least in some places it has solved an old problem endemic to open-access fisheries, namely, slim profits or none and low economic status for the individual fisherman.

One place where this problem has been dramatically solved is in Bristol Bay. Limited-entry permits are transferable at any time, and the best barometer to the sort of money people stand to make in a particular salmon fishery is the current market value of that fishery's permits. In 1975 the price of a Bristol Bay drift gill-net permit was typically a little more than $1000. By 1979, however, such a permit was worth nearly $70,000, and today its value is probably in the neighborhood of $300,000. I've been told that even that isn't so steep, since the permit can pay for itself in only two or three good seasons. Bristol Bay is as much a Yupik place as the Yukon-Kuskokwim Delta, but bonanza money like this — along with the limited-entry system itself — has had a profound effect on the character of its commercial fishing fleet. Some believe the events in Bristol Bay are ominously instructive as to what is happening now even on the Kuskokwim, and now even between brothers. I'm tempted to apply these events more widely: to the worm in the apple of the Alaska Native Claims Settlement Act, and to the general effect — an effect rather like sprinkling salt on soap bubbles — of introducing cash in the first place into systems of exchange and modes of living not designed to rely on cash.

Interestingly enough, Oscar and all his brothers first learned to fish on Bristol Bay, not the Kuskokwim. Their father, James, traveled regularly down there to fish in the sixties and early seventies, and in 1974 he was one of the slightly more than 1700 fishermen awarded Bristol Bay permits by the state. I find this surprising, knowing James. I first met him one afternoon in Bethel after he'd ridden his snow machine into town from Kasigluk and turned up for lunch at Elsie's, on a day when Charlie and Oscar and I were expected as well. The old man sat at Elsie's table like a carnival automaton, a smile frozen on his long white face and his eyes lit with internal fires. His lips seemed to be working of their own accord, thickly dispensing a stream of "Fuck you's" and "Young farts" to his family and me. Elsie paid

him no mind whatsoever, bustling about her kitchen as though
he were an apparition visible only to our eyes, and his sons just
snickered. Afterward, outside in the thin March sunlight, Oscar
found two bottles of whiskey hidden away in James's sled. The
old man staggered out to the porch and stood swaying and grinning and cursing as Oscar opened both bottles and poured them
into the snow.

In Kasigluk last month Oscar stood uneasily by the door of
James's house and listened to the story of his escape from Anchorage, his discovery of the lost ticket. Oscar's face even then,
covered in confusion, reminded me that I can't simplify this escape artist into a hapless drunk. James was, after all, one of the
relatively few Alaskan Natives who were stubborn and insistent
enough to get one of those Bristol Bay permits in the first place,
even though the design of the system appeared to protect the
interests of local — that is to say, Yupik — fishermen foremost.
The state's Limited Entry Commission set up a point system for
determining who was most deserving, and in this it gave greatest
weight to such factors as the number of years an applicant had
fished in a fishery such as Bristol Bay, how much cash that person had invested in fishing, how much that person depended
on fishing for cash employment, and the degree to which he or
she had alternative employment available in another industry.
This seemed propitious for the locals. Fishermen from Bristol
Bay and the delta maybe didn't have as much money invested
in boats and gear as *kass'aq* fishermen from the Lower 48 or
elsewhere in Alaska, but presumably they had a long presence
in the fishery, depended on it almost exclusively for cash income, and certainly had little in the way of other industries to
turn to.

But it was really more complicated than that. Within these
criteria, heaviest point value was assigned for presence in and
dependence on the fishery during the years immediately preceding the application, 1971 and 1972, and particularly for having
fished at least three weeks per season during those years. However, 1971 and 1972 were precisely those years whose poor re-

turns prompted limited entry in the first place, and Yupik fishermen, with their long experience, were probably less surprised
than others, since those years were at the bottom end of a red
salmon cycle that peaks every fifth year in Bristol Bay. Rather
than fish empty waters, many local fishermen from the very first
looked for whatever alternate seasonal employment they could
find, such as firefighting or construction work, or simply concentrated more of their gas and time either in subsistence activities
or in fishing just during the peak ten days or so of the commercial salmon season. But with the point system set up as it was,
Native fishermen who elected not to depend on commercial
salmon income for those years or who elected to fish only during
the short peaks of the runs were later denied a permit.

Other factors as well militated against men who had fished
their entire lives in Bristol Bay. The Limited Entry Commission
defined documented participation in the fishery as holding a license to fish — and in that respect being a boat captain — during the years immediately preceding. But unlike *kass'aq* fishermen, Bristol Bay and delta fishermen rarely entertain formal
captain-crewman relationships. Instead they generally fish in
equal partnerships, as Oscar and Charlie did at Cape Avinof,
and it has never been a matter of much concern as to which
partner holds a license and is the official boat captain, so long
as one of them does. Unfortunately, those who did not hold
licenses themselves in those crucial two years subsequently
found themselves unable to document their participation in the
fishery, and for that reason were also denied a permit. In these
respects the application process in fact ended up selecting
strongly in favor of those professional fishermen, very often
from California, Oregon, and Washington, who were bound to
come to the bay every year, to fish in its waters through the full
extent of the commercial season, and to do so in a formal captain's capacity. Those whose circumstances forced them to be
more opportunistic and diverse than that, and also less formal,
were often excluded from an activity they had considered a
birthright until 1974.

Finally, there was the bureaucratic nature of the process itself, and the complexity of the application. In its original form the application was seven pages long and accompanied by forty-one pages of instructions. In general, the men of James Active's generation had neither the education nor the English-language skills to understand such a document. While the state did provide counselors to help in filling out the applications, many Yupik fishermen found these outsiders from Anchorage or Juneau almost as unfathomable as the form itself, and I'm sure many of the counselors had trouble understanding the fishermen. In any event, many of those who applied ended up distrusting both the counselors' competence and their motives. Eventually, one of those two hundred suits brought against the Limited Entry Commission was filed by Alaska Legal Services on the grounds that the application assistance did not legitimately speak to the needs of local rural fishermen.

In the end, of the 1700 permits awarded, a little less than 700 fell directly into Bristol Bay hands. The rest went to those largely non-Native fishermen who best answered to the application process's implicit assumptions about what a fisherman properly does. I'm surprised that the hard-drinking James Active — and the practical-minded James Active, one and the same — should have put in enough time on the water during those lean years to impress the Limited Entry Commission, though maybe this was a paternal strain of the same clenched-teeth obstinacy that kept us out on the water at Cape Avinof until the tide and the daylight finally ran out beneath us and the processors started running out as well. I'm also surprised that James's application found its way into the commission's offices in time, and properly filled out, but James is a good English speaker who knows his way around *kass'aqs,* and perhaps this is one example of counseling at work.

Be that as it may, Oscar's father was one of the elect in 1974, allowed to run an old wooden gill-netter — which Oscar had to repaint every year, and whose skeletal frame now lies crumbling in the grass across the street from John's house — out among those well-equipped boats from the Pacific coast and the Panhandle and south-central Alaska, and pull in netloads of money from among those fish returning from God-knows-where and running in their ranks of God-knows-how-many up into the Aleutian Range, the Ahklun Mountains, and the Kilbuck Mountains. But only for a few years — James eventually sold his permit for $10,000, and in so doing became one of the unhappy statistics in a 1984 report by the Alaska Commercial Fisheries Entry Commission. That report indicates a 21.3 percent drop in Native ownership of fishing permits in Bristol Bay between 1975 and 1983 (certainly this drop has accelerated since then) and a 13.8 percent drop in Native ownership statewide in all commercial salmon fisheries.

So the slim have become slimmer. But this at least is understandable, and I don't think it's simply a matter of bankrolled *kass'aqs* throwing a one-time windfall at straitened Native fishermen with cash-flow problems, though there is some truth to that. Cash flow is part of it, and most permits are indeed sold in the winter, when there isn't any firefighting or construction work, when cash flow has more or less frozen solid. Also, the enticement of a big score, or a seemingly infinite supply of whiskey, has to be part of it as well.

But ultimately, I suspect, the problem of Native permit alienation has dimensions more fundamental than these. Although in certain respects the cash and subsistence economies seem to complement each other, especially since commercial fishing — or working as a secretary in the village school, for that matter — helps to pay for the gear used for subsistence food-gathering, the two economies are in fact deeply inimical, and maybe salmon and cash in particular, more than labor and cash, form an uneasy and volatile mix in the Yupik psyche. If so, it makes me queasy sometimes just to imagine it, particularly in limited-entry fisheries, where the mere right to fish for money has itself become a substantial unit of individual wealth. I have to suppose that for someone like Oscar, who has moved to Kongiganak to position himself more squarely within Yupik tradition, the simple act of being out in a boat during a commercial period must be something like straddling two running horses, a foot strapped fast to the back of each, knowing all the while that each horse has its own idea about exactly where it should be taking you.

Aataq, who never fished commercially or held a regular job, remembers a much simpler time, and it gives one pause to consider that the delta's cash economy is younger than that man, and younger even than Oscar — is really no more ancient than snow machines and statehood and yesterday's blossoming of the commercial fisheries. You might argue that cash established a beachhead in the mid-1800s with the international market for furs that first brought the Russians in force to Alaska — a market that subsequently brought more Western goods into the delta villages, though items such as tea and tobacco and metal goods had been known for at least a century already through indigenous trading networks. But during the time of the Russians, cash itself was of no use whatsoever in the delta. Yupik Eskimos traded with the Russians as they did with the Inuit or Athabascans or anyone else, by barter, and if there was any one thing that approached the status of a universal medium of exchange, it would have to have been dried salmon.

Lieutenant Zagoskin describes an incident along the Yukon in which an old woman who needed a good hatchet offered to pay him on the following day twenty dried salmon, or twice the customary price, for an Aleut hatchet he had in his possession. "I had become acquainted with the native character, and wishing to test her word, I granted her request," Zagoskin says. The next morning, however, he decided that he didn't have time to land at her camp and that the hatchet therefore would have to be a gift. But the old woman was watching for him, and as the explorer's party floated past she first rushed to a promontory with the promised salmon and then climbed into a canoe with the intent of pursuing them. Finally, "a friendly 'chikikha' ('I give it to you') stopped her."

The dollar bill didn't establish a beachhead until eighty years later. Then, with the boom in fur prices that occurred after World War I, some delta residents (but not really a great many) were content to specialize as trappers and work for cash. And the cash they earned was of nearly bonanza proportions; a single prime red fox pelt, for example, might fetch the modern cash equivalent of $500. Some Eskimo trappers would run lines that extended a hundred miles, take a week to travel from end to end by dog team, and earn in a year as much as $40,000 in today's currency. It was also during this time that the first stores and outboard motors began appearing in the villages.

But in the 1930s the bottom dropped out of the fur market, depressing the price of fox pelts to $25 in modern cash — another boom, another bust, this time with the irony that the formerly rich trappers often found themselves to be poor and unskilled hunters upon their re-entry into the subsistence economy. For the next three decades the time-honored system of barter, supplemented by a system of credit that had evolved with Zagoskin and the Russians, once again prevailed along the Kuskokwim. Money orders and IOUs would grow as grimy and wrinkled as worn-out silver certificates as they passed from hand to hand, and when some storekeepers in Bethel began showing Charlie Chaplin movies, the price of admission was frequently a single dried salmon or a sheaf of the rye grass that women collected for insulating boots or weaving baskets and mats. Elsie remembers that one storekeeper kept a mink, and admission to his movies could be obtained just by cutting some fresh grass for his mink — "But sometimes girls like us were lazy or we didn't have no time, you know, and so we just steal those bundles that the old women collect to dry."

This sort of bartering for Western goods and services was not finally quenched until the fishing money washed in, and until an accompanying surge in the delta's *kass'aq* population took place. But a good many Kuskokwim fishermen found themselves actually perplexed by these new earnings. In Mary Lenz and

James H. Barker's centennial history of Bethel, an anonymous resident recalls:

> When commercial fishing come on, we all thought it would be such a help. But the first couple of years of commercial fishing, when it came time to subsistence fish, many people were drinking. When winter came, they didn't have any tangible benefit from the money, and they didn't have the fish either. There were so many temptations associated with having cash for people who had never had it before. We saw the same thing among non-Natives — the loggers and miners and fishermen and trappers who would come in after a season and party. Money was looked on as something extraneous.

But of course the money wasn't at all extraneous. Firearms and motors and twine nets and textiles and fossil fuels and other goods had long since ceased to be luxury or convenience items; they performed so successfully that they had largely extinguished the Native technologies that preceded them, and suddenly they were becoming increasingly expensive, and appearing in important new refinements such as snow machines. No longer were they available from storekeepers for dried fish or other barter goods.

Given these needs and circumstances, how to dispose of a season's fishing earnings might generally be a fairly plain matter for a *kass'aq,* but for sound enough reasons it was a puzzle for a Yupik fisherman, and continues to be so. In that fisherman's thinking, the goals, values, and strictures of the subsistence economy are more fundamental than those of the cash economy, and in certain respects are in direct opposition. The subsistence economy, in fact, expresses little interest in the private accumulation of money or goods, which in the cash economy is the common denominator of status and success. Instead, individual prestige has more to do with its opposite, sharing, and the resulting accumulation of obligation. In other words, a rich man is he who has at his disposal those ties among individuals and families that support social cooperation, whether it be in hunting, building a new house, or settling a particular matter in village politics. This cooperation is in effect purchased by the disbursement of either food or goods through customary networks of relatives and companions, and occasionally even of strangers. This might occur informally, in an invitation to come pick up some fresh salmon or some herring eggs, for example, or formally, through the gift of new cotton work gloves to all the men who come to visit a house during ritual Russian Orthodox Christmas celebrations.

In pre-Christian days such disbursements took place on a huge scale between villages during winter religious festivals, and Zagoskin was much impressed by how speedily and joyfully the people got rid of whatever a Russian might consider profit.

> There are no poor among them: the wealthy use their possessions for the common good. After a successful transaction that brings them profit, their one ambition is to expend all they have collected in a celebration to honour the dead. Not one or two men, but a whole village, when they have expended all their supplies in one way or another — on games, evening parties, trading — in short, when they have failed to save anything, moves to the nearest village in the conviction that as long as there is food there, their neighbors will share it with them.

Observers at a three-day festival at Napaskiak in 1887 reported the distribution among six hundred people of some three thousand pounds of frozen fish; eighty gallons of *akutaq,* a whipped confection of animal fat and berries; an unnumbered quantity of dried salmon; and dozens and dozens of goods such as grass baskets, fishskin boots, seal-gut rain parkas, grass socks, wooden buckets, loonskin bathing caps, carved ladles, and tin dippers. Himself a careful trader, Zagoskin didn't wholly approve of this behavior, but he admired the wonderful scope of its generosity.

John Kilbuck also admired this generosity, though he eventually condemned it for its religious dimensions. Other Moravian missionaries, extolling thrift and providence, sometimes saw the just hand of God at work whenever such orgies were followed in the spring by hunger or famine. And in the habits of those missionaries who came to live in villages such as Kwigillingok and Quinhagak, villagers saw early applications of an entirely different economic philosophy. In Kwigillingok, Ferdinand Drebert was disturbed by the manner in which people freely partook of the mission rain barrel and woodpile, as he wrote in his memoirs.

> In accordance with their Eskimo philosophy and customs, no one ever lived to himself or hoarded anything. If one had more than the others, he was supposed to share with them, so they did not see why we should have a supply of water on hand to last for weeks and months when they had none. So it was with the woodpile too. . . . We had to convince them that with our mode of living we needed more water and wood than they did. We had to show that it cost the mission a lot of money to have our wood hauled down and we could not afford to give it away or have it stolen.

Although the impulse to share (like the impulse to hoard) can yield to excessive zeal when its reward is prestige or recognition, this Yupik disbursement of profit was not so blindly improvident as some observers believed. John Kilbuck understood, writing:

> Those who do not fully comprehend the conditions prevailing among primitive people often charge improvidence because in seasons of plenty — provision for lean years is not made — as the Egyptians did under Joseph's direction. The two different characteristic kinds of food are lost sight of — fish and grain. Grain, without trouble can be kept for an indefinite time but fish or meats without the modern arts is like the manna of which the Children of Israel could only gather 24 hours' supply, and whatever was over and above this amount was waste. Primitive methods of meat preservation was good for only a year and any remaining over this time was spoiled even for the Eskimos.

Also, while not exactly nomadic, Yupik families often moved to various seasonal camps in the course of a summer, and any more than was necessary in the way of personal goods or preserved foods was burdensome. Possibly even more significant was, and is, the central character of subsistence food-gathering as essentially a cooperative — as opposed to competitive — endeavor. Industrial items have made the solitary hunter more of an economic plausibility now, but still, birds and seals and moose are harvested more efficiently and more safely in partnerships or groups. In this respect the donation of a cut of fresh moose meat to cement a partnership or incur an obligation is more practical than trying to hoard that meat, especially when censure still accrues to those who hoard and status to those who share.

The character of this sharing is also a little different from the sort of quid pro quo implicit in kass'aq sharing. To the Yupik mind, the most important thing is simply the recognition that some sort of exchange has taken place; whether the person who receives the gift responds with a gift of his own, or whether the two are bartering, or whether some other sort of "payment" is subsequently rendered, is generally immaterial. A simultaneous or reciprocal exchange wouldn't cancel obligation, as it does in the cash economy, but rather would aim it in two directions at once. This may have had something to do with that old woman's fierce determination to attend to what Zagoskin viewed as a debt but what she saw as an obligation. The language itself is unconcerned with Western distinctions between a gift and a sale; the essential obligation exists in either case in Yupik exchanges. So the terms tun'uq and navertuq express synonymously the English concepts of selling an item, trading it, and simply giving it away.

Above all, however, the most powerful impetus to share can still be found in the enduring spiritual dimension of the act. It ties directly into the Yupik conviction that the objects of the hunt have given of themselves freely and that that which has come freely must be given away freely in order to ensure its later return. So while Western culture preaches that there is no such thing as a free lunch, Yupik belief maintains that a free lunch is the only imaginable kind. I remember the Kongiganak elder Adolph Jimmie telling cautionary tales of the times when hostilities between villages sometimes made it dangerous to hunt. Eventually, particularly in the lean days of spring, the old man said, some individuals would pretend to have run out of food rather than share their remaining store. Naturally an offense of this sort against the animals who had given of themselves resulted in difficult hunting during later periods of peace or abundance.

And naturally the spiritual aspect of this mandate applied nearly as much to goods as to food, since goods were generally manufactured from animal products. In the end, this ideally unimpeded cycling of foods and goods between the households of a village, and at intervals between villages themselves, ran as the flywheel of the cycling of animals' *yuat* between this world and the next. How could there truly be any need, then, for hoarding or accumulating such capital, when it was certain to be delivered into your hands again next year?

If cash, however, replaces or becomes attached to the elements of such capital — and, quite dramatically, if a fisherman comes home with cash rather than the actual salmon, the staple item of Yupik diet and personal exchanges — then this simultaneous cycling of goods and *yuat* is confused and finally blocked, because money, after all, has no *yua*. Instead it is inanimate. *Kass'aqs* have defined its use, and by definition cash doesn't come freely. Rather, it is something to be won in an adversarial contest with other men or businesses, or in contest with the animals that Western culture and the Alaska constitution define as property, or in contest with the earth, which is similarly defined as property and therefore something always to be strenuously transformed. Giving cash away in no way guarantees its return — quite the reverse, by Western lights.

Cash, moreover, has always been used to cancel obligation rather than establish it. In keeping with this characteristic, cash is entirely abstract and anonymous, lacking any implication of a personal or spiritual relationship between the persons and elements involved in the exchange, lacking even the personal signatures on the money orders and IOUs once passed from hand to hand in Bethel. However, it can be easily carried, doesn't tend to spoil, and lends itself to concealment and hoarding. It could hardly be otherwise that Ferdinand Drebert and indeed all succeeding *kass'aqs* would appear to be grasping and stingy to their Yupik neighbors. Even today some elders simply can't guess at the full extent of this pathology, and are genuinely surprised on their first visit to Anchorage to discover that one actually has to pay for food there, that one may not knock on a stranger's door and expect to be freely and comfortably fed. Rather than drawing people together into a spiritually charged network of interdependence, cash keeps people at a distance and discourages the easy initiation of social relationship.

Even in Western culture, gifts of cash between relatives and friends are considered impersonal and are used as something of a last resort. But as an item of gift exchange between Yupik households, cash, in its soullessness and lack of cultural meaning, is simply impossible. What, then, of items that are bought for cash? The salmon that swims into a fisherman's net may be conceived as having given itself freely, but the money given in exchange for this salmon has nothing to do with this morality, nor, in turn, does the rifle or snow machine or electronic fishfinder or Plymouth Duster procured in exchange for the money. Cash instead short-circuits the cycles of exchange, encouraging the private accumulation of goods such as these and also encouraging status hierarchies based on their accumulation. It blunts and confuses the primary Yupik impetus to share, and implicitly robs the fish and any other creature sold for money of their *yuat*. This transforms them indeed into mere property, and also short-circuits the cycling of their souls.

Although some small store-bought items are being incorporated now into Yupik gift exchanges — the candy and yarn and soap and so forth thrown at seal parties, or the gloves or face towels or combs distributed to visitants at the Russian Orthodox Christmas, or even just a box of stuffing mix brought to a neighbor's birthday party — these function solely as social gestures, not simultaneously as gestures of thanksgiving. Nor do such gifts convey much of the power and status that once earned the messengers who invited one village over to another to feast and receive gifts the ironic sobriquet of *curukat,* or attackers. In fact, I can think of only one class of goods available for cash whose giving seems to convey, at least in some circles, some semblance of the prestige that might attend, say, the gift of a choice portion of bearded seal — maybe because these goods are expensive and can be difficult and even dangerous to obtain, and their consumption, even in atomistic Western culture, is modeled strongly on communal lines: alcohol and other drugs. It probably helps that among the effects of these drugs is at least a temporary abeyance of contradiction and anxiety.

But just the same, cash is now necessary. The men and women of Aataq's generation, who hardly guessed its uses and who know the secrets of sinew-backed bows and fishskin boots and willow-bark nets, are disappearing in droves. Sometimes more cash than a season can provide is necessary, even a season in Bristol Bay, and sometimes permits get sold for cash, often at lower than market prices. In general Native fishermen tend to devalue their permits, partly because their earnings are customarily lower than those of outsiders, who fish in bigger and more capacious boats that can also work in heavier weather than open skiffs, and partly because they are temperamentally uncomfortable with the adversarial process of driving a hard bargain and thus appearing grasping and stingy. James Active probably undersold his permit, but the money is gone now anyway, and would still be gone even if he sold it at five times the price he got. Today Oscar and Charlie and Buzzo and Hippa take note of the prices that Bristol Bay permits command and of the impressive earnings of those who have hung on to theirs — Moses

Strauss, for example, Charlie's former father-in-law, who began his cable TV franchise in Kongiganak with money from Bristol Bay — and the sale of that permit turns slowly in their guts like the loss of an ancestral kingdom.

But James's sons can't afford too much righteous anger. Applications for Bristol Bay permits were so numerous that the commission awarded no more than one per family, but this wasn't the case with the much less lucrative Kuskokwim fishery, where all four natural sons were awarded permits. At some point Hippa sold his Kuskokwim permit, though, and in 1977 Oscar sold his to that woman from Anchorage. Margaret, who wanted him to keep the permit, remembers how he pestered her for advice before he sold it, and then argued against her when she offered advice, so that finally she threw up her hands and told him to do whatever he wanted with it. Now his commercial fishing depends on the grace of those brothers who still have their Kuskokwim permits, and any less than two permits between the four of them would be hard to accommodate peacefully. Oscar worries about the long-term prospects of Charlie's permit, fearing that Charlie will sell it, or even if he doesn't, that the possibility that Charlie hasn't filed tax returns for the past few years means the IRS will seize it; and obviously, the powerlessness and vulnerability of his position in this and other respects is galling to him.

This points to another atomizing effect of these commercial salmon fisheries. Just as the soullessness and anonymity of cash and store-bought goods erect certain barriers between households, so the nature of the limited-entry permits as purely individual units of wealth erects certain barriers within households and families. Traditionally, matters of inheritance and the disposition of wealth were never of great concern; when someone died, such clothes or utensils as he or she might own were customarily either burned or left at the gravesite. It's true that a certain hunting or fishing spot might be thought of as exclusive to a particular hunter, and inheritable, but a place to fish is easily shared among an individual's descendants.

A limited-entry fishing permit, however, bears one name only. If James Active still owned his Bristol Bay permit, and if he were to pass away, to whom would that considerable unit of wealth devolve? His oldest son, John, the adopted one, who is less interested in fishing than the four other brothers? Buzzo, the oldest of James's natural sons? Another son? No matter who ended up with the permit, it would create a sense of privilege that has no traditional counterpart and would inevitably seem arbitrary and unjust. In just this way Jacob and Esau waged a destructive rivalry over Isaac's blessing. Maybe apprehensions such as this even influenced James's decision to sell the permit and be done with it, and maybe the whole philosophical antipathy between fish and money prompts the sale of permits in some cases (though these are just speculations on my part).

But certainly the familiar relationships of fathers to sons and brothers to brothers are being warped and distorted under the pressures of limited entry. And certainly the indivisibility of the permits — and this is perplexing too, because a fish is almost infinitely divisible — is slowly bringing into existence along the Kuskokwim an entire social class whose members are already numerous at Bristol Bay: young men (and sometimes women) who a generation ago would have been fishing equally with their parents and peers, but who, as members of this generation, have neither a commercial permit nor any real prospect of ever owning one — men whose families sold their permits, men whose families have lost their permits as collateral on bad boat loans, men whose families applied for a permit and were denied, men whose families failed to apply, and men simply not chosen as the permit holders from among their relatively numerous siblings. Almost an entire generation is finding itself at odds with its privileged few and generally excluded from a fishery once considered an ancestral birthright. Like Oscar here on the Kuskokwim, these men have little other recourse in the way of necessary cash employment, and a desperate mood is building among the villages around Bristol Bay as a higher and higher proportion of gill-netters and trawlers from the Lower 48 dis-

place their own boats in the summer. The state has initiated a
loan program whose avowed purpose is to help rural fishermen
buy such permits as are offered for sale, but again the application is complex, and it requires collateral and information that
are hard for such fishermen to provide. Many of those who have
successfully won such loans thus far have been urban fishermen
from elsewhere in Alaska.

Although pressures such as these do not exist just yet along
the more marginal Kuskokwim fishery, they are only a generation removed as Oscar's peers wrestle with the problem of which
of their offspring will enjoy privileged commercial status, and
also, in all probability, as an increase in both village populations
and international demand brings about what critics of the commercial fishery feared in the first place: a contest for ever bigger
bites of the resource between commercial and subsistence fishermen.

Thomas R. Berger sees in the manner in which these limited-
entry permits tend to slip away from Native hands a rehearsal
for the probable behavior of the shares of Native corporations,
if they ever become eligible to enter the open market. Berger is
the Canadian jurist who presided over the Alaskan Native Review Commission, a body established by the Inuit Circumpolar
Conference in 1983 to investigate both the current and potential
impact of ANCSA. Whereas the sale of either a fishing permit or
corporate stock by a white man is a morally neutral act consis-
tent with the motions of his economy, Berger recognizes, the sale
of either by an Alaskan Native has potentially profound — and
dispiriting — moral consequences.

> To dismiss the sale of these permits and the sale of shares in
> the Native corporations as a matter of personal choice will not
> do. Permits and shares alike represent the division of what the
> Native peoples have always regarded as a common resource
> into distinct units of individual wealth; these units are passing
> from Natives to non-Natives. The experience with limited-en-
> try permits suggests that shares in the village and regional cor-
> porations will be sold when it becomes possible to alienate

stock freely at the end of 1991. As with limited-entry commercial fishing permits, shareholders who sell their stock after 1991 will be making a choice that must affect all of their descendants.

Currently, individual shareholders in the Native corporations are not allowed to sell their stock. According to the terms of the settlement, this restriction was scheduled to be lifted automatically on December 18, 1991, the twentieth anniversary of the law's enactment. But the Anchorage-based Alaska Federation of Natives (AFN), which negotiated ANCSA in the first place, has recently steered a set of amendments to the settlement through Congress. One of them would allow a Native corporation, through a majority vote of its shareholders, to keep present restrictions against the sale of stock in place. Thanks in part to the impressive example of these limited-entry salmon permits, most Native corporations almost certainly will vote to do that.

And just as limited entry has made the right to fish into a discrete and individual unit of wealth, creating a class excluded from that wealth, so ANCSA has made being Native into a discrete and individual unit of wealth, creating a class excluded from that. This sort of exclusion results from the fact that only Alaskan Natives born prior to the date of enactment in 1971 were issued stock. The corporations' lists of shareholders are the closest things Alaskan Natives have to formal tribal enrollments, but none of the "afterborns" — including all of Oscar's children — will find their names on these lists. Multiple shares of stock are at least more divisible through inheritance or other means than a single limited-entry permit, but at present the afterborns have no guarantees, and are lost if such stock is alienated; they have no corporate voting rights, they may not directly receive corporate dividends, and therefore they enjoy no proprietary relationship whatsoever to corporate lands.

Since the congressional amendments, this too may be remedied. In 1991 a Native corporation could vote to issue additional shares to its afterborns, and to keep doing so with each new birth. This, and a continuation of the restriction on the sale of stock, will help to keep lands and shares securely in Native hands and will ensure a continual distribution of those assets, in smaller and smaller bits, throughout Native communities. The price will be the ability of the corporations to operate in the marketplace as full-fledged business entities, and the original promise of ANCSA as a means of generating necessary cash while sheltering Native subsistence economies.

The problem with ANCSA is precisely what made it so attractive and exciting during the boom times of the sixties: its provision of a ready-made path, a sort of golden road, into a reserved parking place on Wall Street. Instead of those dangerous cash transactions taking place on the Kuskokwim, as they did for at least a while with Lieutenant Zagoskin's furs, Edward W. Nelson's trivia, John Kilbuck's sawmill, Sheldon Jackson's reindeer, they could take place in carpeted offices far away in Anchorage. All that the hunters and fishermen would have to do would be to pick up their dividend checks from the corporations' capital investments elsewhere in Alaska, or the Lower 48, or other countries. But cash is like grain, not manna. There is no limit on its accumulation, no imperative within it to share, and just the touch of it causes that gossamer web that once tied everyone and everything into a single symmetrical design, each strand reinforcing the next, to split, unravel, and collapse. Not even Anchorage — where Calista, the Yupik regional corporation, has put its offices — has been far enough away. All the AFN's amendments have been stop-gap efforts to splice some of those strands back together and still have the web support the lead weight of the settlement.

Out in the rivers and bays the salmon are still running in their eye-popping numbers, and on the Kuskokwim maybe all the more so now, with this strike. Right now nearly everybody is just sitting on the sea wall, but as soon as the strike is squared away, the fishermen will again segregate themselves into permit holders, the helpers of permit holders, and those who have no place out there during the commercial periods, strike or no strike. Oscar still thinks of himself as just a fisherman, and he conceives of his fate in terms of that. "I was born a fisherman," he told me once. "I wish I was born a banker or a lawyer, but I wasn't. I'm glad I wasn't born a doctor — they get sued too much."

It must be hard for a fisherman to sit out a season, or a lifetime, to see the waters of a river or a bay just boil with fish and realize that there isn't enough of that bonanza for everybody, that old-fashioned sharing won't do anymore. But here in the unpopulated bush it's also hard to appreciate just how large a concept this "everybody" has become. As much as Yupik elders are surprised to have to pay for their food and lodging in Anchorage, they're at least equally surprised, despite all that they've heard, by the city's unimagined numbers and concentrations of people — almost ten times as many as inhabit the entire sprawl of the delta.

These urban dwellers are all full-time members of the cash economy, and a concept even more arresting than the prodigious scope of all their various needs is something hardly to be guessed at by the old men and women who little know the uses of cash: the infinite extent of their desires.

2 ◉ WELL, THINGS ARE looking up. Oscar has been out in the apartment parking lot, lovingly topping up the oil and the fluids in the steel-blue '85 Plymouth Duster he bought yesterday, and cheered by rumors that the strike is about to end. There's even a rumor that Fish & Game is considering an emergency commercial period tomorrow in order to allow fishermen to catch up. Oscar is also happy to see Hippa, who came in from the fish camp with Emma

and the kids to do some shopping. Hippa, who is sitting inside Elsie's apartment with his son Mumford, happily wearing one of the green woolen vests Elsie knitted for her three married sons for Father's Day, says he intends to take Buzzo back to camp with him in order to dry him out. "Maybe Charlie will dry out now too," Oscar proposes.

This morning at Charlie's house only Harvey was awake, his eyes flickering and his face puffy. Buzzo lay sprawled on the couch, and Charlie was asleep in the bedroom. The smell inside the house was overpowering. Oscar had given up on any help from Charlie for subsistence fishing, so his interest was largely scientific. "I don't believe you guys," he said. "A whole week, and never stopping. Not even I used to go that long."

Harvey sat in Charlie's recliner and seemed to be looking at a halo above Oscar's head. Oscar said, "You ought to just go home to Kongiganak. You ain't doing nothing here."

Harvey just nodded toward Oscar's baseball cap — a polar bear on its crown, ALASKA written above that — and said, "Oscar, I like your hat."

Oscar and I went subsistence fishing ourselves again yesterday. In the morning, on the news — after President Bush had said that he favored a constitutional amendment against burning the American flag, and Oscar had nodded his approval, saying, "He's right" — we heard that a mediator had arrived in Bethel at the invitation of both Kemp-Paulucci and the fishermen's organizations. Then we watched an interview with Louie Kemp, who sat before the camera in tinted glasses and a leather flight jacket, his dark beard turning prematurely gray. He said, "We aren't ripping anybody off. The fishermen on the Kuskokwim are getting the exact same prices as we pay in Bristol Bay, as they'll soon find out. Are we being hurt financially by this strike? Yes, we are, and so are a lot of other people. A lot of innocent people are being misled here, and a lot of good income is being lost for no real reason."

But all the income that Oscar has lost hasn't thus far eroded his credit — not at the bank, and not with Margaret. The day before yesterday Margaret learned that the First National would give them an unsecured loan of $3000, which would allow them to pay off the $800 they still owed on the Nissan and then, if the owner agreed, drive away with the Duster after making a down payment of, say, $500. There would still be money for some other bills, some money to keep Oscar's fishing going, and some money for whatever payment schedule the owner wanted on the Duster.

"We're going to be broke," Margaret said as they came out of the bank with the loan.

"Like usual," Oscar replied.

Then, to his huge relief, Oscar passed his driver's test, achieving a perfect score on his third and final try. Afterward we drove the old pickup out toward the airport, where the Duster stood on sale in a parking lot in front of the janitorial agency. The big car had a little rust underneath and a long and spidery crack in the windshield, but the engine was sound and the interior clean. Oscar and I each had driven it once, and with its plush seats and clean windows and firm suspension, it had felt like a stretch limo after the lumbering Chevy pickup.

Inside Kuskokwim Janitorial, however, the *kass'aq* watching over the car said that he couldn't take just a down payment for it, since he wasn't the owner. He raised his arms helplessly and said, "I'd like to give you a break, and if Mike was here I'm sure he'd deal with you, but he's on vacation now and he won't be back in town for a month. You could call him, but I don't even have a telephone number for him."

Margaret and Oscar traded swift, despairing glances, and then Margaret turned back toward the counter, lowering her eyes and staring hard into the buttons of the store owner's chamois shirt. A moment later she asked quietly if they could pay $3000 now and the remaining $500 when the owner got back. The *kass'aq* rubbed his chin a moment and then laughed uneasily, saying that Mike probably would be satisfied with that — at least he'd be willing to risk it. Margaret drew from her jacket pocket a rolled cylinder of bills and counted out thirty crisp and immaculate hundreds onto the store counter.

Now Oscar loads the family into the Duster — the delighted children clamber riotously over its soft seats — and drives them down to the smokehouse to work on the kings and chums we caught yesterday. Elsie looks at the fish from last week still hanging on the drying rack and judges that they're far enough along to start smoking. By now the slabs of fish have stiffened, the meat darkening to a burgundy red and acquiring a lacquered sheen. But neither Oscar nor I stay; Oscar drives off to his regular Thursday night AA meeting, and drops me off on the other side of Brown's Slough to listen in at the KUFMA membership meeting.

At the meeting hall, all the anger that crackled through last week's gathering has dissipated into hard-edged resignation. The chairman reports that Whitney Seafoods has made an offer of thirty-one cents per pound on chums, with the prices on the reds and kings to remain as is, and one member responds, "Prices are dropping all over. I suppose we're lucky to get that."

"But Prince William Sound's shut down," another rises to say. "Why the hell aren't prices going up?"

After only a little more discussion, the association votes to accept Whitney's offer and return to the river, with a recommendation to its membership that they continue their boycott of Kemp and sell to other buyers instead. Oscar and I heard on the news coming over that the co-op had also voted to end the strike. "Kemp-Paulucci has met its contractual obligation in matching its Bristol Bay prices," a co-op spokesman said, and he urged their membership to sell preferentially to Kemp as before, in keeping with their side of the contract.

Back at the smokehouse, a homemade weathervane that John Active fashioned some years ago — a two-masted square-rigger with a mizzen, its sails now torn and ragged — rests idly against the sky, and the clouds above it lie like long blue continents, breaking up toward the horizon into smaller pieces with scalloped edges whose shapes and number suggest the islands of Arctic Canada. The islands are washed in peach and salmon as the sun begins to drop, and Elsie regards them admiringly, saying, "Gee, that's a pretty sunset." On the other side of the slough the *Shinmei Maru* has returned to its former berth, having anchored out in the river only so a barge could unload, and now its crew is hoisting bins of fish on board.

When Oscar comes back from the AA meeting, his face is no less radiant than those clouds. Apparently a white man had shown up at the meeting and spoken about his addiction, and Oscar says to me incredulously, "I didn't know *kass'aqs* had alcohol problems. I thought only Eskimos did."

Oscar has backed the Duster down the top of the ramp and parked it a short distance from where Hippa's skiff lies at anchor, full of bags of groceries. He pops open the back of the car and starts loading the groceries into it. "That was a good meeting, a funny meeting. They said alcoholism was a disease, not a profession, and nobody plans on being an alcoholic when they grow up. But one guy, he said he made a New Year's resolution one time to become an alcoholic, and he said it was the only one he ever kept. Then we all started laughing. I almost got ready to speak my piece, but not yet. I was gonna speak up, but then that other guy started talking."

He pauses with a bag of groceries on the Duster's tailgate, arrested in thought, at the same instant that the tatters on John's weathervane stir under a sudden breeze from the south and the ship points squeaking into the wind. "Hippa-Bear's at the drunkhouse," he says mildly. "Emma's drunk too. A cop stopped him and won't let him drive. I got to go get him. I'll let Emma's sister take care of the kids."

3 ⊚ THE TELEPHONE RINGS at 1:00 A.M. and Elsie hobbles stiffly out of her bedroom to answer
it. Oscar sits up barechested and wild-haired
from the mattress on the floor. Elsie says that it's Hippa. "What
you do?" she says sharply into the mouthpiece. "You end up in
jail?"

"Drunk driving, probably," Oscar says. "I told him he'd end
up like me."

"I got no money to bail you!" Elsie says. "Oscar's got no
money either. He never fish that last time. You just spend the
night there. It won't do you no harm." She listens for a moment
more, her face darkening in exasperation, and finally she hangs
up, muttering, "I got bills to pay. I'm not gonna bail him."
When the phone immediately rings again, she says, "Don't answer it."

But Oscar can't stand its ringing. He rises, sighing, picks it up,
and listens for some time in silence to Hippa's drunken plead-
ings. Then, "I'm broke, just like Ma told you. How much is your
bail? Who's got money? You got any money? Okay, I'll call
John Hastie. I'll call John Hastie and we'll come get you. Okay,
hang up so I can call him."

When Oscar finally gets off the phone, he looks up the number for the bail bondsman in Elsie's phone book. The old
woman sits at the supper table opposite him and remarks, "You
shouldn't bail him out. You got to put some money in the bank.
You got to start thinking about your kids."

"How much is his bail?" Margaret asks.

"Two hundred and fifty bucks," Oscar says. "With John Hastie, he just charges twenty-five. But I'm not putting up collateral.
Hippa can do that." He sighs again and says, "Fucking cops just
grab anybody."

"They always pick on you guys, and they leave Charlie," Elsie
observes. "I can't do nothing to get him out of my house. They
took you last summer and Buzzo last winter, but they never take

Charlie, and he's drunk all the time. Crazy. Bootleggers too — they never take 'em."

Oscar dials the bondsman's number, listens a moment, and then leaves a message on John Hastie's answering machine. He runs his hands through his hair in uncertainty and shifts about in his seat. "Well, we'll let him sleep it off, I guess."

Oscar grabs at the phone when it suddenly rings again, expecting it to be the bondsman, but once again it's Hippa. Oscar tells him that there's nothing he can do about his bail tonight. But Hippa isn't so easily discouraged, and while Oscar sits and listens, and listens some more, Elsie says, "Hippa's got to stay away from Charlie's house. There's always trouble there."

Ten minutes pass, and finally Oscar pries himself away by observing that John Hastie won't be able to call back as long as the phone is tied up. He slumps sleepily back in his chair, and Elsie thrusts her chin out at him, saying, "He's gonna get just like Charlie. Charlie, he don't care whether he lives or dies. One time he told me he's not scared to die."

Oscar sits quietly, thinking, and then says, "That time I got my own DWI, Charlie was there in an hour with John Hastie."

The old woman straightens her legs, which are as brown and firm as sumac limbs. The hard glint goes out of her eyes, and finally she suggests, "He misses Curtis too much. He wouldn't be so bad if he just had Curtis."

"Don't make excuses for him," Oscar snaps. "It's his own damn fault. Nobody's making him drink."

Elsie sniffs and falls silent. At last she stands and hobbles into the bathroom. Oscar remains seated by the phone, thinking. Then the phone rings again, and once again it's Hippa, and the rest of us go to sleep with Oscar still on the line with his brother.

In the morning, at nine o'clock, Oscar drives alone to the bondsman's office, which he finds closed. Then he goes to Emma's sister's place to check on the kids and look for Emma. The kids are fine, but the sister, Eleanor, says that Emma never came back last night. Finally he returns to the apartment, picks up everybody except Elsie, who is still asleep, and starts driving

around the streets of the town. "Where the hell's Emma?" he
wonders. "She's probably got all Hippa's money."

At last he sees her, in a bulky gray sweatshirt, her eyes large
and moist behind the great round lenses of her glasses, walking
toward Watson's Corner. In front of her the cable company's
satellite dish throws its rim against a blank blue sky that throbs
with light. Emma climbs wordlessly into the back seat of the
Duster, and Oscar asks, "You got any money?"

Emma shakes her head. "I got a hundred dollars, but I need
seventy-five for my own bail."

"Your own bail?"

"They took me in last night for protective custody. Hippa was
a disorderly conduct."

"How'd you get out if you ain't paid your bail?"

"I told 'em I had to go get my kids."

Oscar chews at his lower lip as he heads the car toward the
Kilbuck Elementary School's playground, where Eleanor said
she would wait with the kids. "Let's see — with my hundred
bucks and her hundred bucks, and maybe fifty bucks from Ma,
maybe we could get him out."

Margaret's eyebrows arch in surprise. "Where'd you get a
hundred bucks?"

"Charlie gave me some money for that VHF antenna."

At the playground, Emma's three children, who apparently
have been through this before, rejoin their mother just as if she'd
gone shopping for an hour. Emma says that Hippa's station
wagon is in front of Bethel's VFW building, where bingo games
are held, and Oscar drops me there with her and her kids while
he drives everybody else down to the smokehouse. Hippa's family piles into the wagon, and I drive to the city jail at the outskirts of town.

We arrive just as a smiling and fresh-faced Hippa climbs out
of the back of a white police van with a group of other men. He
waves cheerfully, holding up some paper in his hand, and then
disappears into the jail. Emma goes in after him, and it turns out
we don't need bail after all; he's being released on his own re-

cognizance. Hippa's smile is white and even and hard to resist, and apparently he has made some friends; he comes out in the company of a bald man in a blue blazer and a nattily dressed blond woman, and these two stand at the door and wave farewell like proud parents as he skips down the steps and out to his car.

He sighs happily as he settles into the front passenger seat of the wagon. "Man, I ain't never gonna do that again," he says. "I couldn't sleep in that little room in the drunk tank. You seen Buzzo? I just want to get back to fish camp and stay there, man."

In the late afternoon, the weather turns: pumice-colored banks of clouds are building up in mountains outside Elsie's apartment window, and an ear-popping stillness has fallen over the town. With Hippa safely out of jail and on his way back to fish camp, taking Buzzo with him, Oscar can start thinking again about tomorrow's commercial period. The rumored emergency makeup period, which would have occurred today, never happened, and Oscar needs a big payday tomorrow. Charlie, however, still hasn't sobered up.

Elsie worries about Charlie's never eating anything. At dinner she prepared a pot of fresh salmon and salmon eggs boiled in broth. Then she prevailed on Oscar to drive her over to Charlie's, where she ran hastily into the house with the pot and then out again. As we pulled into the road, Charlie leaned out his porch door, his head eclipsing the disk of the declining sun in the northwest, the rays of which shot hard and brilliant from his silhouetted skull. He shouted, "You come all the way over here and then you just go off!"

Now Elizabeth stretches out sleepily on the rug and Clayton clambers all over her, as *3-2-1 Contact* ends and the evening news comes on. KYUK says it's official: the strike is over on the Kuskokwim, now that the buyers have raised their price by a nickel per pound for chums, but falling fish prices in Bristol Bay may soon lead to a strike there. Outside, the mounting clouds rumble with thunder, and instantly a drenching rain falls in bayonets across the road and parking lot.

Oscar notes in the *Tundra Drums* that the VFW is having a $10,000 raffle drawing on the Fourth; also that Camai Air is looking for someone to work on their ground crew. "I should apply," he says to Margaret. "Just get out of this fishing business."

4 ⊙ A FEW WHITE CLOUDS are floating like kites along the southwestern horizon, down toward Cape Newenham, but otherwise the sky is a methylene blue vacancy. Some warm puddles of water have congealed on the tarp in the bow, the one that lies under the net when it's hauled in and cleaned, and in two or three of these puddles an occasional silverfish, with what look to be antennae at either end, is swimming awkwardly about. Just below the forward starboard gunwale a fly is cleaning its face, its legs lifting and wiping in machinelike motions of eye-blurring speed. The river is sluggish, almost gelatinous, and along its surface the floats lie slack. "The fish are swimming deep again," Oscar says, looking up at the sun. "This is a perfect time to go down to Jo Jo's Hole, but not without Charlie — too many snags."

In fact Charlie sobered up for this period, but not quite in time, not quite willingly. I stayed at the smokehouse this morning to ready the boat while Oscar went for Charlie, who tried to hide from him, Oscar said, but not quite well enough. Charlie said that by the time Hippa took Buzzo away yesterday, they'd gone through their whole supply of stuff anyway: "Buzzo bought two bottles of Southern Comfort for the Fourth, but we drank 'em both already." He still carried the weight of all that booze in his gut and head, however.

We went just a short distance downriver, down the channel on the Bethel side of the midstream islands, where in the distance a row of bone-white fuel tanks rose above the brush and where two red-and-white radio towers spired into a sky whose gray cover was breaking up under a mild westerly breeze. This time the river was jammed with boats, all speeding calmly to their various destinations, with just a few sentimental orange ribbons in sight. Only two other skiffs, however, set net in the section we were working. It was slack tide, and our floats trailed straight and languid from the boat. Three or four island fish camps, their cabins planted in neat green clearings, floated past our transom, looking from a distance like prosperous vacation homes.

As the sky opened up and the sun beat down, Charlie began pacing back and forth between the thwarts, drinking can after can of Coke Classic and also swigging from the two quarts of Gatorade that he brought with him. "Suffer, suffer, suffer," he said, his face as white as the fuel tanks. "I'm only half alive. I don't know if I'll make it the whole period." He stopped with his hands on the boat's rail, his shoulders hunched, his head hanging over the side. Then he said, "I can't believe Oscar's not drinking yet."

Oscar laughed as he tightened four screws into the base of the new VHF antenna he bought yesterday at Bethel Power Products. "I can't believe it either. I'm proud of myself," he said frankly. "You should stay sober on the Fourth this year, for a change, and do some things."

"Yeah, I'm always passed out on the Fourth of July," Charlie admitted. "I was doing okay yesterday after Buzzo went, until that guy from Kwig showed up again with some more stuff. I got to learn to lock my door and not answer it."

"Now you're talking." Oscar took up the mike to his radio and tried to contact Sam Beaver's boat, but received no answer. "I wonder if this thing is transmitting." He listened for a moment to the chatter of other fishermen, telling Charlie, "They're all selling to Whitney today. Nobody's gonna sell to Kemp." Then he laid the mike aside as the floats in the water trembled slightly. "If you go subsistence fishing for Ma tomorrow, I'll hang that net you got. We'll need that smaller mesh. These big fish ain't gonna be here forever. That second run is always smaller fish."

Charlie nodded but didn't say anything. After a moment he let his head drop down to the level of the gunwale, and then his back jumped and hunched as though an electric charge were running slowly up his spine. His retches were hoarse and deep and regular. Toward the end his throat popped and gasped with the sound of a drain sucking dry. Oscar turned his face away, adjusting the squelch on the VHF. "I better replenish Margaret's checking account," he said, as if Charlie's final heaves were the sound of money running out. "It's pretty far down now."

After that Charlie felt better, at least for a while, and the two brothers sat comfortably in the boat and told stories together. One time near here last summer they took a brand-new net and caught what Oscar described as a "Moby Dick snag." With two boats pulling hard to clear it, they finally ripped the net and snapped the lead line. "You're not a rich man anymore when that happens," Charlie said. Another time near here Oscar's brother-in-law Wassillie, drunk, helped himself to Oscar's boat and net, snagged the net up on the shore, and then just left it there. Oscar said he finally found Wassillie and his boat down around Napakiak, and he was so mad after he had to cut the net free that he made Wassillie walk all the way back to Bethel. And last year way upriver, in country that Oscar said was so beautiful you never want to leave, he shot a black bear, which apparently limped away into the forest, because neither he nor Charlie could find it when they brought the boat in to shore. They camped near that spot, and the next day Charlie nearly jumped out of his skin when he found the bear — dead, but he didn't know that then — beneath a tangle of roots and brush right under his feet at the campsite. Oscar and Charlie laughed mildly together, their laughter sifting into the languorous quiet of the river, where all the boats were waiting at their nets.

After an hour and a half they hauled in. The chums came in with violet stripes cutting through splashes of olive green, in camouflage for a ridge-top attack at dawn. A few were even in combat gear, sprouting fangs, while one already had a leprous patch of rot on its face. There weren't very many chums, however, or many kings either, and after cleaning the net Charlie felt bad again. By then he'd finished off two cups of coffee, three cans of Coke, and both quarts of Gatorade; there wasn't anything left in the boat for him to drink.

At last Oscar took pity on him and we rode back up to town, to that steep grade at the downriver end of the sea wall only a short distance from Charlie's house. We dropped him off, Oscar assuming the risk of a large fine or confiscation of his boat and gear for fishing without a permit holder. "We'll come pick you up at six-thirty so we can sell our fish," he said. Charlie nodded while we cast off, then stared up at the hundred-foot embankment he had to climb as though it were the Alaska Range.

Now Charlie stares in exactly that same way at the ladders on the *Husky II,* the tender to which Oscar has brought him and our fish at the end of the period. After three long drifts of the river, the last one coming up virtually empty, we were able to land only about two hundred fish, and all but twenty or so are low-priced chums. Charlie finally finds a ladder onto the tender low enough for his liking. Later he comes out of the wheelhouse with a little more than $400 in his pocket.

Oscar isn't much pleased with a take like that on the first day that he's been able to spend a whole period out on the water. When two Japanese sailors off the *Shinmei Maru* approach him as he beaches the *Crazy J* at the ramp, holding up a flask of Black Windsor while describing the shape of a fish in the air with their hands, he waves them aside angrily and stalks up to the smokehouse to lock up his gas cans.

At the apartment he complains to Margaret. "If you'd've called that catalogue number today, we coulda had that fish-finder by Monday. The only way we find fish now is by guessing." He sits at the supper table staring darkly into his coffee. "I wouldn't've wasted that third drift today if I had a fish-finder. All you need is three good drifts and they pay for themselves."

Later this evening I go down to the smokehouse in order to fetch the old pickup and bring it back to the apartment parking lot. When I get back I find Elizabeth standing outside the apartment with her face pressed against the corridor wall, her cheeks streaked with tears. Margaret comes out of the apartment and brushes past me, her face rigid with contained emotion, and Oscar follows her. "We're going for a ride," he says. Inside the apartment the sort of silence reigns that follows in the wake of a hurricane.

As the night wears on, the children nervously drop off to sleep, but Elsie waits up, starting at the sound of every tire in the parking lot. She says nothing all evening and keeps her thoughts to herself. Finally she asks me if I know Sam Beaver's phone number, and then she searches in vain for a listing in the phone book. When I tell her the number for directory assistance, she calls and says, "Yeah, you know Sam Beaver's number? What you mean, 'What city?' He lives right here in Bethel." At that moment the Duster pulls into the parking lot, and Elsie is able to see its blue roof as it moves past her window. "Oh, it's okay. Oscar's here right now."

Oscar is alone, and he sweeps wordlessly into the apartment, appropriates his mother's seat by the phone, and then begins dialing — it seems to me — the numbers of various houses where Margaret might be. Elsie moves to the seat opposite and stares at him with her single eye, the lines of her mouth pressed tight and firm.

5 ⊙ ALL SUMMER LONG a partly filled-in sort of classroom workbook has lain on the dashboard of the Chevy pickup: *Living Without Violence: A Handbook for Men*. I don't know what it signifies, if anything, that Oscar hasn't finished the self-analysis he began here. The blank white spaces under the essay questions in the second part of the book remind me of the blanknesses that I see these faces assume — the blankness that Margaret has worn in Charlie's and my presence all summer long, for example; the blankness that Oscar wore on that day during the strike when he walked past Kriska Evans down at the small-boat harbor, or as he brushed past me in the hallway when he went out behind Margaret.

I wonder what the blanks conceal, in the book and in the faces, and how and if they connect. Oscar doesn't mind talking about his boyhood and often refers to it, but only to its sunlit portions. He'll talk about James teaching him how to hang a net at Bristol Bay, for example, attaching a float line or a lead line to the mesh so the lines won't twist and the knots are even and firm, but hardly ever about his father as an alcoholic, and what sort of things happened when James came home drunk. Once Oscar mentioned, under his breath, that his dad used to get the shits sometimes when he was drinking. Once he described how an uncle of his, James's brother, maybe Matthew, said he was going to go out and get a drink when they were staying the summer in Bristol Bay. James said he could get hurt that way, and then proved it by beating his brother up and then tying him down in the bunkhouse. Everything else is blank.

No one tied Oscar down when, years later, he felt like going out for a drink himself, when he jumped of his own accord into the same messy shit his father wallowed in. I've talked with him at some length about my own father's alcoholism, and I wonder now if he was even listening, or if maybe he thought I was making it all up, since he came back from that AA meeting just the other night incredulous that a *kass'aq* could have a drinking problem. I don't know what James was like, but I know what fathers are like, and what loving them is like. Inevitably, I think, the sons of drunks despise themselves. We gave all the love we had to give, absorbed full measure of the pain we had to bear, held them close to us in spite of the shit, and it still wasn't enough. We come at last to a dispiriting suspicion: that an attachment that seems to us no less than elemental in its might and immaculate in its essence is less in our fathers' minds than their attachment to a mere appetite — an appetite, moreover, that removes us from their hearts and robs them of everything we admire them for.

So Oscar is always jealous, always seeing Margaret, whom he loves, as "often like a deer corraled but ever looking for an exit." Sometimes he thinks she gets out of their bed in the middle of the night to go and be with an overnight visitor on their couch. Sometimes he thinks that a neighboring woman's invitation to Margaret to come take a steambath in one of the *maqiviit*, the little household steamhouses in Kongiganak, is really an invitation from the woman's husband. Particularly given his own drinking, and particularly given his recent violence, he finds it impossible that Margaret could still love him and not betray him — particularly since his own father betrayed him when he was only a boy and still innocent. So he imagines Margaret's betrayals whenever he's alone with his thoughts, and the thoughts drive him almost as mad as Othello. Maybe he knows they're crazy, but they don't go away.

For her part, Margaret finds that her loyalty is a matter less of principle than of love, as amazing to her as to Oscar, in his rare lucid moments. Once last fall, after Margaret at last allowed him to come home again, she and Oscar quarreled, and Oscar left the house in a rage to fly up to Bethel. Before he left, however, while Margaret was working up at school, he carefully went through all their family photo albums and took his own pictures out. If she had any doubt that she still loved him, in spite of the handbook of horror now in the pickup, it was answered by the grief that overcame her when she discovered all those mute and empty spaces, all that blankness and nothingness, in their photo albums.

Sometimes when he's mad at her and jealous of her job, Oscar somewhat bitterly calls her a *kass'aq*. Out on the river, of course, he says that he's thankful he doesn't have a job like that,

that he'd feel like he was in jail. But the pleasure Margaret takes in her work at school has nothing to do with being either *kass'aq* or Yupik, she believes; it's just the way she is, on a fundamental level, and doesn't have anything to do with the color of her skin or the values she entertains. All the same, I wonder if the accusation calls to mind a night in Bethel some twenty years ago, after Margaret's curiosity about the world on the other side of the Alaska Range, and her ambition, had prompted her to arrange to stay with a family in Anchorage and go to high school there for her senior year. Aataq and Aanaq and her father, Mills, had given their permission, albeit reluctantly, and Margaret had gotten help in setting everything up from a counselor at the Bethel high school. Afterward she planned to go to college.

At that point the great Oscar Active was a boyfriend whom she regretted leaving, but she was prepared to do so. For that matter, she was still getting letters from Tommy Andrew in Oklahoma, the boy whom Aanaq had picked out for her in the first place. In the fall she made her reservations, packed her luggage, and flew to Bethel in order to spend the night at an uncle's before catching the morning jet to Anchorage. But that night another uncle, exercising his prerogative in a Yupik family, came to say that there was too much trouble for a girl to get into in Anchorage and that she wouldn't be allowed to go after all. Instead of boarding the jet, Margaret flew home to Kongiganak the next day. She returned despondently to Bethel a few days later to report to the high school dorm. That year maybe Oscar came to represent at least a journey beyond the village, if not over the mountains.

A part of Margaret still dreams about that other world, and she reads to keep in touch with it. That's also one of the ways she keeps in touch with God. Her own bookshelf, above a long row of children's books, is largely religious in character, with her New Testament, the *Moravian Daily Text for 1989, God's Psychiatry, Matthew Henry's Commentary on the Whole Bible,* back issues of the Christian magazine *Dove.* There are also such political tracts as Vine DeLoria's *Custer Died for Your Sins,* and a biography of Paul Robeson, whom she admires for his struggle against racism. But there are novels as well, opulent romances set in Paris, New York, San Francisco, all describing places she'd like to visit and lives she'd like to live, at least in part, sometimes so much that it hurts. She'd even like to go to Barrow once, just to see if the sun really hangs in the sky twenty-four hours a day all summer as people say it does.

An opportunity for at least a different sort of life, another kind of identity, presented itself last summer when Oscar was in jail and then subject to the court injunction while he awaited his hearing. But she didn't take it. I don't know the precise answer, but maybe their little house, overstuffed as always with clothes and bedding and dishes and books and photo albums and trophies, seemed cavernously empty without Oscar's considerable presence. When she woke up every morning alone in bed with the two boys, she must have glanced at the clock above their dresser mirror, the one made from a lacquered cross-section of a tree and inscribed in flowing script with their names and marriage vows and the date of their wedding, August 18, 1974. In the other bedroom Elizabeth and Janet woke to a huge computer printout that Elizabeth had made at school the previous spring and tacked to the paneling above her posters of Patrick Swayze and Justin Bateman: I LOVE MOM & DAD.

Up in Bethel, Oscar had been staying dry since he posted bail and got back on the streets. I don't know if he told Margaret then, or indeed has ever told her, about his thoughts of suicide, about not caring whether he lived or died, like Charlie. But he promised her that he would start going to AA meetings and talk regularly with a counselor at the Phillips Alcoholism Treatment Center in Bethel. In September she allowed him to come to Kongiganak briefly, just to see the kids. Did her heart break then, or did it start to be pieced back together when she saw how gratefully the kids went to him, how powerful their love still was, even after what they'd seen? Maybe it was then that Oscar promised Elizabeth that he would never drink again, just as poor Jack Carey once promised me.

In October, as the day of Oscar's hearing approached, Margaret's lawyer called from Bethel. She told him that she wouldn't testify against her husband after all, that she wanted all the charges dropped. The lawyer was disappointed and encouraged her at some length to follow through with the case, but Margaret held firm. Then the lawyer wrote to her, saying that she'd have to make her request in writing and also explain why. This brought her up short, since she found at that moment that she simply couldn't explain why. I don't know how she found her way out of this last conundrum. Maybe she had recourse to the six habits of mind that she finds exemplified in Aanaq — disciplines that she keeps written in a notebook close at hand, that she described once in a letter from her and Oscar, and that she says she tries to uphold every day: "1) A positive mental attitude; 2) Harmony in human relations; 3) An open mind to all subjects; 4) A willingness to share blessings; 5) The capacity to understand people; 6) The labor of love." Or maybe she simply looked up at the placard she has tacked to the wall above their door in Kongiganak — "God's Will: Nothing More, Nothing Less, Nothing Else" — and in some manner found her answer there.

In any event, the letter got written, the lawyer was discharged, and Oscar came home. Since then I think they've shared some of their best times together, and also some of their most difficult. Last year Margaret tried harder than ever to arrange for someone else to look after the boys while she worked at school, not to stick Oscar with the babysitting, but that was hard sometimes; Aanaq is too old and blind to chase toddlers around all day, and Margaret's sister-in-law Sarah has four children of her own. Sometimes Oscar just had to stay home with them, and no doubt that drove him crazy on days when the weather was good for hunting. Then Margaret came home tired from her work at school, only to have to sweep the house, dress the meat, change the diapers, cook dinner, start the laundry up at Safewater, and do the dishes with the water Oscar had hauled in from the rain-barrel or chopped from a lake. "What are you so tired about?"

Oscar would say. "You been sitting all day." When she got mad enough, she would snap right back at him and then retire into one of her silent, brooding rages. Maybe that did Oscar some good, reminding him that even someone as strong as Margaret could lose the handle on her feelings sometimes and say things frankly intended to hurt.

I'm sure some of the spark for that anger was provided by everything that she finds difficult and confining about life in a village such as Kongiganak, even by the irony that this is where she ended up with Oscar. Certain things just wear you out. Even with Safewater, the water-treatment plant (which is often broken down), clean water in Kongiganak is hard work and a constant worry. The rainbarrel outside is convenient through the summer but frequently gets fouled by children playing around it, and Margaret thinks that's how Elizabeth got hepatitis last year. She worries too about sanitation for the whole village, since all the honeybuckets are simply dumped into one of the lakes below their house through the summer or left to freeze on the river ice in winter.

The drudgery and repetition of doing laundry twice each week, lugging the clothes in half a dozen thirty-gallon trash bags up to the washing machines at Safewater, then staying there all night to feed clothes through the dryers and fold them, has to be painful. When Safewater is shut down for repairs, Margaret has to use her small wringer washer, which is even more drudgery. The house can't be kept clean, or the clothes, given the way the river silt and the gluelike mud get tracked over the floor and sifted into everything.

Also there is that scrutinizing way in which everybody watches everybody else in such a little place, and the peril involved in speaking your mind, expressing your feelings, unburdening your heart, even to Oscar, who — like a lot of husbands, particularly threatened ones — prefers not to hear about his wife's troubles. All this sucks the marrow from her dreams and forces on her the impossibility of ever becoming anyone other than the person she's always been.

Margaret has pretty much given up on college now, though she still thinks sometimes about taking some courses, maybe in computer science or business. Even that never happens. Once she was bold enough to tell Oscar that sometimes she feels like she's not even living at all, that she's just existing. In the same letter in which she described her mental disciplines, she talked about attending a secretarial training workshop in Seward, on the eastern side of the Kenai Peninsula in central Alaska. A number of other secretaries from the school district went with her, and she was astonished at how many of her peers, whom she knew and respected, simply got drunk and behaved like animals. She was shaken when one young woman waded out into the icy waters of Resurrection Bay in an attempt to drown herself, and she came away frightened — afraid for Oscar, afraid for herself, and afraid for all her people and what might become of them. She described it as a sense of helplessness and doom, a sense that all their lives are inevitably tragic — a feeling, she wrote, "like this world is full of snarling dogs." She carries the emblem of that feeling on her cheek: the faint, raking pattern of sepia-colored scars that she received as a child from that mauling in Kwigillingok.

But all of this leaves out something else, something that answers to that other urge in her life and has more powerfully governed its shape than her dreams of other lives or her memories of snarling dogs. Maybe it begins in the earliest of her few memories of her mother, Lilly, even then growing thin, with Lilly's warm hand pressed between her thighs at night in order to catch the first drop of incontinence as Margaret slept sideways with Lilly and Mills and her brothers in a double bed. Then Aanaq took her mother's place, and it continues on through the tears the old woman wept as she stood on the riverbank in Kwigillingok each fall to see Margaret, still only in grade school, climb into a float plane and disappear to the federal boarding school in Wrangell. Then it was Oscar, the famous basketball player, who amazed her by even approaching her and courting her, and who did so — even more amazing — with such fumbling shyness and vulnerability, who was so amazed to find her coming to return his love. Now it's her own children, whether the tug of Clayton's hand at her hair as he feeds at her breast or the dozens of "I love you's" that Crazy writes on the papers that she brings home from school, and still Oscar, who can still amaze her, who can place one of his huge arms around her and see her on her own terms for a moment, with the scales of his own grief fallen from his eyes, and thank her for her faithfulness.

This is the thread that has tied her life together, this giving and receiving of love, just as it has run through Aanaq's. Gontran de Poncins, the French adventurer who went to live among the Eskimos of Pelly Bay in Canada in 1938, found "something impalpable" in the women there, "some spring or power which they never reveal, a rumination upon the life of their family or clan which determines to what use they will put their power." Margaret, something like those Pelly Bay women, has little choice but to be circumspect in what she reveals, and I see in her unexpressed rumination something of the apprehension she described once when she told me what it was like to travel by kayak with Aataq and Aanaq when she and Harvey and Paul were still little. The two adults sat back to back in the cockpit, while the children were packed like bundles into the bow and stern of the craft. The kayak's sealskin cover had been cured in urine, and the stench and close air inside were literally stifling. Nonetheless, the children had to be as still as death, as rigid as the blankness now on Margaret's face, lest their least movement upset Aataq's balance and cause the craft to tip.

Through her command of something impalpable, through her grasp of this thread that ties all her actions and choices together, Margaret sustains the family's life and balance. I see in that, or guess in that, the substance of her thoughts, the key to her finesse, the foundation of that urge that finds its best expression, after all, on the coast where she was born. Despite all her dreams about that other world, about that other life, I've heard her wonder aloud why *kass'aqs* are so restless and like to go everywhere. She affirms that she herself couldn't be happy in a place where trees or mountains or buildings hid the sun going up and down, as they do at Wrangell.

In that letter in which she wrote about the snarling dogs, she described as well how she feels at other times, indeed at most times. She said that she knew she couldn't control circumstances or events, but even so she had faith that "love can survive anything and time would cure, not all, but most, and that I will be able to go on."

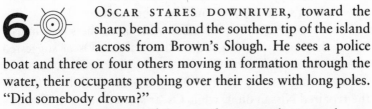

6 OSCAR STARES DOWNRIVER, toward the sharp bend around the southern tip of the island across from Brown's Slough. He sees a police boat and three or four others moving in formation through the water, their occupants probing over their sides with long poles. "Did somebody drown?"

"I wouldn't be surprised," says a *kass'aq* with tattooed arms and a camouflage cap. "I was coming in around midnight last night, and I saw a whole bunch of guys drunk and just running in circles. Somebody ought to shoot out their motors with a high-powered rifle, maybe save their lives."

Elsie was supposed to come down after church this morning to help with the new load of kings Charlie and Harvey brought in yesterday, but it didn't work out that way. Instead John is helping Margaret to cut the fish, while Charlie and Harvey work at installing a new muffler on the Chevy pickup, which can now be yours for $600. Actually the new muffler is an old and sooty but still functional one that Oscar scrounged off the side of the road somewhere. Oscar, meanwhile, is hanging a float line and a lead line on Charlie's new six-inch-mesh nylon filament net.

The green net hangs in the shape of a haycock from a hook on the drying racks, and the float line, scrounged off a net from Adolph Lind's old storehouse up near John's house, stretches down to the sea wall in a gritty trail across the dirt. Dust puffs out in clouds from it as Oscar snaps his knots tight with his shuttle.

The air is a lot better now at Charlie's place, even if it's gotten thick in a different sort of way at Elsie's. Yesterday morning Oscar and I arrived at Charlie's to find the house thrown open, with a breeze blowing through the front door and out the back window and Charlie sweeping the floors. Oscar went inside and with a flourish put on his new baseball cap with the Whitney Seafoods logo on it; all three of us were given these caps the day before at the *Husky II.* Then he took his old ALASKA cap and gave it to an appreciative Harvey. Oscar said, "You're wearing a sober man's hat. Maybe you'll be sober now too."

Then Charlie and Harvey came with us to the smokehouse, where they finally made good on the deal that Oscar suggested more than a week ago: Charlie and Harvey went subsistence fishing, using not the *Crazy J* but Joe Brown's little skiff with the repaired Nissan on it, while Oscar started hanging Charlie's new net. The warranty on the Nissan had in fact saved Oscar a $200 repair bill, though he then spent $100 on a prop with a larger pitch to guard against the motor's being overrevved again.

This morning the clouds burned away like smoke, and now, in the late afternoon, the sun lies hot and hard across the open lots and the river. Charlie has abandoned the muffler project and is climbing up to the roof of the smokehouse with a large American flag, which he lashes to the same piece of lead pipe that supports John's weathervane. "Tell George Bush we'll burn this on the Fourth," he jokes. "We'll blame it on the smokehouse."

Margaret and Oscar smile, but not at each other. Their relations have been brusque since Margaret came in the night before last, only a few minutes after Oscar began his phone calls. They slept together on the mattress on Elsie's floor, the two boys occupying a demilitarized zone between them, and Oscar's foot twitched all through the night as if he were a cat switching its tail.

Since then Elsie has been brusque as well, with just about everybody except her grandchildren, and this morning the annoyances of the past two weeks were given a public hearing at Charlie's place. On Friday, Elsie had thoughtfully given me a pair of socks that she'd knitted in honor of Father's Day, but yesterday she snapped at me for leaving a puddle of water on the bathroom floor after she called me out of the shower for an emergency visit to the toilet, and she snapped at me again today for opening up a packet of instant cream of wheat for breakfast. "If you want that for breakfast, you should buy some of your own!" she said.

Margaret too — yesterday Elsie called Margaret to bring a dress into the bathroom for her and then scolded her for bringing the wrong one. This morning she took bags of last summer's crowberries and salmonberries out of the freezer and curtly told Margaret to make some *akutaq* for lunch today. (The contemporary form of *akutaq* is made from berries and sweetened Crisco whipped together into billows.) Then she went to church, refusing Oscar's offer of a ride in the Duster.

We saw her next at Charlie's place. Oscar was stopping there to pick up Charlie and Harvey and bring them to the smokehouse, and Elsie was picking up some items that had been stored in the porch.

"You got that *akutaq* ready?" she demanded of Margaret.

"Not yet — I couldn't," Margaret said. "The berries were still too frozen when we left a while ago."

Elsie's lips tightened; her chin thrust out. "I bet they're good now. You should go back there right now and do it, then."

Margaret blinked, and explained that Ina Jenkins, a well-known Yupik gospel singer from Nunapitchuk, was singing this morning at the Holiness Pentecostal Church. "They're starting in just a few minutes, and I'm taking the kids to see her. I'll do it as soon as we get back."

Elsie drew a deep breath, her nostrils flaring, and as Oscar approached the step she said something to him that incited him to turn and gesture angrily to the Duster. "There's the truck — *you* use it!"

She required no further provocation. From her place on the top of the steps she launched into a Yupik-language harangue describing for the benefit of all of Weber Circle the nature of the bills that were killing her and the various ways in which her own children, her in-laws — who thought they were better than she was — and a certain freeloading *kass'aq* as well were taking advantage of her. Oscar just turned and got back in the car, and Charlie and Harvey came running out to join us as though fleeing a burning house. We pulled out into the road and left her railing on the steps like Jeremiah.

In the car Oscar said, "Goddamnit, she's been cranky and mumbling all week. I hate it when she starts mumbling."

"I wouldn't call that mumbling," I said.

"Well, maybe we better just get out of her place and move over to Charlie's, or maybe over to Hippa's fish camp, if Buzzo's got his big tent set up."

When we got to the smokehouse, John came out of his house and was apprised of what had happened. He said, "Ever since you guys came to town, I don't get any dinner invites. She says she's got too many mouths to feed."

"I better give her some more money," Oscar said.

"That's probably why she's mumbling," Margaret ventured.

"Fucking shit," Oscar complained, "I give her money and she turns around and spends it on the kids. She complains about bills and then spends everything she's got on candy and clothes for them."

Margaret asked, "What did you used to do when you were kids and she got mad?"

"Just go, right, Charlie?"

Charlie laughed and nodded.

"We just put on our coats and went," Oscar said.

Now Charlie's flag, which John brought home from Swanson's, where he works, hangs limp in the hot, still air. By contrast, the little dime-store flags that Elizabeth and Crazy have attached to the hood ornament and antenna of the Duster stand out straight and starched. Sweat beads on Oscar's brow as he works on Charlie's net, and once in a while he glances over at Margaret at the cutting table. She leans resolutely over her work, though now and then a chill rolls up her spine.

Later Charlie drives off somewhere in the pickup and doesn't come back, and Oscar and I get into the Duster to go look for him. We drive first across the slough and down Third Avenue to Watson's Corner, where opposite the satellite dish stands Twitchell's Music Store with its enigmatic marquee sign:

THE TRAVELING WILBURYS GUITAR
OPEN 12 T
HEE HAW GOSPEL QUARTET

Then we turn and head back to Lousetown, past a gutted building on tall pilings, a sign tacked to it reading ADULT EDUCATION CENTER. Three ravens perch along the eaves of this building. The sun is just as hard and palpable as it was yesterday, beating down out of a white, yawning sky, and the dust turned up from the roads by the traffic hangs over the town like smog.

Maybe it's just the backache that's stayed with me since last night, or maybe it's the embarrassment of having been strafed by Elsie, but in any case, as we circle by the small-boat harbor and continue along the road that winds back to the bridge, it seems to me that at least by its face tonight, Bethel looks a lot like the sets for those post-holocaust Mad Max movies that Oscar and I have seen playing on Charlie's VCR. With its empty freezer vans and bombed-out trailers, its gimcrack cabins and shacks and haphazard storefronts, its random antennas and corrugated metal roofs and helter-skelter power lines, the crazy variety of its three-wheelers and vans and pickups and taxicabs and water trucks, all of them layered with dust and pocked by gravel and corroded by the rain and ice and salt, and all of this festering like a dirty wound beneath this heatlamp of a sun, it looks like a place that might spring up like wormwood in the aftermath of a nuclear winter — a place where our buildings and machines and social forms are only dimly remembered and have been reconstructed in such a way that they are all somehow twisted and edged with malice. I start thinking about that drowned man in the river, imagining the darkness and chill of the water down on the bottom and the slow tug of the current, and I wonder if they've found him.

Oscar decides to check for Charlie at his mom's place, but thinks it might be prudent to keep me out of her way, so he drops me off back at the smokehouse. Charlie returns there with the pickup fifteen minutes later, button-lipped as to where he's been, and Oscar comes back in half an hour. When Charlie asks him if everybody's staying at his place tonight, Oscar says probably not. "I stopped at Ma's place a while ago. We'll stay there, I guess. She's cranky, but not too cranky."

At around 9:00 P.M. Oscar takes Margaret and the kids back to Elsie's, then returns to work some more on Charlie's net. He ties knots until midnight, when we drive back to the apartment through nearly deserted streets in a cool, bright twilight. As we go past the AC store, I notice an old woman in a green Windbreaker walking along through the parking lot with her chin thrust out and her hips rolling in that bowlegged gait characteristic of Elsie.

At the apartment a wide-eyed Margaret comes running out the door at the end of the building just as we pull into the parking lot. "Your mom got really mad and just put on her coat and went out," she says.

Without a word Oscar races into the apartment, where shoes and clothes are stuffed into bags and rucksacks, and sweeps the children out the door, leaving the rooms as empty of our presence and belongings as if we'd been made to vanish. The various bags are crammed into the back of the Duster, and we rumble out of the parking lot like Israel fleeing Pharaoh. Margaret sighs as Oscar pulls out into the street, saying, "She does this every year."

VII
THE TERRACES
OF PURGATORY

1 ◉ HARVEY STANDS BARECHESTED at the top of
the boat ramp and wrings water out of his gloves,
the sky behind him thin with light, the clouds
along the southwestern horizon as pale as gauze. In the boat
Oscar gasps as he and Charlie lift the eighteen-gallon gas tank
over the gunwale. The water from the gloves trickles like sweat
into the sand, and then the gas tank drops down on top of it.
Oscar says, "Geez, it was hot out there."

I didn't fish with Oscar today because I was laid up with a
bad back. That means I didn't run the risk he ran, either. With
both Charlie and Harvey still sober and Oscar growing increasingly desperate for the sort of payday he had ten days ago, the
one that tempted him into buying the Duster, he yielded to
Charlie's suggestion that they run two boats, Charlie and
Harvey in the little aluminum skiff, Oscar in the *Crazy J* with
Rex, Hippa's oldest boy. Then, just before the end of the period
at 7:00 P.M., they met at some hidden spot in the river, where
all of Charlie's fish were hastily thrown into Oscar's boat and
where Charlie replaced Rex for the purpose of selling the combined load.

Once again, Oscar would have had worse problems than he
has now if a Fish & Game agent had paid him a visit. That
didn't happen, but the risk doesn't seem much worth it, in ret-
rospect. When Buzzo and Hippa approach the sea wall and run
their boat into the ramp beside Oscar's, Oscar tells them that he
started out in the channel above Hippa's camp, but he came up

with only fifteen fish there on his first drift. Then he went to a spot below Napakiak and did at least a little better, catching thirty fish on his second drift and ninety on his third. But he also snagged his net three times; he was lucky not to tear it. The combined load that he and Charlie sold to a Whitney tender was worth only a little more than $200, now that the reds and the kings have fallen off. "I only caught two little kings, man, small enough to be chums," Oscar says. "I got more reds than I did kings. Maybe we got three of those."

Buzzo laughs and says that on one of their drifts, he and Hippa caught a nice fat whitefish, which they cleaned and ate right there in the boat. "Then when that *kass'aq* off that tender we sold to was in our boat and putting our fish on his scale, he found the tail of that whitefish. He just held that up and said, 'What the hell is this?' So we told him, and then his eyes all bugged out and he says, 'You eat it raw?' I says, 'Fuck, man, those things swim cooked.'"

Charlie shows me his receipt for the fish he sold, and I notice that the chums are priced at only twenty cents per pound. Oscar says that the other eleven cents are made up in bonus and delivery fees that Charlie signs for and is paid at the end of the season. But Charlie can't find his receipt for these fees, nor for the fees for the fish he sold to Whitney in the last period. His brow creases and he says, "I don't think I ever signed for those."

When the *Crazy J* is cleaned out and anchored, Harvey and Charlie and I pile into the Duster, and Oscar drives across Brown's Slough and over to that section of the waterfront where the *Husky II,* Whitney's main processing ship, is tied up. He and Charlie climb up a ramp and disappear into the ship's wheelhouse. When they return, Charlie's mouth is jammed shut, his features taut. He says that the processor's captain radioed over to the tender where he sold his fish, and that the captain of the tender said that in fact he had signed for his fees. "I didn't believe him, but I didn't want to argue with him."

Charlie looks down the river as Oscar pulls away from the ship. He says, "That guy at the tender pissed me off," and he turns and grins at Harvey, remembering maybe that tomorrow is the Fourth of July and he's got some money in his pocket. Or maybe he's just tired of thinking about that guy on the tender. "Well, Harv, you about ready to resume our normal life?"

Harvey's ready. He grins back and nods.

Oscar suggests that we buy some fried chicken for dinner, and he pulls into the parking lot in front of the Quik Food Center III, just across from the bridge. Four or five people are queued up ahead of us at the cash register, and as Charlie waits in line next to Oscar, his eyes snap suddenly toward the grocery section of the little store. Then he breaks out of line and nearly runs toward the middle aisle. Above the top shelf of the groceries I see the head and shoulders of Linda, Charlie's former girlfriend, moving firmly up the aisle, her face held high but her eyes downcast, as though she knows the ceiling is about to fall in on her but doesn't know exactly when.

But Charlie isn't after Linda. Instead he kneels at the end of the aisle and extends his arms, calling quietly, almost plaintively, "Hi, Curtis. It's me, Curtis. It's me, your daddy. Come on to Daddy, Curtis. Come on and see your daddy."

I move up behind Charlie and see Linda standing almost at bay at the end of the aisle, holding Curtis to her legs, her arms crossed tightly across his chest. The boy gazes back at Charlie with his eyes as wide as quarters, gazing at some wonder that defies explanation, his face otherwise strangely expressionless.

Out in the Duster, Charlie says that Linda has a new court order preventing him from approaching Curtis. He falls silent, staring into the hands that lie slack in his lap. He looks as though he held his own guts in them, and his face is as white and ghastly as it was in the cold off Cape Avinof.

2 ◎ WE NEVER FOUND OUT if Buzzo in fact has set up his big tent over at Hippa's fish camp. But no matter — by now everybody except me has moved back into Elsie's place. We all slept in packed rows across the floor at Charlie's house on the night we abandoned the apartment. The next morning Oscar went to visit his mother, and found her — as he said again — "not too cranky." With that all the gear went back into the Duster and then back into heaps and piles in Elsie's apartment, though my gear went out to a friend's house in Tundra Ridge, a housing development on the outskirts of Bethel. Oscar thought this would help keep his mother less cranky, and I agreed with him.

It isn't a problem of personality. Elsie has known me for years, has generally been kind to me, and I haven't suffered more than anyone else from her temper. Partly it has to do with simple crowding, partly with the expedience of diverting family tensions to the person of a non–family member, and partly with reliable bottom-line economics. In this last respect I'm an obstruction in the cycles of exchange turning (just barely) within this family. Unable independently to contribute quantities of fish and game to my upkeep, I make do with cash, paying Oscar a sum we agreed on for my room and board this summer. At first this offended Margaret's sense of how a guest and a friend should be accommodated, but I was staying an unusually long time with them, and I was more comfortable that way — an example of using cash, I suppose, to cancel obligation.

Also, Oscar needed the cash, or, more precisely, the credit. When we struck our deal in April, he knew he'd need a new snow machine next winter, and he asked that my room and board be applied as credit against my asking price on the snow machine I was selling. That was fine, but it left the problem of how to compensate people such as Elsie and Buzzo's wife, Alice, who would be feeding us both this summer. Oscar said he would contribute extra groceries to those households and so recompense them for what I ate. "I'll have my fishing money then," he said.

But there was hardly a penny for Oscar at Cape Avinof, and there's been only one good payday on the Kuskokwim so far, and it's already the Fourth of July. Margaret has been cajoling Oscar into giving her some money and buying Elsie some groceries, but I'm sure the old woman hasn't gotten as much help as she really needs. For the past two weeks I've tried to help by at least buying quantities of the store-bought foods that I've been eating, though I forgot about the instant cream of wheat.

But I feel the pinch myself. Cash or credit, the money for my room and board is still running out of my pocket, and the groceries that I buy on top of that are breathtakingly expensive here in Bethel: $3.89 for a loaf of bread, $5.98 for a gallon of milk, $8.09 for thirty ounces of peanut butter, and so on. As Elsie said to Oscar the other night, I've got my own family to think about, and every time I've gone into AC or Swanson's lately, I've found myself in a tug-of-war between what Elsie obviously needs and what my household down States needs, especially if I don't find a job down there in the fall. The compromise that I strike results in bags of groceries that I think are a lot better than nothing, but by themselves they seem scanty, even to me. Because I had a job over the winter, no doubt Elsie considers me to be rich, and I don't know if she's even aware of the deal I have going with Oscar.

I don't think it would make any difference to Elsie, however, if she did know. My compromise is different from the one that a Yupik person in the same situation would make. In one way or another, the algebra has always been mutually unintelligible. Mrs. Schwalbe, for example, described the sensation created by such penniless missionaries as John and Lydia Schoechert when they visited the Lower 48: "Mrs. Schoechert was wearing a beaver coat when she reached the States. As they were about to entrain for the East, an obsequious porter took one look at the coat, hurried to Mrs. Schoechert and taking her luggage said,

'Palace car madam?' Later, in Chicago, Brother Schoechert . . . told how people turned to stare at him as he walked down State Street wearing an overcoat made of glossy muskrat skins. For once the missionaries shared Solomon's glory." But the glossy skins that made up such glory could be had then for a few cups of tea leaves, a packet of safety pins.

Just as Yupik people were puzzled by the deeper motives of the missionaries and the interest of *kass'aqs* in skins of relatively little utilitarian value, so were they puzzled by the sort of gift-giving exemplified by Zagoskin's gift of the Aleut axe to the woman on the Yukon. Because it was often cheaper simply to abandon equipment and unused supplies than to ship them out of the region, as was the case at the end of the Western Union Telegraph Expedition in Saint Michael, such giving was sometimes practiced on the wholesale scale characteristic of a Yupik winter feast. Having established their wealth and generosity, however, these *kass'aqs* just sailed away and never came back. In response, Yupik people could only suppose that *kass'aqs* had no sense of the value of their own wealth, and throughout western Alaska this had the effect of driving up the prices on Eskimo goods. In places such as Saint Michael and Bethel, it also encouraged villagers to beg from Westerners, even to camp out in a white man's house until he gave them something as the price of going away.

On the other side of the coin, for a resident *kass'aq*, a member of the cash economy, to formalize such generosity and enter into a village's customary exchange relationships could be a daunting prospect. Ferdinand Drebert had an opportunity to do so in Kwigillingok, when he was expressly invited to join in the village's potlatch and gift-giving feasts, during which a request for a particular gift was accompanied by a kiss. "But if I had taken advantage of such a privilege, I would have automatically accepted all the responsibilities that go with membership in the tribe. Any one of them could have kissed me for some article and I would have been obliged to produce it. So the idea did not

appeal to me. After all I was one among many. In their estima-
tion I was considered rich. But I was not willing to part with any
of my belongings just for the glory of giving."

So it continues today out in the villages. Though more and
more of the certified teachers in the village schools of the Lower
Kuskokwim School District are Yupik, at present the majority
are *kass'aq*. These outsiders admire the still extravagant generosity of the Russian Orthodox Christmas celebrations, for instance, but are largely no more tempted than Drebert was to
throw their own foods and goods into the pool. Their neighbors,
who take such satisfaction in giving and who envy the cash resources that the teachers could bring to bear in it, still wonder
at this hesitancy, and wonder why *kass'aqs* as individuals are
uniformly so stingy. Elsie was probably disappointed by my
puny bags of groceries, but not surprised.

John Kilbuck couldn't help but be uneasy about a prosperity
that depended on good weather and the unpredictable movements of wildlife, but even in famine there was at least the assurance that what little there was would be shared equally. How
much less trustworthy is money? The original balance of trade,
so many pins for so many furs, broke down with the collapse of
the international fur market sixty years ago. Since then salmon
has taken up a bit of the slack, but not a lot. The demand for
Western goods inside the delta now far exceeds the demand for
Yupik goods outside it, and anyway, bartering with salmon
places the subsistence economy at risk.

Somehow it always seems that the money is coming in slower
than it did before, and running out faster, as the price of everything — except Kuskokwim salmon — climbs higher and
higher. Electricity costs in the delta have nearly tripled in the
past fifteen years, fuel costs have better than doubled in the past
ten, and there is always the routine inflationary spiral of the
store-bought goods. Oscar distrusts the whole thing, talks about
it as a sort of conjuror's house of cards, or a game that works
only because everybody agrees to pretend that a picture of
George Washington is worth something. If a card is pulled out

from the bottom, or if a big enough player gets tired of pretending, then it all collapses. "At least I can always eat," Oscar tells me, taking me in the Duster to my temporary residence in Tundra Ridge. "At least I can just go out into the tundra or on the river, and I know I got my dinner."

I'm thinking about last Wednesday night, when Hippa was desperate for bail. I've been loaning Oscar money to buy gas as he needs it, and he has been conscientiously paying me back out of his fishing money, as poor as it's been. That night no one so much as glanced in my direction to suggest that I come up with the money for Hippa, just as a loan. The money was there in my checking account if I wanted to write the check, and I could have volunteered, but I was unimpressed with the glory of giving, was more worried about what my own family might need the money for. I don't know exactly what Oscar was thinking that night, or Elsie.

3 ⊙ ON THE FOURTH, Pinky's Park is jam-packed, milling and jostling and swarming with almost all the population of Bethel as well as a good part of all the villages up and down the river and along the coast. A portable stage has been erected in the shadow of the abandoned Bethel bowling alley, and two or three dozen game and concession booths have been jimmied into the park's outdoor basketball courts. I don't know how much money has been changing hands. Everybody knows that out on the river the biggest kings and the highest concentrations of chums already swam by, during the strike. Now the river will bear smaller and more sporadic runs until the first of the silver salmon hit, late in the month or at the beginning of August.

But all the concession stands have been busy today, and the

288 of RAVEN'S CHILDREN

busiest have been those selling the raffle tickets, the ones dispensing slim shots at prizes that in and of themselves could save a whole fishing season. The Bethel Lions Club is offering a new Isuzu 4 × 4 pickup, while the Alaska Commercial Company has an "Outdoor Adventure Kit" — a sixteen-foot aluminum skiff, a forty-horse motor, an eighteen-gallon gas tank, a propane stove, some fishing tackle, and a picnic basket. The Association of Village Council Presidents offers a series of prizes that includes a twenty-foot Kofler aluminum boat with a ninety-horse Yamaha motor and trailer, a fifty-fathom prehung net, two round-trip tickets to Anchorage, and a ten-by-twelve canvas tent. The Veterans of Foreign Wars sell tickets for straight cash: a first prize of $10,041, two second prizes of $2500, and ten third prizes of $410. There are others as well, maybe a dozen. Oscar has loaded up for shots at them all, visiting the stands throughout the day and buying tickets in big handfuls.

This morning I came out to the park from Tundra Ridge late, but Oscar and Margaret and the kids were late too, and we all caught only the tail end of the parade of trucks and floats coming down Third Avenue and Ridgecrest Drive, then bearing left at the cemetery into the park. Inside the park the cotton grass was blossoming in white bolls around the boardwalks and the margins of the small, glassy ponds. The sky was sheeted over, the sun winking at long intervals out from the clouds and back in again. Another commercial period is scheduled for tomorrow, Wednesday, and Oscar approved of today's cool temperature, saying as we walked into the park, "I hope it's like this for fishing."

After the honor guard stood at attention on the stage as the national anthem played over the loudspeakers, and after a folksinger had taken its place, the crowd dispersed among the booths. Big as he is, Oscar was conspicuous, and it seemed as if almost everybody knew him and exchanged greetings with him. Margaret trailed impatiently far behind, the two boys on either hand, until finally, with a rebuke, she transferred them to Oscar's care, in that way evening out their progress through the quarter-tosses and ticket booths and chili-dog stands. Many of those greeting Oscar were drunk, and a number carried bottles they wanted to share, or else they wanted to share the bottle that Oscar certainly had. He brushed past all these, waving them aside and repeating over and over, like a benediction, "I'm on the wagon." I know Charlie is drunk today too, but he hasn't appeared at the park yet.

I know also that a number of the people staggering around now will roam through the hallways and bedrooms of their apartments or houses tonight like lions loose among the Christians, and on Thursday the weekly crime report in the *Tundra Drums* will describe a dozen or two dozen incidents of assault, burglary, and rape, almost all of that violence directed against immediate family members or close friends; and each description will conclude with an unvarying phrase: "Alcohol involvement was apparent." The perpetrators of these crimes will almost all be Yupik, as nearly all of the staggering drunks are Yupik; that doesn't vary much either. But this isn't a circumstance peculiar to the Kuskokwim. Although Alaskan Natives have made up only about 15 percent of the state's population during this past decade, about 34 percent of all persons incarcerated during that time have been Native. The Alaska Federation of Natives estimates that there is an 80 to 100 percent correlation between drunkenness and the commission of violent crimes by Alaskan Natives. In Bethel, at least, the police blotter would indicate that it hovers close to 100 percent.

A few days ago Evon Alexie, a former mechanic and fisherman who sold his permit and is now a wharf rat, hanging around the sea wall and living from bottle to bottle, described to me certain flasks of whiskey that had fallen into his hands serendipitously over the years, almost like Kilbuck's manna from heaven: one bottle, very old, half buried in the sand of an island in the river; another bottle left hidden and forgotten in the attic of a house he was helping to dismantle. Paradisical is the only word that conveys the sense of bliss that swam into Evon's eyes as he described these unbidden pleasures; maybe

only from the outside does that bliss seem so different from what
it was.

The Russians, to their credit, were for the most part reluctant
to introduce alcohol into Alaskan Native villages. In this they
were unlike the British, French, and American fur traders, who
used alcohol not only as a form of cash with Indian trappers
elsewhere in North America, but also as a means of ensuring
that addicted trappers would come back to the trading posts.
The Russian-American Company, however, forbade the sale of
liquor to Natives in Alaska, and also imposed limits on its availability to the company's traders and soldiers. Of course, on
those occasions when spirits were made available, the Russians
zestfully modeled the sort of spree drinking seen today in Bethel
and elsewhere in Alaska. Lieutenant Zagoskin found the char-
ismatic Aleksandr Baranov, for twenty years the chief manager
of the Russian-American Company, positively heroic in this regard. This is his description of what life was like in the company's main post in Sitka when Baranov nodded to the keeper of
the rum cellar:

> For important holidays, or in the case of some especially happy
> event . . . barrels of rum were poured into an enormous kettle,
> a circle was formed around it, and "the sky was the limit." In
> the meantime, Mr. Baranov, dressed in a raspberry-colored
> frock coat of Utrecht velvet, would disport himself on the tun-
> dra or in his house, surrounded by the boys of the settlement,
> with selected singers, honored officials, and escorted by a
> hunter dressed as a Hussar and acting as the Honor Guard. He
> loved to see his entire suite completely intoxicated — on gen-
> eral holidays nobody should stay sober, according to Mr. Bar-
> anov. Any dissenter was lowered, or rather shoved from a 52-
> foot conical rock [into the sea], or plunged into the kettle of
> rum — the same kettle in which food for 200 employees is
> cooked. Such festivities did not last one day, but three or four,
> or sometimes until the keeper of the rum cellar declared that
> there was not a drop of rum left in the barrels, or of wine in
> the bottles. In those days it could be said that they squandered

their time in drinking, but not their money. Was this not truly
a Golden Age?

Despite Baranov's scruples about offering the elixir of this
Golden Age abroad, a certain amount nonetheless found its way
into Native bellies, more in the southeast than elsewhere. Nor
did the technology for making home brew remain a secret for
long. But some southeastern Indians actually refused the alcohol
offered them by Russian traders, perceiving presciently — or
maybe from word of other Indians' experience with British traders — a threat to their independence. The Americans also forbade by law the sale of alcohol to Alaskan Natives, but the law
was unenforceable, and independent American traders didn't
have to contend with restrictions on their supply, as the Russians did. William H. Dall, the scientific director of the Western
Union Telegraph Expedition, observed in 1868 a *umiak* loaded
with two barrels of rum pulling away from an American trading
schooner off Saint Michael and wrote that this was "already the
beginning of evils whose future growth none could estimate."

Because such schooners were unwilling to assay the mouth of
the Kuskokwim, John Kilbuck saw little evidence of such evils
in his years on the river. Ironically, the Kilbucks, the Weinlands,
and Hans Torgersen might never have reached the region if not
for the fortuitous services of a reformed drunk. Before setting
sail from San Francisco in 1885, the missionaries observed a
shabby, intoxicated man — one who wished to be rid of his "ruining associations," said William Weinland — beg the captain
of the *Lizzie Merrill* for passage to Alaska in exchange for work
aboard ship. Then, out at sea, the churchmen discovered to their
horror that their captain knew scarcely a thing about deep-water
navigation. But as soon as the drunk was sober enough to stand
on deck, they found that this Mr. McDonald just happened to
be very skilled in that area. So it was "by the hand of God,"
declared Weinland, that the party sailed to the Kuskokwim
without mishap.

As traffic began to increase in the region, so did the opportunity for ruining associations. Ferdinand Drebert described his visits to Togiak, a village near Cape Newenham, after the art of home brew had been learned from the white fishermen and cannery workers at Nushagak.

> Every now and then some one would set a barrel with brew and when that was ripe the whole village joined into a drinking spree. I dreaded getting into a village at such a time. I did run into it on two occasions, but each time we still had enough daylight to reach the next village. With it all, however, they had a sort of system. Before they started their carousing they would delegate two of the men to act as policemen and these men would not indulge for the occasion. But from year to year the drinking and carousing seemed to increase.

Drebert and other missionaries condemned these sprees, whether self-policed or not, and their message acquired a more pronounced religious dimension as it was taken up by the Yupik pastors who succeeded them. To this day the strength of church and public opinion against alcohol in such villages as Kongiganak, Kipnuk, and Kwigillingok — communities that are predominantly Moravian, remote from Bethel, and rarely visited by outsiders — provides for an orderliness not radically different from that witnessed by Nelson and Kilbuck.

But from the very first this was a peace somewhat at the expense of Bethel, where a racially mixed and transient population assured that such rectitude would not achieve the hegemony it had elsewhere, and which therefore provided the place for members of those communities to go and drink when the need overcame them — a more urban and anonymous environment, free of the censure, and the risk of violence to their immediate families, that they would have had to face at home. During the World War I years the missionary Arthur Butzin confessed himself disheartened by the increasing number of residents and visitors to Bethel who "caroused and fought night upon night. When real whiskey failed, they brewed their own dope and thus the deviltry went on."

Maybe there was some abatement during the years of the Alaska territory's Prohibition, from 1918 to 1935 — a prohibition that was selectively enforced and applied almost exclusively to Alaskan Natives. But during World War II, when more than a thousand soldiers and airmen descended on Bethel, bottled liquors poured into the town as if through floodgates, as did the ingredients for home brew. Though the MPs kept order on the streets, a whole generation of problem drinkers took shape in Bethel and the surrounding villages, and it was during this time that the Kuskokwim first began to witness with such numbing frequency the deviltry routinely recounted each week in the *Tundra Drums*. Within the past thirty years the wounded children of that generation — Oscar and Charlie and Buzzo, for example — have matured, their sum no doubt including an untold and undiagnosed number of fetal alcohol syndrome victims.

Meanwhile, Bethel has continued to grow and become more volatile, with more and more outsiders moving in, more and more Yupik families coming in from the villages, and steady sources of cash developing in the town's fishing, transportation, social service, and bootleg alcohol industries. Now, on holidays such as this and after the commercial fishing periods, the drunks stagger down the roads, congregate on the steps of Swanson's and the Kusko Inn, and shout and flail bloodily at each other in their houses, beneath the bridge over Brown's Slough, or in ditches by the sides of the roads.

That Bethel is the Kuskokwim's primary arena for this has to do with the same factors that make it such a bootleggers' paradise: not only its mixed population, not only its status as a transportation hub, not only the sobriety of the outlying villages, but also its history of tentativeness and ambivalence in a legal stance toward alcohol. In 1960, a year after statehood, Bethel residents numbered about a thousand and voted against the sale of liquor in the town by a margin of twenty-five votes. Three years later, after city council members observed that while the town was underfunded, bootleggers were racking up profits into the hundreds of thousands of dollars, some members mustered enough voters to narrowly approve a city-operated liquor store, which soon grossed close to $1 million. Originally this revenue was earmarked for financing various young people's activities, but it went instead to paying for expanded police and fire departments, required by the effects of the liquor store. In Lenz and Barker's history of Bethel, state trooper John Malone described the summer of 1967 as a particularly noteworthy liquor-store summer, with forty-two drownings, eleven homicides, and forty attempted suicides: "I think we set all records in violence. The majority of the incidents happened right here within this river system. The draggers we used to use were boys from Napaskiak, called the Napaskiak Draggers in fact. I remember the Fourth of July we had a whole family who got drunk and they ran into a family of six right there in the slough, at the bridge. And all six of them drowned right there in front of everybody."

Citizens had in fact voted to close the city store in January 1966 and to ban liquor sales in Bethel, but another referendum narrowly reversed this decision in October of that year, and through subsequent years the community has flip-flopped between wet and dry by razor-thin majorities. Wet and damp is actually a more precise terminology, since the right to import alcohol for purposes of personal consumption — and for the professional benefit of bootleggers, who can net up to $350 on a case of whiskey — has never been called into question, at least among the town's *kass'aq* electorate, who live largely unmolested by the zombies in the streets. Damp is Bethel's current status; a referendum that would have allowed bars to open was defeated as recently as last August, by a margin of 124 votes.

Why are the effects of alcohol distributed so unevenly between the Kuskokwim's two populations? This question opens up a field fertile for speculation, though asking it is sort of like quantum mechanics in reverse: the mere act subtly changes the posture not so much of the people observed but of those doing the observing. The social and cultural factors that may (or may not) contribute to this epidemic are impressive in their number and range. Maybe it has something to do with the degree to which sharing a bottle of whiskey mediates between the cash economy and the subsistence economy by reflecting the way game is shared by a successful hunter, who thus establishes prestige and authority. Or maybe it has something to do with the parallels that appear, at least superficially, between a drunk's intoxication and a shaman's ecstasy, implying a corresponding acquisition of spiritual insight and influence; or with a more pronounced sense of ease with abnormal states of mind, as is generally characteristic of nonindustrial cultures (Western culture, of course, stigmatizes such states at the very same time that it markets and promotes the means to attain them). Or maybe it has something to do with the degree to which alcohol can be seen as either the purest example of the pleasure-oriented consumer goods offered by Western culture or a symbol of that culture's glamour and technology. Or with the degree to which alcohol consumption was modeled in Bethel by miners, traders, and military personnel who came to town for bouts of spree drinking, not by the missionaries and teachers, who drank either not at all or in moderate quantities at home. Or with the degree to which spree drinking mirrors Yupik patterns of consumption at celebratory feasts and complements Yupik strictures against waste. Or with the degree to which alcohol offers a channel for the aggressiveness and hostilities that previously found outlets not only in the occasional wars fought between nonaffiliated peoples but in the feasts that were contests for prestige among affiliated peoples. Or with the large swaths of idle time that exist for those who don't hold jobs or fishing permits, now that subsistence hunting and fishing are accomplished more swiftly and efficiently, now that the equipment for such activities no longer has to be manufactured in the houses and kashims, now that the traditional feasts and games and dances of winter social and ceremonial life have largely disappeared. Or it could have something to do with the lack of time-tested indigenous structures and values that run counter to alcohol abuse, a sort of social vulnerability corresponding to the physiological vulnerability that offered free play to epidemics of infectious disease; or with

the loss of cultural certainty in general and the decline of male
prestige in particular, and the accompanying despairs, which
spree drinking at least temporarily assuage; or with the degree
to which such drinking patterns and such violence are indulged
as a conscious or unconscious affront to the Western culture —
or even the Christian culture — that condemns them.

Some offer physiological explanations as well, proposing that
certain individuals or certain races are inherently disposed to
alcoholism, possibly for lack of a certain blood enzyme or possibly for presence of a certain neurological receptor. These explanations have the virtue of suggesting why alcohol has been
so uniformly devastating among Native Americans, though it
obscures the variability of individuals' responses within these
peoples. Whatever the answer, I feel a certain discomfort in even
speculating on an etiology of alcoholism in racial or cultural
terms, because of the ease with which such speculations fossilize
into stereotype. Here, the stereotype holds that a Native American will inevitably be a drunk, one whose boozing is sympto-
matic of a sad but irreversible cultural decline, whose society
was demonstrated to be less fit, in the Darwinian sense, because
it couldn't militarily defeat the hordes of settlers and soldiers
that a population-dense agricultural and industrial society threw
against it. So one supposes that it's natural for all Native Americans to get drunk, and for them to commit crimes in which
alcohol involvement is apparent. With this the stereotype slides
consolingly into place, and the real keenness of the human anguish that trails in the wake of the parties is correspondingly
diminished. Ultimately, by emphasizing those issues or circumstances unique to Native Americans' consumption of alcohol,
non-Natives become brittle, and also superficial, in their response to that consumption.

That stereotype and its dimensions of inevitability exert a fatal allure even to its subjects. "I didn't know *kass'aqs* had alcohol problems. I thought only Eskimos did," Oscar said. Well,
though bliss may come in many forms, I never knew any bliss
sadder than my father's. Whenever I can bear to look, I see his

fogged and grieving eyes in the face of any drunk shuffling down Third Avenue and cussing at the traffic. Then Bethel becomes, in my mind's eye, one of the terraces of Purgatory, where the solitary disgrace that he endured — and inflicted — is tuned to a higher, more excruciating pitch and played out on a universal scale. Alcohol abuse is so patently a maladaptive behavior that the question of why it even happens can't help but absorb those who exercise it, those who suffer from its effects, and those who simply observe it from a presumed safe distance.

But at some point the question has to be posed to individuals, where its utterance is most painful. Those who receive a promise that it will never have to be asked again — as I did once, as Elizabeth did last fall, as maybe Oscar did from James, I don't know — take the guilt for the breaking of that promise on themselves, and so accuse themselves in their father's (or mother's) disgrace. But who else is there to blame? What other recourse is there? Only in blaming ourselves, only in our assumption of the responsibility for that failure, can we preserve the fiction (as we secretly fear it to be) of the parental love that should have held that promise inviolate. Maybe in later years we start drinking ourselves in order to stage one last contest, removed now to the next generation, between that love and its nemesis, to see if we can defeat the dragon that ate our fathers, or if not, to find reassurance of their love in the very impossibility of the task.

Now, toward the end of the day, the booths empty out again and the crowd washes back to the stage to watch as the raffle drawings take place. Oscar and Margaret stand in the back, at the rear of a trailer, Oscar's tickets fanned out like poker hands. Some people from Kongiganak do well in the drawings. Robert Otto, a young man who plays basketball with Oscar's Hunters, is the winner of AVCP's round-trip tickets to Anchorage, and Marjorie Strauss, the sister of Charlie's former wife, wins one of the VFW's $410 cash prizes. Oscar's face shows his disappointment, however, as one by one his own fistfuls of tickets come up empty. "Shit, every year we buy *lots* of raffle tickets, and we never win nothing," he says when the drawings are done.

Only a few yards away from us Marjorie Strauss is celebrating her small windfall with some friends, and Margaret smiles as she gestures in Marjorie's direction. "You better snuggle up to Mamie," she says, referring to Charlie's former mother-in-law.

Oscar's loyalty lies with his brother, especially as he listens to Marjorie celebrate, and he spits into the dust and says darkly, "I ain't never gonna do that."

Oscar's friend Jo Jo Green came up empty too. Last week Jo Jo showed up on a three-wheeler down at the smokehouse while everybody was cutting and hanging the kings we caught. Jo Jo is the acknowledged discoverer of Jo Jo's Hole, that spot on the river full of fish and snags, but we hadn't seen him on the Kusko-kwim all summer. "How come you're not fishing?" Margaret called out to him that night. "Aren't you a fisherman?"

Jo Jo stopped his motor and shook his head. "Nope. Sold my permit," he said.

"Are you rich now?" Margaret asked.

"Nope," replied Jo Jo, who in fact wanted to borrow $10 from Oscar. Oscar didn't have any money, but he gave him some gas for his three-wheeler. Now Jo Jo walks sadly past the trailer, and when Oscar says that he's surprised to see him sober on the Fourth, Jo Jo replies that he spent all his money on raffle tickets. "And what do I got? Nothing. Next year I'm gonna get drunk instead."

"At least raffle tickets don't hurt you," Margaret says.

Oscar's out of money and there's nothing to do now but go home, but the family just sits for a time on the bumpers of the trailer, watching the people go back and forth on the road leading out of the park. Onstage the members of a belly-dancing group have assumed position for a performance, but there seems to be a glitch in the loudspeaker system. The five women stand self-consciously beneath the gray sky in their low-slung costumes, their arms slack at their sides, a breeze lifting their veils, as only silence proceeds from the speakers. Oscar spits again and says, "I got a feeling Charlie's gonna be a pain in the ass tomorrow, man."

4 ◉ THURSDAY'S COMMERCIAL PERIOD passes, and another one on Saturday. Buzzo says that there are so few fish in the river because of the drowned man, Andrew Jacob of Napaskiak, whose boat was found empty and circling near the lower part of the sea wall last weekend. Boats have been dragging the deep portion of the river all week, and fishermen have entirely stayed away from that area. "The fish disappear when a man drowns," Buzzo tells me. "At least until they find the body."

On Thursday Oscar and Charlie hauled in only twice during the entire six-hour period, bringing in about 150 fish, nearly all of them chums, worth less than $500, though the weather was as cold as Oscar had hoped. Charlie was drunk, had to be dragged by the scruff of the neck into the boat, and then cussed and complained about the rain the whole time. The next day he and Buzzo got into a quarrel at the smokehouse, and while stomping away from Buzzo, Charlie had yelled out to Oscar, who wasn't even involved, "I'm not fishing anymore, Oscar! You can go out yourself tomorrow, or I don't care what the hell you do, but I quit that fucking job!"

By Saturday Oscar had finished hanging Charlie's net, and we fished with that, hoping that its smaller mesh would catch the valuable reds that we presumed were slipping through Oscar's net. The two brothers took in half a ton of chums, three kings, and exactly two reds, along with a single tiny and bewildered pink salmon, worth twelve cents a pound, for about $300. They cashed in at Inlet Salmon, where we waited in line next to the boat of Ozzie Demientieff, Jerry's brother. Ozzie said that Jerry wasn't even fishing this summer; instead he was over at Valdez, running a winch on a barge housing oil-spill cleanup crews and making good money. When Ozzie gestured in disgust at his load of chums, saying they were trash fish and not worth shit, Oscar told him okay, just load them into his boat.

Oscar is starting to get desperate. There's another opening

today, Tuesday. Because of the generally low harvest volumes, the commercial openings in this district have come thick and fast for the past two weeks. I know Oscar doesn't like messing with Fish & Game, as we did at Charlie's urging the week before last, but this time it's his idea that we run two boats and combine their loads. The only problem is that Harvey is passed out stone cold on Charlie's couch. By the time we get down to the smokehouse with Charlie, Chris Jacobs and everybody else who keeps his boat there is already out on the river. The only warm body in sight belongs to Evon Alexie, who is searching the length of the sea wall for someone who might have a bottle to share. Evon is sober enough today to know what he'd be getting into if he went out alone with Charlie in the aluminum skiff, and not even the prospect of enough money to buy his own bottle can tempt him into fishing with us.

So finally the three of us go out in the *Crazy J*. This time Oscar runs the boat upriver through Straight Slough. When we come out of the northern end, we veer back half a mile in order to pick up the mouth of Church Slough, which takes a more direct path than the river to the point where the Kuskokwim divides, just below Kwethluk. Oscar then steers the boat up the wide northern fork, where the river opens out to a width of about three fourths of a mile and where four other skiffs have already strung their nets. A steady rain is falling, and above us the sky looks drained of light, while the trees and scrub on either side of the river seem oddly luminescent.

Oscar slows the boat to a halt near the fork's eastern bank, then says that he'll set the net if Charlie will take over at the wheel. But Charlie doesn't want to fish here. "Let's go upriver some more, Oscar," he says. "Look at them other boats right there. We're just gonna get corked by their nets. We ain't gonna catch fish here."

Oscar doesn't reply. He goes to the bow and ties a buoy to one end of the new net, throws the buoy overboard, and begins to feed the net over the gunwale. Suddenly Charlie guns the Evinrude and swings the bow upriver, nearly throwing Oscar out of the boat.

"Fuck you! Fuck you!" Oscar cries, catching hold of the gunwale and the forward thwart. "What the fuck are you doing?"

Charlie kills the motor just as suddenly and relinquishes the wheel, standing behind the storage cabinet with his arms crossed. "Take me home!" he says. "If you're gonna get mad at me like that, just take me home! That's what you get for getting mad at me!"

Oscar just stands in the bow, his breath coming hard as he stares at Charlie. Finally, with a visible effort of will, he swallows his anger and cajoles Charlie into helping him set net. But Charlie isn't happy when he sees the floats of the new net trailing slackly out from the boat in a line parallel to the shore. "Just a dead net here. There ain't no fish. We should go down the sandbar around that island over there, that place where you cut the net on that guy when you drove over it drunk."

"They're hitting," Oscar tells him. "I just put too many corks on that net. You can't see 'em hitting."

Charlie sits on the middle thwart, lounging against the side of the boat and spreading his arms out along the gunwale. "These are just junk fish anyway. I don't care about these fish. I'm thinking of transferring my permit over to Oscar anyway. Hey, Oscar, let's go to Fish & Game tomorrow. I'll sign my permit over, okay?"

Oscar receives this largesse without comment; he simply looks at the floats and then the other skiffs.

"Silvers are good," Charlie continues. "We'll probably make lots of money on silvers. We used to make four thousand dollars a period on silvers, one summer. We'll make lots if all those offshore ships don't take 'em. They got a two-hundred-mile limit now, but that's nothing, that's bullshit." He points to the approaching western bank, where the water looks green from the sourceless light glancing off the horsetails growing along its edge. "Considered to me, that two-hundred-mile limit is only the distance from here to that shore. Maybe a five-hundred-mile limit, maybe that's what it should be."

Oscar points to a mug of coffee that he poured from his Thermos a few moments ago and put at Charlie's feet. "Don't forget your coffee."

Charlie grins as he reaches for the mug. "If it were Black Windsor I wouldn't forget it. I better get a jug before we go down to Quinhagak."

All week long Oscar has been talking about going all the way down the river to Quinhagak, where there are supposed to be more reds than here, but he's worried about the gas money in case it doesn't turn out that way, and he hasn't been able to reach a decision yet.

Charlie sips at his coffee and says, "Oscar, we should be using two boats today. We could fill up in just one drift, you know?"

Oscar sighs. "Fish & Game is out today. I heard on the radio they got four boats on the river."

"I don't give a flying fuck."

"Well, I couldn't get a nigger to go with you anyway. Evon wouldn't go."

"Bullshit. That Marvin was gonna go with me," Charlie says, naming another wharf rat, one who hangs around with their brother John whenever John takes up a bottle. "He told me yesterday. It's no sweat to me if we use two boats. I got a permit. You guys are the ones who got to sweat if Fish & Game comes around, man." He laughs, then reaches up and touches his hair, surprised to find it streaming wet. "Shit, I don't have a hat." Then he raises his arms, staring at them in equal surprise. "And here I am wearing my good leather jacket. Shit."

After an hour's slow drift down to the fork in the river, Oscar talks Charlie into hauling in, and we take in about seventy fish, including a couple of fifteen-pound kings and a single enterprising silver, which has arrived three weeks ahead of the rest, more lustrous in its sheen than the nickel-plated kings but similar in the flecks of coal along its spine. "Geez, these are small fish," Oscar says. "We should be using a whitefish net."

Charlie cleans the net with a look on his face as though he were sifting through garbage. "I hate this fucking job." He throws a small chum into the bin and then says once more, "I'll just transfer my permit to you tomorrow." A smile flickers over his face and his eyes go slack, turning inward a moment, as he adds, "Dad sold his Bristol Bay permit about six, seven years ago. I'd have money if he didn't sell that, man. I'd have a two-story house and a Cadillac at my door."

As Oscar prepares to set net again, Charlie says that we should go up the Kwethluk River to fish.

"That's a spawning stream. It's always closed," Oscar says.

Charlie laughs. "We used to cheat all the time — come out at three or four A.M., use a penlight, when they had those nine A.M. periods. We'd fill up, sell those fish right at nine. 'Where'd you get all them fish so fast?' 'The river.'"

Almost on cue with Charlie's suggestion about the Kwethluk River, a Fish & Game float plane with blue pontoons lands noisily downstream from us, near the fork in the river. It turns and taxis slowly up the smaller eastern fork, where the Kwethluk joins the Kuskokwim, the wash from its propellor carving the surface of the river into crisp, sinuous ridges.

Charlie watches the plane through half-shut eyes from his seat on the middle bench and then asks Oscar for more coffee. He warms his fingers around the hot cup and chuckles contentedly, the rain running in beads down his cheeks. "I'm happy, you know that? I got family — nieces and nephews and a son. I got my mom. When she moved out of that house, you know, she begged me to come with her, but I said, 'Mom, I'm thirty-three years old. I got to get out on my own now.' I got no wife, but that's all right — I don't mind being a bachelor. Marianne left me after six years, but I still love her. And the bitch still loves me. I know that. Her friends say she always asks about me."

By now six other skiffs are working this portion of the river, and one of the boats, manned by a lone fisherman, has begun to set net only a hundred yards upstream of us, though a little more toward the center of the channel. Charlie twists around and shouts over his shoulder to the other fisherman, "If you run into us, it's your problem!" When the man in the other skiff proceeds with his net, Charlie shouts again, "Hey, if you run into us, it's your problem!"

"Shut up," Oscar says.

"Gonna cork us, Oscar."

"No, he's not."

Charlie shrugs and lies against the gunwale again. "I don't give a shit. These fish, to me they're just pop and cigarette money. And money means nothing to me, you know that? 'Cause everybody dies broke, no matter who you are, no matter what you got — Cadillacs or bank accounts or big fucking yachts, man. What you got makes no difference on that day when you get called upstairs."

Oscar is working the VHF, trying to find out what anybody knows about Quinhagak. Someone says that Ozzie Demientieff went down there for yesterday's period and made about $700.

"Well, that's better than we're doing here," Oscar says.

"He told me there was a lot o' reds," the voice on the radio says.

I'd like to go down to Quinhagak, to get away from Charlie's rocket fuel and also let Elsie have some peace. I tell Oscar about a Fish & Game report I heard on the radio today; they said about one in every three fish caught in the Quinhagak and Goodnews districts yesterday was red. Then Oscar raises Chris Jacobs, who says that another fisherman, Joe Chief, went down there and got hardly anything.

We get dwindling returns on our drifts here: fifty fish on the second drift, around forty on the third, and an empty net on a ten-minute fourth drift that Oscar tries just before the close of the period. An hour ago a young *kass'aq* tied up to us in his skiff and passed out ham sandwiches and warm cans of Pepsi in exchange for our serious consideration of selling our fish to Kemp-Paulucci. Oscar wolfed down his sandwich and said he'd be sure to consider it, though Charlie told the man more frankly that we'd sell to whoever had the best prices. Now that it's time to sell, Oscar heads for a little J. B. Crow tender with a broken antenna mast and a lot of peeling paint anchored near the fork. A hand-painted sign propped up on the wheelhouse of this tender offers thirty-five cents per pound for chums. Two boats are lined up ahead of us, both with lighter loads than ours. By now the rain has stopped, and the water lies as smooth as poured oil.

"How'd you get to offer thirty-five cents?" Oscar asks the captain of the tender — the only man on the boat — as he throws us a line to tie up with. "I thought Crow was paying thirty-one like all the rest."

"They are," the buyer says. "I'm paying the other four out of my own pocket."

Now the Yupik buyer is recognized by Oscar as a former pilot with one of the bush flight services. "How come you're not still flying?" he asks.

The buyer smiles hesitantly, then says, "Well, I quit when I started having trouble with my wife."

Oscar shakes his head at this, filling in the rest of the story for himself. "Goddamn women, always wanting things."

"You can't live with 'em and you can't live without 'em," Charlie adds.

The two brothers head down the river and back into Church Slough with a little more than $500 from the Crow buyer. Oscar says that since the river is so calm, this might be a good night to head down to Quinhagak. He asks Charlie, "Should we go? We'd have to buy a drum of gas. It's a hundred-dollar gamble."

For the first time all day, Charlie doesn't have anything to say. He stands next to Oscar in the stern of the boat, wearing sunglasses against the spray, his dripping hair blown back by the wind blowing over the bow. The flesh of his face is pressed flat against his bones by the force of that wind, and in the dim, luminous light he wears the gaunt aspect of someone who has already been called upstairs.

5 ☉ AT DAWN a thin light the color of old canvas
glances off the window above Oscar's head. He
listens to the wind tossing the trees outside Tony
Watson's cabin, as it has all night, and says, "More shit weather.
We ain't going nowhere, even if we find Charlie again."

Quinhagak and all them reds. Quinhagak and all them reds.
The phrase keeps popping into my head as it has for Oscar all
week, until by now, at least in our heads, the waters off Warehouse Creek, where supplies for the Moravians and Trader Lind
were once unloaded from deep-draft vessels at high tide, boil as
richly as the waters of Bristol Bay.

Oscar took his gamble late last night, buying a drum of gas
and then stopping at Charlie's place a few hours after we got
back from fishing up near Kwethluk. Charlie was ready: he'd
gotten not just one jug but two, and was nipping at one as he
slipped both flasks into his duffel bag before he went out the
door. Harvey was dewy-eyed, as though he didn't expect ever to
see Charlie again. He put his arm sentimentally around his
friend's shoulder and said to Oscar, "Take care of this guy."

"Hey, Harvey, you lock this fucking door the minute I'm
gone," Charlie said. "Don't let nobody in — don't even answer
the door. And no partying."

Harvey sniffed and nodded, waving disconsolately as we
pulled away in the Duster.

By the time we left Bethel, a misting rain had begun to dapple
the river. The rain came harder the farther we traveled, as did a
scudding south wind, and finally long series of jarring waves
began to punch hard against the *Crazy J*. At that time we were
approaching Fowler Island, about fifteen miles downstream
from Bethel. Oscar chewed his lip and shook his head as the
island hove out of the river in the twilight like the knobby back
of a turtle. On Fowler's northern side the Evinrude whined and
threw up mud. Oscar veered away from the sandbar and then
slowed to a halt, surveying the wind-whipped lower reaches of

the river. At last he threw up his arms, folded his cards, and turned back to Bethel.

Tony Watson, who owes a lot of money on the 120-horse Johnson powering his big aluminum Raider, had also decided to make a run for Quinhagak that night. We ran into him and his girlfriend, Betty, and another boat on our way back. Oscar told Tony and the other boatman what the river looked like below the island and suggested that we just wait out the dark at Tony's camp, leaving at first light in the morning if the wind was down. Tony came back behind Oscar as the other boat disappeared downstream, electing to risk the wind and the dark.

It was probably around 1:00 A.M. when we trailed into town. The rain had stopped, and the clouds were blowing apart like scraps of paper. The lights of Bethel glowed with an orange tint behind the forested humps of the islands as we approached, and red beacons winked high on the radio towers, which stood against a July night sky not so much dark as distilled of light, a starless, fluid vacancy clothed in clarity.

Charlie wanted to go home rather than to Tony's, and Oscar dropped him off at the end of the sea wall near his house, warning him to stay put in case we left again at dawn. At the fish camp Betty vanished into her sleeping bag while Tony and Oscar and I talked and drank coffee all through the night. Now Tony laughs as Oscar reminds him of traveling down to Quinhagak once at night with Charlie and Jo Jo Green, all four of them drunk. "We got out of the river and out on the bay, and then we saw the lights of the village, and we started making for them," Oscar tells me. "And we kept going, and we kept going, and gee, we never got any closer. Tony says, 'Hmm, looks like them lights are running away from us.' Finally we get close to 'em, and it's a big Jap fishing boat. Gee, man, we couldn't believe it. We were *way* out to sea!"

Outside, the dawn slowly wears into morning, and then the morning wears into noon, the wind still blowing. Oscar stands on Tony's front step, pulling at a cigarette, watching the cottonwoods and alders at the water's edge lean away from the wind, lift up briefly, and then lean away again. "Goddamn this shit weather. I got to make some money, and I'm running out of time." He throws his face up to the sky, his nostrils flaring smoke. "It was good all those days when I wanted to go but Charlie wouldn't."

Finally Oscar and I give up and go back to town, stopping at Ted's Deli, across from the Brass Buckle, for doughnuts and some more coffee. Charlie is there for coffee as well, but he's plenty mad. He complains to Oscar that Harvey wouldn't unlock the door when he got back to the house last night.

"Well, that's what you told him to do," Oscar says.

"Yeah, but then I go back later and the door's wide open," Charlie says. "They got a party going on there, and everything in the house is getting all messed up. So I just threw everybody out. I threw Harvey out too, man, just dumped his clothes right out in the street. He ain't living there anymore."

At Elsie's apartment, Margaret says that Elsie has been suffering from chest pains and has gone down to the hospital for a cardiac exam. Margaret sits in the loveseat, and Janet is seated on the floor in front of her, having her mother comb her long black hair.

"I don't know when the next opening's gonna be at Quinhagak," says Oscar. "What's today? Wednesday? Maybe Friday. It's been so bad here, I don't know if they're even gonna have any more periods on the river. Maybe they'll just shut it all down here until silvers start coming."

Crazy's eyes widen and she nearly springs from the floor in her excitement. "We should fly home!" she says.

That was the idea — Margaret and the kids were to fly down to Kongiganak today to wait there while we fished Quinhagak until the beginning of silver season. Certainly Margaret's heart must have sunk deep to see us back this morning. Last week, while we were down at the smokehouse, moving fish in to be smoked, Margaret stiffened as Elsie brushed past her going into the smokehouse. Yesterday Margaret's half-brothers Panta and Leo, visiting from Kwigillingok, stopped at the apartment, but they left after only a few minutes because they felt uncomfortable with Elsie.

Now Margaret mentions guardedly that she called her brother Paul in Kongiganak a while ago. "It's too windy for a plane down there now, but he said he'll call later if it gets good."

Oscar sits preoccupied at the supper table, banging his fingers on its surface in a thumping staccato. "You hear that they found that body yesterday?" he finally asks. "I don't know if they dragged him up or if he just popped up. Maybe it'll finally get good here. Maybe now there'll be more fish."

Margaret's sigh is almost inaudible as she bends to Janet's hair and thinks a little more about the weather in Kongiganak.

 **6** I UNDERSTAND WHAT'S happening now because I've been around all day watching it unfold. But if I forget about that for a minute, this scene on the sea wall has a weird and dreamlike quality. Oscar is standing like a monument on the wall's steel lip, the rain falling in driven nails around him, his eyes staring half a mile away at his own net — or, more precisely, Charlie's net — as it's hauled up empty into the *Crazy J* from the rain-pocked river, his lips drawn tight and grinning as it comes up like that. It must be even stranger for Oscar, almost like an out-of-body experience, this glimpse of his own affairs from a great distance, and the unexpected emotion he feels in watching them.

Oscar is as heedless of the rain as the derelict drunk crumpled in a stupor against the sea wall almost at his feet. A moment ago I watched the drunk, an old man with a week's growth of whiskers, stagger there from the road. His checked wool jacket was sopping wet, and he stopped to pull its sleeves down the stems of his wrists in gestures as fastidious as an aristocrat's. Then he crouched down, laid his neck and skull gently against the sea wall, and at last simply collapsed into the mud, curling up like wadded paper beneath the rain. Neither Oscar nor the drunk is aware of the other. I watch all this comfortably from the passenger seat of the Duster — the old man helpless beneath the emptying sky, Oscar no less helpless on his pedestal.

We swim today in a river of booze. It's Friday the 13th, and Fish & Game has decided to open the river for another commercial period. This morning Charlie was still flying on the R&R that he'd intended to have as comfort in Quinhagak. So was Harvey, who was forgiven, his clothes taken back in, as soon as the both of them got drunk enough yesterday. Oscar grabbed Charlie at his house and drove him down to the smokehouse as usual, but when we got there we found the whole area overrun with drunks — Hippa, Emma, Buzzo, Evon Alexie and his partner, Marvin, a couple of other guest stars unknown to me, all of them lurching about crazily in the rain, clustering into caterwauling groups, then staggering off into solitary orbits. Meanwhile the children from the fish camp — Hippa's sons, Rex and Mumford, and Buzzo's little Alexandra, who'd come back with her father from his last visit to Kipnuk — kept their distance, playing along the length of the sea wall running up Brown's Slough.

Charlie and I got out, then Oscar gathered the kids up into the Duster. He blinked slowly, shaking his head, as he watched Charlie join the others like a sheep joining the fold. Then he said, "I'm taking these kids up to Eleanor's. We'll load the boat when I get back."

I tried to stay out of the way, but they found me. I'd bet Buzzo $5 that he wouldn't be sober on the Fourth, and then I'd paid him when in fact he was. After Oscar had gone, he came up to me sadly and pronounced that he'd have to give me those five bucks back, now that he'd fallen off the wagon again. Hippa was sad too; he said that I was lucky, that I was "living a freebie," since I didn't ever have to get shitfaced like they did. Charlie wondered why Oscar and I kept going out with him on the river. "How do you know I'm not an asshole? How do you know that I won't drown both you guys and come back alone?"

When Oscar returned, the children emptied out of the Duster and scattered like sparrows along the sea wall. "Eleanor's not around right now. I guess I got to check over there again in a while."

Then Oscar and I loaded the boat for what seemed like the thousandth time, navigating our way through drunks as though they were perilous reefs: the eighteen-gallon gas can, the five-gallon gas can, the marine battery, the oars, the Thermoses of coffee, the grub box, the propane tank and stove, the tarpaulin, Charlie's net, the buoys, the tools, the rain gear. Afterward Oscar stood in the boat, took off his glasses, and wiped them clean of rain, his eyes small and sad and bearlike.

"Fuck these goddamn drunks. And fuck Charlie — I don't even want to go out with him. And look at it out there. It's shitty again. When it's calm like that the fish stay down." Then he put his glasses on and sat down heavily on the bow thwart. "But I'm flat broke. I got my VHF down at Greg's Electronics now with a burned-out transmitter, probably 'cause I used that rubber-ducky antenna on it when we were stuck down at the Ishkowik, and I can't even get it out of there. I got to make some money."

He shook his head when I suggested we go out alone and pick up Charlie when it was time to sell. "I'm too scared to do that for a whole period. Remember, I'm still on probation from last summer. If they catch me fishing out there without a permit, they lock me up and throw away the key."

It took some doing to cut Charlie out of the herd and get him into the boat, but no sooner was that done than he looked down at the sneakers on his feet and protested that he'd left his boots back at the house. So Oscar decided to give Eleanor another try and piled the kids into the Duster again, while I drove Charlie home in the old pickup, which still hadn't sold.

"I don't want to go fishing. I hate that fucking job," Charlie said as we turned down Third Avenue. "I don't mind the work, but there's no money in it, you know? And money means nothing to me anyway. But Oscar wants money. He's always complaining about money. I should just transfer my permit to him. Shit, we'll go down to Fish & Game tomorrow and I'll do that, right after we go fishing today." He glanced suddenly from side to side as though he couldn't recognize his surroundings. "Where are we going? My house? For what? Oh yeah, my boots." He laughed, and then he pressed his lips hard together, his chin jutting out. "Shit, man, I'm the captain of that boat. I'm the one with the permit. I'm the one who says if we fish or not. When you got your rain gear on, man, and you're in that boat, you got nothing. It all belongs to me."

At the house Charlie got his boots and then bade me follow him to the willow bush where the sparrows had hatched. The tiny nest now lay empty on its branch. "One time a while ago I chased some kids away that were bothering that nest while them babies were still in it." He peered into the nest and smiled, his eyes blinking slowly. "Later on that mother bird flew down and sort of whistled at me, and it was just like she was saying to me, if you know what I mean, 'Thanks for being my friend.'" He laughed again, embarrassed, shrugging his shoulders dismissively.

Oscar was already back by the time we returned, and this time the kids were gone. But he just sat slumped at the wheel of the Duster, and his face was hollow with despair when he looked up at our approach. "I got stopped and ticketed," he said. "That new cop they hired gave me a ticket for 'unsecured child' 'cause Hippa's two kids in back didn't have their seat belts on. I don't know what they're gonna do to me. I might lose my license with that probation." He sat back against the seat and put his hands around the steering wheel. His knuckles dimpled and turned white. "I got to be in court on July twenty-sixth. I know I sure as hell can't pay that fine."

Hippa looked even worse than Oscar. He staggered up to the driver's window of the Duster with tears streaming down his cheeks. "Was it my kids, Oscar? I'll pay the fine for 'em. How much was it? You're shitting me. Two hundred and fifty? Okay,

I'll pay every penny of that, Oscar. Every penny, Oscar."

Hippa wept in part for Oscar's ticket but mostly for his own boat and motor, which had been stolen from the ramp right beneath everybody's noses sometime this morning. His voice catching with grief, he said, "Buzzo's fired me from fishing with him, and Charlie's fired you. We got to get us a permit, Oscar, and fish together. But I don't even have a boat now. Shit, man, all I had in the world was that boat. What am I gonna do, Oscar?" His tears fell like the rain drumming on the hood of the Duster. Oscar promised him he'd look for the boat when he got a chance, and then sat brooding in his seat, with his face turned away.

Over near the drying rack Charlie and Marvin had hold of each other's jackets and were angrily pushing at each other. Oscar climbed wearily out of the car and helped me to separate them, then stood for a few moments talking with Charlie. Charlie was still mad from his shoving match with Marvin, and the more Oscar had to say to him, the madder he got. Finally he exploded, shouting, "Fuck you, Oscar! I'm not going fishing today!" Then he stalked up the driveway leading away from the ramp and up to the road.

Oscar just stood there, his shoulders stiff, his face black with rage. For a minute I thought he was going to chase after Charlie and finish what Marvin had begun. But finally — in precisely the same manner as Charlie, in almost a parody — he turned and stalked away himself. He jumped into the Duster, shouting to me that he wasn't going fishing today either, and then spun into the driveway and out to the road with his tires skidding in the wet gravel.

Even then, Oscar wasn't entirely ready to quit. Within an hour, after he'd calmed down, he sought me out and said we'd go out alone if the drunks had cleared away from the smokehouse. But we found them still there in full force, like an occupying army. We crouched behind a row of oil drums at Brown Slough Marina, where Oscar sometimes bought gas, and peered clandestinely down at the launch ramp. Oscar said that he was tired of this bullshit and mentioned that somebody who runs some vending machines around town was looking for a driver. "But unless he gives me a job right away, let's just you and me get out of here and go to Quinhagak tomorrow."

I don't know what he intended to do about a permit in that event, but I didn't think it was worth hashing out just then. We went back to those drums again an hour and a half later, and still the drunks held the beach, though Charlie and Marvin had gone off somewhere. By then the period was half over, and there was hardly any point in going out so late anyway.

It was at that moment that something broke in Oscar, or seemed to. He turned to me bleakly and said that everything was falling apart. His voice was filled with a kind of emptiness that I'd never heard from him before as we drove to the section of the sea wall in front of Swanson's Marina to see how the other fishermen were doing. The radio in the Duster said that a huge run of red salmon in southeastern Alaska had contributed to this season's low prices, as had a Japanese overstock from the previous year. Oscar told me that he was going to give up on his AA meetings, and also on the detoxification program he'd started with his counselor at the treatment center. "None of that shit's doing me any good," he said. The whiteness had gone from his knuckles on the wheel; he handled the big car like a sleepwalker, hardly seeming to see the turns in the road or its sparse traffic.

Now an enormous raven lands on the sea wall above the folded drunk. It looks appraisingly at the old man, as though he were meat not quite ripe enough yet, then steps sideways along the wall in Oscar's direction. A few moments earlier, while he was still in the car, Oscar expressed surprise that only two boats were working this section of the river. But then he judged that a lot of fishermen were probably quitting early because they weren't catching anything.

Suddenly he sat bolt upright in his seat as he recognized the blue wooden boat downstream from us. "Shit, man, that's my boat!" he cried. The two men inside it had to be Charlie and

Marvin, unaccounted for earlier at the launch ramp. "Goddamn that shit!" he bellowed. "That's my boat! He took my goddamn boat!"

Oscar still stands in the rain, watching Charlie and Marvin pull in their net and clean it, or rather just pull it in: fathom after fathom, the green nylon mesh comes glistening and empty from the river. Oscar turns and tells me that we're not missing anything by not being out there. The raven lifts croaking into the sky, and on Oscar's face is written the cold cynicism that takes assurance in the failure of good works.

VIII

LIVING WITHOUT
VIOLENCE

1 ☉ IF YOU WALK into the brush beyond the cabin at
Tony Watson's fish camp, you almost immediately
find yourself walking on pavement, though still enclosed by aspens and stunted cottonwoods, beset by fat, solitary
bees and swirling clouds of gnats. This is an odd sort of effect.
The pavement seems to offer hardly any inconvenience at all to
either the tough, elastic trees or the spreading beds of fireweed,
mountain avens, oxytrope, parrya, and creeping willow that
flourish almost as thickly here as they do elsewhere on this big
island — though for all practical purposes this land is just another chunk of the riverbank, skewing the Kuskokwim into an
oxbow, and is strictly an island only by virtue of the narrow,
unnavigable slough that runs between the ends of the oxbow, a
mile away in either direction.

The pavement lies white and smooth between all these trunks
and stems and beds, almost as though it had been dropped like
a precut template upon the forest floor. As you walk on, the
brush and vegetation become sparser, separated by wider swaths
of uninterrupted concrete. In the space of a hundred yards or so
the brush gives out almost entirely, though random patches of
flowers and herbs remain, and you find yourself at the central
junction of the old airstrip's crosshatched runways. The main
runway, as wide as six lanes of an interstate highway, runs out
of sight into the heart of the island. Nothing else remains — no
buildings, no vehicles, no machinery, no explanation, just the
clean, level pavement, slowly losing its battle with the under-

growth, lying as mute beneath the clouds as the architecture of a vanished civilization.

Longtime Bethel residents don't need an explanation; they remember it as the airbase that the U.S. Army built in 1942 following the Japanese bombing of Dutch Harbor in the Aleutians and the accompanying invasion and occupation of the islands of Attu and Kiska. It was called Todd Army Airfield, in honor of Jack Todd, the first American pilot downed by the Japanese over Kiska. The invaders hoped to use the Aleutians as a staging ground for bombing raids down to Seattle's shipyards and airplane factories, but nobody in Bethel knew that, or would have been much reassured by it. During the war, windows in the little town of four hundred were blacked out every night with tarpaper, burlap, or animal hide, and on occasion balloons carrying incendiary bombs were floated up the Kuskokwim valley from Japanese ships lying just off the coast, though none did any damage.

The immediacy of the enemy threat to Bethel at that time influences even today the feelings of many residents about the current Japanese commercial presence in the delta and the manner in which that presence dominates the river's main cash industry. In Oscar's world such tensions are ultimately a corollary of where he is: a place that, precisely because of its remoteness and its relative lack of population, has throughout history defined the single point at which both sets of humanity's great cultural paradigms — not only Old World and New World but also East and West — grind and scrape against each other like vast tectonic plates. They shift under his feet even as he attempts to balance and stand. The heat generated by their friction boils within his own blood.

Oscar recognizes something of the history of his position when he refers to the Japanese, in his delicate phrasing, as cousins. Such an affinity exists for all Native Americans, but it runs close to the surface for Eskimos, because of the position of the Eskimos — well, not of the Eskimos themselves but of their ancestors, those at the tail end of the series of ice age migrations that brought hunting peoples from Asia into the Americas. Most of these migrants (though not Oscar's ancestors) came across the subcontinent of Beringia, a wide and arid landmass uniting Asia and North America on an on-again, off-again basis throughout the eons of the ice sheets' various advances and retreats.

Currently, the earliest undisputed evidence of human presence in the New World dates back 14,000 years, which is 3000 years before the most recent submersion of Beringia. Some argue, however, that the migrations began even longer ago, possibly as far back as 40,000 years ago, during an earlier appearance of the land bridge. But even that amount of time is hardly an eye-blink in the temporal spaces of human physical and cultural history, or prehistory, and the whole question gives to the phrase "New World" a surety undreamed of by Columbus and other Western navigators. Whatever the case, most of the migrants ventured across the bridge centuries in advance of what we now call the agricultural revolution in the Neolithic Middle East, at a time when the economic and social patterns that have prevailed throughout more than 99 percent of human history — that is to say, hunting and gathering in small family groups — also prevailed throughout the whole world, so there was no distinction between Old and New, East and West.

The ancestors of modern Eskimos weren't really the last ones through the door; rather, they arrived after the door had already closed, sort of jimmied it open, and then, finding themselves suitably accommodated on both sides of it, just stayed there, forging a unique racial and cultural identity right on the dividing line. This began somewhere between 5000 and 8000 years ago, long after Beringia had last succumbed, when paleo-Eskimo peoples crossed from Siberia to Alaska in skin boats. In fact, Edward W. Nelson collected a folktale on the delta — an alternative creation story to the one involving Raven — that suggestively describes just such a crossing. It tells of a man who came from the far side of the great water at a time when there was water all over the earth and a deep cold prevailed, and the sea ice ground together into ridges and hummocks. The solitary traveler married a she-wolf on this side of the water, and their children, born in pairs of twins, each pair speaking a different language, peopled the world as the earth's ravines and riverbeds were being carved out by melting snow running down the hillsides.

These migrants were distinguished by an economy and hunting technology that primarily exploited Arctic marine mammals, and no one knows for sure whether this economy first took shape in Alaska after the crossing, in Siberia before the crossing, or even on the retreating southern shores of Beringia. But in small numbers other people who practiced it began to move east along the uninhabited northern coasts of Alaska and Canada, possibly west to Siberia, and south to the Alaska Peninsula, the Aleutians, and south-central Alaska. Then, maybe during the first century after the birth of Christ, there occurred a rich and sudden cultural florescence among the Eskimoan people in the region of the Bering Strait, and it was there that the salient characteristics of what later became known as the Thule culture took shape. Elements of this heightened culture and its superior marine mammal technology diffused rapidly throughout the hunters of the Arctic and sub-Arctic, and thus it was that members of a modern Eskimo race, practitioners of this distinctive and still developing culture, greeted the amazed Norsemen and then the Western European explorers over on the other side of the world. By then there had been no wholesale movement of people between the two worlds for 5000 years, so entrenched and so successful were these occupants of a place defining not only the longitudinal border of East and West but an entirely new latitudinal line dividing the habitable from the uninhabitable.

In the Yukon-Kuskokwim Delta, a salmon-based version of the Thule culture took form and spread down the coast. It also fragmented; an Indian intrusion into southwestern Alaska may have driven a wedge into southern Eskimo populations and re-

sulted in a separate Aleut cultural complex. The culture fragmented in the north as well. As northern Eskimo groups developed economies that were firmly dependent on whaling, and as
cultural differences between northern and southern populations
emerged as a consequence of this and other factors, the original
Eskimo language divided slowly into Inupiaq and Yupik
throughout the first Christian millennium. Eventually, the prev-
alence of Inupiaq on the Seward Peninsula split Yupik villages
in southwestern Alaska away from those in northeastern Siberia.

In precontact times some twelve thousand people lived in the
Yukon-Kuskokwim Delta. This was the largest and densest Eskimo population in existence, making up two thirds of the Eskimo population of Alaska and a quarter that in the entire
world. Relations with the Athabascan Indians of the interior
were friendly, for the most part, and this provided for a powerful Yupik influence on Athabascan culture and the peaceful assimilation of many Indians into Yupik cultural forms during the
Eskimos' unusual inland penetration up the Yukon and Kuskokwim rivers. At the same time a more general diffusion of Yupik
goods, technologies, and ideas took place in trade networks
stretching east to the American Northwest and west through
Siberia to China and Japan. Just like the first *kass'aq* travelers,
individuals would sometimes undertake long summer or winter
journeys for no purpose other than trade, and each summer Yupik and Inupiaq Eskimos, and sometimes also Athabascan Indians and Chukchis from Siberia, would gather in great numbers
for regional trade fairs. In 1881, Nelson was impressed by the
size of one such fair at Hotham Inlet: "This camp was arranged
with almost military precision; along the beach, above the high
water mark, with their sterns to the sea, were ranged between
sixty and seventy umiaks, turned with the bottom upward and
toward the prevailing wind. . . . Seventy-five yards back from
the umiaks, in a line parallel to the beach, were ranged over two
hundred kaiaks, supported about three feet from the ground on
low trestles made of branching stakes."

At such fairs the Yupik traders offered mink, fox, otter, sable, and beaver pelts; seal, walrus, and bird skins; ivory, feathers, and pigments; grass baskets and bentwood bowls and boxes; pokes of seal oil, and quantities of dried salmon. In exchange they wanted Dall sheep horns or baleen; caribou or reindeer skins, particularly the prized white reindeer skins from Siberia; minerals such as chert, nephrite, and jadeite; and above all whatever European goods — tobacco, snuff, firearms, ammunition, hatchets, knives, cloth, iron, or glass beads — might filter through the Chukchi from Russia.

The first white men seen in the delta — the first actual representatives of one of those other paradigms that had recently taken shape — were shipwrecked sailors, who, on the whole, probably met an unhappy fate. "We used to kill them," one Yupik elder reported to the anthropologist Lydia T. Black. Later, however, when Russian traders and explorers were able to provide access to industrial goods, they were integrated into the Eskimo trade networks. But the villages were in no way prepared to relinquish control of these networks and exchange relationships. In fact, an 1836 Yupik attack on a party of Russians from Saint Michael, in which one Russian was killed and seven were wounded, was prompted by the determination of one community to continue to collect an annual tribute of furs exacted from the inhabitants of Sledge Island — a relationship that the new Russian fort had served to weaken. The attack didn't succeed, and probably this tribute relationship ended, though other specimens of exchange did not.

Indeed, the chief purpose of Zagoskin's expedition in 1842, along with identifying portages between the Yukon and the Kuskokwim, was to discover the routes that furs traveled between the delta and Siberia and to arrange for Russian control of those routes and that trade. To that end Zagoskin recommended that Russian-American Company traders buy up all the available furs in the delta and whatever other goods might be traded with the Chukchi and the Siberian Eskimos. But the people of the delta were unwilling to sell exclusively to the Russians, and the Siberian trade simply continued from village to village in paths redirected around the Russian forts.

Even within these channels, however, and even given the importance of this trade, relations between nonaffiliated peoples — that is, people whose villages did not fall within one group's interlocking grid of kin relations — were always prickly, sometimes bloody. These relations were maintained as much by the threat of reprisal as by the diplomatic bonds of obligation, and maybe their volatility owed at least something to the powerful mechanisms in place against expressing antagonism within a village or between neighboring affiliated villages. These included the imperatives inherent within kinship itself; the status accorded those who characteristically displayed self-control, compliance to the general will, and a reluctance to interfere in the affairs of others; the gossip, ridicule, and even ostracism visited on those who departed from such ideals; and finally — if all else failed, and conflict came to a murderous head — the threat of blood feud, the revenge that would be taken at some unspecified time for the murder of a relative. Nelson commented on the gravity of this eventuality.

> Blood revenge is considered a sacred duty among all the Eskimo, and it is a common thing to find men who dare not visit certain villages because a blood feud existing, owing to their having killed some one whose near relatives live in the place. On different occasions I had men go with me where they dared not go without the protection by a white man's presence. In one place a man kept by me like a shadow for two days and slept touching me at night. The man who held the feud against him would come into the house where we stopped and sit for hours watching the one with me like a beast of prey, and the mere fact that my Eskimo companion was with a white man was all that saved him.

Nelson added that people believed that a murderer could be recognized simply by his eyes, which had a restless, searching, and uneasy quality, and he himself came to believe that this was true.

On rare occasions such a feud could open up into widening gyres of violence that might consume entire villages, but the very savagery of this mechanism argued powerfully for the importance of social and psychological skills in avoiding overt conflict, swallowing or redirecting antagonism, and remaining mindful of the economic interdependence of families and households.

From pressure cookers such as these villages could be, finally, war parties sometimes issued, usually against villages or confederations of villages some distance away. Nelson walked in the aftermath of a war along the lower Yukon, and he was told that the several ruined villages whose remains he saw had been destroyed before the Russians came by war parties from the Kuskokwim. During that time, an informant said, the threat of raids had caused people to choose village sites primarily for their defensibility. Folklore relates that Yupik houses were sometimes built with secret compartments for concealing children and with hidden exits and interconnecting tunnels. Raids would only rarely have been the result of territorial or border disputes, however. Instead, fighting customarily revolved around, say, a particular resource in times of famine or harvest disruption, or a contest between jealous shamans, or a blood feud that began with some criminal action by either travelers or their hosts.

In oral tradition, one famous example of a feud that spun out of control was the War of the Eye, which began (in most tellings) with the accidental puncturing of a child's eye with a dart thrown by another boy within a village's kashim. The father of the boy who had thrown the dart offered to placate the father of the injured boy with one of his own son's eyes, but this man instead blinded the offending boy completely. This was the beginning of a blood feud that eventually pitted Yupik against Inupiaq villages, or Kuskokwim against Yukon villages, or coastal villages against upriver communities, according to various versions. Possibly the memorable dart incident was just one episode in a wider series of engagements, and possibly its peculiar vividness and horror recommended it as the starting point in folk memory for other conflicts. In any event, all such hostilities came to an abrupt close with the arrival of the Russians and the heightened trade relations that they fostered.

But the Russians, shipwrecked or not, may not actually have been the first from the Old World to make landfall in Alaska since the end of the migrations. According to the yearbooks of the Sung dynasty in China, a Buddhist monk, Hwui Shan, sailed with four companions out of the Sea of Japan to the Kamchatka Peninsula, and from there to a string of islands that would have to be the Aleutians, and finally up the Aleutians to the Alaskan mainland in A.D. 458. Over the next thirteen hundred years, Alaskan Native folklore recounts, a number of unintended landings occurred elsewhere in Alaska. The Tlingit, Haida, and Tsimshian Indians of southeastern Alaska told stories of lost Chinese sailors and ancient Chinese trade goods washing up on their coast, and also described similar castaways of Western extraction. Of particular note was a young woman with startling red hair, who was taken to wife by a Tlingit chief; allegedly she lived to an extreme old age and had many children, whose red-haired descendants later amazed the Russians.

The Russians had legends as well. Certain Cossack traders claimed to have visited the mainland as early as 1648, and it was their claims — along with the luxuriant furs appearing at the Siberian trade fairs — that prompted Czar Peter the Great to charge a Dane, Vitus Bering, with finding Alaska once and for all and determining whether any overland connection existed between Siberia and North America. There were even rumors of a lost Russian colony in Alaska; these persisted after Bering's official discovery of the mainland, and as late as 1791 Russian explorers went in search of this colony along the western coast.

Half a century earlier, when Bering himself lay shipwrecked and scurvy-ridden on the Komandorskiye Islands, at the close of one of the West's last great voyages of discovery, it was with a perverse sort of irony that he was driven nearly to madness by hordes of marauding foxes: the pelts of these animals made up a good portion of his cargo and much of his reason for being there in the first place. But Vitus Bering's unhappy career was beset with irony. By the time of his death, it had been seventeen years since the czar had given him his charge, and since the huge and kindly navigator had begun the back-breaking task of hauling iron, tools, and rigging across five thousand miles of wilderness in order to build his ships on the Siberian coast. His first voyage, in 1727, was a failure; he indeed sailed north through the narrow strait, fifty-four miles wide, that bears his name today, and indeed sighted one of the Diomede Islands, but in heavy fog he was unable to see the Alaskan mainland. Once into the Chukchi Sea, he concluded to his own satisfaction that the two continents were not joined, and he decided to turn back rather than risk entrapment in the sea ice. But this left unfulfilled the czar's mandate to land on the mainland and make contact with some manner of European settlement or vessel in order to ascertain the claims of other nations.

After wintering in Kamchatka, Bering tried again, but his ship was blown off course by storms. The first verifiable sighting of the mainland seems to have been made four years later, in 1732, by an obscure geodesist named Mikhail Gvozdev, whom a superior officer had unexpectedly charged with exacting tribute in furs from Native populations, and who sailed across the strait in the very ship that Bering had left behind, landed on one of the Diomede Islands, and caught sight of present-day Cape Prince of Wales. Not even Bering's passage through the strait was a verifiable Western first; in 1648 Semen Dezhnev, a Cossack, led a party of fur hunters around the northeastern corner of Siberia in a small boat, thus demonstrating that the continents were in fact divided. Six accompanying vessels were lost, and Dezhnev's own boat was wrecked. Still, it was a considerable feat of navigation, though news of it did not reach Moscow for eighty years, after Bering had already left on his first expedition.

In 1741, after nine troubled years of preparation for a larger and more complex expedition, Bering set sail once more. This time, with two brigs and 150 men, he left Kamchatka on a southerly heading. Within days, however, his flagship and the second brig, commanded by Aleksey Chirikov, lost sight of each other in a storm, and they were never able to rejoin. Both ships made their way into the Gulf of Alaska, where Chirikov was the first to sight the mainland, seeing land at Cape Addington on the western side of Prince of Wales Island on the fifteenth of July. The very next day, on the Feast of Saint Elias, Bering sighted a towering snowcapped peak much farther up the coast, near Icy Bay, which he named in honor of the saint. Chirikov, meanwhile, made landfall, sending his mate, Abraham Dementieff, ashore in a longboat with ten other men armed with muskets. But the longboat never returned, and when a similar fate befell a second boat sent to search for Dementieff, Chirikov just waited offshore a few days, nervously contemplating the silent forest, and finally set sail back to Kamchatka. Twenty of his sailors died of scurvy along the way.

Bering, exhausted and already ill himself, turned back without making landfall, much to the disappointment of his young naturalist, Georg Wilhelm Steller. But Steller found fame anyway with his brilliant observations and descriptions of the islands they visited en route. Then, at one of the tiny Komandorskiye Islands, only 150 miles east of Kamchatka — after the ship's crew had already been racked by thirst, scurvy, gales, and freezing weather — a rogue wave threw Bering's brig over a reef. The survivors took shelter for the winter in dugouts carved from fox dens, although swarms of fearless foxes stole food and chewed at shoes; Steller once killed more than seventy of the beasts in three hours. Bering finally died there, along with a score of his men.

The following summer Steller and forty-five other emaciated and toothless survivors sailed to Kamchatka in a ship built from the wreckage of the *Saint Peter*. They took with them sealskins, fox pelts, and — more immediately impressive than the expedition's treasure trove of scientific data — some nine hundred sea otter pelts. Deep, velvety, durable, and the warmest of all animal furs, these otter skins were subsequently bought by wealthy Chinese mandarins for as much as the modern equivalent of $5000 each. News of this cargo swiftly persuaded a group of *promyshlenniki* — Cossack trappers, hunters, and traders — to descend on the Komandorskiye Islands, and the unfortunate Bering's gravesite, where an easy harvest of 1600 sea otters, 2000 fur seals, and 2000 blue arctic foxes made them as rich as mandarins themselves.

So it was that Bering's third voyage proved a great success, though the commander, who had endured some ignominy following his failure of nerve in the Chukchi Sea, didn't live to enjoy it. But with his voyage the old gate between the two worlds was nudged open once again, though this time by profit-minded Europeans who more or less bypassed the people who had chosen to settle at the gate. Instead the Westerners sailed to the south in their square-masted ships, and it was from the south that they finally approached the Eskimos almost a century later, at a time when the Russian-American Company had failed in its bids for footholds in Hawaii and California and was turning its energies north.

Elsewhere the encounter between Europeans and Alaskan Natives began in earnest. In southeastern Alaska the fate of Chirikov's longboats was never discovered, though it was supposed by the Russians that the men had been murdered by Indians. Certain Tlingit tales indeed describe such ambushes, but others describe boatloads of white sailors fleeing into the forest rather than facing death from disease aboard their ship, and eventually being accepted into the tribe and marrying Tlingit women. Whatever the case, the irrepressible Aleksandr Baranov established the New World headquarters of the Russian-American Company in southeastern Alaska in 1799, and in the area of the Russian fort at Sitka, relations between the intruding Europeans (who in fact paid a small sum for rights to the land they occupied) and the bellicose Tlingits and Haidas were by turns delicate and hostile.

In the Aleutians the advent of the Russians was nothing less than hellish. The Aleuts had the misfortune to be both incomparably skilled in hunting the sea otters that swarmed in their inlets and bays and tactically vulnerable in their island settlements. After looting the Komandorskiye Islands, the ungoverned *promyshlenniki*, operating beyond the pale of both the Russian government and the nascent Russian-American Company, virtually flew to the Aleutians, where a Russian mariner avenged some of his countrymen's deaths by lining up twelve Aleut youths back to back and firing a single bullet, which finally came to rest in the ninth youth. After a series of bloody encounters and savage reprisals — reprisals whose only countenance was found in the chilling phrase "God is high and the czar is far away" — the Aleuts were literally enslaved, and their numbers were reduced as terribly as the sea otters they were compelled to hunt.

Among the uncut spaces of the Bering coast, however, where the dimensions of the land were so vast and the ecology so forbidding (at least to Europeans) as to defy both the gunships of the *promyshlenniki* and anything more than a token Russian military presence, an entirely different sort of ethic prevailed. Here a vigilant sort of diplomacy rather than shows of brute force provided for the best commercial returns, and Naval Lieutenant Zagoskin, who began his explorations into the interior exactly one hundred years after Vitus Bering's death, was one of its wisest practitioners. Certainly it helped that he was circulating among people who already knew and admired European goods, and who therefore provided him with a ready market.

> Our arrival at each village constituted a celebration, but in this and the following receptions the main thanks were due to Kantelnuk [a Yupik trader, guide, and interpreter]. He explained to the natives who had never seen Russians how these guests should be received. . . . We for our part had learned about native customs and tried as much as possible to conform to them: everything we needed we asked for, and placed in sight the goods to be exchanged for it; we lay down to sleep according to their system, which was with the heads toward the center of the kazhim, in spite of the fact that during the night men were apt to walk over our heads; we did not chop the ice with iron axes; we had no relations with women and did not enter a

winter house without an invitation. When we made return gifts
for what we had received we abandoned to old and young our
snuffbox and tobacco pouch, and by this behavior we found
help at every turn the next morning when we were packing.

For all that politeness and good will, however, Zagoskin kept
one member of his party on watch through the nights, just as
Nelson was later to be guarded on King Island. Sometimes he
was questioned by his hosts as to the necessity for this.

I never resorted to subterfuge but answered directly something
like this: "You are good people, but you say yourselves that
you are often incited by an evil spirit to do something wrong.
What if we all went to sleep and an evil spirit should prompt
you to kill us? Afterwards you would be very sorry that you
had killed people who had not done you any harm, but in the
meantime other Russians would want revenge, and it would be
very uneasy for you." "Yes, you are right," the natives would
say. "Please keep your watchman, you will be protecting yourselves and us from bad actions."

The Kuskokwim's first Russian explorer, Ivan Vasilev, had
been glad to be quit of the river in 1830 after conducting a survey made hasty by what he felt to be the constant threat of attack. But Zagoskin's courage, grace, and good sense were one
small element in a large constellation of factors that preserved a
remarkable peace on the Kuskokwim throughout the years of
Russian presence. These included the sacramental dimension of
the guest-host relationship in Yupik ideology; the lack of extensive Russian settlement and commercial threat to the delta's
wildlife resources, which, unlike the sea otter in the Aleutians,
were able to meet the heightened demand for furs comfortably;
the mutual interest of Russian and Yupik in each other's goods
and skills; the potential for deadly military reprisal possessed by
both sides; the many Russian-American Company employees
who were of mixed Russian, Siberian, Yupik, or Aleut descent,
and the willingness of these individuals to form Yupik-style
trading partnerships and marry into Yupik families; the readi-

ness of the Orthodox priests to accommodate their teachings to existing Yupik belief systems; and the abrupt end of the precontact interregional wars, which came about as a result of both heightened trade relationships between regions and the breakdown of regional lines because of smallpox epidemics and subsequent population shifts.

On the young lieutenant's part, the sympathy that he was willing to extend to his hosts may have had something to do with the political ferment of nineteenth-century Russia. Zagoskin was born in 1808 to a family of landed gentry on an estate worked by serfs in the central Russian plains. Though living some five hundred miles from the nearest saltwater, the gentry in this region had made a tradition of sending their sons into naval service, and at the age of fourteen Zagoskin was enrolled in the Naval Cadet Corps. Four years later he entered the Imperial Navy, choosing to serve on the Caspian Sea in the erroneous belief that he would be able to visit his home near the city of Penza on the way to his ship ("Unfortunately they taught me geography in the corps," he later wrote of this navigational error). He served eight years as an officer and ship commander on a body of water known in the navy as "the Siberia of the seas," a reference to the Caspian's severe weather, treacherous coasts, and hostile Muslim tribesmen, but also to the fact that many officers of revolutionary political leanings had been demoted and exiled there. Later service on the Baltic was no great improvement; during the icebound winter months, some officers out of boredom challenged themselves to drink up literally all the wine in the city of Kronshtadt. "Legend has it that this was accomplished," Zagoskin wrote. "The emblem of the group was a wine-bottle cork; it was worn on the ribbon of the Order of Vladimir suspended from a button-hole."

While not averse to wine himself, Zagoskin also entertained himself by reading voraciously the new works of Pushkin and Gogol and the accounts of travelers to the Pacific and Alaska. In 1838, at a time when the navy was suffering under inept ministers and dispiriting economic cutbacks, the young lieutenant joined a number of other officers in transferring his services temporarily to the ships of the Russian-American Company. Fiercely patriotic but by then critical of many czarist policies and particularly sympathetic to the plight of the serfs, among whom he had grown up, Zagoskin was more than willing secretly to carry letters to political exiles in Siberia from their relatives and friends in Moscow on his overland journey to the Pacific coast. He seemed almost to relish the length and difficulty of this journey, though he and his party were shaken by the unexpected death of a twelve-year-old girl, an orphan traveling in the company of a priest to her grandfather's home in Okhotsk, whose dress ignited when she stood by the fire one morning to dry the dew from her bare feet. Zagoskin dressed her burns in cotton, but was unable to save her.

After arriving in Okhotsk, the lieutenant assumed command of small brigs and corvettes plying the North Pacific between Siberia and southeastern Alaska. He also sailed once to Russian settlements in California, a voyage on which he learned the principles of scientific collection and observation from a passenger from the Russian Academy of Sciences. In 1840 Zagoskin proposed that an expedition be undertaken into the Alaskan interior in order to ascertain the routes of the Eskimo fur trade with the Chukchi, routes that had changed since the establishment of Fort Saint Michael. After arriving at Saint Michael in 1842, Zagoskin's explorations in the delta absorbed three years of his life, a time in which the sight of the mountain ash that grew in thickets on the banks of the Yukon, just as it did in central Russia, roused in him a piercing thrill of homesickness.

These explorations did not result in the Russian-American Company's assuming the control it desired over the fur trade, but Zagoskin's published reports attracted a great deal of both popular and scholarly attention. By 1845 his stipulated time of service with the Russian-American Company had long since elapsed, and he returned to Russia and his commission in the Imperial Navy, producing over the next two years the vivid accounts of his travels that quickly won him an Academy of Sci-

332 ✧ RAVEN'S CHILDREN

ences award, membership in the Russian Geographical Society, and a modest amount of fame. Nonetheless, it was not until 1967 that his work was available in English translation in the West, and I think it doubtful that Edward W. Nelson knew anything of his predecessor's work.

Zagoskin never saw Russian America again. In 1848 he abruptly resigned from the navy, for reasons that remain unclear. He served for a time in Russia's forestry service; then, after freeing the serfs who had served his father, now dead, he went to live on a small estate that his wife had inherited. He left to command a troop of militia in the Crimean War, and returned to publish articles bitterly attacking the institution of serfdom in tiny periodicals. When serfdom was eventually abolished, Zagoskin served as an "arbiter of peace," reconciling former serfs and the members of his own class, the landed gentry, in conflicting land claims and using his prestige and authority among landowners to promote the interests of peasants more effectively than other arbiters did. He endured tragedy in his family: his eldest son, at odds with army regulations and his regimental commander, committed suicide, and his second son, bored and depressed by army life, drank himself to an early death.

The sale of Russian America in 1867 also fell upon Zagoskin as a tragedy. The Imperial Navy, jealous of the Russian-American Company's success under Aleksandr Baranov, finally saw to it that the chief manager was dismissed, and over the years the fortunes of the company declined as a consequence of poor management, overharvesting, Alaskan Native unrest, and the disappearance of the rich Chinese fur market when the United States and the Western European powers seized the commerce of that helpless country. In Alaska the Hudson's Bay Company appeared from the east, and the Russian-American Company endured the indignity not only of having the British Fort Yukon on Russian territory but on one occasion of having to purchase food from it.

During the Crimean War the colony proved too costly and

too difficult to defend, and declining company profits persuaded shareholders not to renew their contract with the czar when their original charter expired. Even before the end of the Crimean campaigns in 1856, Czar Alexander II began negotiating secretly with the United States, hoping that in selling Alaska to the Americans, Russia would realize some gain from a land that was irretrievably lost anyway and also secure a friendlier Pacific neighbor than the British promised to be. Alexander was disturbed as well by the possibilities of an unmanageable gold rush in the territory, and by rumors of an impending northward migration of America's polygamous and reviled Mormons.

Immediately after the sale, a group of American businessmen arranged for the purchase of the Russian-American Company's remaining assets and outposts and reincorporated as the Alaska Commercial Company. The news of this sudden divestiture shocked the Russian gentry, and to the end of his days Zagoskin was unable to reconcile himself to the sale, condemning it as a despot's whim and the betrayal of every Russian who had ever labored in Alaska, even though most of the American money went to finance the emancipation of serfs. In a real sense Zagoskin *was* betrayed. With the Treaty of Purchase, his writings on Alaska became, to most of his countrymen, a lamp illuminating little more than a dead end in Russian history, and of course his work was unknown and unappreciated in the country that had assumed dominion there. He lived until 1890, dying at the age of eighty-two, only a few months before the martyrdom of John Kilbuck's helper Brother Hooker at Kwethluk and in the same year that the first corporate salmon canneries appeared in Alaska. The former explorer was left mute at the end of his life, owing to an illness, as though he were filled with trapped speech and finally succumbed to it.

The reaction of Alaskan Natives to the sale, in the vicinity of those outposts where the transfer was even noted, was chiefly one of indifference. Those *kass'aqs* and mixed-blood people who had stronger roots in Alaska than in Russia were allowed to stay and assume American citizenship. Pure-blood Alaskan

Natives assumed no such status, though they had enjoyed Russian citizenship under the czar. At the time there was little concern about this; neither Indians, Eskimos, nor surviving Aleuts had any quarrel with the Americans, and were eager to allow them the same sort of commercial and mediating role the Russians had played — though the historian Hubert Howe Bancroft reports that even then there was some conjecture, and discontent, as to how it came to be that the czar had the right to sell this land in the first place, and why there was no distribution to Native communities of the money paid by the Americans.

But the old trade networks, which the Russians had mapped and shared in but never ruled, still held, and in the delta, especially because of the epidemics, war between the regional confederations remained only a memory. Today, in the villages of the Nelson Island area, where Catholic missionaries were tolerant of the traditional Yupik dances and where the dances therefore are still performed, there is sometimes an event after gift exchanges in which a group of men and a group of women are said to "fight" by means of their dancing. This refers to a Yupik legend that suggests another explanation besides trade and disease for the end of the regional wars: that at some point all the women simply became fed up and joined together to dance, refusing to support their husbands in their military alliances and enmities any longer.

Really, however, such enmities in Yupik life hadn't disappeared; rather, they had slowly assumed global stature and become as pervasive and invisible as air, as the accidents of geography and history turned this obscure corner, which once had provided a sort of highway between the Old World and the New, into the precise point at which those worlds' contending empires drew their hostile borders. Alaska became the point at which even time drew its border: the international date line, today and tomorrow, angles between Big and Little Diomede, then zigs around the Aleutians, and finally drops like a plumb line down the Pacific. First it was the Russians against the British, then the Japanese against the Americans, then the Russians against the Americans, and now maybe also the Japanese once more, though no real battles have been fought in the delta since the women began their dancing and since the shamans sent their power to France to help the Allies win World War I.

But Dutch Harbor was much too close for comfort, and Bethel went through most of World War II trembling under the persistent threat of invasion and occupation. "Daily we scanned the skies and strained our ears to hear the possible droning of a plane above the clouds," Mrs. Schwalbe wrote. Before Pearl Harbor, Japanese agents disguised as fishermen had landed on the coast and questioned Yupik hunters. When war broke out in 1941 there was only one small U.S. military post — Chilkoot Barracks, at Seward — in all of Alaska, and some authorities asked themselves the same question that had troubled Alexander II: whether it was worth it even to try to defend Alaska. Strangely enough, it was Hitler, through his occupation of Norway and Denmark, just over the pole from Alaska, who persuaded the War Department at least to give it a try, and to request funding for bases in the territory. But the Japanese attackers still found Alaskan defenses woefully unprepared. Along the Bering coast adult men were organized hastily into what became known as the Alaska Territorial Guard and issued rifles left over from World War I.

In 1942 the army arrived in Bethel. It attempted first to enlarge the town's small airfield, but finally barged its heavy equipment across the river to the long flat stretch behind Tony Watson's fish camp. Though the town languished under a blackout at night, its dusty roads were jammed all day with the jeeps and trucks and frantic activity — and the sudden, if temporary, tide of money — that attended the construction of the base and the arrival of a garrison big enough to triple the little town's population. Ships coming up the river would run aground on the shifting sandbars and have to drop fifty-five-gallon drums of oil and gas overboard to ease themselves off. The drums slowly collected along the riverbanks, and when spring floods carried some of these into the brush, opportunistic villagers would roll them away. The army wanted sealskin mukluks and other fur products, and Yupik women worked on an assembly-line basis to sew them. More stores started up, including three or four liquor stores, though MPs efficiently kept drunks off the streets. A snapshot exists of a youthful Bob Hope, dressed slickly in a camel-hair coat (the same sort of coat I remember my father wearing), with the overexposed sky a desolate white behind him, eliciting laughs from the troops at Todd Airfield in 1943.

As it turned out, the only casualty of hostile action in Bethel during the war was the unfortunate Tony Sumi. A native of Japan who had come to the United States as a small boy, he arrived in Bethel long before the war as a riverboat cook and prospector, and had taken a Yupik wife. Later he became a freighter, though he also kept a mink farm and maintained a luxuriant vegetable patch across the river. Well liked in Bethel and widely respected as a riverman, he was known affection-ately as Tony the Jap, and it was he who carefully supervised the barging of the army's equipment, although it was his own vegetable garden they were paving over. Shortly after the airfield was completed, however, he was taken from his family by mili-tary officials and sent to an internment camp in the Lower 48 with other Japanese Americans. Mrs. Schwalbe reported that he went willingly and without rancor, and that the entire town pro-tested, and grieved when he was led away. Tony the Jap was in his sixties, and he died a year later, in the internment camp.

After the war the riverman's ashes came back to Bethel and the soldiers left. That was after a decisive event had occurred on the Aleutian island of Akutan: a crippled Japanese Zero, a swift and agile plane thought to be virtually invincible by American pilots, had plowed into the island's soft tundra and remained almost wholly intact. Information gleaned from the captured plane led to the development of fighter tactics crucial to the stunning success of American air power at the Battle of Midway, a defeat from which the Japanese navy was never able to re-cover.

Today, the airfield that Tony the Jap helped to build goes slowly to grass, and the same searching river that uncovered the graves that James Active had to move uncovers hundreds of corroding fifty-five-gallon barrels, stacked neatly on end and buried when the army was clearing out but now coming to light like columns of hard basalt from surrounding softer rock. Some have fallen over and are leaking an unidentified black substance into the river. The air force says that the barrels are the responsibility of whoever presently owns the land they're on.

Wars seem to come to a slow and reluctant closure out here, so far from the corridors of power. The Confederate raider *Shenandoah* captured and burned Yankee whalers for months in the Bering Sea after the Civil War ended at Appomattox. A team of Japanese archaeologists visiting the delta several years after World War II were nearly shot by some Territorial Guard members, who fortunately radioed to Bethel before opening fire. Today, of course, the affluent Japanese play something of the same role that the wealthy Chinese mandarins once did — they bankroll the delta's chief cash enterprise. Their control of that enterprise, and this summer's low fish prices, have led some to suspect that they have found a way to keep most of the bankroll in their own pockets and still get just as many fish. Sailors rarely venture off the *Shinmei Maru,* but when they do, it's to barter, and they usually offer booze. I saw a group walking by Elsie's smokehouse the other day with an enormous rack of moose antlers in hand. They stopped to peer through the windows of the Duster and examine its contents, as though the car were a storefront display. With fish prices as low as they are, fishermen and their families are tempted to see themselves as serfs at the mercy of these cousins, and to see a touch of swagger in the way the Japanese sailors walk through town.

It has been less than two centuries since boatloads of Siberian Yupik warriors, wearing armor made of bone or ivory slats tied together with baleen, sailed like Vikings across the Bering Strait to raid villages on the Alaskan side. Even with all the trade that funneled back and forth across the strait, even before the big empires collided and drew their lines, relations between people on either side of that water were as fraught as the mating dance of spiders. A week ago, watching the evening news, Oscar stared in outrage at a videotape of crewmen aboard a large drift-net vessel on the open seas frantically throwing dead salmon overboard as a U.S. Coast Guard helicopter approached. "Look at those damned Koreans, just throwing fish away!" he said.

"Thailanders," Margaret corrected.

Though well beyond the two-hundred-mile limit, the vessel had been caught fishing in an area through which salmon of American origin are known to migrate and which is therefore closed by treaty to high-seas salmon fishing. But whether the boats contain Koreans or Thailanders or Taiwanese or Japanese, the movements of these cousins in the Bering Sea are now regarded with even more suspicion than the movements of the Soviet navy. Margaret, at least, is scrupulous about who is doing precisely what to whom, and doesn't like to lump her relatives together. Nor does she like to see such resentments build, to see her husband's blood start to boil. When I asked her once about the rural sovereignty movement in the delta, which seeks to abjure ANCSA and establish for villages such as Kongiganak the same sort of sovereign tribal relationship to the federal government that currently exists for Lower 48 Indian nations, she said that she was uneasy with the divisiveness the movement seemed to foster, both within and outside the Native community. "I'm for all people, all peoples of the earth," she said. "Not one group against another."

I see Oscar stagger as the plates move beneath his feet — as a world that now contains four billion more people than it did at the time of Vitus Bering's death looks to these waters as another breadbasket, as the merchants from the other side, who have come first to buy the bread, calculate ways in which to purchase the resource with a minimum of expense, a maximum of profit. When it was fur that the world wanted and the fur was sold by barter, just as it was between the villages, the Russians weren't able to seize control of the trade. Now that it's fish, which is sold only to outsiders and not to other villages or households, and now that cash is the slippery medium of exchange, the Japanese quite possibly have succeeded. "We hear that same old story every year," a fisherman said on the radio recently, in response to dropping prices in Bristol Bay. "Every year we hear about the overstocks from the year before, the strong yen against the dollar, all the farmed salmon on the market, and everything else that's supposed to explain our low prices. Well, if that's the case, how come it's never any cheaper for the housewife buying it in the supermarket?"

Charlie won't fish. Oscar doesn't have a permit. The bills are piling up. The weather's always bum, the fish are somewhere else or swimming too deep or maybe already gone, and even if they aren't, the prices are too low and getting even lower. It damn well pisses you off, drives you to drink — at least you'll have some company there — and your hands all by themselves start to stiffen and ball up. All of a sudden they're at somebody's throat — your distant cousin's, your wife's, maybe even your own. On Nelson Island, meanwhile, the women still dance.

2 ☉ THE WORLD WAR II Quonset hut has a tiny, suburban-style lawn out front, no more than a few square yards in size, but thick and green, bordered with flowers, and trimmed with a pair of white plastic swans. The lawn throws a lush front against the dirt road that runs along the high bluff over the river and then veers between the houses behind the hut. A pretty *kass'aq* girl in a mauve

sweater and a blue tartan skirt, with cascades of red hair and skin like whole milk, skips out the door of the hut. She is followed by two laughing Yupik children, the boy wearing a green tie that hangs well below the belt of his jeans. A Siamese cat crouches warily behind one of the swans as the children race past, then skirrs over the grass toward the door with its tail jabbed straight at the sky. On the doorstep a teenage girl does a little dance as the cat darts between her legs, and calls out to the youngsters that Robert is about to open his presents. The three children turn on their heels, and Elizabeth and Crazy and I abandon our game of hopscotch in the road and press our way into the crowded hut after them.

Inside, Margaret and Oscar and the boys, along with Elsie, are mingled among two dozen other adults and children, both Yupik and *kass'aq,* ranged about the narrow confines of the hut — some on the sofa, some on chairs, many seated on the clean linoleum floor. In the kitchen area in the back of the hut, helped by her grown daughter, an old woman whose face has creased into wide, concentric smiles serves the final portions of this feast: mugs of tea and coffee and bowls of *akutaq* made from frozen strawberries and some of the season's first fresh salmonberries. The children are churchmouse-quiet in the presence of all these adults, and most of them are gathered about Robert, the boy whose ninth birthday this feast celebrates. Elsie watches from the sofa, squeezed in with three other women, as Robert starts on his presents. She holds two plates of food in her lap, which she intends to take to Charlie and Buzzo, who were invited but were too hung over to make it. Hippa and Emma have also sobered up, and this morning they picked up their kids at Eleanor's and went back to the fish camp.

Oscar and Margaret are on their way home too, if not literally, at least in spirit. The weather is fine here, and the weather is fine in Kongiganak too. The Kuskokwim is smooth as lacquer today, and this would have been a good day for traveling, but the forecast for tomorrow is just as good. Since laundry is easier and cheaper to do here than in Kongiganak, and since Quinhagak won't be opening again until Monday, the day after tomorrow, they decided to wait here just one more day.

This morning Oscar and I went over to the island opposite Brown's Slough to cut five green aspens, their bark salt-and-peppered with flecks of green and black lichens, for Elsie to burn while curing the last of the king salmon. Then we picked her up at her apartment in the pickup and went to Charlie's place, where Charlie lay wrapped in a blanket and stretched out corpselike on his carpet. He rose stiffly, blinking, as we came through the door. Elsie went straight to his refrigerator. Immediately she began clearing out food and spreading it on the counters.

"My refrigerator over there's been icing too much, and it don't work too good," she told Charlie. "So I'm gonna take this one instead."

Charlie now stood enrobed in his blanket like a Roman senator. He watched impassively, as though repossessions like this happened every day, while Oscar disconnected the unit and Elsie offered her advice as to how he and I should move it into the pickup. At last Charlie nodded slightly and said, "Goodbye, refrigerator."

"Maybe I'll buy one of them little refrigerators with my dividend check. Then I'll bring this back for you," his mother offered.

Afterward Oscar went off alone to find Buzzo and sober him up. In fact Oscar went to his AA meeting last night, despite yesterday's resolve to give up on all that shit. At some point between watching Charlie and Marvin haul in his empty net and going down to the smokehouse to join all the drunks, he decided to give up instead on all the other shit and just go home, to fish from there with Buzzo during the openings at Quinhagak, if he could talk his older brother into that. On his way back to Elsie's after the meeting, he said he saw Buzzo driving around in the Chevy pickup. "He got pretty pissed off at me when I stopped him and took away the keys," Oscar told me. "But he was gonna get a DWI, no sweat."

Now, having finished his coffee, Oscar sits outside on the steel railing running along the top of the bluff. He looks down at the river and talks to an old man with heavy, sinewy hands who stands at his side. When Oscar mentions that he means to head down to Kongiganak tomorrow, the old man asks, "What you gonna do down coast?"

"Grow old." Oscar sighs, crossing his arms and stretching his legs out straight.

"Nice down there, huh?"

"Yep." He watches as the two girls resume their game of hopscotch in the road, and as Margaret joins them. "I'm gonna try and get Buzzo to come down with me, and we'll fish Quinhagak from there. Last period I heard some guys got six thousand pounds down there."

The old man, like Oscar, has been fishing the portion of the river around Bethel this summer and having a bad season. "Last period here we got about thirty fish, my partner and me — three silvers," he says. "They only paid us forty-five cents a pound for the silvers."

"Forty-five cents?" Oscar blinks like Charlie did this morning, smiling thinly and nodding, as though this too happened every day now. "Last year they paid a buck seventy."

The old man points out over the smooth water. "They found that body here, I guess. They dragged him up."

Oscar hooks his thumbs into his belt loops and looks down at the spot. "I'm tired of fishing with drunks. Maybe I won't even come up here again in August. I'll come up if Charlie swears not to drink for that whole month. But if he don't do that, I'm staying home."

A sudden gust of wind rolls down the road, blowing grit like birdshot into our faces. Oscar raises his head when the gust blows by and sees the sky breaking in blue streaks through the clouds, and the sun, hardly glimpsed since before the Fourth, shining boldly through the disintegrating cover. I remember his telling me once of being thrown out of his boat in the river and having no sense of where the surface lay in the silty underwater darkness. He swam, and nearly panicked, never breaking free until finally he just stopped struggling and let his own buoyancy lift him up to the light, to the surface. Now he stares up into the sky at the sun and asks, "What's that — a UFO?"

3 ⊙ DOWN ON THE COAST is the best place to look for salmonberries. The pale green of the plant's sepals turn to brown as the fruit starts to ripen, and the berries themselves blush to a marmalade pink, just a little bit lighter than the color of salmon eggs. The fruits are the size of wild raspberries and similar to raspberries in appearance, but the salmonberry's lobes, each of which contains a single seed, are bigger and fewer; the berry looks like a basketful of footballs when viewed from above. Salmonberries are also more succulent, with a sweetness like that of apricots, and so are preferred to blueberries, cranberries, and crowberries as a local staple for *akutaq* (though these other fruits find favor as well). Sometimes families will camp out for weeks in the summer, harvesting from morning until late at night, the fathers included, at particular berry-picking grounds. The middle of July is early for salmonberries, though some are already ripe. But next month, if this is a good year, the berries will lie in huge numbers across the frost heaves down at the mouth of the river, nestling among their rough, toothy leaves like congealed drops of light.

Elsie doesn't want to wait that long. She wants to go down to Kongiganak and start picking right now, and she is all dressed and packed for travel, just as she was in May. But now that the *Crazy J* is loaded up again, and now that the drum of gas Oscar bought for our aborted trip to Quinhagak last week has been wrestled into the aluminum skiff, which Buzzo will handle, she decides that she doesn't want to go after all. She tells Oscar, "I got no plane fare home. I might get stuck down there and get homesick."

I think her decision actually has more to do with the weather, which hasn't turned out so fine as predicted. Elsie said just a minute ago that today feels just like October. The wind from the west is slicing off the water like a cold scythe, and the clouds are gray and seamed with light, like gritty ice viewed from underneath. The Kuskokwim looks and feels as if it were on the verge of freeze-up, as if the berries were already past.

Oscar saw the front approaching last night, and when Margaret was done with the laundry we loaded up the boat in order to leave right away. But Buzzo said he still felt too sick to travel. Wearily, Oscar and I hauled all the gear back into the smokehouse and locked it up again, but in the dark and our tiredness we overlooked Oscar's bag of wrenches, his electric bilge pump, and the brand-new marine battery I bought three weeks ago at the request of Margaret's brother Paul over the telephone from Kongiganak. Sure enough, they were all gone in the morning. "I'm going shopping for those things up around Kwethluk sometime," Oscar vowed, reminding us that that was where he found Hippa's stolen boat yesterday, adrift, all its gas used up, but with somebody else's extra gas tank left in its stern. "Somehow seems like everything that gets stolen turns up around there."

The tide is out this morning, and the *Crazy J*, loaded again, sits high and dry in the middle of the launch ramp. Oscar goes across the road to fetch Chris Jacobs and another neighbor, Gabe Kylook, and then he finds Evon and Marvin too, both of them sober today. With Buzzo and Tony Watson — who had a fight with Betty, and who wants to give Quinhagak a try anyway, and who will come with us in his own boat to Kongiganak — there are eight of us to move the boat. We space evenly around it, and the *Crazy J* slides smoothly across the clay and loose gravel, settles into the water, and swings around on its anchor line so that it already points to the coast.

Finally Oscar leads the other two boats out into the roiling waters, Elsie staring like a sentinel from the sea wall. The river is edged with whitecaps that show like mother-of-pearl against their own dark troughs, and the waves almost immediately dislodge all the gear stowed neatly beneath the foredeck. The stove and the propane tank and the rifles and the sleeping bags scatter themselves across the heaped salmon net, and this whole glacial accumulation slides toward the stern, pressing hard against the backs of Margaret, the four kids, and Buzzo's Alexandra. In distress from the waves, pretty Alexandra sits ashen-faced, her knees folded to her chest.

We run down past Hippa's fish camp and Napakiak, where Buzzo, running alongside us, gestures to a lone skiff speeding in the opposite direction along the river's north bank: their father, James, probably with a little money in his pocket, traveling up from Kasigluk to Bethel. Then we run past Fowler's Island, where we turned back last Tuesday, where the sandbars heave up out of the river like rain-splashed deserts. Then, somewhere past the mouth of the Johnson River, Oscar loses his way among the sandbars; the motor whines and kicks up mud no matter where he turns, and the column comes to a baffled halt. For a while the men in all three boats lift their motors and attempt to pole their way with oars into deeper water, but at last Oscar gives up and says we'll just wait for the tide to come in.

Oscar opens a Thermos, Tony opens his, and the boats tie together, the smell of hot coffee mingling with the salt reek of the sandbars and the wet scent of the grass on the riverbank. The children, except for Alexandra, come out like puppies from the tarpaulin they'd hidden under, while Margaret takes some thick crackers from the grub box and starts buttering them. Oscar is embarrassed to be stuck, worried about the weather out on the bay, and mad at Charlie, saying that he wouldn't be gambling like this if it weren't for Charlie's drinking. But there's nothing to be done about any of that now, and he lounges in the stern, comfortable and easy and absolved of regret in a manner that he never quite manages in Bethel. Buzzo climbs into our boat and starts reminiscing with him about all the times they played hooky from school, the whole herd of them at once, Buzzo, Oscar, Mamoo, Hippa, and Charlie. If James didn't find them and take them to school himself, they'd go to where one of their uncles kept his *taluyat*, big wicker traps for catching blackfish under the ice in winter. "We'd climb into them things and pretend they were jails, finally end up breaking 'em all to hell," Buzzo says. "Then our uncle would get really pissed."

The bumping of the three boats' gunwales against each other is regular and soothing, like a heartbeat. I close my eyes and imagine the five of them (six, counting John) as boys. I'm not surprised that they played hooky, or that they found their uncle's fish traps too confining and busted them all to hell. Elsie has lost one of these hell-raisers already, and day by day watches another fade away before her eyes. I think of the old woman's face above the sea wall today, its lines set deep and hard, trenches in her flesh etched almost to the bone. Whenever the boys provoked her, or whenever her own temper managed to provoke itself, the boys just put on their coats and ran out the door, fleeing her like they fled those traps, as I ended up fleeing her myself.

But what if she hadn't ever exploded in front of them like that, raining her shrapnel down on James as well? Maybe in the breathing room afforded by their escapes she managed to preserve some sort of kinship among a crowd of oversized males who were forever crashing into one another and flying apart. Did she ever wish for a daughter? I find Elsie with a little girl hard to imagine, as though she needed boys, Active boys, who were big and rambunctious and primed with testosterone — a lot of them, and a lot of it — to challenge her own obstinacy and fury. She is hard-edged the same way that her town is hard-edged, but through the years those edges have provided something for her children to hold on to, and they are as steely with her affection as they are with her anger. I see her yesterday with the plates of food in her lap for Buzzo and Charlie. I see her today on the sea wall with those hard lines on her face limned with worry as the boats venture out into the whitecaps.

James lives today removed from that sort of kinship. I don't know if it was some climactic horror that finally brought about his and Elsie's separation, or if it was the old woman's conquest of her own drinking habit, or if she just decided that with the boys all raised it was time to watch out for herself. But there's hardly a thing that Oscar does with his hands or with his mind while he's on the tundra or the bay or the river that he didn't learn from his father. When Buzzo once showed me how an extra board placed under a hammer's head provides the sort of leverage that makes pulling nails a lot easier, he said his father taught him that. It was just common sense, after all, which his father had a hell of a lot of, Buzzo said, except when it came to alcohol.

Earlier I saw the strange, slightly troubled expression on Buzzo's face mirrored in Oscar's as they watched James running full throttle to Bethel, his movements now so isolated from their own, and his probable motive — another jug — so neatly expressive of all that they despise about themselves. They hardly see him except when he's in Bethel, and so they hardly see him except when he's drunk. They tease him when they see him like that, and laugh at the cussing out he always gives them, laugh when he tells them that God will help him against them, that God is even bigger than they are; they respond with a queasy mixture of reverence and scorn, as though he were King Lear gone mad. But he knows the bars of this river and the moods of the bays almost as if he'd made them himself. He taught his sons their birthright by taking them out on the water and showing them how to fish, and then he sold their inheritance.

By its very nature the relationship between generations is testy this way, and the bond between father and son is particularly so. In the West it has been burdened since biblical times — since Jacob deceived Isaac to obtain the blessing meant for Esau, his elder brother — with divisive issues of wealth and its disposition, and recently it has become like that on Bristol Bay and the Kuskokwim as well. This morning all of Oscar's extra help — Buzzo, Tony, Gabe, Chris, Evon, and Marvin — appeared around the *Crazy J* simultaneously, almost as if they were convening at that spot for an appointed ceremony. We were sons of fathers, every one of us, evenly spaced and bent to that moment; we lifted in perfect unison and handled the ponderous boat as if it were nothing. In that manner we put Oscar on the water and prepared him for his fishing. Then half our number disappeared again, their individuality reclaimed: Gabe, who works as a guard at the city jail; Evon and Marvin, the wharf rats, forever being warned by Gabe that he hopes he doesn't see them at work; and Chris, the fisherman who still has his permit. But for a minute we were a fellowship, were perfect, even including a *kass'aq*.

It was easy because the task was simple, it just took a moment, we were then free to go our different ways, and we all carried something of the same secret wound that fathers exact from their sons. As sons we received our fathers' help, or the profit from their help, not just for a minute but for as long as our childhood lasted. We watched with a wholesome admiration as they traveled the river, and for James that meant negotiating its light and dark, its heat and cold, its wind and tides, its channels and bars. Finally we learned from them how to travel the river ourselves, and to fish in its recesses. At some point, however, in one way or another, all of us discovered that our fathers, over the duration of their lives, rode in different directions and to different purposes than we supposed. We found that some of those purposes and directions bewildered us, and that some were contrary to our own, answering to our fathers' individual sense of property and appetite. We realized that even in putting out on the river, in their mere participation in a commerce whose principles are property and appetite, they were capable of compromising, abandoning, or even sabotaging us, whether intentionally or not; and that the same sort of greed and personal absorption — just common sense, I suppose —

that has been required of our fathers in this cash-driven commerce since the time of Jacob and Isaac would be required of us as well.

My son, Ryan, has no escape from me, nor I from him. At one time or another, and in some form or another, I — like Isaac — will withhold my blessing from him just to punish him for the independence of his identity, and for the degree to which this identity exists outside my own dreams of succession, of the ultimate disposition of a wealth for which I contested, that in no way was freely given. Of course this is the fate of daughters now too, as participation in this commerce has, in the past few decades, ceased to be solely a male prerogative. Sometimes I wish that I myself drank, that I staggered down the streets for weeks on end, that I scuttled along the floor like Charlie remembers I did once at Napakiak, that all my appetites were focused to the point of that single chemical obsession, just so the injuries that I'll visit on my children — who have no inkling of all my purposes, just as I have no inkling of all theirs — would at least have the pardon of the apparent involvement of alcohol.

All the coffee is gone by the time the tide rolls in beneath us, lifting us out of our labyrinth. Oscar laughs when the mouth of the Tuntutuliak River opens in the bank to the north — "We were right where I thought we were, right above that little slough near the Tuntutuliak." Below this river the lower reaches of the Kuskokwim are relatively calm, though the wind still blows hard from the west. Against the wind, and weaving around more obstructing sandbars, we make slow time to the coast, and the tide is on the way out again by the time we approach the Kuskokwim's mouth. Oscar sounds a low whistle of dismay as he looks into the open water of the bay; it looks like a field of broken glass, the waves are so short and high.

There is no dismay in Margaret's face, nor has there been. Her eyes fairly shining, she has hardly stirred as she has stared over the gunwales at the black scoters veering and dipping before the bow, their wings flashing a pale white, and at the willows thinning and failing along the banks of the river while her own wide and grassy country — with strips of turf hanging like loose bed-spreads over the undercut portions of the bank, with the new salmonberries lurking on the frost heaves beyond — unrolls around her. The tarpaulin snapping above the faces and figures of the children lends their movements the sort of jerky, dis-jointed quality seen under strobe lights. Junior nods, and Margaret jostles him so that he won't sleep and wake up chilled. The boy glances up, looking almost without recognition at Oscar standing straight at the wheel, and then falls sleepily against the warmth of Margaret's side.

IX
THE WILDERNESS ZION

1 ⊚ HANNAH FINALLY CAME HOME this morning from Bethel, on Seagull Air's early run. The same high winds that thwarted our run to Quinhagak for yesterday's commercial period also forced the cancellation of all flights into the village. She actually returned from Washington sometime before last weekend, and I saw her last Saturday night at the Brass Buckle, the discotheque in Bethel.

She looked, well, comely in her tight stone-washed jeans and a denim jacket with white buckskin fringe, the leather as long and soft as a pony's mane. We took a single dance together. The buckskin whirled and switched, and Hannah's eyes roamed across the crowded floor to see who was out there with us, and with whom. A mirrored globe spun directly over our heads, throwing chips of light onto a wall-size blowup of the earth, blue and streaked with clouds, as seen from the moon. From the ceiling over the bar, which sold only soft drinks, hung a sealskin kayak similar to the one Aataq made with some high school students in Kongiganak, and around the corner was a sign assuring all the Buckle's patrons that its proprietor was armed and there was nothing here worth risking your life for. I don't know where Vivian was that night — probably at Margaret's uncle's house, where Margaret stayed that night years ago, before she almost flew to Anchorage. The dance ended and Hannah disappeared with a smile into the throng of dancers and dancers' watchers.

Today she sits at Aanaq's table with Vivian in her lap. The

afternoon is warm and windless, and she wears a white tank top and glossy metallic-blue gym shorts. Aanaq sits on the floor in front of the TV watching *General Hospital,* peering dimly, blindly, down the hospital corridors, her face only a few inches from the screen, her cheeks blue in its light. Behind her Elizabeth sits on the couch reading *The Story of My Life,* by Helen Keller. Hannah laughs as she feeds Vivian bits of dried seal that she has first chewed and softened, and she mimics the terrible face Vivian made last year when she was given her first taste of seal; now the little girl chirps and swallows the shiny black meat like licorice.

Hannah says that Vivian was like that with José, her father, too — at first Vivian didn't like him at all, but she was just starting to get used to him when he had to leave for California to look for work and they had to come back here. She says they stayed with him in a camper next to his sister and brother-in-law's house in Port Angeles, and Vivian took immediately to José's brother-in-law and his two small children. Hannah liked Washington; José took her over to Hurricane Ridge in the Olympic Mountains, and to a rock concert in Seattle. She looks at Vivian and says, "I took her with me to that concert, but I'm never gonna do that again." Vivian chews and swallows and looks around, her eyes like tortoiseshell buttons.

Paul's four-year-old son, Dick, comes into the house, and Vivian squirms out of her mother's lap. Hannah asks after my own family, then talks more about her travels. Last winter she went to Nome when a pilot was flying some guys up from Bethel in his own plane for a big city-league basketball tournament there. Hannah went with another Kongiganak girl, who picked up the wrong boyfriend and came home with two black eyes and a broken nose. Hannah also went to Hawaii on a ticket she bought for $100 from someone who won it in a raffle. There a middle-aged Korean offered her clothes, a car, her own apartment, all the boyfriends she wanted, but she decided against that.

Vivian starts wailing from an accidental poke in the eye from

Dick, and Hannah sighs and lifts her back into her lap. I finish off the tea and fried bread that Aanaq served me and go out and walk the boardwalks to Qemirtalek, the corporation store, where I buy a six-pack of Coke for myself and the kids. I know Oscar, still dreading his July 26 traffic hearing in Bethel, will like the safety slogan printed on all the cans: "Buckle Up, America! A Click Will Do the Trick!" Quinhagak shimmers on the edge of his dreams like an oasis in the desert, a place where the waters run riot in high-priced reds and where he will find some easing of the iron collar of debt, which weighs on him more heavily than ever — his traffic ticket, his car insurance payments, the phone and power bills that were waiting for him here, the money that he still owes Jerry for the *Crazy J,* the money that he still owes on the Duster, and cash return for that drum of gas he bought in Bethel.

Beyond Quinhagak, on the opposite side of the desert, lies Bristol Bay, the city of gold, whose streets Oscar walked before they were paved in gold but whose gates are now barred to him. Monday night he and Margaret performed the same slow ceremony in the grass that they performed at the beginning of the summer, the two of them advancing a net in tandem, then Oscar kneeling at Margaret's feet to repair rips and tears. "We used to do this after every single period in Bristol Bay," he said. "We'd get two thousand fish in a single drift down there. Every single square in the mesh would be filled. The water would be smoking with fish — I mean really smoking. All them fins and tails thrashing in the net would stir the water up so much it looked like it was throwing off smoke."

Elsie had called earlier that day from Bethel, saying that a storm was forecast for Tuesday, and that if we meant to go to Quinhagak for Wednesday's fishing period, we should go a day early so she wouldn't worry as much. But we were all still tired from the nine-hour trip down the Kuskokwim and from the knocking around that we got out on the bay, and Oscar had his nets to mend. "Me and Tony got big boats," he said. "We'll be all right."

But yesterday the whitecaps rolled across the bay at the mouth of the Kongiganak River like the backs of breaching beluga whales, and the wind spun drenched bank swallows cartwheeling through the air. We waited there an hour, hesitating as though on the brink of a cliff. Oscar said he didn't know anybody better at traveling in rough weather than Joe Brown. "Joe said he was going to Quinhagak today. We'll wait for him to come down and just follow his boat across."

So we floated there another thirty minutes, until at last Oscar raised Joe's house on the VHF he'd just gotten on credit from the Kongiganak Trading Company store. Joe's wife, Polly, said that not even Joe was crazy enough to go out on the bay today, and finally we went back to the village, Oscar beside himself, saying that in all his life he'd never seen a summer like this for weather. "It's like this every damn time I travel. If I tell somebody I'm going tomorrow, then the weather's always bum tomorrow. I got to start lying. 'When you going?' 'Day after tomorrow.' Then leave the next day, before the bum weather hits."

The next period in Quinhagak isn't until Friday. Today the river is high with the tide and yesterday's rains, brimming to the very top of its banks below the village, winding away toward the bay like a trail of molten steel drizzled in coils across the grass. Poor Oscar can't even reach the village dump site a mile or so upriver. On my way back from Qemirtalek, I notice him and Tony and Buzzo drifting silently down the river in the *Crazy J*, three men in a tub. The boat is stuffed fore and aft with bulging plastic trash bags, and Oscar calls out to me, "We didn't have enough trash around the house, so we went to the dump and got some more." Then I recognize the bags as the ones Oscar and I filled in June when we cleaned the grounds. The eighteen-gallon can of gas ran dry before the boat reached the dump, Oscar says, and they had no choice but to drift slowly back to the village.

In front of Aataq's house I find Hannah standing as though frozen on the boardwalk, staring down the long walkway leading to the play deck, where a pickup basketball game is taking shape. I follow her gaze and recognize the square, muscular build of John Andrew, the twenty-year-old son of Kongiganak's former Moravian pastor, who now preaches at Manokotak, a village near Bristol Bay. John was Hannah's boyfriend in high school, but that ended when the Andrews moved away. He is here now to visit for a few days, and he turns for only an instant as he hurries down the boardwalk, almost as though he can feel Hannah's eyes. His own eyes just flicker in recognition. Hannah raises her hand, her fingers moving almost unconsciously in a greeting that John doesn't see, as the breeze off the lakes plays with her hair and the hem of her shorts. She gazes after John as though into another life, into a surmised history more in line with what Aanaq (not so bold anymore as to choose husbands for these youngsters) might have hoped for and imagined. Behind her, Margaret begins loading yet another wheelbarrow full of laundry to take up to Safewater.

2 TIME COLLAPSES, accordions together. Here, more than in Bethel, the years fall in on themselves, fracturing one's sense of history, of a progressive and irreversible linear movement. Last night I saw the two elders, Aataq and Aanaq, sitting together in a kayak skimming across the eastern lake below the village. I saw the blade of Aataq's paddle slice into the lake, hardly troubling its surface, as the little boat floated over the water like a hovercraft. I might as easily have watched that same progress a thousand years ago as last night, and to a Western observer the intervening chasm seems plausibly even greater than that, suggesting not just a distance of years but a division of being, a manner of thinking and living extinguished in the Old World at a point much more distant than fifty generations ago.

Margaret's grandfather's kayak, its hand-hewn driftwood frame covered in faded blue canvas, is one of only two such craft remaining in Kongiganak. But I doubt that the old man considers it outmoded, and in respect to what he uses it for — last night, carrying Aanaq and him to the opposite side of the lake so they could pick salmonberries, saving them half an hour's hike — he's entirely right. The kayak's passengers sat in its cockpit back to back, Aanaq facing the stern, the old man leaning toward the bow, working the paddle with his bent back, his wide shoulders. The kayak's ends are equally narrow and tapering, and with its passengers arranged as they were, it reminded me of Janus, the god of gates, indicating directions both backward and forward, both east and west, both before and after.

Time is polychronic here, not so much advancing as rotating, and Yupik verbs rarely trouble themselves with distinctions between past and present. The salmonberries are starting now, and these were the first food that Raven provided the primal man, who sprang unexpectedly from the pod of a beach pea. Raven led this man away from the beach to ground that was high and firm and then changed into a bird, flew away, and returned in four days with precisely four berries, which satisfied the man's hunger. From this point in the summer the other fruits as well — the blueberries, cranberries, crowberries, bearberries, and red currants — begin their ripening. Families will pick as much as a hundred gallons of berries over the summer, using most of them to make *akutaq*, a food that when served to guests is more expressive than any other of a family's sense of prosperity and harmony. This makes it all the more ironic, and maybe understandable as well, that Elsie's tirade on Charlie's steps a few weeks ago began with a debate over exactly when Margaret would begin making their *akutaq*. The midpoint of July trembles on the verge of the berry season, and sits squarely at the midpoint of the salmon season, with the last of the kings and chums going into the smokehouses now and the fish racks slowly emptying, looking like bones picked clean of their meat, just before they are fleshed out again with the arrival of the silver salmon, or cohos, in August.

But the Yupik name for July has to do with birds: Ingun, or "molting time." Until ten or twenty years ago this was the month of the goose drives on the delta that so disturbed Edward W. Nelson. Hunters would travel in squadrons of kayaks down the rivers, driving the molting females and the unfledged goslings away from the water and into the grass. Then other men and boys would strip down to their shorts and run in wide, narrowing fans through the marshes and grasses, driving the geese into flocks that in turn were driven into nets. This midsummer bonanza of waterfowl provided a foretaste of all that would appear on plates and go into storage during the autumn of late August, September, and early October: ducks and geese taken at their staging grounds or along their migratory pathways, and sometimes moose or bear brought back by hunters from the forests upriver. The women, meanwhile, would comb the tundra for greens in the fall, just as many of them do now: sourdock, brook saxifrage, wild celery, Labrador tea, and the sweet, nut-flavored roots of sedge and arctic cotton grass, called *anlleret,* or "mouse food," taken in sproutlike clumps from the caches of lemmings and voles. Aanaq can find these foods by scent and touch.

Food-gathering has always slowed down after freeze-up in October, but it doesn't stop. Needlefish, also known as stickle-backs, are caught in dip nets through the ice and then dipped in seal oil and eaten whole. These spiny little morsels, usually frozen, feel like greasy steel sprockets and gears in your mouth, but then the spines collapse between your teeth and yield to the strong, satisfying taste of the oil and raw fish. *Taluyat,* the big wicker fish traps, are staked beneath the ice in sloughs and left there all winter, but they are chopped out and hauled up at intervals to be emptied of blackfish. These fish are four to eight inches long, oily, and as black as drops of pitch. Once blackfish were caught in huge numbers for dog teams and were also a last line of defense against famine; now they're simply a winter delicacy. The *taluyat* can be checked whenever it's convenient, and the fish are always fresh, because blackfish are almost impossible to kill. They can be kept indefinitely in oxygen-starved water in a trap, or in a pan of water on the porch, or even as pets in an unaerated goldfish bowl. Caught and heaped outside in a mound of snow, the fish on the inside of the mound, insulated against freezing solid, have been known to survive out of water for two weeks. Sometimes they can be seen swarming in schools at holes in the ice of a slough, rising to the surface, seeming to sip directly from the cold air, and then sinking sleepily back down to the depths in a sort of oxygen narcosis.

There are other foods as well, though the land seems as empty as slate. Tomcod, and also burbot weighing up to fifteen pounds, may be taken through the ice by jigging with baitless hooks. Snowshoe hares, and tundra hares as well, little-known animals as big as small dogs, are sometimes hunted at night, chased down by snow machine. The mink, muskrat, and beaver taken by trappers are often eaten. Naked thickets of willow, alder, and dwarf arctic birch are scoured for flocks of ptarmigan, betrayed in their bone-white winter plumage only by the wet black beads of their eyes, their faintly salacious red eyebrows, and their raucous, guttural alarm calls, which seem to warn a hunter to "go back, go back, go back." Then the call dissolves into a maniacal chortling laugh.

Breakup in April, or sometimes May, is the narrow and perilous point upon which the year pivots and turns. No one ever doubted the salmon; the Kuskokwim and the Yukon and certain other rivers always provided enough, more than enough, of this staple to see a village through the winter, even though great quantities were given away during the winter festivals. But if the summer was too wet, preventing the fish from drying properly, or if breakup was too late or the weather too stormy, or if during the days of the great epidemics the adults were simply too sick or too few to accomplish their harvests, then hunger came stalking. It has been seventy years since the famine described by

Ferdinand Drebert in Kwigillingok, but even today, when the shelves of the stores seem to provide assurance of a food supply that has no seasonal basis, apprehensions still exist. People don't trust stores. Nor do they trust items from other sources that have price tags on them, nor the system that produces these items.

But there is some savor to this anxiety, some sort of wholesome thrill in every portion that results from the happy conjunction of the hunter and his prey, the fisherman and his fish. It's a thrill that's foreign to the senses of those for whom neither experience nor culture teaches what hunger is like when it can't be satisfied, or how miraculous the provision of food really is. And the thrill doesn't get any more exquisite than it does in April — Tengmiirvik, "the time of geese coming" — when the year swings as suddenly as a window blind being tugged and snapped open, when the ice and snow and even the air itself seem to leak luminescence. Then everything else comes back in the wake of the geese, and everything that people eat is fresh and rich: the whelping seals, the migrating walrus, the smelt running up the rivers, the herring spawning offshore.

Easter has lent itself well to this round. In Kongiganak the Moravian church celebrates a sunrise service in the little graveyard on top of a bluff a short distance up the river. I remember the air as exceptionally cold on every one of these mornings, the sky overhead green like the Mediterranean. The Kongiganak River is always still frozen; at the end of the service the worshippers just trail in clumps down the bluff and then cut directly across the oxbow of the river to the village. As they do so, the sun breaks over the long margin of the Kilbuck Mountains and the bay to the east, and the light shines in the people's faces as they return to their houses over the ice. They might be the dead themselves, changed in a twinkling and raised incorruptible from the grave — maybe even little Sammy as well, though he's buried in Bethel — all of the lost ones assembling now at this still point for the Second Coming. But there isn't any trumpet, and in Kongiganak there isn't that end to time's linear progress as it is conceived in Western thought; instead there is a change implicit in the movement of time itself as the village goes back and back and back, just as the ptarmigan demand, to events that have no linear definition, no beginning and no end, no *ex nihilo* birth and no punctual finality in death.

The food itself is the sacrament that brings them back, the engine that drives the round. Here people eat not so much to sustain themselves as to sustain an entire universe of life and spirit. Little Vivian Chanigkak happily eats her shoe-leather bits of dried seal like candy. Ryan Carey, who bears the human essence that once resided in old Willie Azean and who ate as many of his childhood meals at Kenneth Igkurak's house as he did at his own, still likes seal oil and other strong-tasting foods more than most of the grocery store items we serve him. Last Sunday night Paul Paul offered to reimburse me the $60 I spent buying him a new marine battery in Bethel, but since it was my own carelessness that resulted in the battery's being stolen, I declined. Instead Paul's wife, Sarah, gave me a large bag of dried salmon to bring back to Ryan, which is certain to provide him more than $60 worth of delight. I've learned myself to enjoy most of the food served at Kongiganak's tables, though certain things — seal oil, blackfish, pike eggs, a few others — I still eat chiefly out of politeness. I've never been offered the most notorious item in the Yupik diet — *tepturyut,* or stinkheads, which are salmon heads that have been buried in earth for a few weeks and allowed to decompose to a cheeselike mass. This is too strong even for many Yupik palates, but is enjoyed as a great delicacy by some.

Certainly store-bought *kass'aq* foods, with their salt and sweeteners, their engineered flavorings, their convenient packagings and preparations, are more immediately ingratiating, and within the past thirty years they have made substantial incursions into the Yupik diet. But by no means do they threaten to replace that diet. Once more I remember Jacob and Esau, whom the *kass'aq* pastor in Bethel preached about, and the beginning of their rivalry in what might be interpreted as the Bible's rendering of the agricultural revolution. Esau was a hunter, and it was he who provided the venison that Isaac, their father, so relished. But one day Esau returned from hunting faint with hunger, and he went for food to Jacob, the farmer who "sod pottage." Jacob would not feed his brother freely; only in exchange for Esau's birthright would he give him bread and pottage of lentils. Thus began the process of disinheritance that was completed with the blessing Jacob later stole from the blind Isaac. But Isaac's preference of venison to lentils reflects a taste that persists very firmly in Kongiganak. Naturally the cultivated and processed foods bought from the store are void of the spiritual dimensions in which wild meat in particular is so rich. But neither do they keep people warm and make them feel as good as fish or wild meat does.

In 1899 a U.S. Army expedition lost among the headwaters of the Kuskokwim was saved because the soldiers packed only *kass'aq* food. Lieutenant Joseph Herron had gone with a party of soldiers, fifteen horses, and three thousand pounds of supplies into the Alaska Range in search of an overland route from Cook Inlet to the Yukon. After crossing the mountains through Simpson Pass, Herron lost his way, wandering first down the Kuskokwim's south fork almost to the present village of McGrath, and then up the north fork. At some point he and his men abandoned their horses; then one night a bear broke into their remaining food supplies. Shortly afterward the bear was killed by an Athabascan hunting party from Telida, and the hunters were surprised to find white man's food in the bear's stomach. The Indians launched a search for the white men, and finally Herron and his bedraggled soldiers were brought back to the safety of the Athabascan village, where they remained for a number of months.

But I can't think of any other instances of *kass'aq* foods outperforming Native ones in matters of survival in the bush or the Arctic. Certainly Herron's supplies didn't do the bear much good. Western explorers in high latitudes, whether European or American, slowly came to recognize the wisdom of Eskimo-style clothing and methods of travel, but food seemed to be a different sort of matter. Many died of cold, inexperience, bad luck, folly, excess zeal, but they died most frequently of hunger and malnutrition. Vitus Bering's final voyage is an especially impressive demonstration of the horrors of scurvy. But maybe in part because most of the foods that make up the Eskimo diet are so excluded from the Western diet, and maybe in part because of the same arrogance that led the first explorers to dismiss Eskimo parkas and dog sleds as well, Westerners seemed blind to the fact that the people living all around them at these latitudes generally enjoyed excellent nutrition. Today, Oscar is speaking not merely from prejudice, sentiment, or religious conviction when he says that the traditional wild foods make him feel better.

In general Yupik foods are high in protein and low in saturated fat, and far outstrip processed foods in their weight of nutritional value. Seal oil, a strong-tasting, all-purpose marinade, condiment, flavoring, and cure-all, is a uniquely concentrated form of energy and warmth, releasing nine calories per gram as a pure fat. As a rendered fat, it is polyunsaturated — so not disposing the consumer to heart disease — and boasts 120 times the vitamin A content of beef. Other foods offer similarly dense packets of nutrition. The Yukon-Kuskokwim Health Corporation has determined that one cup of sourdock leaves contains the vitamin A equivalent of 156 three-inch carrot sticks; one cup of salmonberries contains the vitamin C equivalent of eight oranges; one cup of needlefish contains the calcium equivalent of nine cups of milk; three ounces of seal meat contain the iron equivalent of five and a half hamburger patties. Overall, Yupik foods are comparably rich in thiamine, niacino, riboflavin, ascorbic acid, and fiber, and wild meat, as opposed to meat from domesticated animals, boasts more protein and fewer calories per unit, as well as five times more polyunsaturated fat per gram. Of course such foods fill people up and keep them warm; they represent much more nearly than the modern Western diet the sort of food that people ate through the millennia that preceded Jacob's contest with Esau.

Throughout 300,000 years of human evolution, people hunted like Esau and (like Oscar as well) devoted a large portion of their diet to wild meat — probably as much as 50 percent. That number increased with the development of Cro-Magnon big-game hunting technologies 30,000 years ago, and consisted of as much as 90 percent in high-latitude Eskimo diets. As recently as 12,000 years ago, when the entire world was wilderness and contained fewer people than presently live in New York City, 100 percent of the human population hunted and ate meat, obtaining protein and amino acids in a physiologically more efficient way, and in more concentrated units, than is possible by eating plants. In addition, if modern hunters and gatherers are any indication, these people labored fewer hours for their sustenance, slept longer, and enjoyed more leisure time than the farmers and peasants who immediately succeeded them, or for that matter contemporary farmers, factory workers, teachers, secretaries, and corporate executives. With limited demands for goods and services and a general ability to secure both prosperity and health with a relatively modest amount of effort, members of these societies enjoyed what some have described as affluence. Among delta villages suggestions of such leisure and affluence echo in the Yupik names for the early winter months — Qaariitaarvik, "time of masked festivals" (October), and Cauyarvik, "time of drumming" (November) — when the fierce activity of the summer had tailed into the much-anticipated season of festivals, dances, rituals, séances, steambaths, and games.

The momentous economic shift that occurred first in the Middle East 10,000 to 12,000 years ago may have happened in response to population pressures, game extinctions, climatic changes, or simply a modest effort to stabilize a particular supply of foraged plants. Customarily we conceive of this as a fortunate event, a deliverance from the uncertainties of animal numbers and movements, proof against the faintness that Esau felt, and certainly it represented a more intensive form of land use; the ten square miles that might support a single hunter's household could support up to ten small farmers and still produce a food surplus. But because this new economy so immediately accommodated a more concentrated demography and a larger population, the agricultural revolution was irreversible. So were its subsequent nutritional effects, as the hunter's protein-rich meat diet changed suddenly into a cereal diet consisting of as much as 90 percent vegetable food. Skeletal evidence in Greece and Turkey from shortly before and after the shift indicates not only a five- to six-inch drop in average stature but also, as summarized by the physiologist Jared Diamond, "a nearly 50 per cent increase in enamel defects indicative of malnutrition, a fourfold increase in iron-deficiency anemia . . . , a threefold rise in bone lesions reflecting infectious disease in general, and an increase in degenerative conditions of the spine, probably reflecting a lot of hard physical labor."

Aside from malnutrition and the cultivation in close quarters of the infectious diseases that were later to cut such a wide swath through the New World, there were certain social corollaries of the agricultural revolution, and of the subsequent population booms, that were hard to reverse. These included the development of inequalities in wealth and status, which were eventually elaborated into deep class divisions; the rise of political tyrannies and military despotisms of a kind inconceivable in a hunting society; the redefinition of hunting as a privilege restricted to an élite, leisured class or (more recently) as a primitive and outmoded barbarism; an accelerated pattern of reproduction, with the immediate benefit of providing additional fieldhands and soldiers and the eventual result of sparking demand for additional lands to exploit; the ideological objectification of both land and animals as commodities existing apart from and subservient to humans and subject entirely to their exploitation; and, ironically enough, the concentration of diet into such a narrow band of cultivated crops that unfavorable weather, blight, or harvest disruptions could result in precisely the sort of famine that the agricultural revolution had promised to prevent. While conceding that the agricultural revolution helped bring about the Parthenon and Bach's B-minor Mass, Jared Diamond is sufficiently impressed by its physical and social consequences to describe it as "a catastrophe from which we have never recovered." The anthropologist Lionel Tiger has referred more pithily to this event as "the great leap backward."

In the century and a half since the industrial revolution, some of these unfortunate corollaries have been somewhat ameliorated, at least among the industrialized nations, and at least for the time being. Particularly impressive have been the nutritional benefits of industry's refinements to the agricultural revolution, albeit at the expense of still uncalculated environmental damage. Industrial and scientific techniques applied to agriculture have resulted in agribusiness, the production and processing of foods in unprecedented quantities. These extraordinarily intensive forms of farming and animal husbandry have broadened and enhanced the diets of poor and middle-class people and, most significantly, restored a meaningful amount of animal protein to the Western diet. As a consequence, citizens of the industrialized nations have in just an eyeblink regained almost entirely the average stature of their Neolithic hunter forebears.

Nonetheless, these citizens remain fixed in a diet that is relatively narrow and that still differs substantially in character from a hunter's diet. Although much enhanced in recent years, the Western diet remains, in comparison, low in protein, vitamins, iron, calcium, ascorbic acid, and fiber, high in total fats, saturated fats, and sodium. The term "affluent malnutrition" is still controversial, as some of the links between what people eat and the chronic diseases now endemic to the Western lifestyle — hypertension, obesity, diabetes, coronary heart disease, cancer — have yet to be incontrovertibly demonstrated. But evidence is steadily accumulating that these pathologies, in part or in whole, are rooted ultimately in dietary factors. Anecdotal evidence from Kongiganak tends to confirm that. Dick Kiunya died recently from heart disease, and Willie Azean and Julia Jimmy from cancer; these and similar losses have prompted Aataq to remark that people never used to suffer from such things. There

simply too productive in necessities other than meat, fish, and fruit for it to be relinquished; to do so produces not only food but social forms, family structure, community integration, cultural identity, and a ubiquitous interdependence in which the economic efforts even of the very young and the very old are valued and significant. And preeminently, the economic efforts of a *nukalpiaq*, a hunter in his prime, such as Oscar Active, are valued and significant.

Who is Oscar otherwise? Former basketball star, past his prime. Former Kuskokwim permit holder, with little prospect of ever getting another one. Present alcoholic, with his best boozing still ahead of him unless he wrenches himself out of that spiral. Present resident of Kongiganak, though some still murmur against him here. But when he comes off the Kuskokwim in the summer with a load of kings for Margaret to cut up, at least he doesn't have to put the fish in a buyer's scale and deduct from their falling price the gas he used and the money he owes on his gear or to Margaret's bank account, or regret the various circumstances — those of his own devising, those of Charlie's, those of the river or the weather or the market or the world — that diminish the value of that delivery. Some of these factors still pertain, but for the fish rack the kings are simply necessary, so much so as to render almost any cost or consideration trivial. And in this household, getting the kings, the seals, the birds, the moose is something only Oscar can do. The commercial permit that he sold a decade ago doesn't matter. The drink that he took last summer and what he did after it don't matter. This job, at least, can't be taken away from him, at least not currently. He remains, like his father, a hunter and a fisherman, permit or not.

But Oscar fears the emptiness of his father's boat, the emptiness of his father's bed, the cooking that both James and Charlie now do for themselves, and the look on little Curtis's face in the convenience store. These fears make him jealous of Margaret, and angry, and all the more tempted by actions likely to lead to just such eventualities. Everything else — the political status of subsistence hunting and fishing in Alaska, the ultimate outcome of ANCSA, the tidal movements of international markets, the seeping stains of environmental degradation — combines into a dark-hued backdrop to the issues he wrestles with on a daily basis, within his heart and within his family. Both the scale and the makeup of that backdrop remind him as well on a daily basis of the utter marginality of his own concerns, of Eskimo concerns, of the outcome of these personal struggles, to the suddenly vast stage on which he plays. His is the most subordinate of subplots unfolding now before an audience that, for all its stated admiration of indigenous peoples, is still comfortably absorbed with its own image as the sole fulfillment of human destiny. Concerns such as Oscar's, suggestions of alternative or more time-honored destinies, still rouse a fascination and a sense of the outlandish that are indicative of their presumed triviality.

I doubt that anyone could have been more impressed with his own outlandishness than the six unfortunate Inuit who were brought by the American explorer Robert Peary to New York City in 1897. A married couple with one child, a father and his young son, and a single man, these were people who had helped Peary locate and retrieve a thirty-seven-ton meteorite from the vicinity of Melville Bay in northern Greenland. Peary was bringing the meteorite back to the American Museum of Natural History, and he persuaded these individuals to accompany him by promising guns, knives, needles — not only for themselves, but for their entire village — and a speedy return. On their arrival, Peary told the New York press that his purpose was to provide subjects for the anthropologist Franz Boas to study, but in all likelihood the publicity-minded explorer was really more interested in the sensation that attended the appearance of authentic Greenland Eskimos in America.

At first the Inuit were placed on public exhibition on Peary's ship, where an admission fee was charged. Later they were removed to the basement of the museum, where only those who received the permission of William Wallace, the museum's superintendent, were allowed to inspect them. Throngs of disappointed New Yorkers who were denied permission simply stood on the sidewalk outside, shoving and jostling to peer at the Eskimos through the grating that opened into the basement. In the succeeding months, three adults and one of the children succumbed to pneumonia. The single man, Uisakassaq, was finally returned to Greenland the following summer, and the surviving child, an orphan now, was adopted by Superintendent Wallace and his wife. This boy, Minik Wallace, didn't return home again until 1909. Subsequently he lived a troubled life divided between America and Greenland, suffered the horror of discovering his father's skeleton on display in the American Museum of Natural History, and fell victim to the 1918 influenza epidemic while working in a New Hampshire lumber camp. By then his intention to write his autobiography had captured the interest of a New York publisher, but the young man didn't live long enough to do more than make a start.

This curious episode, however, was only a footnote to a footnote in the history of the encounter between North America's two tides of immigrants, one from the east and one from the west. Precisely because of a remoteness that over the centuries has exceeded even Greenland's, Oscar's adopted village occupies a significant position in this encounter: at land's end of the continent itself, where manifest destiny has reached its utter limit in space, and at time's end in the linear playing-out of that encounter. The colloquy of races whose salient themes were first sounded in seventeenth-century New England, where farmers and hunters first met in North America and inevitably fell out, continues to sound those same themes along the Kuskokwim, even in a place such as Kongiganak, one hundred years after the end of the Indian wars at Wounded Knee, even in places where those wars were never fought, where no disinheritance was ever intended. It's as if we can't help ourselves, any more than we — or the Indians — could in colonial New England three hundred years ago, when the bitter seed was planted.

At first the signs were good. The English religious dissidents who landed on Massachusetts shores in 1620 and the various Algonquian Indian tribes who occupied southern New England

370 of RAVEN'S CHILDREN

met in peace and mutual regard, joined (as were Russians and Eskimos in southwestern Alaska) by their respective interests in trade. As in Alaska, this trade was carried on courteously enough despite the smallpox — probably introduced by European fishermen — that had already harrowed the Indian tribes before the colonists arrived. Lieutenant Zagoskin would take comfort on the Yukon in the proportion of the smallpox epidemics' survivors who were Christian; but the English settlers were more immediately interested in land than in converts, though ultimately they saw New England as the site of a wilderness Zion, where both red man and white man would in time conform joyfully to Puritan religious convictions. During their first year, however, the coasts' abandoned villages and ghostly, empty fields moved the Puritans' governor, John Winthrop, to write, "God [hath] thereby cleared our title to this place."

For some time this was a title that entertained a sense of boundary, particularly as the Pilgrims discovered that the Indians and the trade they conducted with them were necessary to their own survival. The Algonquians were hungry for Western material goods, while the colonists needed not only beaver pelts to export to England as a source of cash but annual quantities of corn to stave off famine. For two generations the wealth and reciprocal nature of this trade preserved mutual respect and a general peace in New England, just as they have in the delta, even as the decades that followed the Pilgrims' landing saw further disease among the Indians, the first depredations of alcoholism, and swelling numbers of white settlers.

Around the middle of the seventeenth century, however, a change in men's fashions in London caused the price of beaver pelts to plummet, and with that the value of Indian wampum — the jewelry and adornments made from seashells and used as a medium of exchange in New England trade — also plummeted. Roger Williams, the founder of the Rhode Island colony, had earned a reputation among that area's Narragansett Indians as an honest trader, but even he was unsuccessful in explaining why he was suddenly willing to pay only half as much for the furs they brought to his post. "The difference comes from the lower value of beaver furs in England," he told them repeatedly. "But although I . . . explained this to the Indians, they [still] felt cheated."

Within the next few decades the original reciprocity of the trade disappeared. Both the Algonquians and the numerous Abenaki tribes of northern New England had become reliant on Western manufactured goods, which had displaced certain traditional Indian technologies, and reliant on Western markets for Native goods that no longer had much value in those markets — not even corn, which the colonists by then had learned to harvest in sufficient quantities for themselves. The only Native commodity that was still of any interest to the colonists was land, and as the various tribes became hopelessly enmeshed in debt, great tracts of this were either sold or appropriated. In the 1660s a maturing generation of Algonquians and Abenakis began to see very clearly that their parents, willingly or not, were in the process of selling off their sole remaining economic resource. In anger and desperation the young Wampanoag sachem Metacomet, dubbed King Philip by the Puritans of the Massachusetts Bay Colony, began a war that very nearly succeeded in pushing the nascent English colonies into the Atlantic Ocean.

King Philip's War raged throughout New England for three years, and on a proportionate basis was bloodier than any other war in American history. In one of its earliest encounters, the savagery that the colonists feared from their adversaries was entirely preempted by the colonists themselves. In 1675 the powerful Narragansett tribe discounted reports of an advancing army of a thousand men, not only because the Narragansetts to that point had peacefully stood apart from the fray, but because no warning had been received from the threatening force. To give warning was a point of honor between warring Algonquian tribes, and allowed women and children to escape to safety before the battle. The subsequent general slaughter not only brought thousands of enraged Narragansett warriors over to Metacomet's side, greatly widening the scope of the war, but left embers that smolder three centuries later. The historian Russell Bourne quotes a present-day Narragansett leader as vowing, "So far as we're concerned, what the Puritans began here has never been forgotten. The war's still on."

Savagery soon became a failing of both sides in the contest, but the treatment of captives remained curiously and resolutely economic. For the most part, captives taken by the Indians were held for ransom; those taken by the colonists were usually sold into slavery, though the Reverend John Eliot protested, writing that "to sell soules for money seemeth to me a dangerous merchandize." The courageous housewife Mary Rowlandson wrote an affecting account of her own Indian captivity, during which she met Metacomet a number of times, and in fact it was he who once lifted her from despair with a hint of her long-awaited release: "At last, after many weary steps, I saw the Wachusett hills, but many miles off. Then we came to a great swamp through which we travelled up to the knees in mud and water, which was heavy going to one tired before. Being almost spent I thought I should have sunk down at last and never got out; but . . . Philip who was in the company came up and took me by the hand and said: 'Two weeks more and you shall be Mistress again.' "

Metacomet did not actually entertain the command over the various Indian tribes that the Puritans ascribed to him, and ultimately disunity, treachery, and lack of coordination were fatal to the Native war effort. But to the Puritans the terrible King Philip was the central symbol of their peril, and in the summer of 1678 the capture of the sachem's wife and nine-year-old son and the assurance of an imminent victory sent a shudder of relief throughout the colonies. These two prominent captives were taken for trial to Plymouth, where most of the clergy urged Old Testament precedents for their execution. Finally, however, they too were sold into slavery in the West Indies. Metacomet is said to have cried out on learning of their capture, "My heart breaks; now I am ready to die." In fact he died soon thereafter, in one of the war's final skirmishes, killed by Indians allied to the colonists. The corpse was beheaded by the English and then quartered. King Philip's head was set on a spike and displayed for decades in Plymouth. The Puritan theologian Cotton Mather wrote that he more than once "took off the jaw from the skull of that blasphemous leviathan."

But it was an expensive victory. By the end of the war more than half New England's towns had been laid to waste, and the Puritans were burdened with such a crushing war debt that it was not until a hundred years later that the region recovered its former prosperity. Ideologically as well the New England colonies were shaken to their very foundations; gone was all hope of a wilderness Zion, a political and religious utopia that would, through force of charity and love, finally establish God's kingdom on earth, a place where one could in fact, like Margaret Active, be in favor of all peoples and not one group against another. For the defeated Indians, particularly the Algonquians, the war resulted in dispersal, enslavement, and virtual annihilation. The historian Douglas Edward Leach, looking back at this first military contest between the two cultural paradigms in North America, neither of which had initially borne the other malice, remarked that "the eternal yardstick of Christian love continues to remind us of another great opportunity lost."

Now and subsequently, at the extreme opposite end of the continent, Oscar Active feels himself dragged closer and closer to the heart of something much colder than his own history has prepared him for. The old Alaskan fur trade exists today only in a vestigial state. Wild salmon are being devalued in commercial markets, and the permits to harvest them are slipping out of Alaskan Native hands. Oscar's ability to harvest waterfowl of any sort may be revoked at any moment, and his legal access to other wildlife resources could very soon be a matter of political regulation and restriction. Even the sort of land alienation from which Inupiaq and Yupik peoples have always been shielded by the unsuitability of the tundra for agriculture is conceivable now, given the mere existence of ANCSA and the struggling Native corporations, the increasing numbers of *kass'aqs* moving into the region, and the potential fuel and mineral wealth of Native lands. Like the Algonquians and the Abenakis, Yupik people have grown reliant on the same artifacts and technologies that Western people rely on, and Oscar would have only the roughest idea of how to go about making the sort of kayak that Aataq can still construct. Non-Natives are tempted to take a certain assurance from this, interpreting it as another guarantee of the prerogatives of their version of Zion, the bankruptcy of alternative versions.

But as long as the land is still there, and as long as the salmon swim up the Kuskokwim, Oscar the Great can practice the essence of what James the Even Greater taught him, and is preserved at least from the despair that settled to the bottom of Metacomet's heart before he even began his war. Maybe Oscar can hear better than I do the friction and stress now squealing from the engines that drive this industrial cash economy and its concomitant agribusiness. The explosive energies of previous Western crises in population, land ownership, waste disposal, and resource distribution were siphoned off by the uninhabited frontiers of the New World — well, inhabited only by a few savages. Now those frontiers have reached their own limits on the Bering Sea and the Arctic Ocean, and the Prudhoe Bay oil strike may be the last paltry specimen of their promise of limitless growth and infinite wealth.

Some version of the following thought is always in the back of Oscar's mind, especially as he observes my clumsy motions on the tundra or the river and in his overbearing way tries to teach me otherwise — that in the end it may be just as it was at the very beginning, on the shores of Massachusetts in 1620. So the Canadian anthropologist Hugh Brody, impressed with the long and fortunate residence of Athabascan peoples in northwestern British Columbia, suggests: "With limited needs and a careful protection of their resources, they are the peoples who have prospered. Perhaps it is not entirely fanciful to echo the thoughts of every important Indian leader since the first treaties were being negotiated: in the end, they may have to teach us the crucial lessons of survival."

3 ⊙ QUINHAGAK, QUINHAGAK, Quinhagak — the village on the graveled side of the bay, where the delta abuts the Kilbuck Mountains, which twist and dwindle into the Akhluns, has become Oscar's obsession. He hardly thinks of anything else but getting over there before Friday's period and then tapping into those schools of reds, of fishing for entire periods with the relatively reliable Buzzo and finally getting a leg up on his bills. Just to keep the bad weather off balance, he's not telling anybody when we're going.

I don't think much about it myself, and in fact I'm so drunk with the summer in Kongiganak that I find it hard to think at all. My shoes are falling apart, so I just go barefoot all day on the boardwalk. The planks are usually moist and cool from dew or showers, and the wood has been worn smooth and splinterless by many feet, the same feet, walking their many circuits. Beyond the houses, on the other side of the river, the grasses run to the bluffs and ripple in the wind the way a horse's flank ripples when the muscles move underneath. From the crests of those bluffs the grasses run similarly to the next horizon, suggesting a world without end carpeted in grass, in tiny alpine blossoms the size of a thumbnail, in rootless strands of reindeer moss and berries small as raindrops. The village seems extraordinary, perched on the cusp between this sea of grass and the puddled mercury of the bay, and the space on either side is of such persuasive dimensions that it looks as if Aataq indeed found the still point of the turning earth when he first brought his house here in pieces. The images of other worlds on the TVs and the VCRs seem like wormholes in space and time leading to parallel universes. They pertain to places that are curious, exotic, inaccessible, and inconsequential.

I actually see fairly little of Oscar and Margaret, or Tony and Buzzo. The smokehouses and the food caches are too full now, and they demand to be shared. I eat my meals by invitation at the houses of old friends, or of the kids I once taught at school, many of them married now and with kids of their own; yesterday I was at Gabriel and Evelyn Andrew's for lunch, last night at Roxanne Jimmy's for dinner, after dinner at Evon Azean's for a steambath, after the bath at Peter and Carrie Daniel's for coffee and a movie, today at Tommy and Christina Andrew's for lunch, an invitation tonight to Gideon and Alice Azean's for dinner. The children of young men and women whom I remember as children drool at me in amazement from their parents' laps or scuttle like seal pups across the floor, the extravagant fat of their cheeks jiggling, their legs brown and smooth as Formica.

Maybe old Mary Worm is the oldest woman in Kongiganak now, and one night I heard her unconsciously echoing Ecclesiastes, pronouncing that people are like grass, that one generation dies and the next one just takes its place. I wonder at the death of my father, twenty years ago last month. Jack Carey's end was prepared for him on the day that he took a drunken fall from a ladder, like his fellow Irishman Tim Finnegan. He broke a hip and subsequently suffered numbness and poor circulation in his leg. One night three years later, while he was living alone in a Hartford apartment, a blood clot formed in his leg and traveled to his heart like an insuperable grief. I imagine him alone in his car, driving past us in an opposite lane on Farmington Avenue, the elms on either side of the road full and lush, his hair still youthfully black, his eyes looking blankly past us to a place that appeared only to him beyond the stoplights and crosswalks — a destination at which he could no longer do himself or us any harm, no longer inflict on his family any losses.

On Monday a crew of workmen from the village began building a new boardwalk out between the two lakes below Oscar's house. This is to provide access to a new dump site, and the bright new boards are being laid wide enough to accommodate three-wheeler traffic going both ways. The boardwalk grows by leaps and bounds, and it's taken on the look of a road being built to the horizon, the very road that my father drove away on. Margaret is still surprised every time she looks out the south window, and she pauses a moment now in her cleaning to watch the crew at work. The light comes like clean water through the window, splashing over her glasses and high cheekbones and her soft, sloping shoulders.

Oscar sits at the supper table, waiting to go to Quinhagak, thumbing idly though a Cabela's catalogue that came in the mail today. "Look at this," he says to Margaret. "Here's a sixteen-by-twenty tent for sale for five hundred and twenty-nine dollars. That'd be good for a fish camp. You know those sloughs around Angyartuli? That's a good spot — you can fish right there, and the tide don't get too low. Then we wouldn't have to stay in town. I should clear it off — next year, maybe."

"Clear it off this year," urges Margaret, who is so happy in this interlude that she dreads all the more profoundly going back to Bethel in August for silvers, as she knows they will, and living again with fear inside her every day, as she knows she will. She goes through the porch door to shake out her mop, and at the top of the outside steps she pauses again, gazing down at the lakes, before Oscar trails out after her.

A little green-winged teal, with five juveniles following behind it, has ventured from the sedges at the margin of the eastern lake. The birds seem almost haughty in their stately, placid movement, scornful of any danger in this nest of Eskimo hunters.

Oscar laughs quietly, watching the ducks, his eyes brimming with pleasure, and then lays a large and affectionate arm on his wife's shoulder. "There's some eggs you missed," he says.

Margaret laughs quietly herself, and leans just for a moment into his side.

ANNOTATED BIBLIOGRAPHY

ANNOTATED
BIBLIOGRAPHY

I. GOING BLUE

The Alaska Geographic Society publishes a series of books on
various regions of Alaska and aspects of Alaska life. The books
are most striking for their photographs, but the texts are always
well written and well researched. Two books that provided information in this chapter and elsewhere on the history and character of this region are *The Yukon-Kuskokwim Delta,* edited by
Henning, Loken, Olds, Morgan, and Rearden (Anchorage,
1979), and *The Kuskokwim,* edited by Penny Rennick (Anchorage, 1988).

II. FIVE BUCKS

Gontran de Poncins was a restless French aristocrat who, to my
knowledge, never visited Alaska and knew nothing of its southern Eskimos. But he learned a great deal about the Netsilik Eskimos of the Canadian Arctic from the year that he devoted to
the adventure of living among them. His account of that year,
Kabloona (Paris: Reynal, 1941), is a strange and wonderful
book, animated by incantory prose and what Lewis Galantière,
de Poncin's editor, has described accurately as an "alert, quiv-
ering sensibility."

The citation from Bernhard Bendel's journal is taken from the
pamphlet "Bernhard Bendel: 1870 Kuskokwim Expedition,"

edited by Kurt H. Vitt (Bethel: Moravian Seminary and Archives, 1987). Bendel was a German immigrant who was working as an agent in southeastern Alaska for a San Francisco trading firm in 1869. While there he became involved in a scuffle with a Tlingit Indian chieftain; this led to a series of other incidents and eventually to the bombardment of Tlingit villages by the U.S. Navy — one of the very few military engagements between Alaskan Natives and the U.S. armed forces. Bendel was transferred the next year to the Aleutians, and it was from there that he became one of the first Americans to travel up the Kuskokwim. His visit was brief and his observations of Yupik life are superficial, but his journal shows a nice attention to physical detail. Bendel died in San Francisco in 1876, at the age of thirty, of unknown causes.

Some of the place-names that I mention and describe I know from my own travels and conversations, but others I found in *Kuigilinguum Nunain Atrit Anguyiit-Llu Qanemciit (Place-Name and War Stories of the Kwigillingok Area),* a book that was the result of an ambitious Foxfire-type folklore project at the Kwigillingok school. The project was headed by teachers Dennis Ronsse and Noah Andrew and involved some fifty elders and students in the roles of informants, translators, and artists. The book was printed privately (in English) by the Lower Kuskokwim School District in the mid-1980s and has received hardly any distribution. Nonetheless, this is an exceptionally accurate and arresting collection of folklore. Other excellent collections include *Yupik Lore: Oral Traditions of an Eskimo People,* edited by Edward A. Tennant and Joseph N. Bitar and also published by the Lower Kuskokwim School District (Bethel, 1981), and various editions of *Kalikaq Yugnek (The Book of the People),* a magazine published biannually by the Bethel Regional High School in the late 1970s.

John T. Andrew's testimony on the land is culled from *Village Journey* (New York: Hill & Wang, 1985). Its author, Thomas Berger, was chairman of the Alaska Native Review Commission, and *Village Journey* is an analysis of the Alaska Native Claims Settlement Act in light of the testimony submitted to that commission. Unimpressed by ANCSA, Berger recommends that corporate lands be transferred to village tribal governments and that these governments should have exclusive jurisdiction over fish and wildlife on their lands. His proposals do not sit well with the state government, nor with that portion of the Native leadership still committed to ANCSA; but these ideas are central to the philosophy of the sovereignty movement in rural Alaska — a movement whose political center lies in such Kuskokwim villages as Akiachak and Akiak. An interesting and similarly critical commentary on ANCSA voiced by an Alaskan Native during the process of negotiation is to be found in Fred Bigjim's *Letters to Howard* (Anchorage: Alaska Methodist University Press, 1974).

The first and all subsequent citations from Zagoskin are drawn from *Lieutenant Zagoskin's Travels in Russian America, 1842–1844,* edited by Henry N. Michael (Toronto: University of Toronto Press, 1967). Zagoskin wrote more to inform than to entertain, and the accounts of his expedition are generally fragmentary and episodic in themselves, but his warmth is always on display, as is occasionally his humor. He was the first and only explorer of his era to make observations in any detail of a Yupik world that was already changing irrevocably. I think Zagoskin would be surprised, however, to discover how many of his comments find corroboration even today in the social and economic life of the delta.

May Wynne Lamb's response to the aurora borealis comes from *Life in Alaska: The Reminiscences of a Kansas Woman, 1916–1919.* Mrs. Lamb was unable to find a publisher for her memoir during her lifetime, but the manuscript was finally edited by her niece, Dorothy Wynne Zimmerman, a professor of English at the University of Nebraska, and brought out by the University of Nebraska Press in Lincoln in 1988. These reminiscences are vivid and well drawn, and are particularly valuable for the author's impressions of Akiak during the years of John and Edith Kilbuck's residency there.

III. YOUR EVIL FATE

There are now a number of important sources describing, from various perspectives, the founding of Bethel and the course of the cultural encounter that is discussed more fully in Chapter IV. The point of view of the Moravian church is represented by two important church histories which are discussed in the notes to the next chapter. A more bipartisan perspective can be found in the work of the anthropologist Wendell H. Oswalt, who initiated modern ethnographic research on the Kuskokwim in the 1950s. Oswalt's *Mission of Change in Alaska* (San Marino, Calif.: Huntington Library, 1963) devotes itself specifically to that encounter in a manner equal to its complexity. Other important works by Oswalt include *Alaskan Eskimos* (New York: Chandler, 1967), a general reference work containing reliable Yupik ethnographic material, and *Napaskiak: An Alaskan Eskimo Community* (Tucson: University of Arizona Press, 1963), a comprehensive ethnography of a village in which the Russian Orthodox church has always been a stronger presence than the Moravian church.

Another approach — not a churchman's, not a scientist's — is offered by an examination of Bethel's history from the multiple perspectives of its present residents. This is the case with Mary Lenz and James H. Barker's remarkable centennial history of the town, *Bethel: The First Hundred Years* (City of Bethel, 1985). The authors orchestrate scores of archival photographs and the voices of a hundred or so colorful interviewees into a gritty portrait of a town unlike any other in America — one that has largely succeeded in melding its disparate elements into a single rich and functioning community.

The voice of Maggie Lind, along with those of other singers and storytellers, both Yupik and Inupiaq, may be heard on the album *Alaskan Eskimo Songs and Stories,* compiled and recorded by Lorraine Donoghue Koranda (Seattle: University of Washington Press, 1966). The record is accompanied by a booklet offering transcriptions of each performance and an analysis of the structure and purposes of Eskimo music.

The wisest and most accomplished anthropologist currently doing work in the delta is Ann Fienup-Riordan. I agree with Ernest S. Burch, Jr.'s assessment of her monograph, *The Nelson Island Eskimo: Social Structure and Ritual Distribution* (Anchorage: Alaska Pacific University Press, 1983), as "probably the best account of Eskimo ritual that has been produced." In this work Fienup-Riordan undertakes a structural analysis of the *uqiquq,* that ritual distribution of goods following a child's first harvest of a seal or some other wild food. This small ceremony is her point of entry into a gradual revelation of the still-vigorous ideology of subsistence and the degree to which that economy both reproduces and maintains a community's social forms. The book is academic and technical, but very well written and beautifully representative of the subtlety and intricacy of that ideology. Also valuable in this respect is Fienup-Riordan's *When Our Bad Season Comes: A Cultural Account of Subsistence Harvesting and Harvest Disruption on the Yukon Delta* (Anchorage: Alaska Anthropological Association, 1986).

Edward W. Nelson's great monograph, *The Eskimo About Bering Strait* (Washington D.C.: Smithsonian Institution Press, 1983), cannot be described as easy bedtime reading. The book is basically a large and capacious reference work, as comprehensive as the tireless Nelson could make it and invaluable in its minute physical attention to the world that immediately succeeded the milieu that Zagoskin observed. Nelson is genuinely entertaining, however, in his descriptions of the delta's ingenious hunting and fishing technologies, in his anecdotal discussion of Yupik "moral characteristics," and in his accurate transcriptions of many lengthy and subtle Yupik folktales, including a number of Raven stories.

A more accessible rendering of Nelson's work, extensively illustrated with objects from the Smithsonian's Nelson collection, is to be found in *Inua: Spirit World of the Bering Sea Eskimo,* by William W. Fitzhugh and Susan A. Kaplan (Washington D.C.: Smithsonian Institution Press, 1982). The title is a little dissonant to me, since *inua* is an Inupiaq and not a Yupik term, but otherwise the book offers a good overview of Yupik culture, a description of Nelson's career in Alaska, and a great deal of material on the shamanism and ceremonial practices that so beguiled and mystified the young scientist.

The quotation from Robert McGhee about the richness of Yupik culture comes from McGhee's *Canadian Arctic Prehistory* (Toronto: Van Nostrand Reinhold, 1978). I came across the quote in Barry Lopez's *Arctic Dreams: Imagination and Desire in a Northern Landscape* (New York: Scribner's, 1986), the emphasis of which lies in more northerly regions than the Yukon-Kuskokwim Delta. But the book is pertinent to the ecology of the region, and I can think of no work that captures in a more luminous way the long interplay of the human mind — in both its Eskimo and its Western manifestations — with the climate, terrain, and wildlife of the tundra.

IV. THE SUPERIOR COMMUNITY OF FAITH

The first of the two important church sources on the contest between the shamans and the missionaries, and also on the simultaneous struggle between the Moravian and the Russian Orthodox missionaries, is Anna Buxbaum Schwalbe's *Dayspring on the Kuskokwim* (Bethlehem, Pa.: Moravian Church in America, 1951). This book reflects a strong Moravian bias, of course, but Mrs. Schwalbe is a good storyteller, and she recounts her history in a generous spirit, one full of affection for the people of the delta and not wholly insensitive to virtues other than those defined by the strictures of Protestant Christianity.

Harmonious to Dwell: The History of the Alaska Moravian Church, 1885–1985 (Bethel: Moravian Seminary and Archives, 1985), by James W. Henkelman and Kurt H. Vitt, is not so readable as Mrs. Schwalbe's history but is generally more even-handed, more current, and presents a wealth of original documentary material. The authors have also read far beyond their own archives, and the Catholic priest Bellarmine LaFortune's attack on the shamans as a class is quoted in this source.

Neither this history nor Mrs. Schwalbe's has anything to say about the circumstances of what Henkelman and Vitt describe only as the Kilbucks' "retiring" from mission service, nor about the philosophical differences between John Kilbuck and the church leadership in Pennsylvania. I found the best discussion of these matters, and of the Kilbucks' entire career, in Ann Fienup-Riordan's introduction to *The Yup'ik Eskimos: As Described in the Travel Journals and Ethnographic Accounts of John and Edith Kilbuck* (Kingston, Ontario: Limestone, 1988). This book, edited by Fienup-Riordan, presents a vast quantity of the Kilbucks' own writings. A much more detailed examination of their career and the nature of their interaction with Yupik belief systems is offered, I'm sure, in a recent book by Fienup-Riordan, which I haven't yet seen but which I feel confident in recommending: *The Real People and the Children of Thunder: The Yup'ik Eskimo Encounter With the Moravian Missionaries John and Edith Kilbuck* (Norman: University of Oklahoma Press, 1991).

The Kwigillingok missionary Ferdinand Drebert was as good a storyteller as Mrs. Schwalbe, and a much keener student of Yupik mores. His buoyant memoir, valuable for its depiction of the struggle of conversion out on the fringes of the Moravian church's diocese, is entitled *Alaska Missionary* (Bethlehem, Pa.: Moravian Book Shop, 1959).

The shamans' side of this struggle is now largely inaccessible, even through folklore, but an important reconstruction of Yupik ceremonialism is available in the form of Elsie P. Mather's *Cauyarnariuq (It Is Time for Drumming)*, which was published by the Lower Kuskokwim School District (Bethel, 1985) as a high school Yupik-language text. An English summary of this mate-

388 ❖ ANNOTATED BIBLIOGRAPHY

rial is presented by the anthropologist Phyllis Morrow as one of
the articles in *Etudes/Inuit/Studies,* vol. 8 (Quebec: Université
Laval, 1984). This volume of the biannual journal is devoted
entirely to the Central Yupik and boasts a number of well-in-
formed articles on their history, culture, and language.

These materials and oral testimony on shamanism as it was
practiced prior to missionization suggest that Yupik shamanism
had much in common with shamanism elsewhere. Mircea
Eliade's fascinating study of the practice in Siberia, the Americas, the Pacific, and among ancient Indo-European peoples —
Shamanism: Archaic Techniques of Ecstasy (Princeton, N.J.:
Princeton University Press, 1964) — proposes a common root-
stock for this religious complex in central Asia. Eliade's book is
particularly rich in material on Siberian and northern Eskimo
shamanism, much of which I believe is relevant to the delta.
Also, Robert F. Spencer's *The North Alaskan Eskimo: A Study
in Ecology and Society* (Washington, D.C.: U.S. Government
Printing Office, 1959) has contributed some anecdotal material
to this chapter.

A general description of the Russian Orthodox missionary effort in the delta and elsewhere in Alaska may be found in Bishop
Gregory Afonsky's *A History of the Orthodox Church in Alaska*
(Kodiak: St. Herman of Alaska Seminary, 1977). Also important is Michael J. Oleksa's *Alaska Missionary Spirituality* (New
York: Paulist Press, 1987), a collection of letters, reports, ex-
tracts, petitions, and other original documents of the Orthodox
church in Alaska. In his provocative introduction, Oleksa con-
trasts the policies of his own church with the period of "American assimilation" as practiced by Protestant missionaries and
teachers, and he writes knowingly of the degree to which the
Orthodox church has been unjustly discounted in standard
American versions of Alaskan history.

The anthropologist Lydia T. Black writes more dispassion-
ately of how elements of Orthodox practice were incorporated
so fully, and so seamlessly, into Yupik culture as eventually to

be assumed to be indigenous. Her article "The Yup'ik of Western Alaska and Western Impact" may be found in the previously cited issue of *Etudes/Inuit/Studies*. Useful chapters on the Orthodox church are also contained in the handsome *Russian America: The Forgotten Frontier,* edited by Barbara Sweetland Smith and Redmond J. Barnett (Tacoma: Washington State Historical Society, 1990). Wendell Oswalt's material also contains brief surveys of the Orthodox effort, and cool-headed assessments of its encounter with Moravianism.

Libby Beaman's observations of ecstasy and clairvoyance are drawn from *Libby: The Alaskan Diaries & Letters of Libby Beaman, 1879–1880* (Boston: Houghton Mifflin, 1989). These materials were discovered in a trunk by Betty John, Libby Beaman's granddaughter, and then prepared for publication. John writes that her grandmother's journal wasn't quite complete, and she notes in her introduction, "I've had to fill in some gaps by conjuring up memories of the stories she told me and by doing research into her times." I'm disappointed that there is no distinction in the text between the original material and John's interpolations, but this book has the narrative pull of a novel and is an eloquent recounting of an extraordinary year.

The role played by epidemic disease and Western medicine in the collapse of shamanism is treated not only in the preceding church histories but in the two Alaska Geographic publications on the delta, and also in Lenz and Barker's history of Bethel. Robert Fortuine's *Chills and Fever: Health and Disease in the Early History of Alaska* (Fairbanks: University of Alaska Press, 1989), however, is more comprehensive than these, describing the impact of the epidemics on all Alaskan Native populations. Fortuine's book is particularly interesting for its description, based on current paleopathological research, of the general health of these populations before Western contact.

Richard K. Nelson's report of an Athabascan shaman's views on the loss of his powers comes from *Make Prayers to the Raven* (Chicago: University of Chicago Press, 1983), which offers a good description of an Alaskan Indian spirituality closely allied to that of Yupik peoples. Another book by Nelson, *Hunters of the Northern Ice* (Chicago: University of Chicago Press, 1969), describes a wide range of Inupiaq Eskimo hunting techniques, a number of which are also used in the delta and are often surprising in their inventiveness.

Christian marriage and household living patterns have had a revolutionary impact on Yupik family life, and the nature of this impact is one of the subjects examined in a paper by the anthropologists Anne D. Shwinkin and Mary C. Pete, "Homes in Disruption: Spouse Abuse in Yupik Eskimo Society" (Fairbanks: University of Alaska, 1983). Shwinkin and Pete suggest that a disjunction between traditional Yupik mores and systems of social control and those inherent in the institution of Christian marriage contributes — on an underlying basis — to the current high rate of spouse abuse. The authors find, however, that alcohol exists "in a nearly perfect relationship" with the incidence of abuse as its immediate precipitating cause.

The citations from the sociologists Max Weber and Peter Berger are both culled from Lionel Tiger's *The Manufacture of Evil: Ethics, Evolution, and the Industrial System* (New York: Harper & Row, 1987). This somewhat chilling book traces in general historical terms the same transition on the Kuskokwim that I try to describe — that from a morality based on kinship relationships diffused throughout close-knit family groups to a morality based on broader and more abstract ethical concerns, transcending family relationships and serving much larger social organizations. Tiger notes that these latter ethics are exclusively the products of agricultural and industrial societies, and suggests that in altering the moral structures under which we live, industrialism has also in effect mass-produced evil, generating vast moral outcomes that no one wanted in the first place and creating conditions under which these outcomes elude responsibility.

V. WHICH SIDE ARE YOU ON?

John Active's essay is entitled "Yup'ik: The Western Eskimos," and *Alaska's Native People* was edited by Lael Morgan (Anchorage, 1979). The essay recounts both the old and the new version of Bethel's cultural roots — that is, the Raven creation myth and the Moravians' historical founding of Bethel — and concludes on a note of pride: "Whatever the missionaries might say about us now, Bethel is the hub of a sizable area. As for the Yup'ik, the western Eskimo who lives [sic] in that sizable area, we seem to be doing all right, whatever the young people and the old people may tell us about our origins." Since the completion of *Raven's Children*, incidentally, John Active has regained his former job at KYUK and is once again playing a prominent role in the production and broadcast of that station's radio and television programming.

VI. THERE ARE NO POOR AMONG THEM

The negotiation of ANCSA is a fascinating story in itself, one that I've learned on a piecemeal basis, but a reliable general account is to be found in *Alaska Native Land Claims,* by Robert D. Arnold et al. (Anchorage: Alaska Native Foundation, 1976). A useful retelling is also contained in a good textbook on Alaskan history, Claus-M. Naske and Herman E. Slotnick's *Alaska: A History of the 49th State* (Grand Rapids, Mich.: Eerdmans, 1979).

Bound up with the land claims movement was the momentous oil strike near Prudhoe Bay in 1968. A book that surveys Alaska's mineral resources in general, details the mechanics and economics of extracting them, reviews the history of these resources in Alaska's economy, and devotes particular attention to North Slope oil exploration is the Alaska Geographic Society's *Alaska's Oil/Gas & Minerals Industry,* edited by Robert A. Henning (Anchorage, 1982). A more skeptical view of the oil industry is to be found in Kenneth Andrasko and Marina Halevi's *Alaska*

Crude: Visions of the Last Frontier (Boston: Little, Brown, 1977), which offers an almost hallucinogenic portrait of the irony, excess, valor, and madness that went into the building of the Trans-Alaska Pipeline. A book that specifically addresses the Prudhoe strike's role in the land claims movement is Mary Clay Berry's *The Alaskan Pipeline: The Politics of Oil and Native Land Claims* (Bloomington: Indiana University Press, 1975).

The nature of the uneasy relationship between the cash and subsistence economies is addressed in one way or another by all of the insightful articles in *Contemporary Alaskan Native Economies,* edited by Steve J. Langdon (Lanham, Md.: University Press of America, 1986). Of particular note here are the editor's own "Contradictions in Alaskan Native Economy and Society," which details the manner in which ANCSA is inimical to the subsistence economy; J. Anthony Koslow's "Limited Entry Policy and Impacts on Bristol Bay Fishermen," which describes the development of the limited-entry system in Alaska and the current straits of Native fishermen; and Ann Fienup-Riordan's "Symbolic and Social Aspects of the Nelson Island Eskimo Subsistence System," which describes the inability of the cash economy to mesh with the mechanisms of social integration established by the subsistence economy.

VII. THE TERRACES OF PURGATORY

Within any family group, and particularly within cultures built around family groups, the projection of internal tensions onto an individual who is external or marginal to the group is a time-honored expedient for managing those tensions. Therefore, for example, the position of an orphan within a Yupik village has traditionally been difficult, and so many Yupik folktales describe the exploits of orphans, for what could be more marvelous than that an orphan should rise to a position of prestige and influence? For a sensitive examination of this expedient at work in a small Inupiaq community, see the anthropologist Jean

Briggs's fine monograph, *Never in Anger: Portrait of an Eskimo Family* (Cambridge: Harvard University Press, 1970).

William H. Dall's observation of a *umiak* loaded with rum off Saint Michael is drawn from Dorothy Jean Ray's *The Eskimos of Bering Strait, 1650–1898* (Seattle: University of Washington Press, 1975), a detailed history of Russian and American interactions with both the Yupik and the Inupiaq peoples of the region. An excellent survey of the historical role of alcohol in white interactions with both Eskimo and northern Indian populations is to be found in John Hamer and Jack Steinbring's introduction to *Alcohol and Native Peoples of the North,* edited by Hamer and Steinbring (Washington, D.C.: University Press of America, 1980). I remain unconvinced, however, by one of this book's central premises: that alcoholism in the sense of addiction rarely occurs in Native populations, and that what we mistake for alcoholism is simply the customary use of alcohol as a medium of exchange in social relationships. In the affecting memoir *The Broken Cord: A Family's Ongoing Struggle with Fetal Alcohol Syndrome* (New York: Harper Collins, 1989), author Michael Dorris acknowledges this use of alcohol among the Lakota Sioux and other Indian groups, but asserts that as it becomes customary, the alcohol also becomes addictive. A harrowing memoir composed by an Inupiaq Eskimo who is an alcoholic is to be found in Anthony Apakark Thrasher's *Thrasher: Skid Row Eskimo* (Toronto: Griffin House, 1976). Lenz and Barker's *Bethel: The First Hundred Years* is the best single source for the history of alcohol in Bethel.

VIII. LIVING WITHOUT VIOLENCE

Some material on the prehistory of the delta exists in such works as *Inua, The Kuskokwim, Alaskan Eskimos,* and *Arctic Dreams,* which I have already cited. To my knowledge, however, the best single reference for the Bering Strait region as a whole is to be found in *Crossroads of Continents: Cultures of Siberia and Alaska,* edited by Fitzhugh and Crowel (Washington, D.C.:

Smithsonian Institution Press, 1988). Particularly useful essays in this volume are "Beringia: An Ice-Age View," by Steven B. Young; "Prehistory of Siberia and the Bering Sea," by S. A. Arutionov and William W. Fitzhugh; and "War and Trade," by Ernest S. Burch, Jr. An excellent overview of our current understanding of the genesis and diffusion of Eskimo culture as a whole, with a refreshing emphasis on Yupik groups, exists in Ernest S. Burch, Jr.'s *The Eskimos* (Norman: University of Oklahoma Press, 1988).

Pertinent information on the career of Vitus Bering and the Russian period in Alaska may be found in virtually any of the historical works cited thus far, as well as in Hubert Howe Bancroft's *History of Alaska, 1730–1885* (San Francisco: A. L. Bancroft, 1886); Hector Chevigny's *Russian America* (New York: Viking, 1965); Raymond H. Fisher's *Bering's Voyages: Whither and Why* (Seattle: University of Washington Press, 1977); and the Alaska Geographic Society's *The Aleutians,* edited by Lael Morgan (Anchorage, 1980). My biographical material on Zagoskin is drawn from M. Chernenko's "Lavrentiy Alekseyevich Zagoskin, An Account of His Life and Works," contained in *Lieutenant Zagoskin's Travels in Russian America, 1842–1844.* I owe my description of World War II in the region to information in Lenz and Barker's history of Bethel, and also in *The Aleutians.*

IX. THE WILDERNESS ZION

My information on the nutritional content of specific Yupik foods comes by way of an article by Barbara Knapp and Peter Panruk, "Southwest Alaska Eskimo Dietary Survey of 1978" (Bethel: Yukon Kuskokwim Health Corporation, 1978), public information materials distributed as part of the 1988 Nutrition Improvement Project of the Yukon Kuskokwim Health Corporation, and *The Yukon-Kuskokwim Delta.* More general information on nutrition and the character of human life under subsistence (as opposed to agricultural or industrial) economic modes is derived from the article "Paleolithic Nutrition: A Consideration of Its Nature and Current Implications," by S. Boyd Eaton and Melvin Konner (*New England Journal of Medicine,* vol. 312, no. 5); the article "The Worst Mistake In the History of the Human Race," by Jared Diamond (*Discover,* May 1987); and *Cannibals and Kings: The Origins of Cultures,* by Marvin Harris (New York: Random House, 1977).

Estimates of the cash value of a household's annual subsistence harvest come from the work of Robert J. Wolfe: "Norton Sound/Yukon Delta Sociocultural Systems Baseline Analysis: Technical Report No. 72" (Anchorage: Alaska Outer Continental Shelf Office, 1981), and "The Economic Efficiency of Food Production in a Western Eskimo Population," in the previously cited *Contemporary Alaskan Native Economies.*

The strange and tragic story of Minik Wallace, whose brief life touched on those of such luminaries of Arctic exploration and study as Robert Peary, Franz Boas, Peter Freuchen, and Knud Rassmussen, is skillfully related in Kenn Harper's fine biography, *Give Me My Father's Body: The Life of Minik, The New York Eskimo* (Frobisher Bay, NWT: Blacklead Books, 1986).

My chief source on King Philip's War is Russell Bourne's fine history, *The Red King's Rebellion: Racial Politics in New England 1675–1678* (New York: Atheneum, 1990). Also useful were Douglas Edward Leach's *Flintlock and Tomahawk: New England in King Philip's War* (New York: Norton, 1958) and James Truslow Adams's *The Founding of New England* (Boston: Little, Brown, 1921).

Hugh Brody's statement is taken from the conclusion to his *Maps and Dreams* (New York: Random House, 1981). This perceptive description of a modern Athabascan hunting society was written as part of a land-use project that preceded the construction of a natural gas pipeline through Athabascan lands. Brody notes here the self-fulfilling nature of stereotype, pointing

396 ❖ ANNOTATED BIBLIOGRAPHY

out that if the bush ceases to be a place into which Native peoples can withdraw and on whose wildlife resources they can rely, "then they have lost their economy and are exposed forever to the stereotype that portrays them as impoverished. Such loss and exposure would mean that, finally, the stereotype would become the truth."

ARCTIC O

East Siberian
Sea

Chukchi
Sea

RUSSIA

Chukchi
Peninsula

Barrow

Wainwright

AL

Noatak R.

Hotham Inlet

Kobuk R.

Cape Prince
of Wales

Big
Diomede I.

Seward
Peninsula

Bering Strait

Little
Diomede I.

King I.

NOME

Sledge I.

Unalakleet

Saint
Lawrence I.

Norton Sound

Saint
Michael

Russian
Mission

Kuskok

RUSSIA
UNITED STATES

Hooper
Bay

Kuskokwim R.

Kolm

Bethel

Kongiganak

Nunivak
Island

Togiak

Kuskokwim
Bay

AREA OF INSET

Komandorskiye
Islands

Bering

Bristol
Bay

INTERNATIONAL DATE LINE

Sea

Pribilof
Islands

Alaska Peninsula

False
Pass

Dutch   Akutan
Harbor

Aleutian Islands